HANDBOOK OF TEXTURE ANALYSIS

HANDBOOK OF TEXTURE ANALYSIS

edited by

Majid Mirmehdi
University of Bristol, UK

Xianghua Xie
University of Swansea, UK

Jasjit Suri
Eigen LLC, USA

ICP

Imperial College Press

Published by

Imperial College Press
57 Shelton Street
Covent Garden
London WC2H 9HE

Distributed by

World Scientific Publishing Co. Pte. Ltd.
5 Toh Tuck Link, Singapore 596224
USA office: 27 Warren Street, Suite 401-402, Hackensack, NJ 07601
UK office: 57 Shelton Street, Covent Garden, London WC2H 9HE

British Library Cataloguing-in-Publication Data
A catalogue record for this book is available from the British Library.

HANDBOOK OF TEXTURE ANALYSIS

ISBN-13 978-1-84816-115-3
ISBN-10 1-84816-115-8

Printed in Singapore by Mainland Press Pte Ltd

Preface

The main purpose of this book is to bring together a collection of defining works that span the breadth of knowledge in texture analysis - from 2D to 3D, from feature extraction to synthesis, from texture image acquisition to classification, and much more. The works presented in this book are from some of the most prominent international researchers in the field. The reader will find each chapter a defining testament to the state of the art in the area of texture analysis describe therein, as well as a springboard for further investigation into it.

Chapter 1 provides an introduction to texture analysis, reviewing some of the fundamental techniques, amongst them more traditional methods such as co-occurrence matrices and Laws energy measures, and pointers to some of the more recent techniques based on Markov Random Fields (MRFs) and Fractals.

Chapter 2 sees an exposition of the concepts engaging researchers today in modelling and synthesising textures, as well as a comprehensive review of some of the key works in this area in recent years.

The topic of texture classification is arguably one of the most popular areas of computer vision. In Chapter 3, a novel texton based representation suited to modelling the distribution of intensity values over extremely compact neighbourhoods for MRFs is presented. There is also a comparative study of this texton based model against filter bank approaches to texture classification.

Not all textures exhibit a regular structure and therefore some researchers have focused on the analysis of randomly formed textures, such as random patterns printed on a variety of materials. In Chapter 4 a statistical model to represent random textures is outlined which is used for novelty detection in a quality inspection task, and further developed for general image segmentation.

In Chapter 5, a colour image segmentation technique is presented which is a prime example of how texture can be combined adaptively with other key image information, i.e. colour. Several application areas, including medical imaging, are shown to benefit from using such a combination as a compound image descriptor.

There has been significant advance recently in the practical implementation and investigation of theoretical methods in the area of 3D texture analysis, mainly fuelled by the amazing growth in the computational power of desktop machines. This in turn has permitted further advances in the theoretical study of 3D texture analysis. To reflect the extent of these advances, there are three chapters on 3D texture analysis in this book.

In Chapter 6, the theory of a surface-to-image function is developed to show that sidelighting acts as a directional filter of the surface height function. A simplified version of this theory is then exploited via a classifier that estimates the illumination direction of various textures. Chapter 7 deals with physics based 3D texture models in computer vision and psychophysics, for example showing how the spatial structure of 3D texture provides cues about the material properties and the light field. In Chapter 8, topics in modelling texture with the bidirectional reflectance distribution function (BRDF) and the bidirectional texture function (BTF) are presented. Two particular methods for recognition described in detail are bidirectional feature histograms and symbolic primitives that are more useful for recognising subtle differences in texture.

In Chapter 9, dynamic textures, such as smoke, talking faces, or flowers blowing in the winds, are investigated for which the global statistics of the image signal are modelled, learned, and synthesised to create video sequences that exhibit statistical regularity properties, using tools from time series analysis, system identification theory, and finite element methods.

Chapter 10 returns to the problem of texture synthesis. The method presented considers a hierarchical approach where textures are regarded as composites of simpler subtextures. These subtextures are studied in terms of their own statistics, interactions, and layout to generate highly realistic synthesised scenes such as landscapes.

In Chapter 11, a detailed case study of the Trace transform is presented which not only describes the general concept of the technique, but outlines its implementation in the digital domain, such that the desirable and invariant properties of the features (triple functionals) of the image or texture data are preserved.

Local Binary Patterns have recently become an extremely useful texture analysis tool in a variety of applications, and the second case study of the book in Chapter 12, they are shown in action for a variety of face analysis applications.

Chapter 13 presents a plethora, or what the authors like to call a galaxy, of texture features. This however should be regarded an inexhaustive list of the multitude of texture features available in the literature. Apologies in advance to anyone wondering why his or her favourite feature has not made it into this chapter!

The authors of the various chapters have been tremendously generous with their time and effort, and we thank each and every one heartily. In no particular order, these are Stefano Soatto, Rupert Paget, Maria Petrou, Manik Varma, Luc Van Gool, Roy Davies, Alexey Zalesny, Geert Caenen, Matti Pietikäinen, Kristin Dana, Paul Whelan, Abdenour Hadid, Oana Cula, Andrew Zisserman, Jan Koenderink, Sylvia Pont, Ovidiu Ghita, Mike Chantler, Gianfranco Doretto, Guoying Zhao, Fang Wang, and Timo Ahonen. The staff at World Scientific, Katie Lydon, Lizzie Bennett, and Lance Suchrov, were always a quick email away and a pleasure to deal with, and we are very grateful for their advice and help in putting this book together.

Majid Mirmehdi
Xianghua Xie
Jasjit Suri

Contents

Chapter 1

Introduction to Texture Analysis

E. R. Davies
Machine Vision Group, Department of Physics
Royal Holloway, University of London
Egham, Surrey, TW20 0EX, UK
e.r.davies@rhul.ac.uk

Textures are characteristic intensity (or colour) variations that typically originate from roughness of object surfaces. For a well-defined texture, intensity variations will normally exhibit both regularity and randomness, and for this reason texture analysis requires careful design of statistical measures. While there are certain quite commonly used approaches to texture analysis, much depends on the actual intensity variations, and methods are still being developed for ever more accurately modelling, classifying and segmenting textures. This introductory chapter explores and reviews some fundamental techniques.

1.1. Introduction — The Idea of a Texture

Most people understand that the human eye is a remarkable instrument and value highly the gift of sight. However, because the human vision system (HVS) permits scene interpretation 'at a glance', the layman has little appreciation of the amount of processing involved in vision. Indeed, it is largely the case that only those working on the brain—or those trying to emulate its capabilities in areas such as machine vision—have any idea of the underlying processes. In particular, the human eye 'sees' not scenes but sets of objects in various relations to each other, in spite of the fact that the ambient illumination is likely to vary from one object to another—and over the various surfaces of each object—and in spite of the fact that there will be secondary illumination from one object to another.

In spite of these complications, it is sometimes reasonable to make the assumption that objects, or object surfaces, can be segmented from each other according to the degree of uniformity of the light reflected from them. Clearly, this is only possible if a surface is homogeneous and has uniform reflectivity, and is subject to uniform illumination. In that case not only will the intensity of the reflected light be constant, but its colour will also be unvarying.

In fact, it will rarely be the case that objects, or their surfaces, can be segmented in this way, as almost all surfaces have a texture that varies the reflectance locally, even if there is a global uniformity to it. One definition of texture is the property of the surface that gives rise to this local variability. In many cases this property arises because of surface roughness, which tends to scatter light randomly, thereby enhancing or reducing local reflectance in the viewing direction. Even white paper has this property to some extent, and eggshell more so. In many other cases, it is not so much surface roughness that causes this effect but surface structure—as for a woven material, which gives rise to a periodic variation in reflectance. There are other substances, such as wood, which may appear rough even if they are smooth, because of the grain of the intrinsic material, and their texture can vary from a fine to a coarse pattern. Ripples on water can appear in the form of a relatively coarse texture, albeit in this case it will have a rapidly varying temporal development. Other sorts of texture or textured appearance arise for sand on the seashore, or a grass lawn, or a hedge. In such cases the textured surface is a composite of grains or leaves, i.e. it is composed of separate objects, but for image interpretation purposes it is usual to regard the surface as having a unique texture. On the other hand, if the scale is altered, so that we see relatively few component objects, as for a pile of large chickpeas—and certainly for a pile of potatoes—the illusion of a texture evaporates. To some extent, then, a texture may be a fiction created by the HVS, and is not unrelated to the limited resolution available in the human eye. All these points are illustrated in Figs. 1.1 and 1.2.

In practice, a surface is taken to be textured if there is an uncountably large number of texture elements (or 'texels'), and a set of objects if the opposite is true. In general, the components of a texture, the texels, are notional uniform micro-objects which are placed in an appropriate way to form any particular texture. The placing may be random, regular, directional and so on, and also there may be a degree of overlap in some cases—as in the case of a grass lawn. It is also possible to vary the sizes and shapes of the texels, but doing this reduces the essential simplicity of the concept. Actually, what we are seeing here is the possibility of recognition by reconstruction: if a texture can be reconstructed, it will almost certainly have

Fig. 1.1. A variety of textures. (a) Tarmac, (b) brick, (c) carpet, (d) cloth, (e) wood, (f) water. These textures demonstrate the wide variety of familiar textures that are easily recognised from their characteristic intensity patterns.

been interpreted correctly. However, while recognition by reconstruction is generally a sound idea, it is much more difficult with textures because of the random element. Nevertheless, the idea is of value when scene generation has to be performed in a realistic manner, as in flight simulators.

What we have come up with so far is the idea of textured surface ap-

Fig. 1.2. Textured surfaces as composites. In this figure the lentils in (a) and the slice of bread in (c) are shown in (b) and (d) with respective linear magnifications of 4 and 2. Such magnifications often appear to change the texture into a set of composite objects.

pearance, which can be imagined as due to appropriate placement of texels; this texture is a property by which the surface can be recognised; in addition, when different regions of an image have different textures, this can be used to segment objects or their surfaces from each other.

We have also seen that, whatever their source, textures may vary according to randomness, regularity (or periodicity), directionality and orientation. Notice that we are gradually moving away from texture as a property of the surface (the physical origin of the texture) to appearance in the image, as that is what concerns us in image texture analysis. Of course, once image textures have been identified, we can relate them back to the original scene and to the original object surfaces. This distinction is important, because it is sometimes the case (see Fig. 1.3) that 3D object structures can be discerned from information about texture variations.

At this point it is useful to say what is and what is not a texture. If an intensity variation appears to be perfectly periodic, it would normally

(a) (b)

Fig. 1.3. Views of a grass lawn. View (a) is taken from directly above, while view (b) is taken at an angle of about 40° to the vertical. Notice how the texture gives useful information on the viewing angle.

be described as a 'periodic pattern' and would not be called a texture. Likewise, any completely random pattern would probably be called a 'noise pattern' rather than a texture—though this may be a subjective judgement, and might depend on scale or colour. However, if a pattern has both randomness and regularity, then this is probably what most people would call a texture, and is the definition that we adhere to here. In fact, these intellectual niceties will normally be largely irrelevant, as any algorithm designed for texture analysis will almost certainly be able to make some judgements about periodic patterns and about noise patterns. However, the inverse will not be the case: for example, an algorithm designed to discern periodic patterns may give inappropriate answers when presented with textures, because the randomness could partially cancel out the periodicity.

Another feature of a texture is its 'busyness': this applies whatever the degree of mix between randomness and regularity, and is not made substantially different if the texture is directional. To a large extent we can characterise textures as having busy microstructures but uniform macrostructures. We can even envisage identifying the busy components and then averaging them in some way to produce uniform measures of macrostructure. As we shall see below, this concept underlines many approaches to texture analysis—at least as a first approximation.

Overall, we have found in this introduction that texture offers another way to segment and recognise surfaces. It will not be useful when surfaces have constant reflectance, in which case the amount of reflected light and its colour will be the sole means by which the surface can be characterised. But when this is not so, texture adds significant further discriminatory information by which to perform recognition and segmentation tasks. Indeed, certain textures, such as directional ones, provide very considerable amounts of additional information, and it is very beneficial being able to use this for image interpretation; and in the cases where the texture reflects the 3D shapes of objects, even more can be learnt about the scene—albeit not without significant algorithmic and computational effort.

In the remainder of this chapter, we will first examine how effective the busyness idea is when used to perform texture analysis. We will then turn to obvious rigorous approaches such as autocorrelation and Fourier methods. After noting their limitations, we will examine co-occurrence matrices, and then consider the texture energy method which gradually took over, culminating in the eigenfilter approach. After considering potential problems with texture segmentation, an X-ray inspection application will be taken as a practical example of texture analysis in action. At this point the chapter will broaden out to deal with the wider scene—fractals, Markov models, structural techniques, and 3D shape from texture—together with outlines of recent novel approaches. The chapter will close with a summary, and with a forward look to later chapters.

1.2. A Simple Texture Analysis Technique and Its Limitations

In this section we start with the 'busyness' idea outlined in the previous section, and see how far it can be taken in a practical situation. In particular, we consider how to discriminate two types of seeds—rape seeds and charlock seeds, the former being used for the production of rape seed oil, and the latter counting as weeds. Rape seeds are characterised by a peaked, almost prickly surface, while charlock seeds have a smooth surface.[a] When seen in digital images, the rape seeds exhibit a speckled surface texture, and the charlock seeds have very little texture. Figure 1.4 illustrates a simple procedure for discriminating between the two types of seed. First, non-maximum intensities are suppressed and a non-critical threshold is applied to eliminate low-level peaks due to noise. Then mere counting of intensity peaks in the vicinity of centre locations clearly leads to accurate discrimination between the two types of seed. In this application, intensity and colour alone are unreliable indicators of seed identity, while size is a relatively good indicator, but would almost certainly lead to one error for the image shown in Fig. 1.4.

[a]Most rape seeds will have similar numbers of peaks on their surface: hence their appearance exhibits both the randomness and the regularity expected of a texture.

(a)

(b)

Fig. 1.4. Texture processing to discriminate between two types of seed. (a) Original image showing 4 rape seeds (speckled) and 6 charlock seeds (dark and smooth). (b) Processed image showing approximate centre locations (red crosses) and bright peaks of intensity (green dots). Simple counting of intensity peaks in the vicinity of centre locations clearly leads to accurate discrimination between the two types of seed.

While the texture analysis technique described above fulfils the immediate demands of the application, it can hardly be described as general or generic. In particular, the seeds are located prior to their classification by texture analysis, and in the majority of applications methods are needed that perform segmentation as an intrinsic part of the analysis. Furthermore, only intensity maxima are considered, and thus the richness of information available in many textures would be disregarded. Nevertheless, the method acts as a powerful existence theorem spurring detailed further study of the many techniques now available to workers in this important area.

1.3. Autocorrelation and Fourier Methods

In Section 1.1 texture emerged as the characteristic variation in intensity of a region of an image which should allow us to recognise and describe it and to outline its boundaries. In view of the statistical nature of textures, this prompts us to characterise texture by the variance in intensity values taken over the whole region of the texture.[b] However, such an approach will not give a rich enough description of the texture for most purposes, and will certainly not provide any possibility of reconstruction: it will also be especially unsuitable in cases where the texels are well defined, or where there is a high degree of periodicity in the texture. On the other hand, for highly periodic textures such as those that arise with many textiles, it is natural to consider the use of Fourier analysis. Indeed, in the early days of image analysis, this approach was tested thoroughly, though the results were not always encouraging. (Considering that cloth can easily be stretched locally by several weave periods, this is hardly surprising.)

Bajcsy (1973)[1] used a variety of ring and orientated strip filters in the Fourier domain to isolate texture features—an approach that was found to work successfully on natural textures such as grass, sand and trees. However, there is a general difficulty in using the Fourier power spectrum in that the information is more scattered than might at first be expected. In addition, strong edges and image boundary effects can prevent accurate texture analysis by this method, though Shaming (1974)[2] and Dyer and Rosenfeld (1976)[3] tackled the relevant image aperture problems. Perhaps more important is the fact that the Fourier approach is a global one which

[b] We defer for now the problem of finding the region of a texture so that we can compute its characteristics in order to perform a segmentation function. However, some preliminary training of a classifier may clearly be used to overcome this problem for supervised texture segmentation tasks.

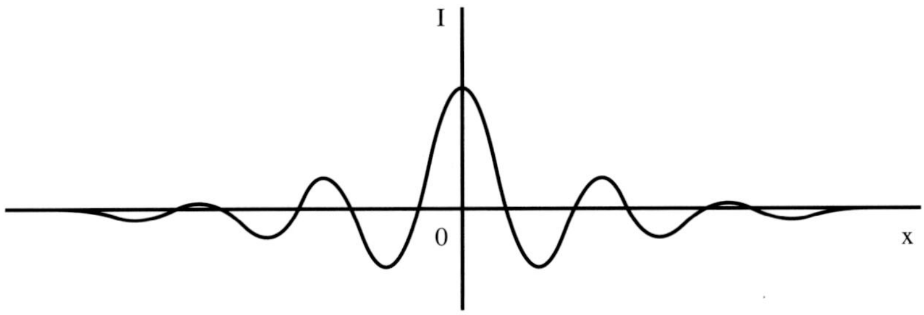

Fig. 1.5. Use of autocorrelation function for texture analysis. This diagram shows the possible 1D profile of the autocorrelation function for a piece of material in which the weave is subject to significant spatial variation: notice that the periodicity of the autocorrelation function is damped down over quite a short distance. © Elsevier 2005.

is difficult to apply successfully to an image that is to be segmented by texture analysis (Weszka *et al.*, 1976).[4]

Autocorrelation is another obvious approach to texture analysis, since it should show up both local intensity variations and also the repeatability of the texture (see Fig. 1.5). In particular, it should be useful for distinguishing between short-range and long-range order in a texture. An early study was carried out by Kaizer (1955).[5] He examined how many pixels an image has to be shifted before the autocorrelation function drops to $1/e$ of its initial value, and produced a subjective measure of coarseness on this basis. However, Rosenfeld and Troy (1970)[6,7] later showed that autocorrelation is not a satisfactory measure of coarseness. In addition, autocorrelation is not a very good discriminator of isotropy in natural textures. Hence workers were quick to take up the co-occurrence matrix approach introduced by Haralick *et al.* in 1973:[8] in fact, this approach not only replaced the use of autocorrelation but during the 1970s became to a large degree the 'standard' approach to texture analysis.

1.4. Grey-Level Co-Occurrence Matrices

The grey-level co-occurrence matrix approach[c] is based on studies of the statistics of pixel intensity distributions. As hinted above with regard to the variance in pixel intensity values, single pixel statistics do not provide rich enough descriptions of textures for practical applications. Thus it is natural

[c]This is also frequently called the spatial grey-level dependence matrix (SGLDM) approach.

to consider second order statistics obtained by considering pairs of pixels in certain spatial relations to each other. Hence, co-occurrence matrices are used, which express the relative frequencies (or probabilities) $P(i, j|d, \theta)$ with which two pixels having relative polar coordinates (d, θ) appear with intensities i, j. The co-occurrence matrices provide raw numerical data on the texture, though this data must be condensed to relatively few numbers before it can be used to classify the texture. The early paper by Haralick *et al.* (1973)[8] gave fourteen such measures, and these were used successfully for classification of many types of material (including, for example, wood, corn, grass and water). However, Conners and Harlow (1980)[9] found that only five of these measures were normally used, viz. 'energy', 'entropy', 'correlation', 'local homogeneity' and 'inertia' (note that these names do not provide much indication of the modes of operation of the respective operators).

To obtain a more detailed idea of the operation of the technique, consider the co-occurrence matrix shown in Fig. 1.6. This corresponds to a nearly uniform image containing a single region in which the pixel intensities are subject to an approximately Gaussian noise distribution, the

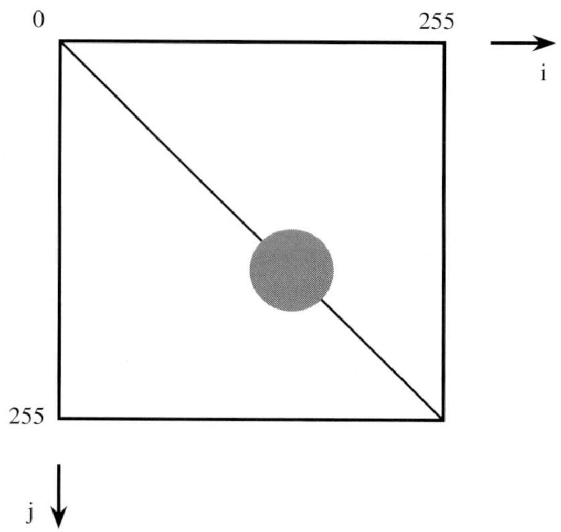

Fig. 1.6. Co-occurrence matrix for a nearly uniform grey-scale image with superimposed Gaussian noise. Here the intensity variation is taken to be almost continuous: normal convention is followed by making the j index increase downwards, as for a table of discrete values (cf. Fig. 1.8). © Elsevier 2005.

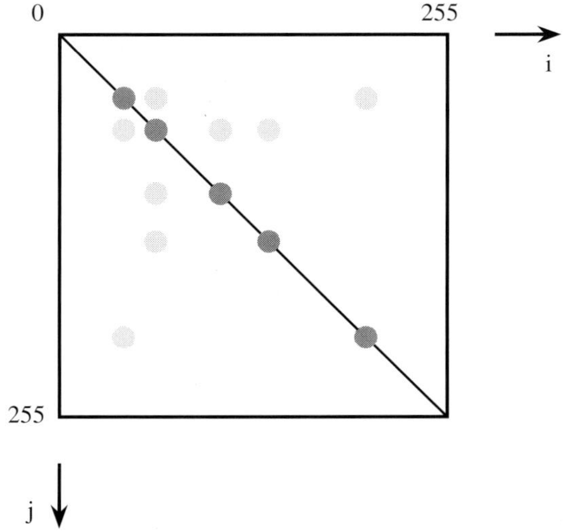

Fig. 1.7. Co-occurrence matrix for an image with several distinct regions of nearly constant intensity. Again, the leading diagonal of the diagram is from top left to bottom right (cf. Figs. 1.6 and 1.8). © Elsevier 2005.

attention being on pairs of pixels at a constant vector distance $\mathbf{d} = (d, \theta)$ from each other. Next consider the co-occurrence matrix shown in Fig. 1.7, which corresponds to an almost noiseless image with several nearly uniform image regions. In this case the two pixels in each pair may correspond either to the same image regions or to different ones, though if d is small they will only correspond to adjacent image regions. Thus we have a set of N on-diagonal patches in the co-occurrence matrix, but only a limited number L of the possible number M of off-diagonal patches linking them, where $M = \binom{N}{2}$ and $L \leq M$ (typically L will be of order N rather than N^2). With textured images, if the texture is not too strong, it may by modelled as noise, and the $N + L$ patches in the image will be larger but still not overlapping. However, in more complex cases the possibility of segmentation using the co-occurrence matrices will depend on the extent to which $\mathbf{d}$ can be chosen to prevent the patches from overlapping. Since many textures are directional, careful choice of θ will clearly help with this task, though the optimum value of d will depend on several other characteristics of the texture.

As a further illustration, we consider the small image shown in Fig. 1.8(a). To produce the co-occurrence matrices for a given value of

0	0	0	1
1	1	1	1
2	2	2	3
3	3	4	5

(a)

	0	1	2	3	4	5
0	2	1	0	0	0	0
1	1	3	0	0	0	0
2	0	0	2	1	0	0
3	0	0	1	1	1	0
4	0	0	0	1	0	1
5	0	0	0	0	1	0

(b)

	0	1	2	3	4	5
0	0	3	0	0	0	0
1	3	1	3	1	0	0
2	0	3	0	2	1	0
3	0	1	2	0	0	1
4	0	0	1	0	0	0
5	0	0	0	1	0	0

(c)

Fig. 1.8. Co-occurrence matrices for a small image. (a) shows the original image; (b) shows the resulting co-occurrence matrix for $\mathbf{d} = (1, 0)$, and (c) shows the matrix for $\mathbf{d} = (1, \pi/2)$. Note that even in this simple case the matrices contain more data than the original image.

$\mathbf{d}$, we merely need to calculate the numbers of cases for which pixels a distance $\mathbf{d}$ apart have intensity values i and j. Here, we content ourselves with the two cases $\mathbf{d} = (1, 0)$ and $\mathbf{d} = (1, \pi/2)$. We thus obtain the matrices shown in Fig. 1.8(b) and (c).

This simple example demonstrates that the amount of data in the matrices is liable to be many times more than in the original image—a situation which is exacerbated in more complex cases by the number of values of d and θ that are required to accurately represent the texture. In addition, the number of grey-levels will normally be closer to 256 than to 6, and the amount of matrix data varies as the square of this number. Finally, we should notice that the co-occurrence matrices merely provide a new representation: they do not themselves solve the recognition problem.

These factors mean that the grey-scale has to be compressed into a much smaller set of values, and careful choice of specific sample d, θ values must be made: in most cases it is not at all obvious how such a choice should be made, and it is even more difficult to arrange for it to be made automatically. In addition, various functions of the matrix data must be tested before the texture can be properly characterised and classified.

These problems with the co-occurrence matrix approach have been tackled in many ways: just two are mentioned here. The first is to ignore the distinction between opposite directions in the image, thereby reducing storage by 50%. The second is to work with differences between grey-levels; this amounts to performing a summation in the co-occurrence matrices along axes parallel to the main diagonal of the matrix. The result is a set of first order difference statistics. While these modifications have given some additional impetus to the approach, the 1980s saw a highly significant diversification of methods for the analysis of textures. Of these, Laws' approach (1979, 1980)[10–12] is important in that it has led to other developments which provide a systematic, adaptive means of tackling texture analysis. This approach is covered in the following section.

1.5. The Texture Energy Approach

In 1979 and 1980 Laws presented his novel texture energy approach to texture analysis (1979, 1980).[10–12] This involved the application of simple filters to digital images. The basic filters he used were common Gaussian, edge detector and Laplacian-type filters, and were designed to highlight points of high 'texture energy' in the image. By identifying these high energy points, smoothing the various filtered images, and pooling the information from them he was able to characterise textures highly efficiently and in a manner compatible with pipelined hardware implementations. As remarked earlier, Laws' approach has strongly influenced much subsequent work and it is therefore worth considering it here in some detail.

The Laws' masks are constructed by convolving together just three basic 1×3 masks:

$$\mathrm{L3} = \begin{bmatrix} 1 & 2 & 1 \end{bmatrix} \tag{1.1}$$

$$\mathrm{E3} = \begin{bmatrix} -1 & 0 & 1 \end{bmatrix} \tag{1.2}$$

$$\mathrm{S3} = \begin{bmatrix} -1 & 2 & -1 \end{bmatrix} \tag{1.3}$$

The initial letters of these masks indicate *L*ocal averaging, *E*dge detection and *S*pot detection. In fact, these basic masks span the entire 1×3 subspace and form a complete set. Similarly, the 1×5 masks obtained by convolving pairs of these 1×3 masks together form a complete set:[d]

$$\mathrm{L5} = \begin{bmatrix} 1 & 4 & 6 & 4 & 1 \end{bmatrix} \tag{1.4}$$

$$\mathrm{E5} = \begin{bmatrix} -1 & -2 & 0 & 2 & 1 \end{bmatrix} \tag{1.5}$$

$$\mathrm{S5} = \begin{bmatrix} -1 & 0 & 2 & 0 & -1 \end{bmatrix} \tag{1.6}$$

$$\mathrm{R5} = \begin{bmatrix} 1 & -4 & 6 & -4 & 1 \end{bmatrix} \tag{1.7}$$

$$\mathrm{W5} = \begin{bmatrix} -1 & 2 & 0 & -2 & 1 \end{bmatrix} \tag{1.8}$$

(Here the initial letters are as before, with the addition of *R*ipple detection and *W*ave detection.) We can also use matrix multiplication to combine the 1×3 and a similar set of 3×1 masks to obtain nine 3×3 masks—for example:

$$\begin{bmatrix} 1 \\ 2 \\ 1 \end{bmatrix} \begin{bmatrix} -1 & 2 & -1 \end{bmatrix} = \begin{bmatrix} -1 & 2 & -1 \\ -2 & 4 & -2 \\ -1 & 2 & -1 \end{bmatrix} \tag{1.9}$$

The resulting set of masks also forms a complete set (Table 1.1): note that two of these masks are identical to the Sobel operator masks. The corresponding 5×5 masks are entirely similar but are not considered in detail here as all relevant principles are illustrated by the 3×3 masks.

All such sets of masks include one whose components do not average to zero. Thus it is less useful for texture analysis since it will give results dependent more on image intensity than on texture. The remainder are sensitive to edge points, spots, lines and combinations of these.

Having produced images that indicate local edginess, etc., the next stage is to deduce the local magnitudes of these quantities. These magnitudes are then smoothed over a fair-sized region rather greater than the basic filter mask size (e.g. Laws used a 15×15 smoothing window after applying his 3×3 masks): the effect of this is to smooth over the gaps between the texture edges and other micro-features. At this point the image has been transformed into a vector image, each component of which represents energy of a different type. While Laws (1980)[12] used both squared magnitudes and absolute magnitudes to estimate texture energy, the former corresponding

[d]In principle nine masks can be formed in this way, but only five of them are distinct.

to true energy and giving a better response, the latter are useful in requiring less computation:

$$E(l,m) = \sum_{i=l-p}^{l+p} \sum_{j=m-p}^{m+p} |F(i,j)| \tag{1.10}$$

$F(i,j)$ being the local magnitude of a typical microfeature which is smoothed at a general scan position (l,m) in a $(2p+1) \times (2p+1)$ window.

Table 1.1. The nine 3×3 Laws masks.
© Elsevier 2005.

$\mathbf{L3}^{\top}\mathbf{L3}$			$\mathbf{L3}^{\top}\mathbf{E3}$			$\mathbf{L3}^{\top}\mathbf{S3}$		
1	2	1	–1	0	1	–1	2	–1
2	4	2	–2	0	2	–2	4	–2
1	2	1	–1	0	1	–1	2	–1
$\mathbf{E3}^{\top}\mathbf{L3}$			$\mathbf{E3}^{\top}\mathbf{E3}$			$\mathbf{E3}^{\top}\mathbf{S3}$		
–1	–2	–1	1	0	–1	1	–2	1
0	0	0	0	0	0	0	0	0
1	2	1	–1	0	1	–1	2	–1
$\mathbf{S3}^{\top}\mathbf{L3}$			$\mathbf{S3}^{\top}\mathbf{E3}$			$\mathbf{S3}^{\top}\mathbf{S3}$		
–1	–2	–1	1	0	–1	1	–2	1
2	4	2	–2	0	2	–2	4	–2
–1	–2	–1	1	0	–1	1	–2	1

A further stage is required to combine the various energies in a number of different ways, providing several outputs which can be fed into a classifier to decide upon the particular type of texture at each pixel location (Fig. 1.9): if necessary, principal components analysis is used at this point to help select a suitable set of intermediate outputs.

To understand the process more clearly, consider the use of masks $\mathrm{L3}^{\top}\mathrm{E3}$ and $\mathrm{E3}^{\top}\mathrm{L3}$. If their responses are squared and added, we have a very similar situation to a Sobel operator. An alternate result can be obtained for directional textures by using the same mask responses and applying the arctan function—which can be regarded as enhancing the classifier (Fig. 1.9) in a particular way.

Laws' method resulted in excellent classification accuracy quoted at (for example) 87% compared with 72% for the co-occurrence matrix method,

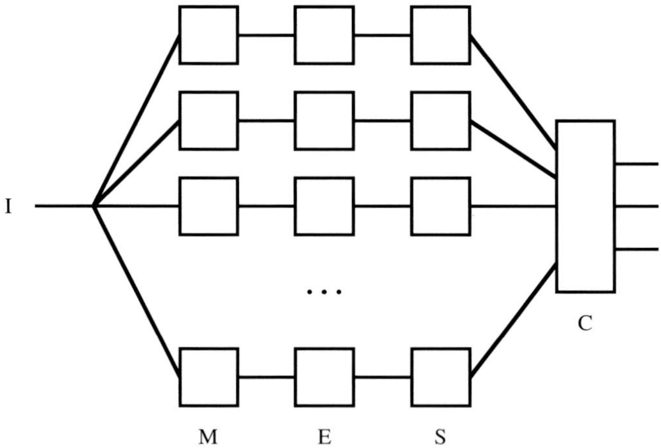

Fig. 1.9. Basic form for a Laws texture classifier. Here I is the incoming image, M represents the microfeature calculation, E the energy calculation, S the smoothing, and C the final classification. © Elsevier 2005.

when applied to a composite texture image of grass, raffia, sand, wool, pigskin, leather, water and wood (Laws, 1980).[12] He also found that the histogram equalisation normally applied to images to eliminate first-order differences in texture field grey-scale distributions gave little improvement in this case.

Research was undertaken by Pietikäinen *et al.* (1983)[13] to determine whether the precise coefficients used in the Laws' masks are responsible for the performance of his method. They found that so long as the general forms of the masks were retained, performance did not deteriorate, and could in some instances be improved. They were able to confirm that Laws' texture energy measures are more powerful than measures based on pairs of pixels (i.e. co-occurrence matrices).

1.6. The Eigenfilter Approach

In 1983 Ade[14] investigated the theory underlying the Laws' approach, and developed a revised rationale in terms of eigenfilters. He took all possible pairs of pixels within a 3×3 window, and characterised the image intensity data by a 9×9 covariance matrix. He then determined the eigenvectors required to diagonalise this matrix. These correspond to filter masks similar to the Laws' masks, i.e. use of these 'eigenfilter' masks produces images which are principal component images for the given texture. Furthermore, each eigenvalue gives that part of the variance of the original image that can be extracted by the corresponding filter. Essentially, the variances give an exhaustive description of a given texture in terms of the texture of the images from which the covariance matrix was originally derived. Clearly, the filters that give rise to low variances can be taken to be relatively unimportant for texture recognition.

It will be useful to illustrate the technique for a 3×3 window. Here we follow Ade (1983)[14] in numbering the pixels within a 3×3 window in scan order:

1	2	3
4	5	6
7	8	9

This leads to a 9×9 covariance matrix for describing relationships between pixel intensities within a 3×3 window, as stated above. At this point we recall that we are describing a texture, and assuming that its properties are not synchronous with the pixel tessellation, we would expect various coefficients of the covariance matrix C to be equal: for example, C_{24} should equal C_{57}; in addition, C_{57} must equal C_{75}. It is worth pursuing this matter, as a reduced number of parameters will lead to increased accuracy in determining the remaining ones. In fact, there are $\binom{9}{2} = 36$ ways of selecting pairs of pixels, but there are only 12 distinct spatial relationships between pixels if we disregard translations of whole pairs—or 13 if we include the null vector in the set (see Table 1.2). Thus the covariance matrix takes the form:

$$C = \begin{bmatrix} a & b & f & c & d & k & g & m & h \\ b & a & b & e & c & d & l & g & m \\ f & b & a & j & e & c & i & l & g \\ c & e & j & a & b & f & c & d & k \\ d & c & e & b & a & b & e & c & d \\ k & d & c & f & b & a & j & e & c \\ g & l & i & c & e & j & a & b & f \\ m & g & l & d & c & e & b & a & b \\ h & m & g & k & d & c & f & b & a \end{bmatrix} \tag{1.11}$$

C is symmetric, and the eigenvalues of a real symmetric covariance matrix are real and positive, and the eigenvectors are mutually orthogonal. In addition, the eigenfilters thus produced reflect the proper structure of the texture being studied, and are ideally suited to characterising it. For example, for a texture with a prominent highly directional pattern, there will be one or more high energy eigenvalues with eigenfilters having strong directionality in the corresponding direction.

Table 1.2. Spatial relationships between pixels in a 3 × 3 window.

a	b	c	d	e	f	g	h	i	j	k	l	m
9	6	6	4	4	3	3	1	1	2	2	2	2

This table shows the number of occurrences of the spatial relationships between pixels in a 3 × 3 window. Note that a is the diagonal element of the covariance matrix C, and that all others appear twice as many times in C as indicated in the table.

1.7. Appraisal of the Texture Energy and Eigenfilter Approaches

At this point, it will be worthwhile to compare the Laws and Ade approaches more carefully. In the Laws approach standard filters are used, texture energy images are produced, and then principal component analysis may be applied to lead to recognition; whereas in the Ade approach, special filters (the eigenfilters) are applied, incorporating the results of principal component analysis, following which texture energy measures are calculated and a suitable number of these are applied for recognition.

The Ade approach is superior to the extent that it permits low-value energy components to be eliminated early on, thereby saving computation. For example, in Ade's application, the first five of the nine components contain 99.1% of the total texture energy, so the remainder can definitely be ignored; in addition, it would appear that another two of the components containing respectively 1.9% and 0.7% of the energy could also be ignored, with little loss of recognition accuracy. However, in some applications textures could vary continually, and it may well not be advantageous to fine-tune a method to the particular data pertaining at any one time.[e] In addition, to do so may prevent an implementation from having wide generality or (in the case of hardware implementations) being so cost-effective.

[e]For example, these remarks apply (1) to textiles, for which the degree of stretch will vary continuously during manufacture, (2) to raw food products such as beans, whose sizes will vary with the source of supply, and (3) to processed food products such as cakes, for which the crumbliness will vary with cooking temperature and water vapour content.

There is therefore still a case for employing the simplest possible complete set of masks, and using the Laws approach.

In 1986, Unser[15] developed a more general version of the Ade technique. In this approach not only is performance optimised for texture classification but also it is optimised for discrimination between two textures by simultaneous diagonalisation of two covariance matrices. The method has been developed further by Unser and Eden (1989, 1990):[16,17] this work makes a careful analysis of the use of non-linear detectors. As a result, two levels of non-linearity are employed, one immediately after the linear filters and designed (by employing a specific Gaussian texture model) to feed the smoothing stage with genuine variance or other suitable measures, and the other after the spatial smoothing stage to counteract the effect of the earlier filter, and aiming to provide a feature value that is in the same units as the input signal. In practical terms this means having the capability for providing an r.m.s. texture signal from each of the linear filter channels.

Overall, the originally intuitive Laws approach emerged during the 1980s as a serious alternative to the co-occurrence matrix approach. It is as well to note that alternative methods that are potentially superior have also been devised—see for example the local rank correlation method of Harwood *et al.* (1985),[18] and the forced-choice method of Vistnes (1989)[19] for finding edges between different textures which apparently has considerably better accuracy than the Laws approach. Vistnes's (1989)[19] investigation concludes that the Laws approach is limited by (a) the small scale of the masks which can miss larger-scale textural structures, and (b) the fact that the texture energy smoothing operation blurs the texture feature values across the edge. The latter finding (or the even worse situation where a third class of texture appears to be located in the region of the border between two textures) has also been noted by Hsiao and Sawchuk (1989)[20,21] who applied an improved technique for feature smoothing; they also used probabilistic relaxation for enforcing spatial organisation on the resulting data.

1.8. Problems with Texture Segmentation

As noted in the previous section, when texture analysis algorithms such as the Laws' method are used for texture segmentation, inappropriate regions and classifications are frequently encountered. These arise because the statistical nature of textures means that spatial smoothing has to be done at a certain stage of the process: as a result, the transition region between

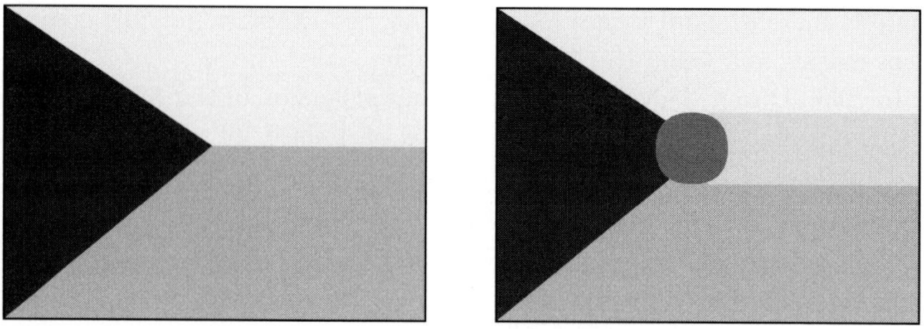

(a) (b)

Fig. 1.10. Problems with texture segmentation. (a) depicts an original texture where darkness indicates the density of peaks near each pixel. (b) shows where spurious classifications can occur between (in this case) one pair of regions and also between a triplet of regions.

textures may be classified as a totally different texture. For example, if one texture T_1 has n_1 intensity peaks over a smoothing area A, and another texture T_2 has n_2 such peaks over a corresponding area, then a transition region can easily have $(n_1 + n_2)/2$ intensity peaks over an intermediate smoothing area. If this is close to the number of peaks expected for a third texture T_3 on which the classifier has been trained, the transition region will be classified as type T_3.

The situation will be even more complicated where three textures T_1, T_2, T_3 come together at a point P. Not only can the texture regions between pairs of textures be segmented and classified erroneously, but a further texture region may also appear around P. Figure 1.10 shows a possible scenario for this. In this case, if there are n_1, n_2, n_3 peaks over the corresponding smoothing areas, T_4 appears if $n_4 \simeq (n_1 + n_2)/2$ and T_5 appears if $n_5 \simeq (n_1 + n_2 + n_3)/3$. Note that such situations will not arise if the classifier has not been trained on the additional textures T_4 and T_5. However, the output of the smoothing area will still change gradually from n_1 to n_2 on moving from T_1 to T_2, and similarly for the other cases. (Note that the scenario depicted in Fig. 1.10 is not the worst possible, as additional textures could appear in all three transition regions T_1–T_2, T_2–T_3, T_3–T_1, and also in the triple transition region T_1–T_2–T_3.)

Fortunately, these types of misclassification scenario should appear less often than indicated above. This is because we have assumed that just one microfeature is being measured: but in fact, as Fig. 1.9 shows, there will normally be nine or more microfeatures, and each should lead to different

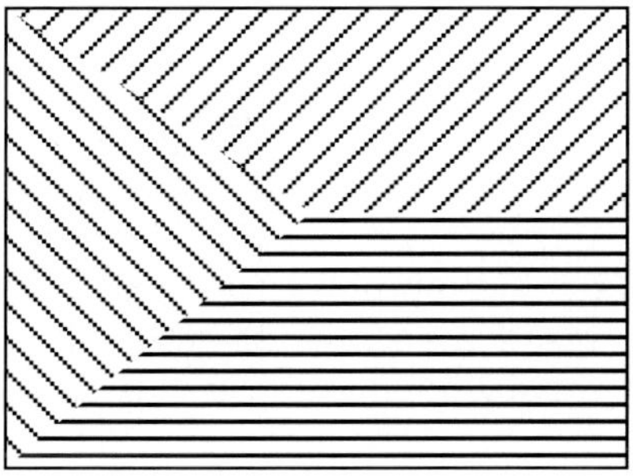

(a) (b)

Fig. 1.11. Texture segmentation with directional textures. This figure shows that with perfect pattern structure, particularly good segmentation can be performed—though this may well not apply for less artificial textures or when the boundaries between textures are at all crinkly.

ways in which textures such as T_1 and T_2 differ. There will therefore be less likelihood that spurious regions such as T_4 will occur. However, regions such as T_5 have a higher probability of occurring, because there are so many combinations of textures that can arise in the many sampling regions surrounding P. Again, generalisation is difficult because a lot depends on the exact training that the classifier has been subjected to.

Overall, we can say that while any individual microfeature may allow a texture to be misclassified in a particular transition region, there is much less likelihood that a number of them will act coherently in this way, though the possibility is distinctly enhanced where three textures meet at a point.

Finally, we enquire whether it is ever impossible for such spurious regions to occur. Take, for example, the case of a set of three directional textures meeting at a point, as in Fig. 1.11. Analysis of the patterns could then yield strict boundaries between them without the possibility of spurious regions being introduced. However, such accurately constructed patterns lack the partial randomness characteristic of a texture; thus it is difficult to envisage smoothing areas not being needed for real textures. For further enlightenment on such points, see Vistnes (1989)[19] and Hsiao and Sawchuk (1989).[20,21]

1.9. An X-Ray Inspection Application

The application outlined in this section relates to the inspection of bags of frozen vegetables such as peas, sweetcorn or stir-fry (Patel *et al.* 1996).[22]

In the past it has been usual to use X-rays for this purpose, as 'hard' contaminants such as pieces of metal can be located in the images by global thresholding. However, such schemes are very poor at locating 'soft' contaminants such as wood, plastic and rubber; in addition, they are often unable to detect small stones even though these are commonly classed as hard contaminants. One basic problem is the high level of intensity variation in the X-ray image of the substrate vegetable matter: the fact that several layers of vegetables contribute to the same image means that the latter appears highly textured, and it is rather ineffective to apply simple thresholding.

In this application, no assumptions can be made about the individual foreign objects that might occur, so the usual algorithms for locating defects cannot be used. In particular, shape analysis and simple measures of intensity are mostly inappropriate, and thus it is necessary to recognise foreign objects by the fact that they disrupt the normal (textural) intensity pattern of the substrate. *A priori*, it might have been thought that a set of feedforward artificial neural networks (ANNs), each adapted to detect a particular foreign object, would be useful. However, so many types of foreign object with so many possible shapes and sizes can occur that this is not a viable approach except for certain crucial contaminants.

To solve this problem Laws' approach to texture analysis was adopted. The reasons for this choice were (a) ease of setting up and (b) the fact that Laws' approach is well adapted to hardware implementation as it employs small neighbourhood convolutions to obtain a set of processed images. Summing the 'textural energies' in these images permits any foreign objects to be detected by thresholding coupled with a minor amount of further processing.

Following Ade's (1983)[14] modification of the Laws' schema, it was found that sensitivity is enhanced by making use of principal components analysis (PCA). However, instead of using conventional diagonalisation procedures, the Hebbian type of ANN (Oja 1989)[23] was adopted. A major advantage of the Hebbian approach is that it permits PCA to be applied without the huge computational load that would be expected when dealing with large matrices.

Finally, by adopting a statistical pattern recognition approach, it is possible to classify the images into three regions—background region, food-bag region, and any foreign object regions. Thus it is unnecessary to have a preliminary stage of bag location—with the result that the whole inspection algorithm becomes significantly more efficient.

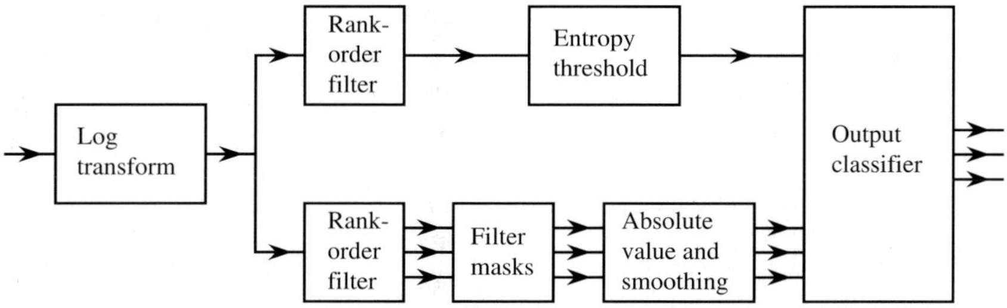

Fig. 1.12. Foreign object detection system. The input image comes in on the left, and the output classification (which is not an image) emerges on the right. © World Scientific 2000.

1.9.1. *Further details of the algorithm*

The considerations mentioned above lead to a system design of the form shown in Fig. 1.12. In particular, the initial acquisition stage is followed by a preprocessing stage, a feature extraction stage and a decision stage. For simplicity, the Hebbian training paths are not shown in this figure, which just includes the data paths for normal testing of the input images.

A major part of Fig. 1.12 that has not been covered by the earlier discussion is the preprocessing stage. In fact, this has several components. The first is the log transform, which compensates for the non-linearity of the image acquisition process, thereby making the occupation levels of the grey-levels more uniform and the subsequent processing more reliable. Rank-order filtering provides further capabilities for preprocessing. In particular, local intensity minimisation operations have been found valuable for expanding small dark foreign objects in order to make them more easily discernible. In some cases the same operation has also been found useful for enhancing the contrast between soft contaminants and the food substrate. Finally, thresholding is added to the texture analysis scheme, both to provide the capability for locating contaminants directly and as the final decision-making stage of the texture analysis process.

It was found to be both effective and computationally efficient to use Laws' masks of size 3×3 to form the microfeatures, and, following absolute value determination, to use smoothing masks of size 5×5 to obtain the texture energy macrofeatures. The tests were made with 1 lb. bags of frozen sweetcorn kernels into which foreign objects of various shapes, sizes and origins were inserted: specifically, foreign objects consisting of small pieces of glass, metal and stone and larger pieces of plastic, rubber and wood were used for this purpose (Fig. 1.13).

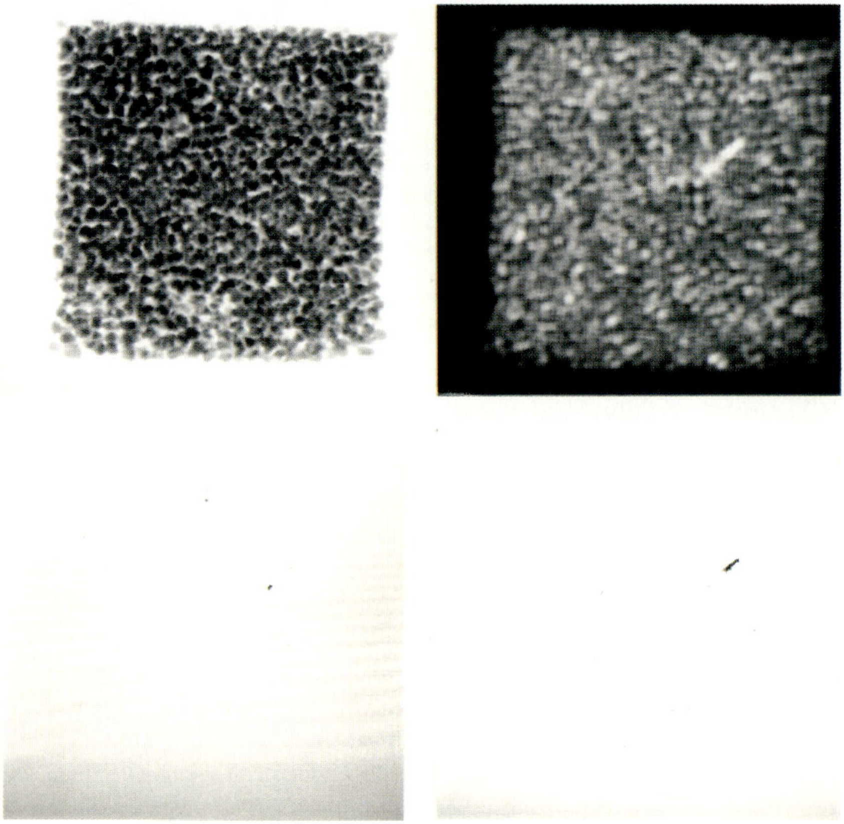

Fig. 1.13. Foreign object detection using texture analysis. (top left) Original X-ray image of a packet of frozen sweetcorn. (top right) An image in which any foreign objects (here a splinter of glass) have been enhanced by texture analysis. (bottom left and right) The respective thresholded images. Notice that false alarms are starting to arise in the bottom left, whereas in the bottom right there is much increased confidence in the detection of foreign objects. © MCB University Press 1995.

1.10. Other Approaches to Texture Analysis

1.10.1. *Fractal-based measures of texture*

An important new approach to texture analysis that arose in the 1980s was that of fractals. This incorporates the observation due to Mandelbrot (1982)[24] that measurements of the length of a coastline (for example) will vary with the size of the measuring tool used for the purpose, since details smaller than the size of the tool will be missed. If the size of the measuring tool is taken as λ, the measured quantity will be $M = n\lambda^D$, where D is known as the fractal dimension and must in general be larger than the immediate geometric dimension if correct measurements are to result (for a coastline we will thus have $D > 2$). Thus, when measurements are being made of 2D textures, it is found that D can take values from 2.0 to at least 2.8 (Pentland, 1984).[25] Interestingly, these values of D have been found to correspond roughly to subjective measures of the roughness of the surface being inspected (Pentland, 1984).[25]

Since the fractal approach was put forward by Pentland (1984),[25] other workers have expressed certain problems with it. For example, reducing all textural measurements to the single measure D clearly cannot permit all textures to be distinguished (Keller *et al.*, 1989).[26] Hence there have been moves to define further fractal-based measures. Mandelbrot himself brought in the concept of lacunarity and in 1982 provided one definition, while Keller *et al.* (1989)[26] and others provided further definitions.

Finally, note that Gårding (1988)[27] found that fractal dimension is not always equivalent to subjective judgements of roughness: in particular he found that a region of Gaussian noise of low amplitude superimposed on a constant grey-level will have a fractal dimension that approaches 3.0—a rather high value, which is contrary to our judgement of such surfaces as being quite smooth. (An interpretation of this result is that highly noisy textures appear exactly like 3D landscapes in relief!)

1.10.2. *Markov random field models of texture*

Markov models have long been used for texture synthesis, to help with the generation of realistic images. However, they have also proved increasingly useful for texture analysis. In essence a Markov model is a 1D construct in which the intensity at any pixel depends only upon the intensity of the previous pixel in a chain and upon a transition probability matrix. For images this is too weak a characterisation, and various more complex constructs have been devised. Interest in such models dates from as early as 1965 (Abend *et al.*, 1965),[28] and during the 1980s a considerable amount of further work was being published (e.g. Geman and Geman, 1984; Derin and Elliott, 1987).[29,30] Space does not permit details of these algorithms to be given here. Suffice it to say that by 1987 impressive results for texture segmentation of real scenes were being achieved using this approach (Derin and Elliott, 1987).[30]

1.10.3. *Structural approaches to texture analysis*

It has already been remarked that textures approximate to a basic textural element or primitive that is replicated in a more or less regular manner. Structural approaches to texture analysis aim to discern the textural primitive and to determine the underlying gross structure of the texture. Early work (e.g. Pickett, 1970)[31] suggested the structural approach, though little research on these lines was carried out until the late 1970s—e.g. Davis (1979).[32] An unusual and interesting paper by Kass and Witkin (1987)[33] shows how orientated patterns from wood grain, straw, fabric and fingerprints, and also spectrograms and seismic patterns can be analysed: the method adopted involves building up a flow coordinate system for the image, though the method rests more on edge pattern orientation analysis than on more usual texture analysis procedures. A similar statement may be made about the topologically invariant texture descriptor method of Eichmann and Kasparis (1988),[34] which relies on Hough transforms for finding line structures in highly structured textiles. More recently, pyramidal approaches have been applied to structural texture segmentation (Lam and Ip, 1994).[35]

1.10.4. *3D shape from texture*

This is another topic in texture analysis that developed strongly during the 1980s. After early work by Bajcsy and Liebermann (1976)[36] for the case of planar surfaces, Witkin (1981)[37] significantly extended this work and at the same time laid the foundations for general development of the whole subject. Many papers followed (e.g. Aloimonos and Swain, 1985; Stone, 1990)[38,39] but there is no space to cover them all here. In general, workers have studied how an assumed standard texel shape is distorted and its size changed by 3D projections; they then relate this to the local orientation of the surface. Since the texel distortion varies as the cosine of the angle between the line of sight and the local normal to the surface plane, essentially similar 'reflectance map' analysis is required as in the case of shape-from-shading estimation. An alternative approach adopted by Chang *et al.* (1987)[40] involves texture discrimination by projective invariants. More recently, Singh and Ramakrishna (1990)[41] exploited shadows and integrated the information available from texture and from shadows.

1.10.5. *More recent developments*

Recent developments include further work on automated visual inspection (e.g. Davies, 2000; Pun and Lee, 2003),[42,43] medical, remote sensing and other applications. The paper by Pun and Lee is specifically aimed at rotation-invariant texture classification but also aims at scale invariance. Other work (Clerc and Mallat, 2002)[44] is concerned with recovering shape from texture via a texture gradient equation, while Ma *et al.* (2003)[45] are particularly concerned with person identification based on iris textures. Mirmehdi and Petrou (2000)[46] describe an in-depth investigation of colour texture segmentation. In this context, the importance of 'wavelets'[f] as an increasingly used technique of texture analysis with interesting applications (such as human iris recognition) should be noted (e.g. Daugman, 2003).[48] Note that they solve in a neat way the problems of Fourier analysis that were noted in Sec. 1.3 (essentially, they act as local Fourier transforms).

Finally, in a particularly exciting advance, Spence *et al.* (2003)[49] managed to eliminate texture by using photometric stereo to find the underlying surface shape (or 'bump map'), following which they were able to perform impressive reconstructions, including texture, from a variety of viewpoints; McGunnigle and Chantler (2003)[50] have shown that this sort of technique is also able to reveal hidden writing on textured surfaces, where only pen pressure marks have been made. Similarly, Pan *et al.* (2004)[51] have shown how texture can be eliminated from ancient tablets (in particular those made of lead and wood) to reveal clear images of the writing underneath.

1.11. Concluding Remarks

This chapter started by exploring the meaning of texture—essentially by asking "What is a texture and how is a texture formed?" Typically, a texture starts with a surface[g] that exhibits local roughness or structure, which is then projected to form a textured image. Such an image exhibits both regularity and randomness to varying degrees: directionality and orientation will also be relevant parameters in a good many cases. However, the essential feature of randomness means that textures have to be characterised by statistical techniques, and recognised using statistical

[f]Wavelets are directional filters reminiscent of the Laws edges, bars, waves and ripples, but have more rigorously defined shapes and envelopes, and are defined in multiresolution sets (Mallat, 1989).[47]

[g]Naturally, textures also arise inside solid bodies, seen through the medium of X-rays.

classification procedures. Techniques that have been used for this purpose have been seen to include autocorrelation, co-occurrence matrices, texture energy measures, fractal-based measures, Markov random fields, and so on. These aim both to analyse and to model the textures. Indeed, it can be said that workers in this area spend much time striving to achieve ever-improved models of the textures they are working with in order to better recognise and segment them. Failure to model accurately in the end means failure to perform the requisite classification tasks. And, as elsewhere in vision, modelling is the key: we need to be able to generate accurate look-alike scenes in order to succeed with classification. Nevertheless, an additional ingredient is necessary—the ability to infer the parameters that permit the currently viewed scene to be modelled. In fact, using different techniques, different representations and procedures will be necessary in order to perform the optimisations, and, again, workers have to strive to make their own techniques work well. The early success with PCA (cf. the Unser and Ade enhancement of the Laws approach) reflects this, but at the same time this approach has its limitations. This is why so many other methods are described by the authors of the later chapters in this book. Not only do we find Markov random field models, but also local statistical operators, 'texems', hierarchical texture descriptions, bidirectional reflectance distribution functions, trace transforms, structural approaches, and more. The developing methodology is so wide and so varied[h] that it seems difficult to consider texture analysis as a mature subject: but yet, in terms of the ideas outlined above, it is clear that each of the authors has been able to find generic statistical approaches that match some important subset of the wide and complex range of textures that exist in the real world.

Acknowledgements

The work on this chapter has been supported by Research Councils UK, under Basic Technology Grant GR/R87642/02. Tables 1.1 and 1.2, and Figs. 1.5, 1.6, 1.7, 1.8 and 1.9, and some of the text are reproduced from Chapter 26 of: E.R. Davies *Machine Vision: Theory, Algorithms, Practicalities* (3rd edition, 2005), with permission from Elsevier. Figure 1.12 and some of the text are reproduced from Chapter 11 of: E.R. Davies *Image Processing for the Food Industry* (2000), with permission from World Scientific. Figure 1.13 is reproduced from: D. Patel, E.R. Davies, and

[h]See also the recent book by Petrou and Sevilla (2006).[52]

I. Hannah *Sensor Review* 15(2):27–28 (1995), with permission from MCB University Press.

References

1. R.K. Bajcsy. Computer identification of visual surfaces. *Computer Graphics and Image Processing*, 2:118–130, October 1973.
2. W.B. Shaming. Digital image transform encoding, 1974. RCA Corp. paper no. PE-622.
3. C.R. Dyer and A. Rosenfeld. Fourier texture features: Suppression of aperture effects. *IEEE Trans. Systems, Man and Cybernetics*, 6:703–705, 1976.
4. J.S. Weszka and A. Rosenfeld. An application of texture analysis to materials inspection. *Pattern Recognition*, 8(4):195–200, October 1976.
5. H. Kaizer. *A Quantification of Textures on Aerial Photographs.* MS thesis, Boston University, 1955.
6. A. Rosenfeld and E.B. Troy. Visual texture analysis, 1970. Computer Science Center, Univ. of Maryland Techn. Report TR-116.
7. A. Rosenfeld and E.B. Troy. Visual texture analysis. In *Conf. Record for Symposium on Feature Extraction and Selection in Pattern Recogn. IEEE Publication 70C-51C, Argonne, Ill., Oct.*, pages 115–124, 1970.
8. R.M. Haralick, K. Shanmugam, and I. Dinstein. Textural features for image classification. *IEEE Trans. Systems, Man and Cybernetics*, 3(6):610–621, November 1973.
9. R.W. Conners and C.A. Harlow. A theoretical comparison of texture algorithms. *IEEE Trans. Pattern Analysis and Machine Intelligence*, 2(3):204–222, May 1980.
10. K.I. Laws. Texture energy measures. In *Proc. Image Understanding Workshop, November*, pages 47–51, 1979.
11. K.I. Laws. Rapid texture identification. *SPIE*, 238:376–380, 1980.
12. K.I. Laws. *Textured Image Segmentation.* PhD thesis, University of Southern California, LA, 1980.
13. M. Pietikäinen, A. Rosenfeld, and L.S. Davis. Experiments with texture classification using averages of local pattern matches. *IEEE Trans. Systems, Man and Cybernetics*, 13:421–426, 1983.
14. F. Ade. Characterization of textures by 'eigenfilters'. *Signal Processing*, 5:451–457, 1983.
15. M. Unser. Local linear transforms for texture measurements. *Signal Processing*, 11:61–79, July 1986.
16. M. Unser and M. Eden. Multiresolution feature extraction and selection for texture segmentation. *IEEE Trans. Pattern Analysis and Machine Intelligence*, 11(7):717–728, July 1989.
17. M. Unser and M. Eden. Nonlinear operators for improving texture segmentation based on features extracted by spatial filtering. *IEEE Trans. Systems, Man and Cybernetics*, 20(4):804–815, 1990.
18. D. Harwood, M. Subbarao, and L.S. Davis. Texture classification by lo-

cal rank correlation. *Computer Vision Graphics and Image Processing*, 32(3):404–411, December 1985.
19. R. Vistnes. Texture models and image measures for texture discrimination. *International Journal of Computer Vision*, 3(4):313–336, November 1989.
20. J.Y. Hsiao and A.A. Sawchuk. Supervised textured image segmentation using feature smoothing and probabilistic relaxation techniques. *IEEE Trans. Pattern Analysis and Machine Intelligence*, 11(12):1279–1292, December 1989.
21. J.Y. Hsiao and A.A. Sawchuk. Unsupervised textured image segmentation using feature smoothing and probabilistic relaxation techniques. *Computer Vision Graphics and Image Processing*, 48(1):1–21, October 1989.
22. D. Patel, E.R. Davies, and I. Hannah. The use of convolution-operators for detecting contaminants in food images. *Pattern Recognition*, 29(6):1019–1029, June 1996.
23. E. Oja. A simplified neuron model as a principal component analyzer. *J. Math. Biol.*, 15:267–273, 1982.
24. B.B. Mandelbrot. *The Fractal Geometry of Nature*. Freeman, 1982.
25. A.P. Pentland. Fractal-based description of natural scenes. *IEEE Trans. Pattern Analysis and Machine Intelligence*, 6(6):661–674, November 1984.
26. J.M. Keller, S.S. Chen, and R.M. Crownover. Texture description and segmentation through fractal geometry. *Computer Vision Graphics and Image Processing*, 45(2):150–166, February 1989.
27. J. Gårding. Properties of fractal intensity surfaces. *Pattern Recognition Letters*, 8:319–324, December 1988.
28. K. Abend, T.J. Harley, and L.N. Kanal. Classification of binary random patterns. *IEEE Trans. Information Theory*, 11(4):538–544, October 1965.
29. S. Geman and D. Geman. Stochastic relaxation, Gibbs distributions, and the bayesian restoration of images. *IEEE Trans. Pattern Analysis and Machine Intelligence*, 6(6):721–741, November 1984.
30. H. Derin and H. Elliott. Modelling and segmentation of noisy and textured images using Gibbs random fields. *IEEE Trans. Pattern Analysis and Machine Intelligence*, 9(1):39–55, January 1987.
31. R.M. Pickett. Visual analysis of texture in the detection and recognition of objects. In *Picture Processing and Psychopictorics*, pages 289–308, 1970.
32. L.S. Davis. Computing the spatial structures of cellular texture. *Computer Graphics and Image Processing*, 11(2):111–122, October 1979.
33. M. Kass and A.P. Witkin. Analyzing oriented patterns. *Computer Vision Graphics and Image Processing*, 37(3):362–385, March 1987.
34. G. Eichmann and T. Kasparis. Topologically invariant texture descriptors. *Computer Vision Graphics and Image Processing*, 41(3):267–281, March 1988.
35. S.W.C. Lam and H.H.S. Ip. Structural texture segmentation using irregular pyramid. *Pattern Recognition Letters*, 15(7):691–698, July 1994.
36. R.K. Bajcsy and L.I. Lieberman. Texture gradient as a depth cue. *Computer Graphics and Image Processing*, 5(1):52–67, 1976.
37. A.P. Witkin. Recovering surface shape and orientation from texture. *Artificial Intelligence*, 17(1-3):17–45, August 1981.

38. Y. Aloimonos and M.J. Swain. Shape from texture. In *Proc. IJCAI*, pages 926–931, 1985.
39. J.V. Stone. Shape from texture: textural invariance and the problem of scale in perspective images of textured surfaces. In *Proc. British Machine Vision Assoc. Conf., Oxford, 24–27 Sept.*, pages 181–186, 1990.
40. S. Chang, L.S. Davis, S.M. Dunn, A. Rosenfeld, and J.O. Eklundh. Texture discrimination by projective invariants. *Pattern Recognition Letters*, 5:337–342, May 1987.
41. R.K. Singh and R.S. Ramakrishna. Shadows and texture in computer vision. *Pattern Recognition Letters*, 11:133–141, 1990.
42. E.R. Davies. Resolution of problem with use of closing for texture segmentation. *Electronics Letters*, 36(20):1694–1696, 2000.
43. C.M. Pun and M.C. Lee. Log-polar wavelet energy signatures for rotation and scale invariant texture classification. *IEEE Trans. Pattern Analysis and Machine Intelligence*, 25(5):590–603, May 2003.
44. M. Clerc and S. Mallat. The texture gradient equation for recovering shape from texture. *IEEE Trans. Pattern Analysis and Machine Intelligence*, 24(4):536–549, April 2002.
45. L. Ma, T.N. Tan, Y. Wang, and D. Zhang. Personal identification based on iris texture analysis. *IEEE Trans. Pattern Analysis and Machine Intelligence*, 25(12):1519–1533, December 2003.
46. M. Mirmehdi and M. Petrou. Segmentation of colour textures. *IEEE Trans. Pattern Analysis and Machine Intelligence*, 22(2):142–159, 2000.
47. S.G. Mallat. A theory for multiresolution signal decomposition: The wavelet representation. *IEEE Trans. Pattern Analysis and Machine Intelligence*, 11(7):674–693, July 1989.
48. J.G. Daugman. Demodulation by complex-valued wavelets for stochastic pattern recognition. *Int. J. of Wavelets, Multiresolution and Information Processing*, 1(1):1–17, 2003.
49. A. Spence, M. Robb, M. Timmins, and M. Chantler. Real-time per-pixel rendering of textiles for virtual textile catalogues. In *Proc. INTEDEC, Edinburgh, 22–24 Sept.*, 2003.
50. G. McGunnigle and M.J. Chantler. Resolving handwriting from background printing using photometric stereo. *Pattern Recognition*, 36(8):1869–1879, August 2003.
51. X.B. Pan, M. Brady, A.K. Bowman, C. Crowther, and R.S.O. Tomlin. Enhancement and feature extraction for images of incised and ink texts. *Image and Vision Computing*, 22(6):443–451, June 2004.
52. M. Petrou and P.G. Sevilla. *Image Processing: Dealing with Texture.* Wiley, Chichester, UK, 2006.

Chapter 2

Texture Modelling and Synthesis

Rupert Paget
Computer Vision Group
Gloriastrasse 35
ETH-Zentrum, CH-8092 Zurich
rpaget@texturesynthesis.com

Texture describes a myriad of spatial patterns. Some can be quite simple, for example a checker board pattern, while others can exhibit extremely complex behaviour, as seen in nature. The science of texture analysis has been on the search for a model that can give a mathematical description to these patterns, and thus, a definition, for currently no precise definition of texture exists. However it is generally accepted that texture is a pattern that can be characterised by its local spatial behaviour, and is statistically stationary. The second pillar implies that all local spatial extents of a texture exhibit like behaviour. These sound like obvious pillars, but what this means is that the Markov Random Field model is very applicable to modelling texture. Today, it is the Markov Random Field model, or variations of it, that is most often used in modelling texture. However when applying the model to a texture, there are still some specific questions that do not have complete answers. Firstly, given a texture, what local spatial characteristics need to be modelled, and secondly, what is local? Complete answers to these questions are not currently available, so generally these questions are rephrased to ask, what model gives us the result we want? That is, if given say a classification problem, which model best discriminates between the desired texture classes? Or given say a synthesis problem, which model best replicates the desired texture (where "best" has its own qualities of measure)? Unfortunately, these two model driving forces, produce opposingly different model formulations. To really understand texture, the "Holy Grail" of texture models would be one that could uniquely describe a texture, giving both optimal discrimination and synthesis properties. To date, this has only really been achieved for a select few textures.

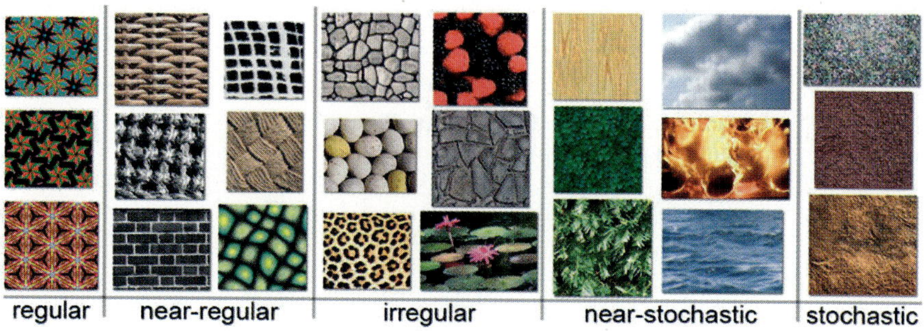

Fig. 2.1 Texture spectrum on which textures are arranged according to the regularity of their structural variations. Image courtesy of Lin *et al.*[1]

2.1. Introduction

Texture is a ubiquitous cue in visual perception, and therefore an important topic within the science of vision. In particular, it has been studied in the fields of visual perception, computer vision and computer graphics. Although these fields tend to view texture with sometimes opposing purposes, they all require that texture can in some way be mathematically modelled. However how can one model a phenomena, for which a proper definition does not exist.

The problem is that texture is quite varied, and can exhibit a myriad of properties. These properties can cover a complete plethora of possibilities, from smooth to rough, coarse to fine, soft to hard, *etc.* However, from a mathematical perspective it is usual to view texture as a spectrum of stochastic to regular.

Stochastic textures These textures look like noise: colour dots that are randomly scattered over the image, barely specified by attributes such as minimum and maximum brightness and average colour. Many textures look like stochastic textures when viewed from a distance.

Regular textures These textures simply contain periodic patterns, where the color/intensity and shape of all texture elements are repeated in equal intervals.

These extremes are connected by a smooth transition, as visualized in Figure 2.1

Natural scenes contain a huge number of visual patterns generated by various stochastic and structural processes. How to represent and model these diverse visual patterns, and how to learn and compute these visual patterns efficiently is a fundamental problem in computer vision.

2.1.1. *Texture perception*

One of the most influential pieces of work in the area of human textural perception was contributed by Julesz. Julesz's[2] classic approach for determining if two textures were alike was to embed one texture in the other. If the embedded patch of texture visually stood out from the surrounding texture, then the two textures were deemed to be dissimilar. Julesz found that texture with similar first order statistics, but different second-order statistics, were easily discriminated. However Julesz could not find any textures with the same first and second-order statistics, but different third-order statistics, that could be discriminated. This led to the Julesz conjecture that,

> "Iso-second-order textures are indistinguishable."
> — Julesz 1960s-1980s

However, later Caelli, Julesz, and Gilbert[3] did produce iso-second-order textures that could be discriminated with pre-attentive human visual perception. Further work by Julesz[4] revealed that his original conjecture was wrong. Instead, he found that the human visual perception mechanism did not necessarily use third-order statistics for the discrimination of these iso-second-order textures, but rather used the second order statistics of features he called *textons*. These textons he described as being the fundamentals of texture. Julesz revised his original conjecture to state that,

> "The human pre-attentive visual system cannot compute statistical parameters higher than second order."
> — Julesz 1960s-1980s

He further conjectured that the human pre-attentive visual system actually uses only the first order statistics of these textons.

Since these pre-attentive studies into the human visual perception, psychophysical research has focused on developing physiologically plausible models of texture discrimination. These models involved determining which measurements of textural variations humans are most sensitive to. Textons were not found to be the plausible textural discriminating measurements as envisaged by Julesz.[5] On the other hand, psychophysical research has provided evidence that the human brain does a spatial frequency analysis of the image.[6] Chubb and Landy[7] observed that the marginal histogram of Gabor filtered images seemed to provide sufficient statistics in human texture perception. However the current opinion in Neurobiology, is that the visual cortex performs sparse coding, whereby an image is represented by only a small number of simultaneously active neurons.[8]

2.2. Texture Analysis

The vague definition of texture leads to a variety of different ways to analyse texture. In which case, the analysis tends to be more driven by the desired application rather than any pure fundamentals. A summary of possible approaches can be found in the following literature.[9–14] These approaches may be broken down into the following classes:

(1) **Statistical methods:** A set of features is used to represent the texture. Generally it is not possible to reconstruct the texture from the features, so these types of methods are usually only used for classification purposes. Haralick[12] is renowned for providing such a feature set, which was derived from the Grey level co-occurrence matrices (GLCM).
(2) **Spectral methods:** Like statistical methods, spectral methods collect a distribution of filter responses as input to further classification or segmentation. Gabor filters are particularly efficient and precise for detecting the frequency channels and orientations of a texture pattern.[15] However be aware, that in this case, more does not necessarily mean better.[16]
(3) **Structural methods:** Some textures can be viewed as two dimensional patterns consisting of a set of primitives or subpatterns (*i.e.*, textons[4]) which are arranged according to certain placement rules. Correct identification of these primitives is difficult. However if the primitives completely captivate the texture, then it is possible to re-create the texture from the placement rules. A survey of structural approaches for texture is given by Haralick.[12] Haindl[17] also covers some models used for structural texture analysis.
(4) **Stochastic methods:** The texture is assumed to be the realisation of a stochastic process which is governed by some parameters. Analysis is performed by defining a model and estimating the associated parameters. Although defining the correct model is still a "black art", there are some rigourous methods for estimating the parameters, *e.g.*, Seymour[18] used maximum-likelihood estimation, or there is the ever popular Monte Carlo method.[19] Alternatively, one may choose a non-parametric model.[20]

Irrespective of the approach used, the problem with using a model to define a texture is in determining when the model has captured all the significant visual characteristics of that texture. The conventional method is to use the models to actually classify a number of textures, the idea being to heuristically increase (or decrease) the model complexity until the textures in the training set can be successfully classified.

An ideal texture model is one that completely characterises a particular texture, hence it should be possible to reproduce the texture from such a model. If this could be done, we would have evidence that the model has indeed captured the full underlying mathematical description of the texture. The texture would then be uniquely characterised by the structure of the model and the set of parameters used to describe the texture.

2.3. Texture Synthesis Modelling

Unfortunately, with the present knowledge of texture, obtaining a model that captures *all* the unique characteristics specific to a particular texture is an open problem.[21] Texture is not fully understood, and therefore, what constitutes the unique characteristics has not been defined. However, a reasonable way to test whether a model has captured all the unique characteristics is to use the same model to synthesise the texture and subjectively judge the similarity of the synthetic texture to the original.

There has been quite a history of texture models designed to capture the unique characteristics of a texture. These models have ranged from the fractal,[22] auto-models,[23] autoregressive (AR),[24–26] moving average (MA),[17] autoregressive moving average (ARMA),[27] Markov,[28] autobinomial MRF,[29,30] auto-normal MRF,[31,32] Derin-Elliott,[33] Ising,[34–36] and log-SAR model[37] which was used to synthesise synthetic aperture radar images. A summary of these texture synthesis models is provided by Haindl,[17] Haralick,[38] and Tuceryan and Jain.[13]

These models were successful at modelling the stochastic type textures, but when it came to the natural textures with more structural characteristics, these models were deemed inadequate. The next generation of texture models used a multi-resolution approach. De Bonet,[39] Heeger and Bergen,[40] Navarro and Portilla,[41] Zhu, Wu and Mumford,[42] based their models on the stochastic modelling of various multi-resolution filter responses. These types of models could capture a certain degree of structure from the textures, and therefore were quite successful at synthesising natural textures. These approaches were obviously dependent on choosing the correct filters for the texture that was to be modelled.

Julesz[2] had suggested that there was textural information in the higher order statistics. Gagalowicz and Ma[19] used third order statistics to generate some natural textures. Popat and Picard,[43] and Paget and Longstaff[20] successfully used high-order, nonparametric, multiscale MRF models to synthesise some highly structured natural textures. Later it was shown through other researchers' results, that the nonparametric MRF models were the most versatile and reliable for synthesising natural textures. However these models proved less than successful at segmentation and classification.[44]

Although the synthesis test may indicate if a model has captured the specific characteristics of a texture, it does not determine whether the model is suitable for segmentation and classification. Based on Zhu, Wu and Mumford's philosophy,[42] a texture model should maximise its entropy while retaining the unique characteristics of the texture. The principle behind this philosophy is that a texture model should only model known characteristics of a texture and no more. The model should remain completely noncommittal towards any characteristics that are not part of the observed texture. Zhu, Wu, and Mumford[42] used this philosophy to build their *minimax* model, which was designed to obtain low entropy for characteristics seen in the texture while maintaining high entropy for the rest, thereby sustaining a model that infers little information about unseen characteristics. This minimax entropy philosophy is equivalent to reducing the statistical order of a model while retaining the integrity of the respective synthesised textures.[16,45]

2.4. Milestones in Texture Synthesis

The following is a collection of work that show the progression of texture models that were driven by synthesis performance. This is by no means a complete collection, but it provides a brief overview of the history of texture synthesis modelling. The following were chosen on the basis that they are fairly well known within the texture synthesis community. However this should not detract from other well deserving models that do not appear in this list. Obviously space prevents a complete listing of all relevant models. The list begins with Popat and Picard for the reason that they were one of the first to present a decent synthesis of a natural texture.

2.4.1. *Popat and Picard, '93: Novel cluster-based probability model for texture synthesis, classification, and compression.*[43]

This texture synthesis algorithm can be best classified as a nonparametric Markov chain synthesis algorithm. The basis of the algorithm was to order the pixels and then synthesise a new pixel from a nonparametric representation of the conditional probability function derived from samples of the input texture. Popat and Picard proposed to use stochastic sampling of

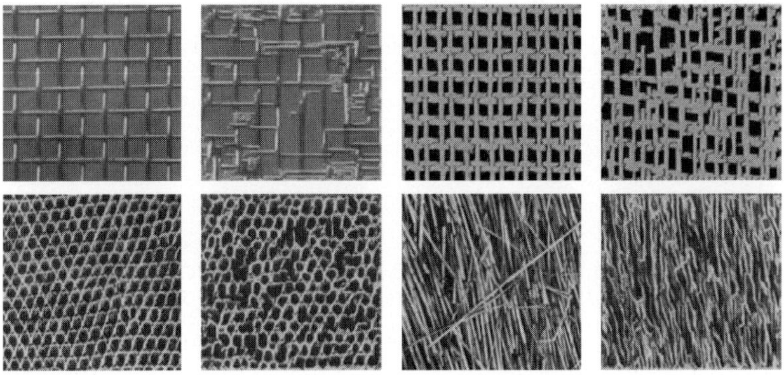

Fig. 2.2 Popat and Picard results for hierarchical synthesis of 4 Brodatz textures. In each pair left image is original and right image is synthetic. Images courtesy the Popat and Picard.[43]

the conditional probability function and also to compress the conditional probability function via a set of Gaussian kernels. This compression allowed for fast look ups, but limited the neighbourhood order that could be successfully modelled.

The one problem in Popat and Picard's approach was that it was causal. That is the synthesis was performed in a sequential sequence starting from a "seed" and gradually moving further away. This meant that if the past pixels start to deviate from those seen in the input image, then the synthesis algorithm tends to get lost in a domain that is not properly modelled, causing garbage to be produced. To alleviate the cause of this problem, Popat and Picard proposed a top-down multi-dimensional synthesis approach on a decimated grid. Results are shown in Figure 2.2.

2.4.2. *Heeger and Bergen, '95: Pyramid based texture analysis/synthesis*[40]

Heeger and Bergen were one of the first to synthesise coloured textures. They did it using a combination of Laplacian and Steerable pyramids to deconstruct an input texture. The histograms from each of the pyramid levels were used to reconstruct a similar pyramid. However the deconstruction was not orthogonal, which meant that Heeger and Bergen had to use an iterative approach of matching the histograms and expanding and reducing the pyramid. With this method, Heeger and Bergen achieved some very nice results, but their technique was limited to synthesising basically stochastic homogeneous textures with minimal structure, Figure 2.3.

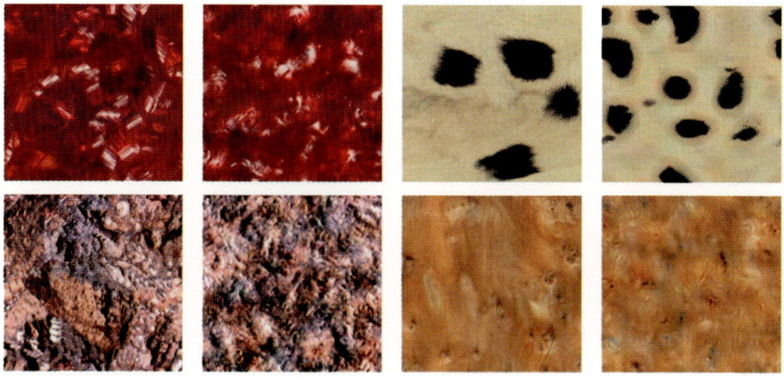

Fig. 2.3 Heeger and Bergen. In each pair left image is original and right image is synthetic: iridescent ribbon, panda fur, slag stone, figured yew wood. Images courtesy of Heeger and Bergen.[40]

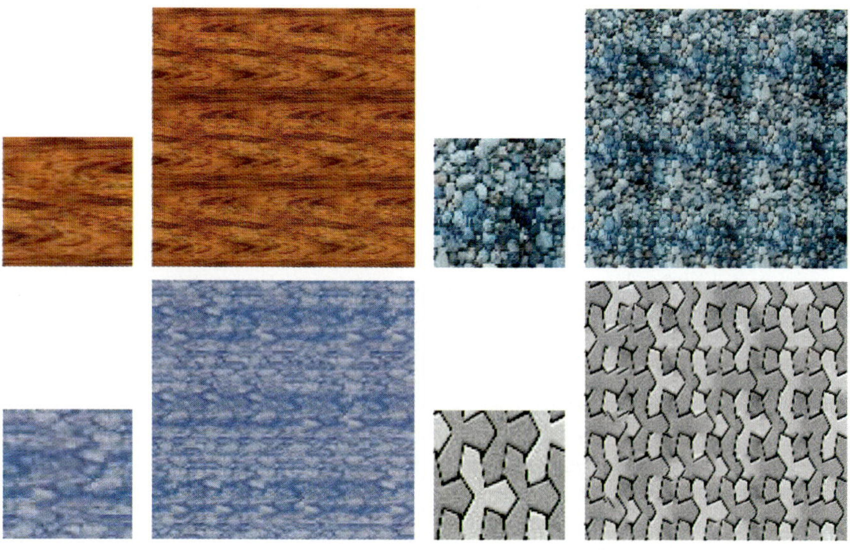

Fig. 2.4 DeBonet's texture synthesis results. Images courtesy of DeBonet.[39]

2.4.3. *De Bonet, '97: Multiresolution sampling procedure for analysis and synthesis of texture images*[39]

De Bonet's method could be considered a variant of Heeger and Bergen's pyramid based texture analysis/synthesis method. It overcomes the iterative requirement of Heeger and Bergen's method by enforcing a top-down

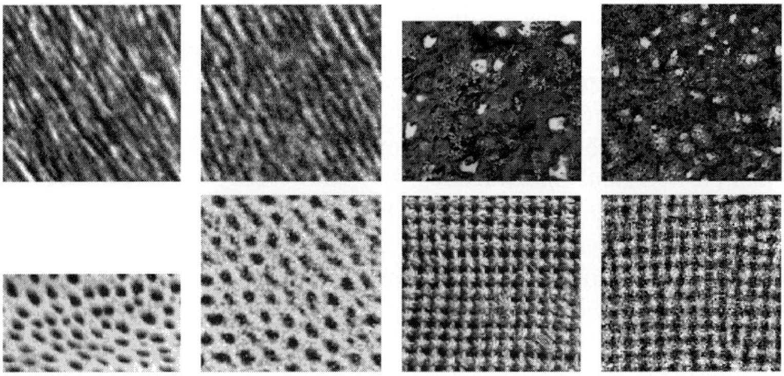

Fig. 2.5 Zhu, Wu, and Mumford: FRAME texture modelling results. In each pair left image is original and right image is synthetic. Images courtesy of Zhu *et al.*[46,47]

philosophy. That is, restricting the sampling procedure by conditioning it on the previous results from coarser resolutions in the decomposed pyramid. In De Bonet's method, the texture structure is also better handled than in Heeger and Bergen's method by further restricting the sampling procedure to pixels that fall within a threshold determined by texture features. Although De Bonet's method performed better than Heeger and Bergen's method for a wider variety of textures, the tuning of the threshold parameters was not exactly intuitive. This was problematic as synthesis results were highly sensitive to the choice of these threshold parameters, which if chosen incorrectly, detrimentally affected the synthesised texture.

2.4.4. *Zhu, Wu, and Mumford, '97, '98: FRAME: Filters, random fields and maximum entropy towards a unified theory for texture modelling*[46,47]

Zhu, Wu, and Mumford amalgamated the filter technology and MRF technology to produce the so-called FRAME model. They did this by comparing the histograms of both the filter responses from the original texture and that of the synthetic. The synthetic texture was then continually updated with respect to an evolving MRF probability function, that was defined with respect to modulated filter responses. The modulation was defined with respect to differences between the expected filter response using the current MRF probability function and the filter response from the original texture. All this avoided the messy process of trying to reconstruct a texture from arbitrary filter responses and wrapped it all up in some nice clean mathematics, but the synthesis/modelling process was very slow, Figure 2.5.

As part of the model learning process Zhu, Wu, and Mumford[46,47] presented the minimax entropy learning theory. Its basic intention was to rigourously formulate the requirements of the model when dealing with data in high dimensional domains (commonly known as the curse-of-dimensionality). The high dimensional data is best observed via lower dimensional marginal distributions, but these have to be selected so as to be as informative as possible. This is done by choosing the features and statistics that minimize the entropy of the model. While the unobserved marginal distributions are modelled by choosing the parameters to the previous features that maximises the models entropy. Basically this means the model describes the most informative features, and leaves everything else as noncommittal.

2.4.5. *Simoncelli and Portilla, '98: Texture characterisation via joint statistics of wavelet coefficient magnitudes*[48]

Simoncelli and Portilla proposed a similar technique to that of Heeger and Bergen, but where Heeger and Bergen updated the complete filter response using histogram equalisation, Simoncelli and Portilla updated each point in the pyramid of filter responses with respect to the correlations using a method similar to projection onto convex sets (POCS). They did this by finding an orthogonal projection from the filter response of the synthetic texture to that of the original. After the projection of all filter responses, the wavelet pyramid was collapsed, further projection was performed, and then the pyramid was reconstructed. This iteration continued until a convergence was reached. Simoncelli and Portilla found that only a few minutes of processing time was required to produce reasonable results. However they still had some failures, and had difficulty maintaining fidelity with textures containing structure.

2.4.6. *Paget and Longstaff, '98: Texture synthesis via a nonparametric Markov random field model*[20]

Similar to Popat and Picard's top-down approach,[43] Paget and Longstaff also used a nonparametric Markov random field model to gradually introduce the spatial components of a texture into a synthesised image, from the gross to the fine detail. They also used the same multiscale structure of a decimated grid, to sample and synthesise the texture. Where the two models differed was in how they modelled the high dimensional probability density function. Popat and Picard used a Gaussian mixture model, whereas Paget and Longstaff used Parzen density estimation and a method they termed "local annealing", to slowly refine the estimated density as the

Fig. 2.6 Simoncelli and Portilla's texture synthesis results. In each pair left image is original and right image is synthetic. Images courtesy of Simoncelli and Portilla.[48]

Fig. 2.7 Paget and Longstaff texture synthesis results. In each pair left image is original and right image is synthetic. Images courtesy of Paget and Longstaff.[44]

synthesis progressed towards a more stable state. This annealing process kept the synthesis algorithm from wandering off into a non-recoverable "no man's land."

As the synthesis algorithm used a top-down approach with a noncausal model that maintained a viable probability density function, it could be reliably used to synthesise texture to any size. This was a marked difference to the sequential approaches which were susceptible to small errors cascading the synthesis process off course and producing rubbish. The number and range of textures that could be synthesised by their scheme also showed that nonparametric Markov random field models were the models of choice for natural textures that included both stochastic and structural properties. However, the one draw back to their scheme was speed.

The results shown here, are not from the algorithm as published in Paget and Longstaff's paper,[20] but a modified version as discussed in Paget's thesis.[44]

- Sampling is not performed over all possible colour values, but only over those values that occur within the original input texture[44] [Section 7.6.1].
- Given the sampling method of iterative condition modes (ICM) and the large sparse nature of the local conditional probability density function (LCPDF), the sampling algorithm is computationally approximated as a minimum distance look up algorithm.

2.4.7. *Efros and Leung, '99: Texture synthesis by non-parametric sampling*[49]

Efros and Leung also followed the work of Popat and Picard.[43] However in their case they did not do any probability density estimation or modelling, but instead simply used the nearest neighbour look up scheme to sample the texture. This proved quite effective for synthesising new textures. However their synthesis algorithm was causal, and not multi-scaled, which meant that it had inherent stability problems. Small errors in the synthesis process would precipitate a cascading effect of errors in the output image.

2.4.8. *Wei and Levoy, '00: Fast texture synthesis using tree-structured vector quantisation*[50]

Wei and Levoy, also used Popat and Picard's approach.[43] They also used the same sequential based synthesis scheme as proposed by Popat and Picard. Although this scheme (as discussed earlier) had inherent stability problems, they kept it for a very good reason, speed. Under this scheme the Markov neighbourhood structure stayed fairly consistent over the whole synthesis process, which in turn allowed for data compression. Popat and Picard used Gaussian kernels to define a probability density function. Wei and Levoy used tree-structured vector quantisation to quickly search for the nearest neighbour.

Fig. 2.8 Efros and Leung's texture synthesis results. Images courtesy of Efros's web site.[49]

Fig. 2.9 Wei and Levoy's texture synthesis results. Images courtesy of Wei and Levoy's web site.[50]

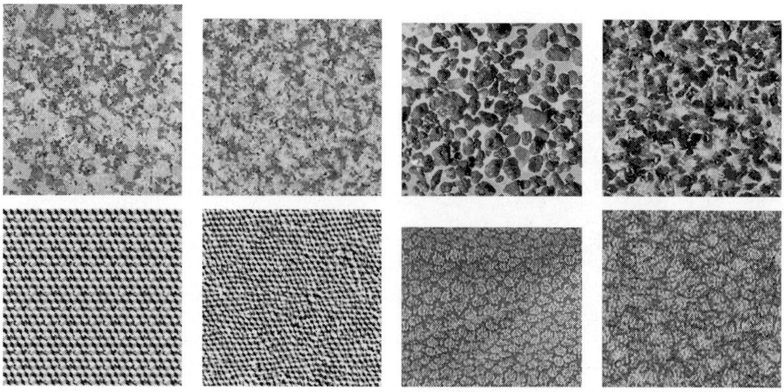

Fig. 2.10 Zhu, Liu and Wu: Julesz ensemble texture modelling results. The left image is observed and the right one is sampled. Images courtesy of Zhu, Liu and Wu.[51,52]

2.4.9. *Zhu, Liu and Wu, '00: Julesz ensemble*[51]

This is basically a cut down version of their previous FRAME model.[46] In this case they propose a slightly faster algorithm for synthesis, one that does not need to estimate the model parameters. Instead of creating a probability density function for a Gibbs ensemble, they directly compare the statistics from the filters applied to both the original and synthesised texture. The synthesised texture is progressively updated via the Markov chain Monte Carlo algorithm until the statistics match, see Figure 2.10. The procedure is also controlled by a minimax entropy principle.[46]

Wu, Zhu and Liu[52] proved the equivalence between the Julesz ensemble and the Gibbs (FRAME) models.[46,47] This equivalence theorem proved the consistence between conceptualisation in terms of the Julesz ensemble and modelling in terms of the Gibbs and FRAME models. Therefore unifying two main research streams in vision research: MRF modeling, and matching statistics.

2.4.10. *Xu, Guo and Shum, '00: Chaos mosaic: fast and memory efficient texture synthesis*[53] *and Y. Q. Xu, S. C. Zhu, B. N. Guo, and H. Y. Shum, '01 "Asymptotically Admissible Texture Synthesis"*[54]

These two papers saw the birth of the so-called "patch-based" texture synthesis. Instead of copying one pixel at a time from an input image, they copied whole patches. In this case, these algorithms randomly distribute patches from an input texture onto an output lattice, smoothing the re-

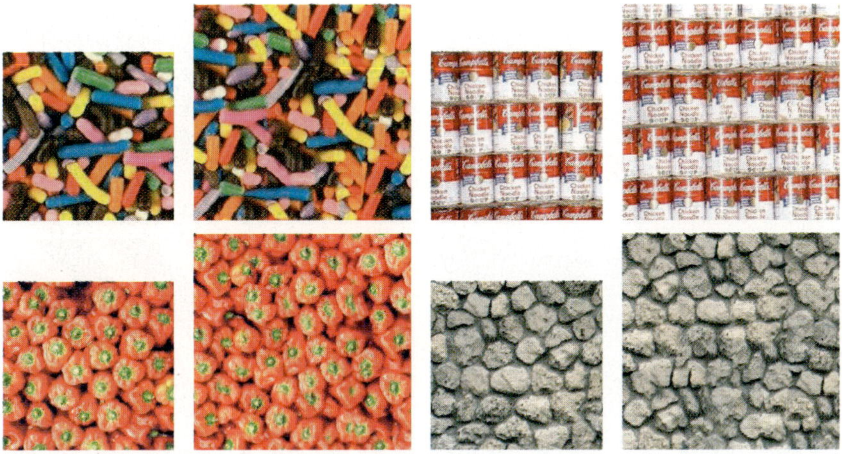

Fig. 2.11 Zhu *et al.*'s Chaos Mosaic: Fast and Memory Efficient Texture Synthesis, and Asymptotically Admissible Texture Synthesis. Images courtesy of Zhu *et al.*[53,54]

sulting edges between overlapping patches with simple cross-edge filtering. Figure 2.11 shows texture synthesis results. The synthesis can be computed in about 1 second. The one drawback to patch based synthesis is that the technique obviously produces large chunks of just plain verbatim copying.

2.4.11. *Liang et al., '01: Real-time texture synthesis by patch-based sampling*[55]

Liang *et al.* also developed a patch based synthesis algorithm. In their scheme they included a fast nearest neighbour search algorithm based on a quad-tree pyramid structure of the input texture. This allowed for fast texture synthesis by sequentially laying down the best fitting texture patch one after the other. As it was a complete patch (or tile) that was being laid down, the synthesis scheme did not suffer from stabililty problems as with the other sequential based schemes of Efros and Leung[49] and Wei and Levoy.[50] This fact was highlighted within their paper, showing comparisons between the three schemes.

2.4.12. *Ashikhmin, '01: Synthesising natural textures*[56]

Ashikhmin presented the first real solution to the time consuming procedure of exhaustive nearest neighbour searching, without loss of quality as with Wei and Levoy's approach.[50] In fact Ashikhmin's method actually

Fig. 2.12 Patch-based sampling. Images courtesy of Liang *et al.*'s paper.[55]

gave both an increase in synthesis quality and speed. In his seminal paper, he proposed a new measure of nearest neighbour instead of either the Manhatten or Euclidean distance, as he suggested that these may not be the best measure to test for perceptual similarity. He notes that if we are only taking pixel colours from the input image (and not sampling from a larger distribution), then when we synthesise a pixel colour, we can be assured that each of its defined neighbours corresponds to a pixel within the input image. Speed can be gained if, instead of doing an exhaustive search, we only sample from those pixels with a corresponding neighbour.

Ashikhmin applied this new search method to Wei and Levoy's synthesis algorithm, and obtained the results shown in Figure 2.13. As observed, the sequential synthesis order induces quite a number of phase discontinuities in the synthesised texture leaving the final texture looking broken or shattered. In Figure 2.14 the results of applying Ashikhmin's neighbourhood searching scheme to Paget and Longstaff's algorithm[20,44] are shown. Here phase is maintained giving the final synthetic textures a high fidelity look.

2.4.13. *Hertzmann et al., '01 Image analogies: A general texture transfer framework*[57]

Although Ashikhmin's technique does very well for natural textures, sharp phase discontinuities can occur with textures that contain a high degree of structure. In these cases, the Euclidean distance combined with exhaustive nearest neighbour searching gives a smoother transition between these

Fig. 2.13 Ashikhmin's synthesis of natural textures. Images courtesy of Ashikhmin.[56]

discontinuities. Hertzmann *et al.* recognised this and proposed their algorithm which uses both measures of perceptual similarity. They then used a heuristic measure to decide when to use one method over the other. Results are presented in Figure 2.15.

2.4.14. *Efros and Freeman, '01: Image quilting: stitch together patches of input image, texture transfer*[58]

Developed concurrently with Liang *et al.*'s approach,[55] Efros and Freeman took patch-based texture synthesis a step further. Instead of blending overlapping edges with a filter, they propose cutting and joining the respective patches along a boundary for which the difference in pixel values is minimal. A minimum error boundary cut is found via dynamic programming. Results are shown in Figure 2.16.

2.4.15. *Zelinka and Garland, '02: Towards Real-Time Texture Synthesis with the Jump Map*[59]

What if nearest neighbour comparisons could be avoided during synthesis? This is what Zelinka and Garland tried to accomplish by creating a k nearest neighbour lookup table as part of an input texture analysis stage. They

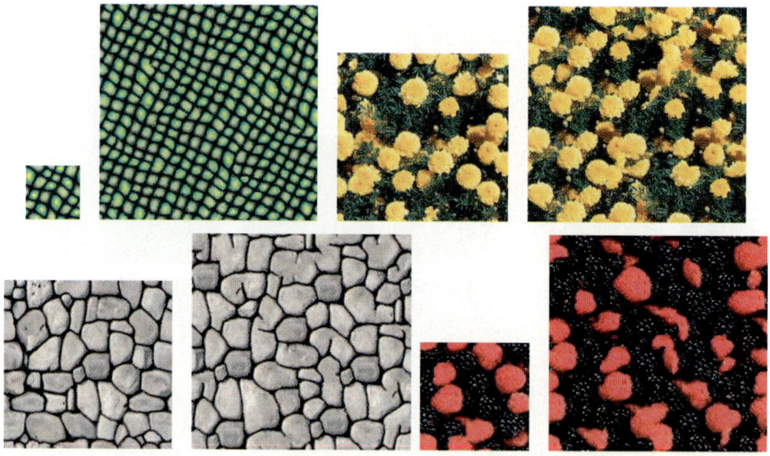

Fig. 2.14 Ashikhmin's neighbourhood searching scheme using Paget and Longstaff's algorithm. Images courtesy of Paget.[44]

Fig. 2.15 Hertzmann's image analogies: texture synthesis. Images courtesy of Hertzmann *et al.*[57]

then used this table to make random jumps (like as in Schödl *et al.*'s video textures[60]) during their sequential texture synthesis stage. No neighbourhood comparisons are done during synthesis, which makes the algorithm very fast. Synthesis examples are shown in Figure 2.17.

2.4.16. *Tong et al., '02: Synthesis of bidirectional texture functions on arbitrary surfaces*[61]

Tong *et al.* also used a k nearest neighbour lookup table, but instead of defining random jump paths like Zelinka and Garland,[59] they simply used the list of k nearest neighbours as a sample base from which to choose the neighbourhood that gave the minimal Euclidean distance measure. When k equals one, this method is comparable to Ashikhmin's method.[56]

Fig. 2.16 Efros and Freeman's Image quilting. Images courtesy of Efros and Freeman.[58]

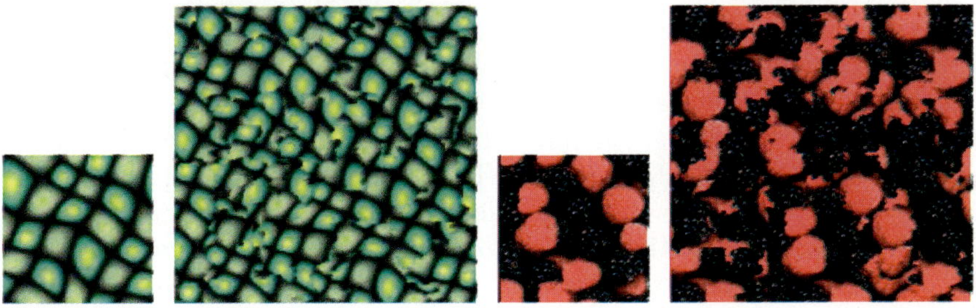

Fig. 2.17 Zelinka and Garland, Jump Map Results. Images courtesy of Zelinka and Garland.[59]

Tong *et al.* noted that k should be set depending on the type of texture being synthesised. For natural textures where the high frequency component is desired, a low k should be used, and for other textures where better blending is required, then a relatively high k should be used.

2.4.17. *Nealen and Alexa, '03: Hybrid texture synthesis*[62]

The hybrid texture synthesis algorithm presented by Nealen and Alexa is a combination of patch-based synthesis and pixel based synthesis. The idea

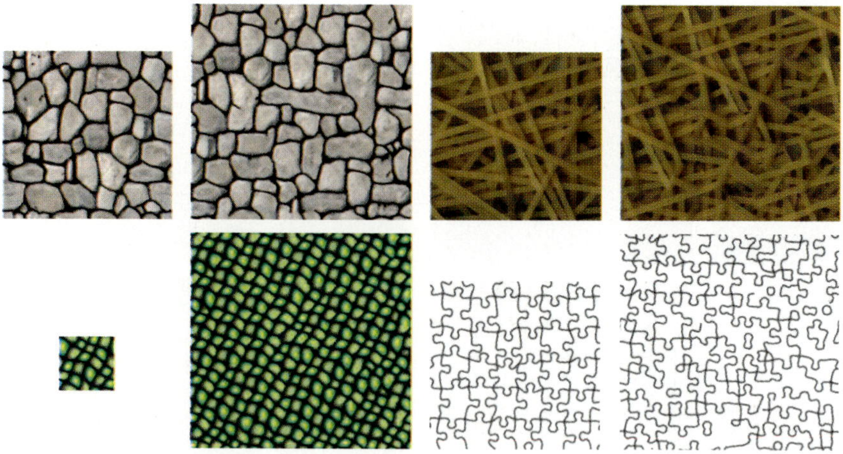

Fig. 2.18 Nealen and Alexa's Hybrid Texture Synthesis results: the original texture (left), the tileable result (right). Images courtesy of Nealen and Alexa.[62]

was to use the advantages of each process to suppress the disadvantages of both. Patch-based synthesis is good at maintaining the structure of a texture, but at the cost of artefacts along the patch boundaries and verbatim copying. Pixel-based synthesis is good at presenting a consistent visual impression, but can lose long range structure.

Nealen and Alexa's algorithm is based on Soler, Cani and Angelidis's "Hierarchical Pattern Mapping".[63] They used adaptive patches to fill a lattice. The patches are chosen to minimise a boundary error. This error is quickly calculated in the Fourier domain. Mismatches between pixels in the overlapping border that exceed a given threshold are then resynthesised using an algorithm similar to Efros and Leung's pixel-based texture synthesis algorithm.[49] Results are shown in Figure 2.18.

2.4.18. *Kwatra et al., '03: Graphcut textures: Image and video synthesis using graph cuts*[64]

This is an advanced version of Efros and Freeman's image quilting.[58] Kwatra *et al.* used a graphcut algorithm called min-cut or max-flow, Kwatra *et al.* also used Soler *et al.*'s[63] FFT-based acceleration of patch searching via sum-of-squared differences. The main advantage of their algorithm over Efros and Freeman's image quilting was that the graphcut technique allowed for re-evaluation of old cuts compared to new. Therefore their synthesis algorithm could take an iterative approach and continu-

Fig. 2.19 Kwatra *et al.*'s Graphcut textures. The smaller images are the example images used for synthesis. Images courtesy the Graphcut Texture's web site.[64]

ally refine the synthesised image with additional overlayed texture patches. Their algorithm was also adept at video texture synthesis. Texture synthesis results are presented in Figure 2.19.

2.5. Further Developments

The previous section reviewed a few prominent articles on texture synthesis. In the beginning, texture synthesis was viewed as a methodology to verify a texture model. As these models became more successful, the focus became less on modelling, but more on quality of synthesis. Now the focus has changed again. Today's texture synthesis research is currently driven by new and exciting applications. There has been a lot of work in applying texture to 3D surfaces. This sort of began with Turk, '01: "Texture synthesis on surfaces".[65] A noteworthy contribution in this area was Zhang *et al.*'s "Synthesis of Progressively-Variant Texture on Arbitrary Surfaces"[66] who added an extra layer to the synthesis to help guide it through transitions. This idea was also taken up by Wu and Yu in their paper "Feature Matching and Deformation for Texture Synthesis"[67] in which they used a feature mask to help guide the synthesis.

Another large area of investigation is in the area of dynamic texturing, the texturing of temporally varying objects. Here Bar-Joseph *et al.* '01: "Texture mixing and texture movie synthesis using statistical learning"[68] and Soatto and Doretto, '01: "Dynamic textures"[69] were two influential pieces of work. Further developments have seen the synthesis of texture guided by flow,[70] and on liquids.[71,72] These types of applications tend to see synthesis algorithms use more modelling. For example, Kwatra *et al.* [70] used an optimisation approach that is more reminiscent of early texture synthesis modelling algorithms.

A lot of this texture synthesis research has been propelled by advances in CPU capabilities. We are now seeing similar advances in the GPU. This has spawned a number of texture synthesis algorithms that are designed to take advantage of these new capabilities. Lefebvre and Hoppe have produced two exciting papers showing the possibilities of using the GPU to perform real-time texture synthesis.[73,74] In their papers, they demonstrate interactive texture synthesis, and synthesis on 3D surfaces.

2.6. Summary

This presentation of texture synthesis algorithms and the forces that drove them, is not intended to be a complete survey of the work. Instead what has been presented is a brief summary of the evolution of texture synthesis algorithms, highlighting the more well known advancements. Hopefully this has given you a taste of what has been going on in the field, and may even provoked your interest. If so, I encourage you to delve further, and explore the many hidden gems that litter this field of research. It is interesting and amazing to see how many disciplines have contributed to our understanding of texture, from which a bigger picture is emerging.[75] There are now many avenues in which texture synthesis is heading, from small beginnings as a tool to prove the validity of a model, progressing to high fidelity computer graphics. The future is bright for many more advances in the application of texture synthesis in varying disciplines.

References

1. W.-C. Lin, J. H. Hays, C. Wu, V. Kwatra, and Y. Liu. A comparison study of four texture synthesis algorithms on regular and near-regular textures. Technical report, Carnegie Mellon University, (2004). URL `http://www.cs.nctu.edu.tw/~wclin/nrt.htm`.
2. B. Julesz, Visual pattern discrimination, *IRE transactions on Information Theory*. **8**, 84–92, (1962).
3. T. Caelli, B. Julesz, and E. Gilbert, On perceptual analyzers underlying visual texture discrimination: Part II, *Biological Cybernetics*. **29**(4), 201–214, (1978).
4. B. Julesz, Textons, the elements of texture perception, and their interactions, *Nature*. **290**, 91–97 (Mar., 1981).

5. J. R. Bergen and E. H. Adelson, Early vision and texture perception, *Nature.* **333**, 363–364 (May, 1988).
6. M. A. Georgeson. Spatial Fourier analysis and human vision. In ed. N. S. Sutherland, *Tutorial Essays, A Guide to Recent Advances*, vol. 2, chapter 2. Lawrence Erlbaum Associates, Hillsdale, NJ, (1979).
7. C. Chubb and M. S. Landy. Orthogonal distribution analysis: a new approach to the study of texture perception. In eds. M. S. Landy and J. A. Movshon, *Computational Models of Vision Processing*, pp. 291–301. Cambridge MA: MIT Press, (1991).
8. A. Olshausen and D. J. Field, Sparse coding with over-complete basis set: A strategy employed by v1?, *Vision Research.* **37**, 3311–3325, (1997).
9. N. Ahuja and A. Rosenfeld, Mosaic models for textures, *IEEE Transactions on Pattern Analysis and Machine Intelligence.* **PAMI–3**, 1–10, (1981).
10. C.-C. Chen. *Markov random fields in image processing.* PhD thesis, Michigan State University, (1988).
11. R. C. Dubes and A. K. Jain, Random field models in image analysis, *Journal of Applied Statistics.* **16**(2), 131–164, (1989).
12. R. M. Haralick, Statistical and structural approaches to texture, *Proceedings of IEEE.* **67**(5), 786–804, (1979).
13. M. Tuceryan and A. K. Jain. Texture analysis. In eds. C. H. Chen, L. F. Pau, and P. S. P. Wang, *Handbook of Pattern Recognition and Computer Vision*, pp. 235–276. World Scientific, Singapore, (1993).
14. H. Wechsler, Texture analysis – a survey, *Signal Processing.* **2**, 271–282, (1980).
15. B. Manjunath and W. Ma, Texture features for browsing and retrieval of image data, *IEEE Transactions on Pattern Analysis and Machine Intelligence.* **18**(8), 837–842, (1996). ISSN 0162-8828. doi: http://doi.ieeecomputersociety.org/10.1109/34.531803.
16. G. Gimel'farb, L. V. Gool, and A. Zalesny. To frame or not to frame in probabilistic texture modelling? In *ICPR '04: Proceedings of the Pattern Recognition, 17th International Conference on (ICPR'04) Volume 2*, pp. 707–711, Washington, DC, USA, (2004). IEEE Computer Society. ISBN 0-7695-2128-2. doi: http://dx.doi.org/10.1109/ICPR.2004.920.
17. M. Haindl, Texture synthesis, *CWI Quarterly.* **4**, 305–331, (1991).
18. L. Seymour. *Parameter estimation and model selection in image analysis using Gibbs–Markov random fields.* PhD thesis, The University of North Carolina, Chapel Hill, (1993).
19. A. Gagalowicz and S. Ma, Sequential synthesis of natural textures, *Computer Vision, Graphics, and Image Processing.* **30**(3), 289–315 (June, 1985).
20. R. Paget and D. Longstaff, Texture synthesis via a noncausal nonparametric multiscale Markov random field, *IEEE Transactions on Image Processing.* **7** (6), 925–931 (June, 1998).
21. D. Geman. Random fields and inverse problems in imaging. In *Lecture Notes in Mathematics*, vol. 1427, pp. 113–193. Springer–Verlag, (1991).
22. A. P. Pentland, Fractal–based description of natural scenes, *IEEE Trans-*

actions on Pattern Analysis and Machine Intelligence. **6**(6), 661–674 (Nov., 1984).
23. J. E. Besag, Spatial interaction and the statistical analysis of lattice systems, *Journal of the Royal Statistical Society, series B.* **36**, 192–326, (1974).
24. R. Chellappa. *Stochastic Models in Image Analysis and Processing.* PhD thesis, Purdue University, (1981).
25. R. Chellappa and R. L. Kashyap, Texture synthesis using 2–D noncausal autoregressive models, *IEEE Transactions on Acoustics, Speech, and Signal Processing.* **ASSP–33**(1), 194–203, (1985).
26. E. J. Delp, R. L. Kashyap, and O. R. Mitchell, Image data compression using autoregressive time series models, *Pattern Recognition.* **11**(5–6), 313–323, (1979).
27. R. L. Kashyap, Characterization and estimation of two–dimensional ARMA models, *IEEE Transactions on Information Theory.* **30**, 736–745, (1984).
28. M. Hassner and J. Sklansky, The use of Markov random fields as models of texture, *Computer Graphics and Image Processing.* **12**, 357–370, (1980).
29. C. O. Acuna, Texture modeling using Gibbs distributions, *Computer Vision, Graphics, and Image Processing: Graphical Models and Image Processing.* **54**(3), 210–222, (1992).
30. G. C. Cross and A. K. Jain, Markov random field texture models, *IEEE Transactions on Pattern Analysis and Machine Intelligence.* **5**, 25–39, (1983).
31. R. Chellappa and S. Chatterjee, Classification of textures using Gaussian Markov random fields, *IEEE Transactions on Acoustics, Speech, and Signal Processing.* **ASSP–33**(4), 959–963, (1985).
32. F. S. Cohen and D. B. Cooper, Simple parallel hierarchical and relaxation algorithms for segmenting noncausal Markovian random fields, *IEEE Transactions on Pattern Analysis and Machine Intelligence.* **9**(2), 195–219 (Mar., 1987).
33. H. Derin and H. Elliott, Modelling and segmentation of noisy textured images using Gibbs random fields, *IEEE Transactions on Pattern Analysis and Machine Intelligence.* **PAMI–9**(1), 39–55, (1987).
34. R. Kindermann and J. L. Snell, *Markov Random Fields and their applications.* (American Mathematical Society, 1980).
35. D. K. Picard, Inference for general Ising models, *Journal of Applied Probability.* **19A**, 345–357, (1982).
36. F. Spitzer, Markov random fields and Gibbs ensembles, *American Mathematical Monthly.* **78**, 142–154, (1971).
37. R. T. Frankot and R. Chellappa, Lognormal random–field models and their applications to radar image synthesis, *IEEE Transactions on Geoscience and Remote Sensing.* **25**(2), 195–207 (Mar., 1987).
38. R. M. Haralick. Texture analysis. In eds. T. Y. Young and K.-S. Fu, *Handbook of pattern recognition and image processing*, chapter 11, pp. 247–279. Academic Press, San Diego, (1986).
39. J. S. D. Bonet. Multiresolution sampling procedure for analysis and synthesis of texture images. In *Computer Graphics*, pp. 361–368. ACM SIGGRAPH, (1997). URL `http://www.debonet.com`.

40. D. J. Heeger and J. R. Bergen. Pyramid-based texture analysis and synthesis. In *Proceedings of SIGGRAPH*, pp. 229–238, (1995). URL http://www.cns.nyu.edu/~david.
41. R. Navarro and J. Portilla. Robust method for texture synthesis–by–analysis based on a multiscale Gabor scheme. In eds. B. Rogowitz and J. Allebach, *SPIE Electronic Imaging Symposium, Human Vision and Electronic Imaging '96*, vol. 2657, pp. 86–97, San Jose, Calfornia, (1996).
42. S. C. Zhu, Y. Wu, and D. Mumford, FRAME: filters, random fields, rnd minimax entropy towards a unified theory for texture modeling, *Proceedings 1996 IEEE Computer Society Conference on Computer Vision and Pattern Recognition.* pp. 686–693, (1996).
43. K. Popat and R. W. Picard. Novel cluster–based probability model for texture synthesis, classification, and compression. In *Proceedings SPIE visual Communications and Image Processing*, Boston, (1993).
44. R. Paget. *Nonparametric Markov random field models for natural texture images.* PhD thesis, University of Queensland, St Lucia, QLD Australia (Dec., 1999). URL http://www.texturesynthesis.com.
45. R. Paget, Strong Markov random field model, *IEEE Transactions on Pattern Analysis and Machine Intelligence.* (2001). submitted for publication, http://www.texturesynthesis.com/papers/Paget_PAMI_2004.pdf
46. S. C. Zhu, Y. N. Wu, and D. B. Mumford, Minimax entropy principle and its applications to texture modeling, *Neural Computation.* **9**, 1627–1660 (November, 1997). URL http://civs.stat.ucla.edu/Texture/Gibbs/Gibbs_results.htm.
47. S. C. Zhu, Y. N. Wu, and D. B. Mumford, Frame : Filters, random fields and maximum entropy—towards a unified theory for texture modeling, *International Journal of Computer Vision.* **27**(2), 1–20, (1998). URL http://civs.stat.ucla.edu/Texture/Gibbs/Gibbs_results.htm.
48. E. P. Simoncelli and J. Portilla. Texture characterization via joint statistics of wavelet coefficient magnitudes. In *Fifth International Conference on Image Processing*, vol. 1, pp. 62–66 (Oct., 1998). URL http://www.cns.nyu.edu/~eero/texture/.
49. A. Efros and T. Leung. Texture synthesis by non-parametric sampling. In *International Conference on Computer Vision*, vol. 2, pp. 1033–1038 (Sept., 1999). URL http://graphics.cs.cmu.edu/people/efros/research/EfrosLeung.html.
50. L.-Y. Wei and M. Levoy. Fast texture synthesis using tree-structured vector quantization. In *SIGGRAPH 2000, 27th International Conference on Computer Graphics and Interactive Techniques*, pp. 479–488, (2000). URL http://graphics.stanford.edu/projects/texture/.
51. S. C. Zhu, X. W. Liu, and Y. N. Wu, Exploring julesz ensembles by efficient markov chain monte carlo—towards a trichromacy theory of texture, *IEEE Transactions on Pattern Analysis and Machine Intelligence.* **22** (6), 554–569, (2000). URL http://civs.stat.ucla.edu/Texture/Julesz/Julesz_results.htm.
52. Y. N. Wu, S. C. Zhu, and X. W. Liu, Equivalence of julesz ensemble and frame

models, *International Journal of Computer Vision.* **38**(3), 247–265, (2000). URL http://civs.stat.ucla.edu/Texture/Julesz/Julesz_results.htm.
53. B. Guo, H. Shum, and Y.-Q. Xu. Chaos mosaic: Fast and memory efficient texture synthesis. Technical report, Microsoft Research (April, 2000). URL http://civs.stat.ucla.edu/Texture/MSR_Texture/Homepage/datahp1.htm.
54. Y. Q. Xu, S. C. Zhu, B. N. Guo, and H. Y. Shum. Asymptotically admissible texture synthesis. In *Proc. of 2nd Int'l Workshop on Statistical and Computational Theories of Vision*, Vancouver, Canada (July, 2001). URL http://civs.stat.ucla.edu/Texture/MSR_Texture/Homepage/datahp1.htm.
55. L. Liang, C. Liu, Y.-Q. Xu, B. Guo, and H.-Y. Shum, Real-time texture synthesis by patch-based sampling, *ACM Trans. Graph.* **20**(3), 127–150, (2001). ISSN 0730-0301. doi: http://doi.acm.org/10.1145/501786.501787. URL http://research.microsoft.com/research/pubs/view.aspx?msr_tr_id=MSR-TR-2001-40.
56. M. Ashikhmin. Synthesizing natural textures. In *SI3D '01: Proceedings of the 2001 symposium on Interactive 3D graphics*, pp. 217–226, New York, NY, USA, (2001). ACM Press. ISBN 1-58113-292-1. doi: http://doi.acm.org/10.1145/364338.364405. URL http://www.cs.utah.edu/~michael/ts/.
57. A. Hertzmann, C. E. Jacobs, N. Oliver, B. Curless, and D. H. Salesin. Image analogies. In *SIGGRAPH '01: Proceedings of the 28th annual conference on Computer graphics and interactive techniques*, pp. 327–340, New York, NY, USA, (2001). ACM Press. ISBN 1-58113-374-X. doi: http://doi.acm.org/10.1145/383259.383295. URL http://mrl.nyu.edu/projects/image-analogies/.
58. A. A. Efros and W. T. Freeman. Image quilting for texture synthesis and transfer. In *SIGGRAPH '01: Proceedings of the 28th annual conference on Computer graphics and interactive techniques*, pp. 341–346, New York, NY, USA, (2001). ACM Press. ISBN 1-58113-374-X. doi: http://doi.acm.org/10.1145/383259.383296. URL http://graphics.cs.cmu.edu/people/efros/research/quilting.html.
59. S. Zelinka and M. Garland. Interactive texture synthesis on surfaces using jump maps. In *EGRW '03: Proceedings of the 14th Eurographics workshop on Rendering*, pp. 90–96, Aire-la-Ville, Switzerland, Switzerland, (2003). Eurographics Association. ISBN 3-905673-03-7. URL http://graphics.cs.uiuc.edu/~zelinka/jumpmaps/images.html.
60. A. Schödl, R. Szeliski, D. H. Salesin, and I. Essa. Video textures. In *Proceedings of SIGGRAPH 2000*, pp. 489–498, New Orleans, LA (July, 2000). http://www.cc.gatech.edu/perception/projects/videotexture/index.html.
61. X. Tong, J. Zhang, L. Liu, X. Wang, B. Guo, and H.-Y. Shum. Synthesis of bidirectional texture functions on arbitrary surfaces. In *SIGGRAPH '02: Proceedings of the 29th annual conference on Computer graphics and interactive techniques*, pp. 665–672, New York, NY, USA, (2002). ACM Press. ISBN 1-58113-521-1. doi: http://doi.acm.org/10.1145/566570.566634. URL

`http://online.cs.nps.navy.mil/DistanceEducation/online.siggraph.org/2002/Papers/12_TextureSynthesis/Presentation01.html`.

62. A. Nealen and M. Alexa. Hybrid texture synthesis. In *EGRW '03: Proceedings of the 14th Eurographics workshop on Rendering*, pp. 97–105, Aire-la-Ville, Switzerland, Switzerland, (2003). Eurographics Association. ISBN 3-905673-03-7. URL `http://www.nealen.com/prof.htm`.
63. C. Soler, M.-P. Cani, and A. Angelidis. Hierarchical pattern mapping. In *SIGGRAPH '02: Proceedings of the 29th annual conference on Computer graphics and interactive techniques*, pp. 673–680, New York, NY, USA, (2002). ACM Press. ISBN 1-58113-521-1. doi: http://doi.acm.org/10.1145/566570.566635.
64. V. Kwatra, A. Schödl, I. Essa, G. Turk, and A. Bobick, Graphcut textures: image and video synthesis using graph cuts, *ACM Trans. Graph.* **22**(3), 277–286, (2003). ISSN 0730-0301. doi: http://doi.acm.org/10.1145/882262.882264. URL `http://www-static.cc.gatech.edu/gvu/perception//projects/graphcuttextures/`.
65. G. Turk. Texture synthesis on surfaces. In *SIGGRAPH '01: Proceedings of the 28th annual conference on Computer graphics and interactive techniques*, pp. 347–354, New York, NY, USA, (2001). ACM Press. ISBN 1-58113-374-X. doi: http://doi.acm.org/10.1145/383259.383297. URL `http://www.gvu.gatech.edu/people/faculty/greg.turk/texture_surfaces/texture.html`.
66. J. Zhang, K. Zhou, L. Velho, B. Guo, and H.-Y. Shum, Synthesis of progressively-variant textures on arbitrary surfaces, *ACM Trans. Graph.* **22**(3), 295–302, (2003). ISSN 0730-0301. doi: http://doi.acm.org/10.1145/882262.882266.
67. Q. Wu and Y. Yu, Feature matching and deformation for texture synthesis, *ACM Transactions on Graphics (SIGGRAPH 2004)*. **23**(3), 362–365 (August, 2004). URL `http://www-sal.cs.uiuc.edu/~yyz/texture.html`.
68. Z. Bar-Joseph, R. El-Yaniv, D. Lischinski, and M. Werman, Texture mixing and texture movie synthesis using statistical learning, *IEEE Transactions on Visualization and Computer Graphics*. **7**(2), 120–135 (April–June, 2001).
69. S. Soatto, G. Doretto, and Y. N. Wu. Dynamic textures. In *IEEE International Conference Computer Vision (ICCV '01)*, vol. 2, pp. 439–446, Vancouver, BC, Canada (July, 2001).
70. V. Kwatra, I. Essa, A. Bobick, and N. Kwatra, Texture optimization for example-based synthesis, *ACM Transactions on Graphics, SIGGRAPH 2005* (August. 2005). URL `http://www-static.cc.gatech.edu/gvu/perception/projects/textureoptimization/`.
71. A. W. Bargteil, F. Sin, J. E. Michaels, T. G. Goktekin, and J. F. O'Brien. A texture synthesis method for liquid animations. In *Proceedings of the ACM SIGGRAPH/Eurographics Symposium on Computer Animation* (Sept, 2006). URL `http://www.cs.berkeley.edu/b-cam/Papers/Bargteil-2006-ATS/`.
72. V. Kwatra, D. Adalsteinsson, T. Kim, N. Kwatra, M. Carlson, and M. Lin, Texturing fluids, *IEEE Transactions on Visualization and Computer Graphics (TVCG)*. (2007). URL `http://gamma.cs.unc.edu/TexturingFluids/`.

73. S. Lefebvre and H. Hoppe, Parallel controllable texture synthesis, *ACM Transactions on Graphics, SIGGRAPH 2005*. pp. 777–786 (August, 2005). URL `http://research.microsoft.com/projects/ParaTexSyn/`.
74. S. Lefebvre and H. Hoppe, Appearance-space texture synthesis, *ACM Transactions on Graphics, SIGGRAPH 2006*. **25**(3), 541–548, (2006). URL `http://research.microsoft.com/projects/AppTexSyn/`.
75. S. C. Zhu, Statistical modeling and conceptualization of visual patterns, *IEEE Transactions on Pattern Analysis and Machine Intelligence*. **25**(6), 691–712, (2003).

Chapter 3

Local Statistical Operators for Texture Classification

Manik Varma
Microsoft Research India
manik@microsoft.com

Andrew Zisserman
University of Oxford, UK
az@robots.ox.ac.uk

We investigate texture classification from single images obtained under unknown viewpoint and illumination. It is demonstrated that materials can be classified using the joint distribution of intensity values over extremely compact neighbourhoods (starting from as small as 3×3 pixels square), and that this outperforms classification using filter banks with large support. It is also shown that the performance of filter banks is inferior to that of image patches with equivalent neighbourhoods.

We develop novel texton based representations which are suited to modelling this joint neighbourhood distribution for MRFs. The representations are learnt from training images, and then used to classify novel images (with unknown viewpoint and lighting) into texture classes. Three such representations are proposed, and their performance is assessed and compared to that of filter banks.

The power of the method is demonstrated by classifying 2806 images of all 61 materials present in the Columbia-Utrecht database. The classification performance surpasses that of recent state of the art filter bank based classifiers such as Leung and Malik (IJCV 01), Cula and Dana (IJCV 04), and Varma and Zisserman (IJCV 05). We also benchmark performance by classifying all the textures present in the Microsoft Textile database as well as the San Francisco outdoor dataset.

We conclude with discussions on why features based on compact neighbourhoods can correctly discriminate between textures with large global structure and why the performance of filter banks is not superior to the source image patches from which they were derived.

3.1. Introduction

Our objective is the classification of materials from their appearance in single images taken under unknown viewpoint and illumination conditions. The task is difficult as materials typically exhibit large intra-class, and small inter-class, variability (see Figure 3.1) and there aren't any widely applicable yet mathematically rigorous models which account for such transformations. The task is made even more challenging if no *a priori* knowledge about the imaging conditions is available.

Early interest in the texture classification problem focused on the pre-attentive discrimination of texture patterns in binary images [Bergen and Adelson (1988); Julesz *et al.* (1973); Julesz (1981); Malik and Perona (1990)]. Later on, this evolved to the classification of textures in grey scale images with synthetic 2D variations [Greenspan *et al.* (1994); Haley and Manjunath (1995); Smith and Chang (1994)]. This, in turn, has been superseded by the problem of classifying real world textures with 3D variations due to changes in camera pose and illumination [Broadhurst (2005); Cula and Dana (2004); Konishi and Yuille (2000); Leung and Malik (2001); Schmid (2004); Varma and Zisserman (2005)]. Currently, efforts are on extending the problem to the accurate classification of entire texture categories rather than of specific material instances [Caputo, Hayman and Mallikarjuna (2005); Hayman, E., Caputo, B., Fritz and Eklundh (2004)].

A common thread through this evolution has been the success that filter bank based methods have had in tackling the problem. As the problem has

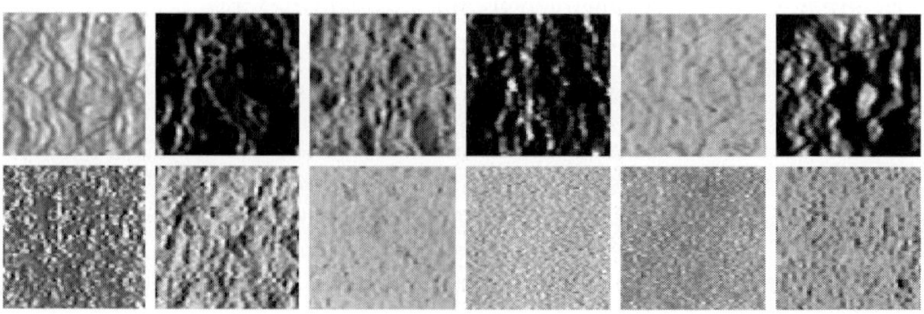

Fig. 3.1. Single image classification on the Columbia-Utrecht database is a demanding task. In the top row, there is a sea change in appearance (due to variation in illumination and pose) even though all the images belong to the same texture class. This illustrates large intra-class variation. In the bottom row, several of the images look similar and yet each belongs to a different texture class. This illustrates that the database also has small inter-class variation.

become more difficult, such methods have coped by building richer representations of the distribution of filter responses. The use of large support filter banks to extract texture features at multiple scales and orientations has gained wide acceptance and popularity.

In this chapter, we question the dominant role that filter banks have come to play in the field of texture classification. Instead of applying filter banks, we develop a direct representation of the image patch based on the joint distribution of pixel intensities in a neighbourhood.

We first investigate the advantages of this image patch representation empirically. The VZ algorithm [Varma and Zisserman (2005)] gives one of the best 3D texture classification results on the Columbia-Utrecht database using the Maximum Response 8 (MR8) filters with support as large as 49×49 pixels square. We demonstrate that substituting the new patch based representation in the VZ algorithm leads to the following two results: (i) very good classification performance can be achieved using extremely compact neighbourhoods (starting from as small as 3×3); and (ii) for any fixed size of the neighbourhood, image patches lead to superior classification as compared to filter banks with the same support. The superiority of the image patch representation is empirically demonstrated by classifying all 61 materials present in the Columbia-Utrecht database and showing that the results outperform the VZ algorithm using the MR8 filter bank. Classification results are also presented for the San Francisco [Konishi and Yuille (2000)] and Microsoft Textile [Savarese and Criminsi (2004)] databases.

We then discuss theoretical reasons as to why small image patches can correctly discriminate between textures with large global structure and also challenge the popular belief that filter bank features are superior for classification as compared to the source image patches from which they were derived.

3.2. Background

Texture research is generally divided into five canonical problem areas: (i) synthesis; (ii) classification; (iii) segmentation; (iv) compression; and (v) shape from texture. The first four areas have come to be heavily influenced by the use of wavelets and filter banks, with wavelets being particularly effective at compression while filter banks have lead the way in classification and synthesis.

The success in these areas was largely due to learning a fuller statistical representation of filter bank responses. It was fuller in three respects: first, the filter response *distribution* was learnt (as opposed to recording just the low order moments of the distribution); second, the *joint* distribution, or co-occurrence, of filter responses was learnt (as opposed to independent distributions for each filter); and third, simply more filters were used than before to measure texture features at many scales and orientations.

These filter response distributions were learnt from training images and represented by clusters or histograms. The distributions could then be used for classification, segmentation or synthesis. For instance, classification could be achieved by comparing the distribution of a novel texture image to the model distributions learnt from the texture classes. Similarly, synthesis could be achieved by constructing a texture having the same distribution as the target texture. As such, the use of filter banks has become ubiquitous and unquestioned.

However, even though there has been ample empirical evidence to suggest that filter banks and wavelets can lead to good performance, not much rigorous theoretical justification has been provided as to their optimality or, even for that matter, their necessity for texture classification or synthesis. In fact, the supremacy of filter banks for texture synthesis was brought into question by the approach of Efros and Leung [Efros and Leung (1999)]. They demonstrated that superior synthesis results could be obtained using local pixel neighbourhoods directly, without resorting to large scale filter banks. In a related development, Zalesny and Van Gool [Zalesny and Van Gool (2000)] also eschewed filter banks in favour of a Markov random field (MRF) model.

Both these works put MRFs firmly back on the map as far as texture synthesis was concerned. Efros and Leung gave a computational method for generating a texture with similar MRF statistics to the original sample, but without explicitly learning or even representing these distributions. Zalesny and Van Gool, using a subset of all available cliques present in a neighbourhood, showed that it was possible to learn and sample from a parametric MRF model given sufficient computational power.

In this chapter, it is demonstrated that the second of the canonical problems, texture classification, can also be tackled effectively by employing only local neighbourhood distributions, with representations inspired by MRF models.

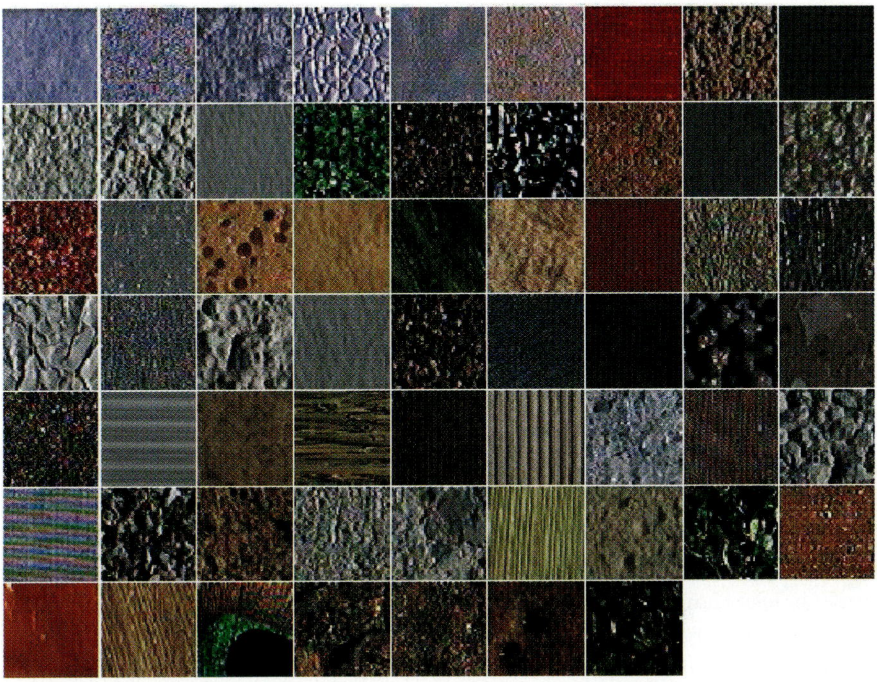

Fig. 3.2. One image of each of the materials present in the Columbia-Utrecht (CUReT) database. Note that all images are converted to grey scale in our classification scheme and no use of colour information is made whatsoever.

3.3. Databases

We now describe the Columbia-Utrecht [Dana *et al.* (1999)], San Francisco [Konishi and Yuille (2000)] and Microsoft Textile [Savarese and Criminsi (2004)] databases that are used in the classification experiments.

3.3.1. *The Columbia-Utrecht database*

The Columbia-Utrecht (CUReT) database contains images of 61 materials which span the range of different surfaces that one might commonly see in our environment. It has examples of textures that are rough, have specularities, exhibit anisotropy, are man-made, and many others. The variety of textures present in the database is shown in Figure 3.2.

Each of the materials in the database has been imaged under 205 different viewing and illumination conditions. The effects of specularities, inter-reflections, shadowing and other surface normal variations are plainly evident and can be seen in Figure 3.1 where their impact is highlighted due to varying imaging conditions. This makes the database far more challenging for a classifier than the often used Brodatz collection where all such effects are absent.

While the CUReT database has now become a benchmark and is widely used to assess classification performance, it also has some limitations. These are mainly to do with the way the images have been photographed and the choice of textures. For the former, there is no significant scale change for most of the materials and very limited in-plane rotation. With regard to choice of texture, the most serious drawback is that multiple instances of the same texture are present for only a few of the materials, so intra-class variation cannot be thoroughly investigated. Hence, it is difficult to make generalisations. Nevertheless, it is still one of the largest and toughest databases for a texture classifier to deal with.

All 61 materials present in the database are included in our experimental setup. For each material, there are 118 images where the azimuthal viewing angle is less than 60 degrees. Out of these, 92 images are chosen for which a sufficiently large region of texture is visible across all materials. A central 200×200 region is cropped from each of these images and the remaining background discarded. The selected regions are converted to grey scale and then intensity normalised to have zero mean and unit standard deviation. Thus, no colour information is used in any of the experiments and we make ourselves invariant to affine changes in the illuminant intensity. The cropped CUReT database has a total of $61 \times 92 = 5612$ images. These are evenly split into two disjoint sets of 2806 images each, one for training and the other for testing.

We will use this database to illustrate the methods throughout this chapter unless stated otherwise.

3.3.2. *The San Francisco database*

The San Francisco database has 37 images of outdoor scenes taken on the streets of San Francisco. It has been segmented by hand into 6 classes: Air, Building, Car, Road, Vegetation and Trunk. Note that this is slightly different from the description reported in [Konishi and Yuille (2000)] where only 35 images were used and the classes were: Air, Building, Car, Road, Vegetation and Other. Figure 3.3 shows some sample images from the database. The images all have resolution 640×480.

Fig. 3.3. Sample images from the San Francisco database.

As can be seen, the database is easy to classify on the basis of colour alone – the sky is always blue, the road mostly black and the vegetation green. Therefore, the images are once again converted to grey scale to make sure classification is done only on the basis of texture and not of colour. Also, when the database is used in subsection 3.6.3.2, each image patch is normalised by subtracting off the median value and dividing by the standard deviation. This further ensures that classification is actually carried out on the basis of textural information and not just intensity differences (i.e. a bright sky versus a dark road).

The database is challenging because individual texture regions can be small and irregularly shaped. The images of urban scenes are also quite varied. However, the three main classes, Air, Road and Vegetation, tend not to change all that much from image to image (the database does not include any images taken at night or under artificial illumination). The other shortcoming of the database is its small size.

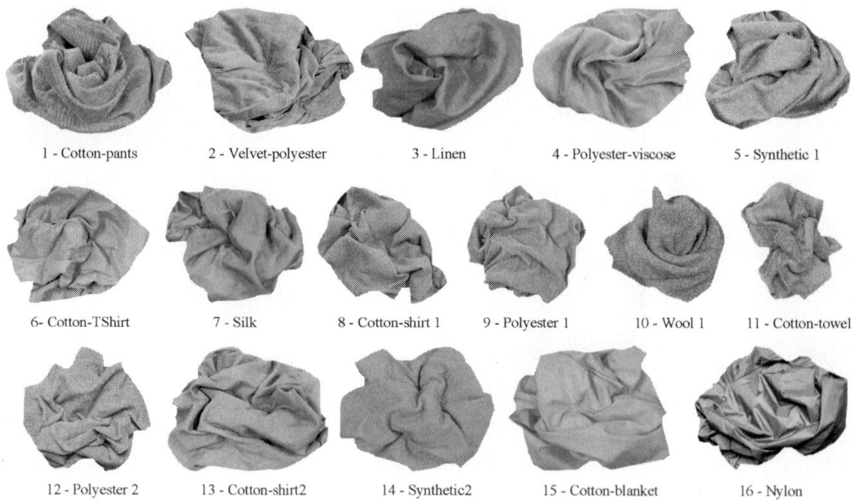

Fig. 3.4. Textures present in the Microsoft Textile database.

3.3.3. *The Microsoft Textile database*

The Microsoft Textile database has 16 folded materials with 20 images available of each taken under diffuse artificial lighting. This is one of the first attempts at studying non-planar textures and therefore represents an important step in the evolution of the texture analysis problem.

Figure 3.4 shows one image from each of the 16 materials present in the database. All the images have resolution 1024×768. The foreground texture has been segmented from the background using GrabCut [Rother *et al.* (2004)]. The impact of non-Lambertian effects is plainly visible as in the Columbia-Utrecht database. The variation in pose and the deformations of the textured surface make it an interesting database to analyse. Furthermore, additional data is available which has been imaged under large variations in illumination conditions.

3.4. A review of the VZ Classifier

The classification problem being tackled is the following: given an image consisting of a single texture obtained under unknown illumination and viewpoint, categorise it as belonging to one of a set of pre-learnt texture classes. Leung and Malik's influential paper [Leung and Malik (2001)] established much of the framework for this area – filter response textons, nearest neighbour classification using the χ^2 statistic, testing on the CUReT database, etc. Later algorithms such as the BFH classifier [Cula and Dana (2004)] and the VZ classifier [Varma and Zisserman (2005)] have built on this paper and extended it to classify single images without compromising accuracy. In turn, [Broadhurst (2005); Caputo, Hayman and Mallikarjuna (2005); Hayman, E., Caputo, B., Fritz and Eklundh (2004)] have achieved even superior results by keeping the MR8 filter bank representation of the VZ algorithm but replacing the nearest neighbour classifier with SVMs or Gaussian-Bayes classifiers.

The VZ classifier [Varma and Zisserman (2005)] is divided into two stages: a learning stage where texture models are learnt from training examples by building statistical descriptions of filter responses, and a classification stage where novel images are classified by comparing their distributions to the learnt models.

In the learning stage, training images are convolved with a chosen filter bank to generate filter responses. These filter responses are then aggregated over images from a texture class and clustered. The resultant cluster centres form a dictionary of exemplar filter responses which are called textons. Given a texton dictionary, a model is learnt for a particular training image by labelling each of the image pixels with the texton that lies closest to it in filter response space. The model is the normalised frequency histogram of pixel texton labellings, i.e. an S-vector of texton probabilities for the image, where S is the size of the texton dictionary (see Figure 3.6). Each texture class is represented by a number of models corresponding to training images of that class.

In the classification stage, the set of learnt models is used to classify a novel (test) image, e.g. into one of the 61 textures classes in the case of the CUReT database. This proceeds as follows: the filter responses of the test image are generated and the pixels labelled with textons from the texton dictionary. Next, the normalised frequency histogram of texton labellings is computed to define an S-vector for the image. A nearest neighbour classifier is then used to assign the texture class of the nearest model to the test image. The distance between two normalised frequency histograms is measured using the χ^2 statistic [Press *et al.* (1992)].

In [Varma and Zisserman (2005)], the performance of four filter banks was contrasted (including the filter bank used by Leung and Malik (LM) [Leung and Malik (2001)] and Cula and Dana [Cula and Dana (2004)], as well as the one used by Schmid (S) [Schmid (2001)]) and it was demonstrated that the rotationally invariant, multi-scale, Maximum Response MR8 filter bank (described below) yields better results than any of the other three. Hence, in this chapter, we present comparisons with the MR8 filter bank.

3.4.1. *Filter bank*

The MR8 filter bank consists of 38 filters but only 8 filter responses. The filters include a Gaussian and a Laplacian of a Gaussian (LOG) filter both at scale $\sigma = 10$ pixels, an edge (first derivative) filter at 6 orientations and 3 scales and a bar (second derivative) filter also at 6 orientations and the same 3 scales $(\sigma_x,\sigma_y)=\{(1,3), (2,6), (4,12)\}$. The response of the isotropic filters (Gaussian and LOG) are used directly. However, in a manner somewhat similar to [Riesenhuber and Poggio (1999)], the responses of the oriented filters (bar and edge) are "collapsed" at each scale by using only the maximum filter responses across all orientations. This gives 8 filter responses in total and ensures that the filter responses are rotationally invariant. The MR4 filter bank only employs the $(\sigma_x, \sigma_y) = (4, 12)$ scale. Another 4 dimensional variant, MRS4, achieves rotation and scale invariance by selecting the maximum response over both orientation and scale [Varma (2004)]. Matlab code for generating these filters, as well as the LM and S sets, is available from [Varma and Zisserman (2004a)].

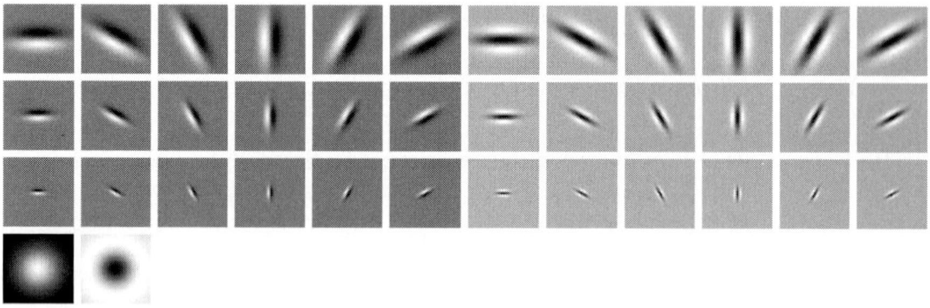

Fig. 3.5. The MR8 filter bank consists of 2 anisotropic filters (an edge and a bar filter, at 6 orientations and 3 scales), and 2 rotationally symmetric ones (a Gaussian and a Laplacian of Gaussian). However only 8 filter responses are recorded by taking, at each scale, the maximal response of the anisotropic filters across all orientations.

3.4.2. *Pre-processing*

The following pre-processing steps are applied before going ahead with any learning or classification. First, every filter in the filter bank is made mean zero. It is also L_1 normalised so that the responses of all filters lie roughly in the same range. In more detail, every filter F_i is divided by $\|F_i\|_1$ so that the filter has unit L_1 norm. This helps vector quantisation, when using Euclidean distances, as the scaling for each of the filter response axes becomes the same [Malik *et al.* (2001)]. Note that dividing by $\|F_i\|_1$ also scale normalises [Lindeberg (1998)] the Gaussians (and their derivatives) used in the filter bank.

Second, following [Malik *et al.* (2001)] and motivated by Weber's law, the filter response at each pixel $\mathbf{x}$ is (contrast) normalised as

$$\mathbf{F}(\mathbf{x}) \leftarrow \mathbf{F}(\mathbf{x}) \left[\log\left(1 + L(\mathbf{x})/0.03\right)\right] / L(\mathbf{x}) \tag{3.1}$$

where $L(\mathbf{x}) = \|\mathbf{F}(\mathbf{x})\|_2$ is the magnitude of the filter response vector at that pixel. This was empirically determined to lead to better classification results.

3.4.3. *Implementation details*

To learn the texton dictionary, filter responses of 13 randomly selected images per texture class (taken from the set of training images) are aggregated and clustered via the *K-Means* algorithm [Duda *et al.* (2001)]. For example, if $K = 10$ textons are learnt from each of the 61 texture classes present in the CUReT database, then this results in a dictionary comprising $61 \times 10 = 610$ textons.

Under this setup, the VZ classifier using the MR8 filter bank achieves an accuracy rate of 96.93% while classifying all 2806 test images into 61 classes using 46 models per texture. This will henceforth be referred to as VZ Benchmark. The best classification results for MR8 are 97.43% obtained when a dictionary of 2440 textons is used, with 40 textons being learnt per texture class. For the other three filter banks investigated in [Varma and Zisserman (2005)], the classification results for 61 textures using 610 textons are as follows: Maximum Response 4 (MR4) = 91.70%, MRS4 = 94.23%, Leung and Malik (LM) = 94.65% and Schmid (S) = 95.22%.

3.5. The Image Patch Based Classifiers

In this section, we investigate the effect of replacing filter responses with the source image patches from which they were derived. The rationale for doing so comes from the observation that convolution to generate filter responses can be rewritten as an inner product between image patch vectors and the filter bank matrix. Thus, a filter response is essentially a lower dimensional projection of an image patch onto a linear subspace spanned by the vector representation of the individual filters (obtained by row reordering each filter mask).

The VZ algorithm is now modified so that filter responses are replaced by their source image patches. Thus, the new classifier is identical to the VZ algorithm except that, at the filtering stage, instead of using a filter bank to generate filter responses at a point, the raw pixel intensities of an $N \times N$ square neighbourhood around that point are taken and row reordered to form a vector in an N^2 dimensional feature space. All pre and post processing steps are retained and no other changes are made to the classifier. Hence, in the first stage of learning, all the image patches from the selected training images in a texture class are aggregated and clustered. The cluster centres from the various classes are grouped together to form the texton dictionary. The textons now represent exemplar image patches rather than exemplar filter responses. However, the model corresponding to a training image continues to be the histogram of texton frequencies, and novel image classification is still achieved by nearest neighbour matching using the χ^2 statistic. This classifier will be referred to as the Joint classifier. Figure 3.6 highlights the main difference in approach between the Joint classifier and the VZ classifier using the MR8 filter bank.

We also design two variants of the Joint classifier – the Neighbourhood classifier and the MRF classifier. Both of these are motivated by the recognition that textures can often be considered realisations of a Markov random field. In an MRF framework [Geman and Geman (1984); Li (2001)], the probability of the central pixel depends only on its neighbourhood. Formally,

$$p(I(\mathbf{x}_c)|I(\mathbf{x}), \forall \mathbf{x} \neq \mathbf{x}_c) = p(I(\mathbf{x}_c)|I(\mathbf{x}), \forall \mathbf{x} \in \mathcal{N}(\mathbf{x}_c)) \tag{3.2}$$

where $\mathbf{x}_c$ is a site in the 2D integer lattice on which the image I has been defined and $\mathcal{N}(\mathbf{x}_c)$ is the neighbourhood of that site. In our case, $\mathcal{N}$ is defined to be the $N \times N$ square neighbourhood (excluding the central pixel). Thus, although the value of the central pixel is significant, its distribu-

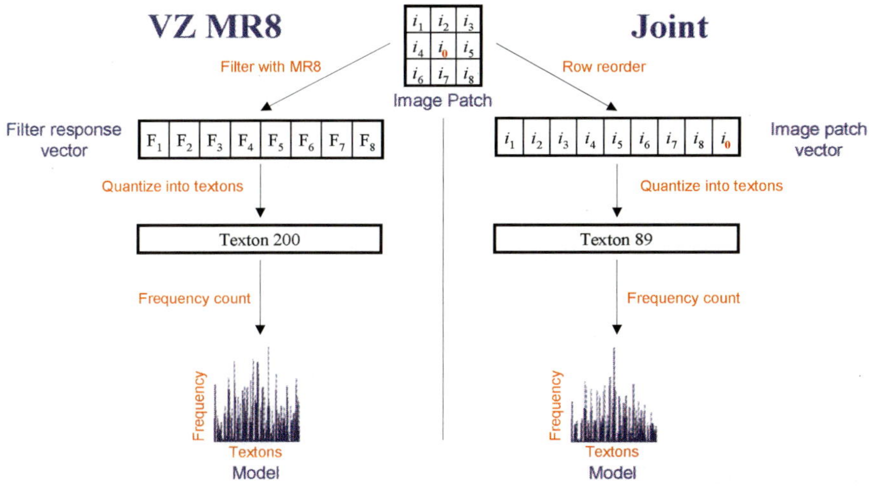

Fig. 3.6. The only difference between the Joint and the VZ MR8 representations is that the source image patches are used directly in the Joint representation as opposed to the derived filter responses in VZ MR8.

tion is conditioned on its neighbours alone. The Neighbourhood and MRF classifiers are designed to test how significant this conditional probability distribution is for classification.

For the Neighbourhood classifier, the central pixel is discarded and only the neighbourhood is used for classification. Thus, the Neighbourhood classifier is essentially the Joint classifier retrained on feature vectors drawn only from the set of $\mathcal{N}$: i.e. the set of $N \times N$ image patches with the central pixel left out. For example, in the case of a 3×3 image patch, only the 8 neighbours of every central pixel are used to form feature vectors and textons.

For the MRF classifier we go to the other extreme and, instead of ignoring the central pixel, explicitly model $p(I(\mathbf{x}_c), I(\mathcal{N}(\mathbf{x}_c)))$, i.e. the joint distribution of the central pixels and its neighbours. Up to now, textons have been used to implicitly represent this joint PDF. The representation is implicit because, once the texton frequency histogram has been formed, neither the probability of the central pixel nor the probability of the neighbourhood can be recovered straightforwardly by summing (marginalising) over the appropriate textons. Thus, the texton representation is modified slightly so as to make explicit the central pixel's PDF within the joint and to represent it at a finer resolution than its neighbours (in the Neighbour-

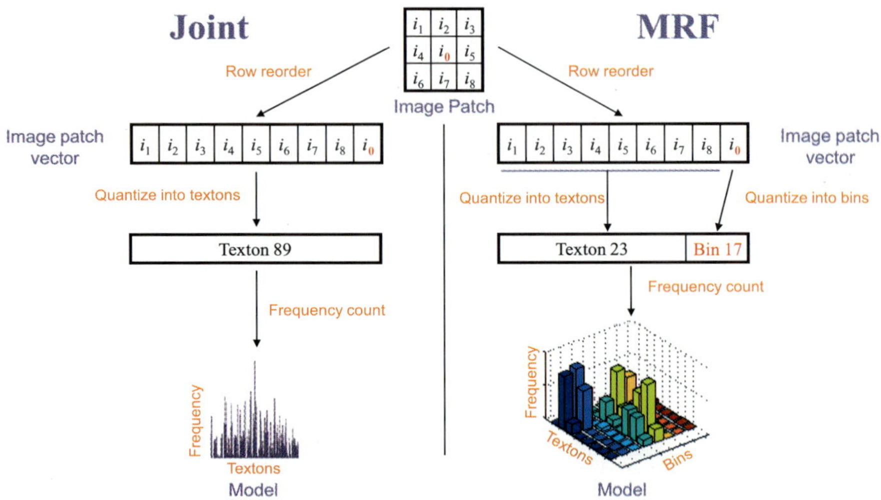

Fig. 3.7. MRF texture models as compared to those learnt using the Joint representation. The only point of difference is that the central pixel PDF is made explicit and stored at a higher resolution. The Neighbourhood representation can be obtained from the MRF representation by ignoring the central pixel.

hood classifier, the central pixel PDF was discarded by representing it at a much coarser resolution using a single bin).

To learn the PDF representing the MRF model for a given training image, the neighbours' PDF is first represented by textons as was done for the Neighbourhood classifier – i.e. all pixels but the central are used to form feature vectors in an N^2-1 dimensional space which are then labelled using the same dictionary of 610 textons. Then, for each of the S_N textons in turn ($S_N = 610$ is the size of the neighbourhood texton dictionary), a one dimensional distribution of the central pixels' intensity is learnt and represented by an S_C bin histogram. Thus the representation of the joint PDF is now an $S_N \times S_C$ matrix. Each row is the PDF of the central pixel for a given neighbourhood intensity configuration as represented by a specific texton. Figure 3.7 highlights the differences between MRF models and models learnt using the Joint representation. Using this matrix, a novel image is classified by comparing its MRF distribution to the model MRF distributions (learnt from training images) by computing the χ^2 statistic over all elements of the $S_N \times S_C$ matrix.

Table 3.1 presents a comparison of the performance of the Joint, Neighbourhood and MRF classifiers when classifying all 61 textures of the

Table 3.1. Classification results on the CUReT database for different patch sizes.

$N \times N$	Joint Classifier (%)	Neighbourhood Classifier (%)	MRF with 90 bins (%)
3×3	95.33	94.90	95.87
5×5	95.62	95.97	97.22
7×7	96.19	96.08	97.47
	(a)	(b)	(c)

CUReT database. Image patches of size 3×3, 5×5 and 7×7 are tried while using a dictionary of 610 textons. For the Joint classifier, it is remarkable to note that classification results of over 95% are achieved using patches as small as 3×3. In fact, the classification result for the 3×3 neighbourhood is actually better than the results obtained by using the MR4, MRS4, LM or S filter banks. This is strong evidence that there is sufficient information in the joint distribution of the nine intensity values (the central pixel and its eight neighbours) to discriminate between the texture classes. For the Neighbourhood classifier, as shown in column (b), there is almost no significant variation in classification performance as compared to using all the pixels in an image patch. Classification rates for $N = 5$ are slightly better when the central pixel is left out and marginally poorer for the cases of $N = 3$ and $N = 7$. Thus, the joint distribution of the neighbours is largely sufficient for classification. Column (c) presents a comparison of the performance of the Joint and Neighbourhood classifiers to the MRF classifier when a resolution of 90 bins is used to store the central pixels' PDF. As can be seen, the MRF classifier does better than both the Joint and Neighbourhood classifiers. What is also very interesting is the fact that using 7×7 patches, the performance of the MRF classifier (97.47%) is at least as good as the best performance achieved by the multi-orientation, multi-scale MR8 filter bank with support 49×49 (97.43% using 2440 textons).

This result showing that image patches can outperform filters raises the important question of whether filter banks are actually providing beneficial information for classification, for example perhaps by increasing the signal to noise ratio, or by extracting useful features. We first address this issue experimentally, by determining the classification performance of filter banks across many different parameter settings and seeing if performance is ever superior to equivalent patches.

In order to do so, we take the CUReT database and compare the performance of the VZ classifier using the MR8 filter bank (VZ MR8) to that of the Joint, Neighbourhood and MRF classifiers as the size of the neighbourhood is varied. In each experiment, the MR8 filter bank is scaled down so that the support of the largest filters is the same as the neighbourhood size. Once again, we emphasise that the MR8 filter bank is chosen as its performance on the CUReT database is better than all the other filter banks studied. Figure 3.8 plots the classification results. It is apparent that for any given size of the neighbourhood, the performance of VZ MR8 using 610 textons is worse than that of the Joint or even the Neighbourhood classifiers also using 610 textons. Similarly, VZ MR8 Best is always inferior not

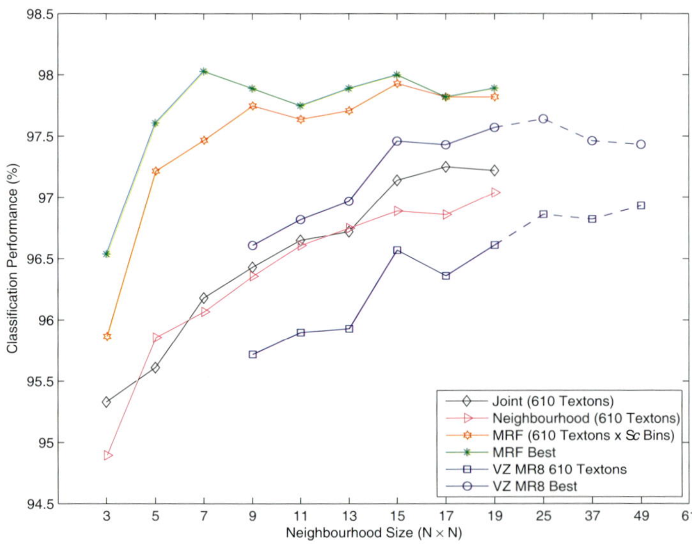

Fig. 3.8. Classification results as a function of neighbourhood size. The MRF Best curve shows results obtained for the best combination of texton dictionary and number of bins for a particular neighbourhood size. For neighbourhoods up to 11×11, dictionaries of up to 3050 textons and up to 200 bins are tried. For 13×13 and larger neighbourhoods, the maximum size of the texton dictionary is restricted to 1220 because of computational expense. Similarly, the VZ MR8 Best curve shows the best results obtained by varying the size of the texton dictionary. However, in this case, dictionaries of up to 3050 textons are tried for all neighbourhoods. The best result achieved by the MRF classifiers is 98.03% using a 7×7 neighbourhood with 2440 textons and 90 bins. The best result for MR8 is 97.64% for a 25×25 neighbourhood and 2440 textons. The performance of the VZ algorithm using the MR8 filter bank (VZ MR8) is always worse than any other comparable classifier at the same neighbourhood size. VZ MR8 Best is inferior to the MRF curves, while VZ MR8 with 610 textons is inferior to the Joint and Neighbourhood classifiers also with 610 textons.

just to MRF Best but also to MRF. This would suggest that using all the information present in an image patch is more beneficial for classification than relying on lower dimensional responses of a pre-selected filter bank. A classifier which is able to learn from all the pixel values is superior.

These results demonstrate that a classification scheme based on MRF local neighbourhood distributions can achieve very high classification rates and can outperform methods which adopt large scale filter banks to extract features and reduce dimensionality. Before turning to discuss theoretical reasons as to why this might be the case, we first explore how issues such as rotation and scale impact the image patch classifiers.

3.6. Scale, Rotation and Other Datasets

Three main criticisms can be levelled at the classifiers developed in the previous section. Firstly, it could be argued that the lack of significant scale change in the CUReT textures might be the reason why image patch based classification outperforms the multi-scale MR8 filter bank. Secondly, the image patch representation has a major disadvantage in that it is not rotationally invariant. And thirdly, the reason why small image patches do so well could be because of some quirk of the CUReT dataset and that classification using small patches will not generalise to other databases. In this section, each of these three issues is addressed experimentally and it is shown that the image patch representation is as robust to scale changes as MR8, can be made rotationally invariant and generalises well to other datasets.

3.6.1. *The effect of scale changes*

To test the hypothesis that the image patch representation will not do as well as the filter bank representation in the presence of scale changes, four texture classes were selected from the CUReT database (material numbers 2, 11, 12 and 14) for which additional scaled data is available (as material numbers 29, 30, 31 and 32).

Two experiments were performed. In the first, models were learnt only from the training images of the original textures while the test images of both the original and scaled textures were classified. In the second experiment, both test sets were classified once more but this time models were learnt from the original as well as the scaled textures. Table 3.2 shows the results of the experiments. It also tabulates the results when the experiments are repeated but this time with the images being scaled synthetically by a factor of two.

Table 3.2. Classification of scaled images.

	Naturally Scaled		Synthetically Scaled ×2	
	Original (%)	Original + Scaled (%)	Original (%)	Original + Scaled (%)
MRF	93.48	100	65.22	99.73
MR8	81.25	99.46	62.77	99.73

In the naturally scaled case, when classifying both texture types using models learnt only from the original textures, the MRF classifier achieves 93.48% while VZ MR8 (which contains filters at three scales) reaches only 81.25%. This shows that the MRF classifier is not being adversely affected by the scale variations. When images from the scaled textures are included in the training set as well, the accuracy rates go up 100% and 99.46% respectively. A similar trend is seen in the case when the scaled textures are generated synthetically. Both these results show that image patches cope as well with scale changes as the MR8 filter bank, and that features do not have to be extracted across a large range of scales for successful classification.

3.6.2. *Incorporating rotational invariance*

The fact that the image patch representation developed so far is not rotationally invariant can be a serious limitation. However, it is straight forward to incorporate invariance into the representation. There are several possibilities: (i) find the dominant orientation of the patch (as is done in the MR filters), and measure the neighbourhood relative to this orientation; (ii) marginalise the intensities weighted by the orientation distribution over angle; (iii) add rotated patches to the training set so as to make the learnt decision boundaries rotation invariant [Simard *et al.* (2001)]; etc. In this chapter, we implement option (i), and instead of using an $N \times N$ square patch, the neighbourhood is redefined to be circular with a given radius. Table 3.3 lists the results for the Neighbourhood and MRF classifiers when classifying all 61 textures using circular neighbourhoods with radius 3 pixels (corresponding to a 7×7 patch) and 4 pixels (9×9 patch).

Using the rotationally invariant representation, the Neighbourhood classifier with a dictionary of 610 textons achieves 96.36% for a radius of 3

Table 3.3. Comparison of classification results of the Neighbourhood and MRF classifiers using the standard and the rotationally invariant image patch representations.

	Neighbourhood Classifier		MRF Classifier	
	Rotationally Invariant (%)	Not Invariant (%)	Rotationally Invariant (%)	Not Invariant (%)
7×7	96.36	96.08	97.07	97.47
9×9	96.47	96.36	97.25	97.75

pixels and 96.47% for a radius of 4 pixels. This is slightly better than that achieved by the same classifier using the standard (non invariant) representation with corresponding 7×7 and 9×9 patches. The rates for the rotationally invariant MRF classifier are 97.07% and 97.25% using 610 textons and 45 bins. These results are slightly worse than those obtained using the standard representation. However, the fact that such high classification percentages are obtained strongly indicates that rotation invariance can be successfully incorporated into the image patch representation.

3.6.3. *Results on other datasets*

We now show that small image patches can also be used to successfully classify textures other than those present in the CUReT database. It is demonstrated that the Joint classifier with patches of size $3 \times 3, 5 \times 5$ and 7×7 is sufficient for classifying the Microsoft Textile [Savarese and Criminsi (2004)] and San Francisco [Konishi and Yuille (2000)] databases. While the MRF classifier leads to the best results in general, we show that on these databases the Joint classifier already achieves very high performances (99.21% on the Microsoft Textile database and 97.9% on the San Francisco database using only a single training image).

3.6.3.1. *The Microsoft Textile database*

For the Microsoft Textile database, the experimental setup is kept identical to the one used by [Savarese and Criminsi (2004)]. Fifteen images were selected from each of the sixteen texture classes to form the training set. While all the training images were used to form models, textons were learnt from only 3 images per texture class. Various sizes of the texton dictionary $S = 16 \times K$ were tried, with $K = 10, \ldots, 40$ textons learnt per textile. The test set comprised a total of 80 images. Table 3.4 shows the variation in

Table 3.4. Classification results on the Microsoft Textile database

$N \times N$	Size of Texton Dictionary S 160 (%)	320 (%)	480 (%)	640 (%)
3×3	96.82	96.82	96.82	96.82
5×5	99.21	99.21	99.21	99.21
7×7	96.03	97.62	96.82	97.62

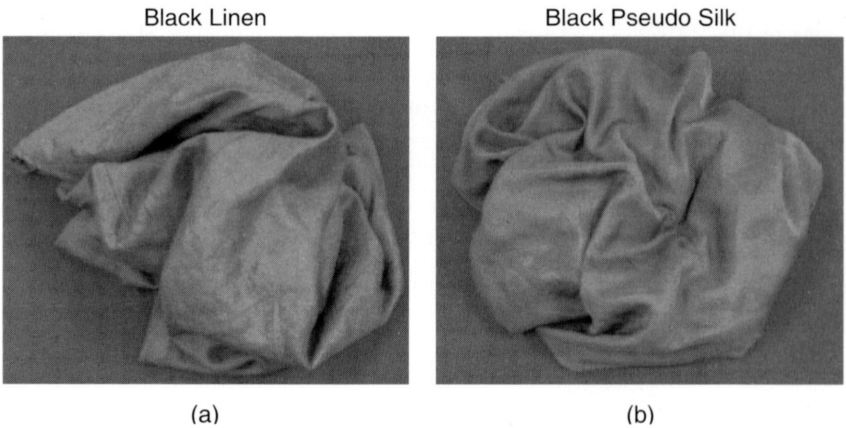

Fig. 3.9. Only a single image in the Microsoft Textile database is misclassified by the Joint classifier using 5×5 patches: (a) is an example of Black Linen but is incorrectly classified as Black Pseudo Silk (b).

performance of the Joint classifier with neighbourhood size N and texton dictionary size S.

As can be seen, excellent results are obtained using very small neighbourhoods. In fact, only a single image is misclassified using 5×5 patches (see Figure 3.9). These results reinforce the fact that very small patches can be used to classify textures with global structure far larger than the neighbourhoods used (the image resolutions are 1024×768).

3.6.3.2. *The San Francisco database*

For the San Francisco database, a single image is selected for training the Joint classifier. Figure 3.10 shows the selected training image and its associated hand segmented regions. All the rest of the 36 images are kept as the test set. Performance is measured by the proportion of pixels that

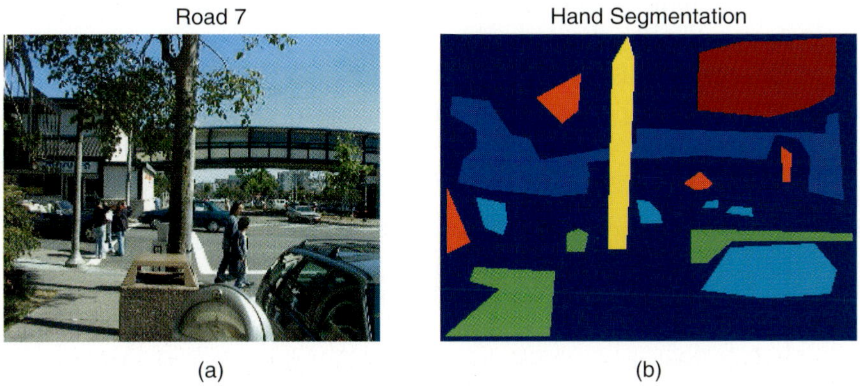

Fig. 3.10. The single image used for training on the San Francisco database and the associated hand segmented regions.

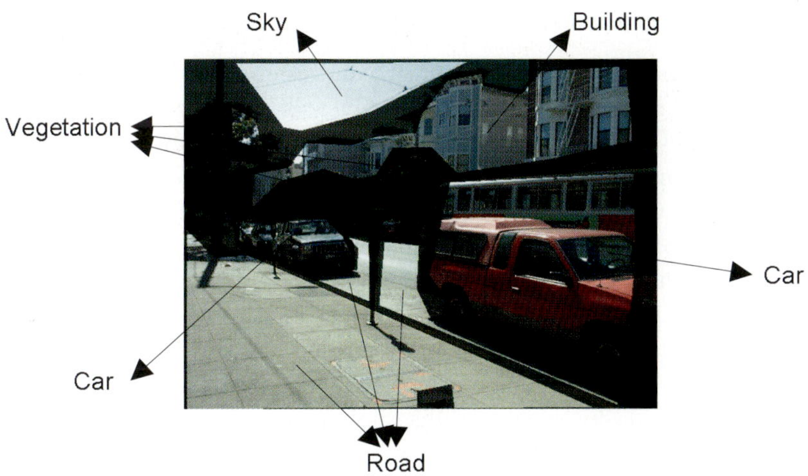

Fig. 3.11. Region classification results using the Joint classifier with 7×7 patches for a sample test image from the San Francisco database.

are labelled correctly during classification of the hand segmented regions. Using this setup, the Joint classifier achieves an accuracy rate of 97.9%, i.e. almost all the pixels are labelled correctly in the 36 test images. Figure 3.11 shows an example of a test image and the regions that were classified in it. This result again validates the fact that small image patches can be used to successfully classify textured images. In fact, using small patches is particularly appealing for databases such as the San Francisco set because large scale filter banks will have problems near region boundaries and will also not be able to produce many measurements for small, or irregularly shaped, regions.

3.7. Why Does Patch Based Classification Work?

The results of the previous sections have demonstrated two things. Firstly, neighbourhoods as small as 3×3 can lead to very good classification results even for textures whose global structure is far larger than the local neighbourhoods used. Secondly, classification using image patches is superior to that using filter banks with equivalent support. In this section, we discuss some of the theoretical reasons as to why these results might hold.

3.7.1. *Classification using small patches*

The results on the CUReT, San Francisco and Microsoft Textile databases show that small image patches contain sufficient information to discriminate between different textures. One explanation for this is illustrated in Figure 3.12. Three images are selected from the Limestone and Ribbed Paper classes of the CUReT dataset, and scatter plots of their grey level co-occurrence matrix shown for the displacement vector $(2, 2)$ (i.e. the joint distribution of the top left and bottom right pixel in every 3×3 patch). Notice how the distributions of the two images of Ribbed Paper can easily be associated with each other and distinguished from the distribution of the Limestone image. Thus, 3×3 neighbourhood distributions can contain sufficient information for successful discrimination.

To take a more analytic example, consider two functions $f(x) = A\sin(\omega_f t + \delta)$ and $g(x) = A\sin(\omega_g t + \delta)$, where ω_f and ω_g are small so that f and g have large structure. Even though f and g are very similar (they are essentially the same function at different scales) it will be seen that they are easily distinguished by the Joint classifier using only two point neighbourhoods. Figure 3.13 illustrates that while the intensity distributions of f and g are identical, the distributions of their derivatives, f_x and g_x, are not. Since derivatives can be computed using just two points, these functions can be distinguished by looking at two point neighbourhoods alone.

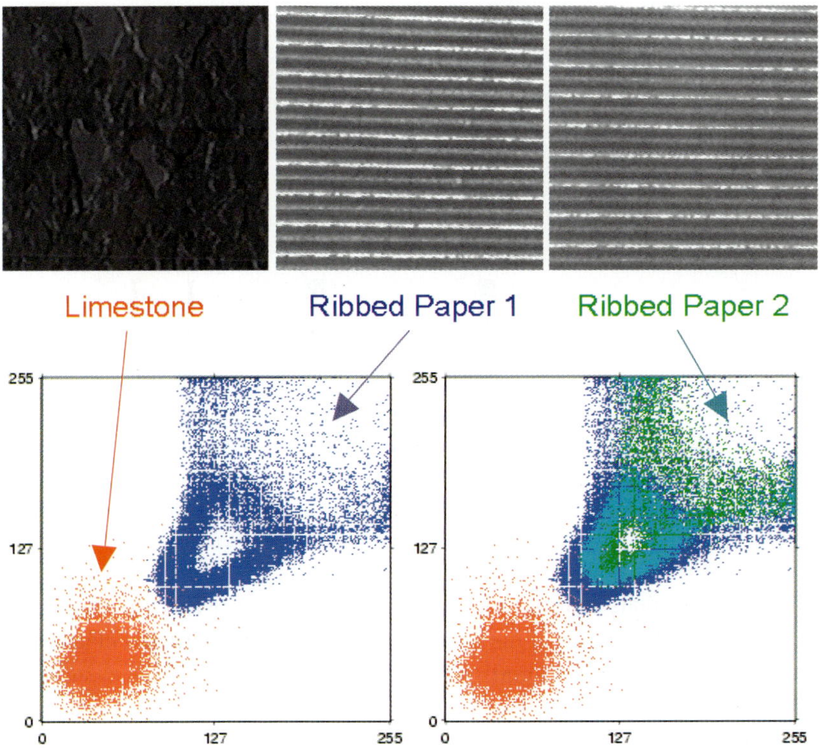

Fig. 3.12. Information present in 3×3 neighbourhoods is sufficient to distinguish between textures. The top row shows three images drawn from two texture classes, Limestone and Ribbed Paper. The bottom row shows scatter plots of $I(\mathbf{x})$ against $I(\mathbf{x}+(2,2))$. On the left are the distributions for Limestone and Ribbed Paper 1 while on the right are the distributions for all three images. The Limestone and Ribbed Paper distributions can easily be distinguished and hence the textures can be discriminated from this information alone.

In a similar fashion, other complicated functions such as triangular and saw tooth waves can be distinguished using compact neighbourhoods. Furthermore, the Taylor series expansion of a polynomial of degree $2N - 1$ immediately shows that a $[-N, +N]$ neighbourhood contains enough information to *determine* the value of the central pixel. Thus, any function which can be locally approximated by a cubic polynomial can actually be synthesised using a $[-2, 2]$ neighbourhood. Since, in general, synthesis requires much more information than classification it is therefore expected

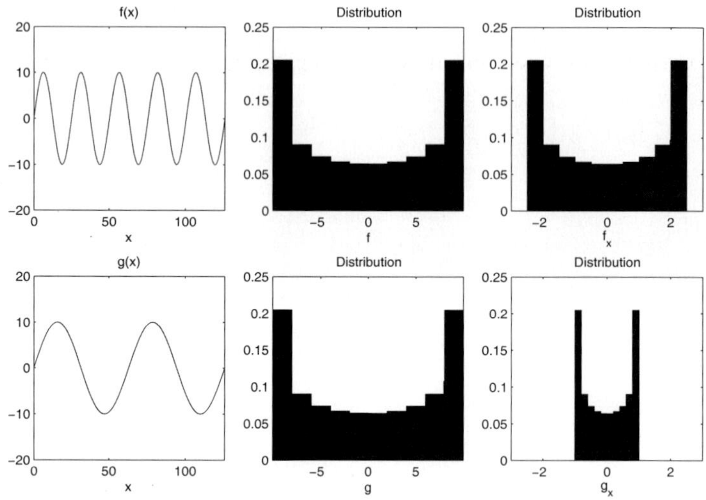

Fig. 3.13. Similar large scale periodic functions can be classified using the distribution of their derivatives computed from two point neighbourhoods.

that more complicated functions can still be distinguished just by looking at small neighbourhoods. This illustrates why it is possible to classify very large scale textures using small patches.

There also exist entire classes of textures which can not be distinguished on the basis of local information alone. One such class comprises of textures made up of the same textons and with identical first order texton statistics, but which differ in their higher order statistics. To take a simple example, consider texture classes generated by the repeated tiling of two textons (a circle and a square for instance) with sufficient spacing in between so that there is no overlap between textons in any given neighbourhood. Then, any two texture classes which differ in their tiling pattern but have identical frequencies of occurrence of the textons will not be distinguished on the basis of local information alone. However, the fact that classification rates of nearly 98% have been achieved using extremely compact neighbourhoods on three separate data sets indicates that real textures do not follow such patterns.

The arguments in this subsection indicate that small patches might be effective at texture classification. The arguments do not imply that the performance of small patches is superior to that of arbitrarily large filter banks. However, in the next subsection, arguments are presented as to why filter banks are not superior to equivalent sized patches.

3.7.2. *Filter banks are not superior to image patches*

We now turn to the question of why filter banks do not provide superior classification as compared to their source image patches. To fix the notation, $\mathbf{f}_+$ and $\mathbf{f}_-$ will be used to denote filter response vectors generated by projecting $N \times N$ image patches $\mathbf{i}_+$ and $\mathbf{i}_-$, of dimension $d = N^2$, onto a lower dimension N_f using the filter bank $\mathbf{F}$. Thus,

$$\mathbf{f}_{\pm_{N_f \times 1}} = \mathbf{F}_{N_f \times d}\ \mathbf{i}_{\pm_{d \times 1}} \tag{3.3}$$

In the following discussion, we will focus on the properties of linear (including complex) filter banks. This is not a severe limitation as most popular filters and wavelets tend to be linear. Non linear filters can also generally be decomposed into a linear filtering step followed by non linear post-processing. Furthermore, since one of the main arguments in favour of filtering comes from dimensionality reduction, it will be assumed that $N_f < d$, i.e. the number of filters must be less than the dimensionality of the source image patch. Finally, it should be clarified that throughout the discussion, performance will be measured by classification accuracy rather than the speed with which classification is carried out. While the time complexity of an algorithm is certainly an important factor and can be critical for certain applications, our focus here is on achieving the best possible classification results.

The main motivations which have underpinned filtering (other than biological plausibility) are: (i) dimensionality reduction, (ii) feature extraction at multiple scales and orientations, and (iii) noise reduction and invariance. Arguments from each of these areas are now examined to see whether filter banks can lead to better performance than image patches.

3.7.2.1. *Dimensionality reduction*

Two arguments have been used from dimensionality reduction. The first, which comes from optimal filtering, is that an optimal filter can increase the separability between key filter responses from different classes and is therefore beneficial for classification. The second argument, from statistical machine learning, is that reducing the dimensionality is desirable because of better parameter estimation (improved clustering) and also due to regularisation effects which smooth out noise and prevent over-fitting. We examine both arguments in turn to see whether such factors can compensate for the inherent loss of information associated with dimensionality reduction.

Increasing separability: Since convolution with a linear filter is equivalent to linearly projecting onto a lower dimensional space, the choice of projection direction determines the distance between the filter responses. Suppose we have two image patches $\mathbf{i}_\pm$, with filter responses $\mathbf{f}_\pm$ computed by orthogonal projection as $\mathbf{f}_\pm = \mathbf{F}i_\pm$. Then the distance between $\mathbf{f}_+$ and $\mathbf{f}_-$ is clearly less than the distance between $\mathbf{i}_+$ and $\mathbf{i}_-$ (where the rows of $\mathbf{F}$ span the hyperplane orthogonal to the projection direction). The choice of $\mathbf{F}$ affects the separation between $\mathbf{f}_+$ and $\mathbf{f}_-$, and the optimum filter maximises it, in the manner of a Fisher Linear Discriminant, but the scaled distance between the projected points cannot exceed the original. This result holds true for many popular distance measures including the Euclidean, Mahalanobis and the signed perpendicular distance used by linear SVMs and related classifiers (analogous results hold when $\mathbf{F}$ is not orthogonal). It is also well known [Kohavi and John (1997)] that under Bayesian classification, the Bayes error either increases or remains at least as great when the dimensionality of a problem is reduced by linear projection. However, the fact that the Bayes error has increased for the low dimensional filter responses does not mean the classification is necessarily worse. This is because of issues related to noise and over-fitting which brings us to the second argument from dimensionality reduction for the superiority of filter banks.

Improved parameter estimation: The most compelling argument for the use of filters comes from statistical machine learning where it has often been noted that dimensionality reduction can lead to fewer training samples being needed for improved parameter estimation (better clustering) and can also regularise noisy data and thereby prevent over-fitting. The assumptions underlying these claims are that textures occupy a low dimensional subspace of image patch space and if the patches could be projected onto this true subspace (using a filter bank) then the dimensionality of the problem would be reduced without resulting in any information loss. This would be particularly beneficial in cases where only a limited amount of training data is available as the higher dimensional patch representation would be prone to over-fitting (see figure 3.14).

While these are undoubtedly sound claims there are three reasons why they might not lead to the best possible classification results. The first is due to the great difficulty associated with identifying a texture's true subspace (in a sense, this itself is one of the holy grails of texture analysis). More often than not, only approximations to this true subspace can be

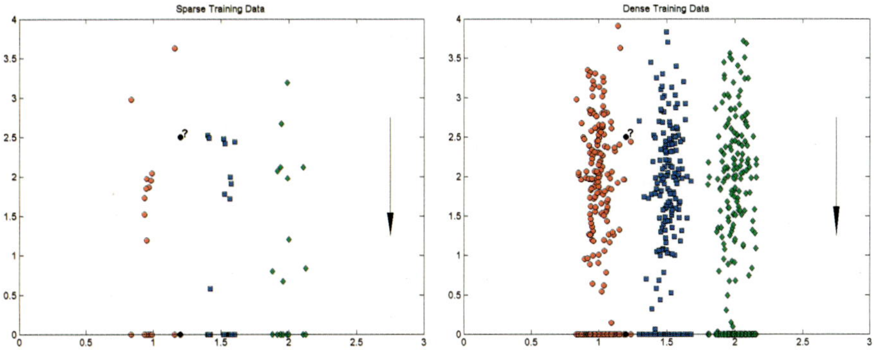

Fig. 3.14. Projecting the data onto lower dimensions can have a beneficial effect when not much training data is available. A nearest neighbour classifier misclassifies a novel point in the original, high dimensional space but classifies it correctly when projected onto the x axis. This problem is mitigated when there is a lot of training data available. Note that it is often not possible to know *a priori* the correct projection directions. If it were, then misclassifications in the original, high dimensional space can be avoided by incorporating such knowledge into the distance function. Indeed, this can even lead to superior classification unless *all* the information along the remaining dimensions is noise.

made and these result in a frequent loss of information when projecting downwards.

The second counter argument comes from the recent successes of boosting and kernel methods. Dimensionality reduction is necessary if one wants to accurately model the true texture PDF. However, both boosting and kernel methods have demonstrated that for classification purposes a better solution is to actually project the data non-linearly into an even higher (possibly infinite) dimensional space where the separability between classes is increased. Thus the emphasis is on maximising the distance between the classes and the decision boundary rather than trying to accurately model the true texture PDF (which, though ideal, is impractical). In particular, the kernel trick, when implemented properly, can lead to both improved classification and generalisation without much associated overhead and with none of the associated losses of downward projection. The reason this argument is applicable in our case is because it can be shown that χ^2, with some minor modifications, can be thought of as a Mercer kernel [Wallraven *et al.* (2003)]. Thus, the patch based classifiers take the distribution of image patches and project it into the much higher dimensional χ^2 space where classification is carried out. The filter bank based VZ algorithm does the same but it first projects the patches onto a lower dimensional space which results in a loss of information. This is the reason why the performance of filter banks, such as MR8, is consistently inferior to their source patches.

The third argument is an engineering one. While it is true that clustering is better and that parameters are estimated more accurately in lower dimensional spaces, Domingos and Pazzani [Domingos and Pazzani (1997)] have shown that even gross errors in parameter estimation can have very little effect on classification. This is illustrated in Figure 3.15 which shows that even though the means and covariance matrices of the true likelihood are estimated incorrectly, 98.6% of the data is still correctly classified, as the probability of observing the data in much of the incorrectly classified regions is vanishingly small.

Another interesting result, which supports the view that accurate parameter estimation is not necessary for accurate classification, is obtained by selecting the texton dictionary at random (rather than via *K-Means* clustering) from amongst the filter response vectors. In this case, the classification result for VZ MR8 drops by only 5% and is still well above 90%. A similar phenomenon was observed by [Georgescu *et al.* (2003)] when *Mean-Shift* clustering was used to approximate the filter response PDF. Thus accurate parameter estimation does not seem to be essential for accurate

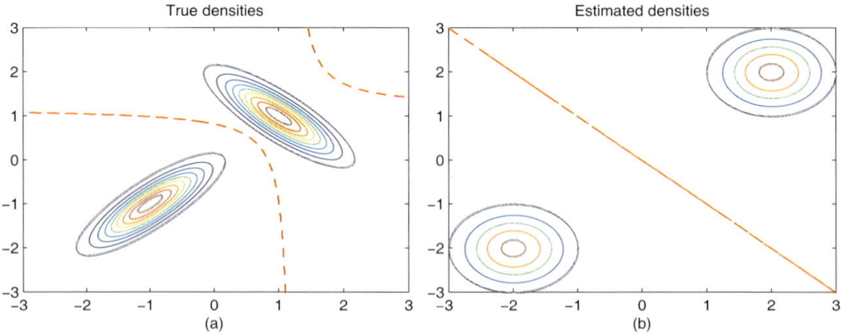

Fig. 3.15. Incorrect parameter estimation can still lead to good classification results: the true class conditional densities of two classes (defined to be Gaussians) are shown in (a) along with the MAP decision boundary obtained using equal priors (dashed red curves). In (b) the estimated likelihoods have gross errors. The estimated means have relative errors of 100% and the covariances are estimated as being diagonal leading to a very different decision boundary. Nevertheless the probability of misclassification (computed using the true Gaussian distributions for the probability of occurrence, and integrating the classification error over the entire 2D space) is just 1.4%. Thus, 98.6% of all points submitted to the classifier will be classified correctly despite the poor parameter estimation.

texture classification and the loss due to inaccurate parameter estimation in high dimensions might be less than the loss associated with projecting into a lower dimensional subspace even though clustering may be improved.

3.7.2.2. *Feature extraction*

The main argument from feature extraction is that many features at multiple orientations and scales must be detected accurately for successful classification. Furthermore, studies of early vision mechanisms and pre-attentive texture discrimination have suggested that the detected features should look like edges, bars, spots and rings. These have most commonly come to be implemented using Gabor or Gaussian filters and their derivatives. However, results from the previous sections have shown that a multi-scale, multi-orientation large support filter bank is not necessary. Small image patches can also lead to successful classification. Furthermore, while an optimally designed bank might be maximising some measure of separability in filter space, it is hard to argue that "off the shelf" filters such as MR8, LM or S (whether biologically motivated or not) are the best for any given classification task. In fact, as has been demonstrated, a classifier which *learns* from all the input data present in an image patch should do better than one which depends on these pre-defined features bases.

3.7.2.3. *Noise reduction and invariance*

Most filters have the desirable property that, because of their large smoothing kernels (such as Gaussians with large standard deviation), they are fairly robust to noise. This property is not shared by image patches. However, pre-processing the data can solve this problem. For example, the classifiers developed in this chapter rely on vector quantisation of the patches into textons to help cope with noise. This can actually provide a superior alternative to filtering, because even though filters reduce noise, they also smooth the high frequency information present in the signal. Yet, as has been demonstrated in the 3×3 patch case, this information can be beneficial for classification. Therefore, if image patches can be denoised by pre-processing or quantisation without the loss of high frequency information then they should provide a superior representation for classification as compared to filter banks.

Virtually the same methods can be used to build invariance into the patch representation as are used for filters – without losing information by projecting onto lower dimensions. For example, patches can be preprocessed to achieve invariance to affine transformations in the illuminant's intensity. Similarly, as discussed in section 3.6.2, to achieve rotational invariance, the dominant orientation can be determined and used to orient the patch.

3.8. Conclusions

We have described a classification method based on representing textures as a set of exemplar patches. This representation has been shown to be superior to one based on filters banks.

Filter banks have a number of disadvantages compared to smaller image patches: first, they often require large support, and this means that far fewer samples of a texture can be learnt from training images (there are many more 3×3 neighbourhoods than 50×50 in an 100×100 image). Second, the large support is also detrimental in texture segmentation, where boundaries are localised less precisely due to filter support straddling region boundaries; A third disadvantage is that the blurring (e.g. Gaussian smoothing) in many filters means that fine local detail can be lost.

The disadvantage of the patch representation is the quadratic increase in the dimension of the feature space with the size of the neighbourhood. This problem may be tackled by using a multi-scale representation. For instance, an image pyramid could be constructed and patches taken from several layers of the pyramid if necessary. An alternative would be to use large neighbourhoods but store the pixel information away from the centre at a coarser resolution. Finally, a scheme such as Zalesny and Van Gool's [Zalesny and Van Gool (2000)] could be implemented to determine which long range interactions were important and use only those cliques.

Before concluding, it is worth while to reflect on how the image patch algorithms and their results relate to what others have observed in the field. In particular, [Fowlkes *et al.* (2003); Levina (2002); Randen and Husoy (1999)] have all noted that in their segmentation and classification tasks, filters with small support have outperformed the same filters at larger scales. Thus, there appears to be emerging evidence that small support is not necessarily detrimental to performance.

It is also worth noting that the "new" image patch algorithms, such as the synthesis method of Efros and Leung and the Joint classifier developed in this chapter, have actually been around for quite a long time. For instance, Efros and Leung discovered a strong resemblance between their algorithm and that of [Garber (1981)]. Furthermore, both the Joint classifier and Efros and Leung's algorithm are near identical in spirit to the work of Popat and Picard [Popat and Picard (1993)]. The relationship between the Joint classifier and Popat and Picard's algorithm is particularly close as both use clustering to learn a distribution over image patches which then forms a model for novel texture classification. Apart from the choice of neighbourhoods, the only minor differences between the two methods are in the representation of the PDF and the distance measure used during classification. Popat and Picard use a Gaussian mixture model with diagonal covariances to represent their PDF while the texton representation used in this chapter can be thought of as fitting a spherical Gaussian mixture model via *K-Means*. During classification, Popat and Picard use a *naïve* Bayesian method which, for the Joint classifier, would equate to using nearest neighbour matching with KL divergence instead of the χ^2 statistic as the similarity measure [Varma and Zisserman (2004b)].

Certain similarities also exist between the Joint classifier and the MRF model of Cross and Jain [Cross and Jain (1983)]. In particular, Cross and Jain were the first to recommend that the distribution of central pixels and their neighbours could be compared using the χ^2 statistic and thereby the best fit between a sample texture and a model could be determined. Had they actually used this for classification rather than just model validation of synthesised textures, the two algorithms would have been very similar apart from the functional form of the PDFs learnt (Cross and Jain treat the conditional PDF of the central pixel given the neighbourhood as a unimodal binomial distribution).

Thus, alternative approaches to filter banks have been around for quite some time. Perhaps the reason that they didn't become popular then was due to the computational costs required to achieve good results. For instance, the synthesis results of [Popat and Picard (1993)] are of a poor quality which is perhaps why their theory didn't attract the attention it deserved. However, with computational power being readily accessible today, MRF and image patch methods are outperforming filter bank based methods.

Acknowledgements

We are grateful to Alexey Zalesny, David Forsyth and Andrew Fitzgibbon for many discussions and some very valuable feedback. We would also like to thank Alan Yuille for making the San Francisco database available, and Antonio Criminisi and Silvio Savarese for the Microsoft Textile database.

The investigations reported in this contribution have been supported by a University of Oxford Graduate Scholarship in Engineering at Jesus College, an ORS award and the European Union (FP5-project 'CogViSys', IST-2000-29404).

References

Bergen, J. R. and Adelson, E. H. (1988). Early vision and texture perception, *Nature* **333**, pp. 363–364.

Broadhurst, R. E. (2005). Statistical estimation of histogram variation for texture classification, in *Proceedings of the Fourth International Workshop on Texture Analysis and Synthesis* (Beijing, China), pp. 25–30.

Caputo, B., Hayman, E. and Mallikarjuna, P. (2005). Class-specific material categorisation, in *Proceedings of the International Conference on Computer Vision*, Vol. 2 (Beijing, China), pp. 1597–1604.

Cross, G. K. and Jain, A. K. (1983). Markov random field texture models, *IEEE Transactions on Pattern Analysis and Machine Intelligence* **5**, 1, pp. 25–39.

Cula, O. G. and Dana, K. J. (2004). 3D texture recognition using bidirectional feature histograms, *International Journal of Computer Vision* **59**, 1, pp. 33–60.

Dana, K. J., van Ginneken, B., Nayar, S. K. and Koenderink, J. J. (1999). Reflectance and texture of real world surfaces, *ACM Transactions on Graphics* **18**, 1, pp. 1–34.

Domingos, P. and Pazzani, M. J. (1997). On the optimality of the simple bayesian classifier under zero-one loss, *Machine Learning* **29**, 2-3, pp. 103–130.

Duda, R. O., Hart, P. E. and Stork, D. G. (2001). *Pattern Classification*, 2nd edn. (John Wiley and Sons).

Efros, A. and Leung, T. (1999). Texture synthesis by non-parametric sampling, in *Proceedings of the International Conference on Computer Vision*, Vol. 2 (Corfu, Greece), pp. 1039–1046.

Fowlkes, C., Martin, D. and Malik, J. (2003). Learning affinity functions for image segmentation: Combining patch-based and gradient-based approaches, in *Proceedings of the IEEE Conference on Computer Vision and Pattern Recognition*, Vol. 2 (Madison, Wisconsin), pp. 54–61.

Garber, D. D. (1981). *Computational Models for Texture Analysis and Texture Synthesis*, Ph.D. thesis, University of Southern California.

Geman, S. and Geman, D. (1984). Stochastic relaxation, Gibbs distributions, and the Bayesian restoration of images, *IEEE Transactions on Pattern Analysis and Machine Intelligence* **6**, 6, pp. 721–741.

Georgescu, B., Shimshoni, I. and Meer, P. (2003). Mean shift based clustering in high dimensions: A texture classification example, in *Proceedings of the International Conference on Computer Vision*, Vol. 1 (Nice, France), pp. 456–463.

Greenspan, H., Belongie, S., Perona, P. and Goodman, R. (1994). Rotation invariant texture recognition using a steerable pyramid, in *Proceedings of the*

International Conference on Pattern Recognition, Vol. 2 (Jerusalem, Israel), pp. 162–167.

Haley, G. M. and Manjunath, B. S. (1995). Rotation-invariant texture classification using modified gabor filters, in *Proceedings of the IEEE International Conference on Image Processing*, Vol. 1 (Washington, DC), pp. 262–265.

Hayman, E., Caputo, B., Fritz, M. and Eklundh, J.-O. (2004). On the significance of real-world conditions for material classification, in *Proceedings of the European Conference on Computer Vision*, Vol. 4 (Prague, Czech Republic), pp. 253–266.

Julesz, B. (1981). Textons, the elements of texture perception, and their interactions, *Nature* **290**, pp. 91–97.

Julesz, B., Gilbert, E. N., Shepp, L. A. and Frisch, H. L. (1973). Inability of humans to discriminate between visual textures that agree in second-order statistics – revisited, *Perception* **2**, 4, pp. 391–405.

Kohavi, R. and John, G. H. (1997). Wrappers for feature subset selection, *Artificial Intelligence* **97**, 1-2, pp. 273–324.

Konishi, S. and Yuille, A. L. (2000). Statistical cues for domain specific image segmentation with performance analysis, in *Proceedings of the IEEE Conference on Computer Vision and Pattern Recognition*, Vol. 1 (Hilton Head, South Carolina), pp. 125–132.

Leung, T. and Malik, J. (2001). Representing and recognizing the visual appearance of materials using three-dimensional textons, *International Journal of Computer Vision* **43**, 1, pp. 29–44.

Levina, E. (2002). *Statistical Issues in Texture Analysis*, Ph.D. thesis, University of California at Berkeley.

Li, S. Z. (2001). *Markov Random Field Modeling in Image Analysis* (Springer-Verlag).

Lindeberg, T. (1998). Feature detection with automatic scale selection, *International Journal of Computer Vision* **30**, 2, pp. 77–116.

Malik, J., Belongie, S., Leung, T. and Shi, J. (2001). Contour and texture analysis for image segmentation, *International Journal of Computer Vision* **43**, 1, pp. 7–27.

Malik, J. and Perona, P. (1990). Preattentive texture discrimination with early vision mechanism, *Journal of the Optical Society of America* **7**, 5, pp. 923–932.

Popat, K. and Picard, R. W. (1993). Novel cluster-based probability model for texture synthesis, classification, and compression, in *Proceedings of the SPIE Conference on Visual Communication and Image Processing* (Boston, Massachusetts), pp. 756–768.

Press, W., Teukolsky, S., Vetterling, W. and Flannery, B. (1992). *Numerical Recipes in C*, 2nd edn. (Cambridge University Press).

Randen, T. and Husoy, J. H. (1999). Filtering for texture classification: A comparative study, *IEEE Transactions on Pattern Analysis and Machine Intelligence* **21**, 4, pp. 291–310.

Riesenhuber, M. and Poggio, T. (1999). Hierarchical models of object recognition in cortex, *Nature Neuroscience* **2**, 11, pp. 1019–1025.

Rother, C., Kolmogorov, V. and Blake, A. (2004). GrabCut - interactive foreground extraction using iterated graph cuts, in *Proceedings of the ACM SIGGRAPH Conference on Computer Graphics* (Los Angeles, California).

Savarese, S. and Criminsi, A. (2004). Classification of folded textiles, Personal communications.

Schmid, C. (2001). Constructing models for content-based image retrieval, in *Proceedings of the IEEE Conference on Computer Vision and Pattern Recognition*, Vol. 2 (Kauai, Hawaii), pp. 39–45.

Schmid, C. (2004). Weakly supervised learning of visual models and its application to content-based retrieval, *International Journal of Computer Vision* **56**, 1, pp. 7–16.

Simard, P., LeCun, Y., Denker, J. and Victorri, B. (2001). Transformation invariance in pattern recognition – tangent distance and tangent propagation, *International Journal of Imaging System and Technology* **11**, 2, pp. 181–194.

Smith, J. R. and Chang, S. F. (1994). Transform features for texture classification and discrimination in large image databases, in *Proceedings of the IEEE International Conference on Image Processing*, Vol. 3 (Austin, Texas), pp. 407–411.

Varma, M. (2004). *Statistical Approaches To Texture Classification*, Ph.D. thesis, University of Oxford.

Varma, M. and Zisserman, A. (2004a). Texture classification, Web page, http://www.robots.ox.ac.uk/~vgg/research/texclass/filters.html.

Varma, M. and Zisserman, A. (2004b). Unifying statistical texture classification frameworks, *Image and Vision Computing* **22**, 14, pp. 1175–1183.

Varma, M. and Zisserman, A. (2005). A statistical approach to texture classification from single images, *International Journal of Computer Vision: Special Issue on Texture Analysis and Synthesis* **62**, 1–2, pp. 61–81.

Wallraven, C., Caputo, B. and Graf, A. (2003). Recognition with local features: the kernel recipe, in *Proceedings of the International Conference on Computer Vision*, Vol. 1 (Nice, France), pp. 257–264.

Zalesny, A. and Van Gool, L. (2000). A compact model for viewpoint dependent texture synthesis, in *Proceedings of the European Workshop on 3D Structure from Multiple Images of Large-Scale Environments* (Dublin, Ireland), pp. 124–143.

Chapter 4

TEXEMS: Random Texture Representation and Analysis

Xianghua Xie and Majid Mirmehdi*

Department of Computer Science, University of Bristol
Bristol BS8 1UB, England
E-mail: {xie,majid}@cs.bris.ac.uk

Random textures are notoriously more difficult to deal with than regular textures particularly when detecting abnormalities on object surfaces. In this chapter, we present a statistical model to represent and analyse random textures. In a two-layer structure a texture image, as the first layer, is considered to be a superposition of a number of texture exemplars, possibly overlapped, from the second layer. Each texture exemplar, or simply texem, is characterised by mean values and corresponding variances. Each set of these texems may comprise various sizes from different image scales. We explore Gaussian mixture models in learning these texem representations, and show two different applications: novelty detection and image segmentation.

4.1. Introduction

Texture is one of the most important characteristics in identifying objects and understanding surfaces. There are numerous texture features reported in the literature, with some covered elsewhere in this book, used to perform texture representation and analysis: co-occurrence matrices, Laws texture energy measures, run-lengths, autocorrelation, and Fourier-domain features are some of the most common ones used in a variety of applications.

Some textures display complex patterns but appear visually regular on a large scale, e.g. textile and web. Thus, it is relatively easier to extract their dominant texture features or to represent their characteristics by exploiting their regularity and periodicity. However, for textures that exhibit complex, random appearance patterns, such as marble slabs or printed ceramic tiles

*Portions reprinted, with permission, from Ref. 1 by the same authors.

(see Fig. 4.1), where the textural primitives are randomly placed, it becomes more difficult to generalise texture primitives and their spatial relationships.

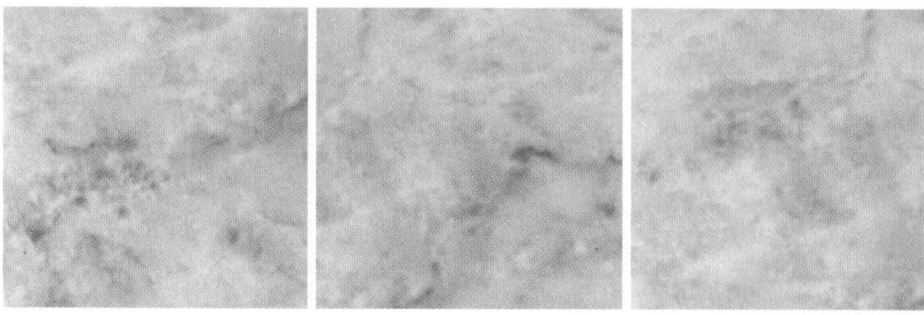

Fig. 4.1. Example marble tiles from the same family whose patterns are different but visually consistent.

As well as pixel intensity interactions, colour plays an important role in understanding texture, compounding the problem when random textures are involved. There has been a limited but increasing amount of work on colour texture analysis recently. Most of these borrow from methods designed for graylevel images. Direct channel separation followed by linear transformation is the common approach to adapting graylevel texture analysis methods to colour texture analysis, e.g. Caelli and Reye[2] processed colour images in RGB channels using multiscale isotropic filtering. Features from each channel were then extracted and later combined for classification. Several works have transformed the RGB colour space to other colour spaces to perform texture analysis so that chromatic channels are separated from the luminance channel, e.g. Refs. 3–6. For example, Liapis *et al.*[6] transformed colour images into the $L^*a^*b^*$ colour space in which discrete wavelet frame transform was performed in the L channel while local histograms in the a and b channels were used as chromatic features.

The importance of extracting correlation between the channels for colour texture analysis has been widely addressed with one of the earliest attempts reported in 1982.[7] Panjwani and Healey[8] devised an MRF model to encode the spatial interaction within and between colour channels. Thai and Healey[9] applied multiscale opponent features computed from Gabor filter responses to model intra-channel and inter-channel interactions. Mirmehdi and Petrou[10] perceptually smoothed colour image textures in a multiresolution sense before segmentation. Core clusters were then obtained from the coarsest level and initial probabilities were propagated through finer levels until full segmentation was achieved. Simultaneous auto-regressive models and co-occurrence matrices have also been used to extract the spatial relationship within and between RGB channels.[11,12]

There has been relatively limited effort to develop fully 3D models to represent colour textures. The 3D data space is usually factorised, i.e. involving channel separation, then the data is modelled and analysed using lower dimensional methods. However, such methods inevitably suffer from some loss of spectral information, as the colour image data space can only be approximately decorrelated. The epitome[13] provides a compact 3D representation of colour textures. The image is assumed to be a collection of epitomic primitives relying on raw pixel values in image patches. The neighbourhood of a central pixel in a patch is assumed statistically conditionally independent. A hidden mapping guides the relationship between the epitome and the original image. This compact representation method inherently captures the spatial and spectral interactions simultaneously.

In this chapter, we present a compact mixture representation of colour textures. Similar to the epitome model, the images are assumed to be generated from a superposition of image patches with added variations at each pixel position. However, we do not force the texture primitives into a single patch representation with hidden mappings. Instead, we use mixture models to derive several primitive representation, called texems, at various sizes and/or various scales. Unlike popular filter bank based approaches, such as Gabor filters, "raw" pixel values are used instead of filtering responses. This is motivated by several recent studies using non-filtering local neighbourhood approaches. For instance, Varma and Zisserman[14] have argued that textures can be analysed by just looking at small neighbourhoods, such as 7×7 patches, and achieve better performance than filtering based methods. Their results demonstrated that textures with global structures can be discriminated by examining the distribution of local measurements. Ojala *et al.*[15] have also advocated the use of local neighbourhood processing in the shape of local binary patterns as texture descriptors. Other works based on local pixel neighbourhoods are those which apply Markov Random Field models, e.g. Cohen *et al.*[16]

We shall demonstrate two applications of the texem model to analyse random textures. The first is to perform novelty detection in random colour textures and the second is to segment colour images.

4.2. The Texem Model

In this section, we present a two-layer generative model (see Fig. 4.2), in which an image in the first layer is assumed to be generated by superposition of a small number of image patches of various sizes from the second layer with added Gaussian noise at each pixel position. We define each texem as a mean image patch associated with a corresponding variance which controls its variation. The form of the texem variance can vary according to the learning scheme used. The generation process can be naturally modelled by mixture models with a bottom-up procedure.

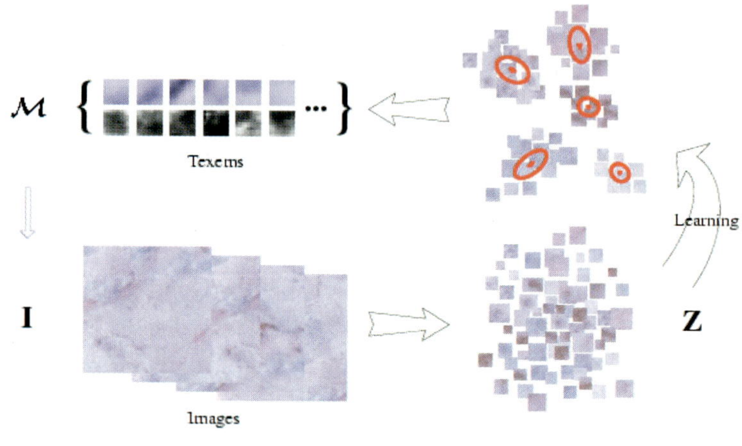

Fig. 4.2. An illustration of the two-layer structure of the texem model and its bottom-up learning procedure.

Next, we detail the process of extracting texems from a single sample image with each texem containing some of the overall textural primitive information. We shall use two different mixture models. The first is for graylevel images in which we vectorise the image patches and apply a Gaussian mixture model to obtain the texems. In the second, colour textures are represented by texems using a mixture model learnt based on joint Gaussian distributions within local neighbourhoods. This extension of texems to colour analysis is examined against other alternatives based on channel separation. We also introduce multiscale texem representations to drastically reduce the overall computational effort.

4.2.1. *Graylevel texems*

For graylevel images, we use a Gaussian mixture model to obtain the texems in a simple and efficient manner.[17] The original image $\mathbf{I}$ is broken down into a set of P patches $\mathbf{Z} = \{\mathbf{Z}_i\}_{i=1}^{P}$, each containing pixels from a subset of image coordinates. The shape of the patches can be arbitrary, but in this study we used square patches of size $d = N \times N$. The patches may overlap and can be of various sizes, e.g. as small as 5×5 to as large as required (however, for large window sizes one should ensure there are enough samples to populate the feature space). We group the patches of sample images into clusters, depending on the patch size, and describe the clusters using the Gaussian mixture model. Here, each texem, denoted as $\mathbf{m}$, is defined by a mean, $\boldsymbol{\mu}$, and a corresponding covariance matrix, $\boldsymbol{\omega}$, i.e. $\mathbf{m} = \{\boldsymbol{\mu}, \boldsymbol{\omega}\}$. We assume that there exist K texems, $\boldsymbol{\mathcal{M}} = \{\mathbf{m}_k\}_{k=1}^{K}$, $K \ll P$, for image $\mathbf{I}$ such that each patch in $\mathbf{Z}$ can be generated from a texem $\mathbf{m}$ with certain added variations.

To learn these texems the P patches are projected into a set of high dimensionality spaces. The number of these spaces is determined by the number of different patch sizes and their dimensions are defined by the corresponding value of d. Each pixel position contributes one coordinate of a space. Each point in a space corresponds to a patch in $\mathbf{Z}$. Then each texem represents a class of patches in the corresponding space. We assume that each class is a multivariate Gaussian distribution with mean $\boldsymbol{\mu}_k$ and covariance matrix $\boldsymbol{\omega}_k$, which corresponds to $\mathbf{m}_k$ in the patch domain. Thus, given the kth texem the probability of patch $\mathbf{Z}_i$ is computed as:

$$p(\mathbf{Z}_i|\mathbf{m}_k, \psi) = \mathcal{N}(\mathbf{Z}_i; \boldsymbol{\mu}_k, \boldsymbol{\omega}_k)\,, \tag{4.1}$$

where $\psi = \{\boldsymbol{\alpha}_k, \boldsymbol{\mu}_k, \boldsymbol{\omega}_k\}_{k=1}^{K}$ is the parameter set containing $\boldsymbol{\alpha}_k$, which is the *prior* probability of kth texem constrained by $\sum_{k=1}^{K} \boldsymbol{\alpha}_k = 1$, the mean $\boldsymbol{\mu}_k$, and the covariance $\boldsymbol{\omega}_k$. Since all the texems $\mathbf{m}_k$ are unknown, we need to compute the density function of $\mathbf{Z}$ given the parameter set ψ by applying the definition of conditional probability and summing over k for $\mathbf{Z}_i$,

$$p(\mathbf{Z}_i|\psi) = \sum_{k=1}^{K} p(\mathbf{Z}_i|\mathbf{m}_k, \psi)\boldsymbol{\alpha}_k\,, \tag{4.2}$$

and then optimising the data log-likelihood expression of the entire set $\mathbf{Z}$, given by

$$\log p(\mathbf{Z}|K, \psi) = \sum_{i=1}^{P} \log\left(\sum_{k=1}^{K} p(\mathbf{Z}_i|\mathbf{m}_k, \psi)\boldsymbol{\alpha}_k\right). \tag{4.3}$$

Hence, the objective is to estimate the parameter set ψ for a given number of texems. Expectation Maximisation (EM) can be used to find the maximum likelihood estimate of our mixture density parameters from the given data set $\mathbf{Z}$. That is to find $\hat{\psi}$ where

$$\hat{\psi} = \arg\max \log(\mathcal{L}(\psi|\mathbf{Z})) = \arg\max_{\psi} \log p(\mathbf{Z}|K, \psi) . \tag{4.4}$$

Then the two steps of the EM stage are as follows. The E-step involves a soft-assignment of each patch $\mathbf{Z}_i$ to texems, $\boldsymbol{\mathcal{M}}$, with an initial guess of the true parameters, ψ. This initialisation can be set randomly (although we use K-means to compute a simple estimate with K set as the number of texems to be learnt). We denote the intermediate parameters as $\psi^{(t)}$ where t is the iteration step. The likelihood of kth texem given the patch $\mathbf{Z}_i$ may then be computed using Bayes' rule:

$$p(\mathbf{m}_k|\mathbf{Z}_i, \psi^{(t)}) = \frac{p(\mathbf{Z}_i|\mathbf{m}_k, \psi^{(t)})\boldsymbol{\alpha}_k}{\sum_{k=1}^{K} p(\mathbf{Z}_i|\mathbf{m}_k, \psi^{(t)})\boldsymbol{\alpha}_k} . \tag{4.5}$$

The M-step then updates the parameters by maximising the log-likelihood, resulting in new estimates:

$$\begin{aligned} \hat{\boldsymbol{\alpha}}_k &= \frac{1}{P}\sum_{i=1}^{P} p(\mathbf{m}_k|\mathbf{Z}_i, \psi^{(t)}) , \\ \hat{\boldsymbol{\mu}}_k &= \frac{\sum_{i=1}^{P} \mathbf{Z}_i p(\mathbf{m}_k|\mathbf{Z}_i, \psi^{(t)})}{\sum_{i=1}^{P} p(\mathbf{m}_k|\mathbf{Z}_i, \psi^{(t)})} , \\ \hat{\boldsymbol{\omega}}_k &= \frac{\sum_{i=1}^{P} (\mathbf{Z}_i - \hat{\boldsymbol{\mu}}_k)(\mathbf{Z}_i - \hat{\boldsymbol{\mu}}_k)^T p(\mathbf{m}_k|\mathbf{Z}_i, \psi^{(t)})}{\sum_{i=1}^{P} p(\mathbf{m}_k|\mathbf{Z}_i, \psi^{(t)})} . \end{aligned} \tag{4.6}$$

The E-step and M-step are iterated until the estimations stabilise. Then, the texems can be easily obtained by projecting the learnt means and covariance matrices back to the patch representation space.

4.2.2. *Colour texems*

In this section, we explore two different schemes to extend texems to colour images with differing computational complexity and rate of accuracy.

4.2.2.1. *Texem analysis in separate channels*

More often than not, colour texture analysis is treated as a simple dimensional extension of techniques designed for graylevel images, and so

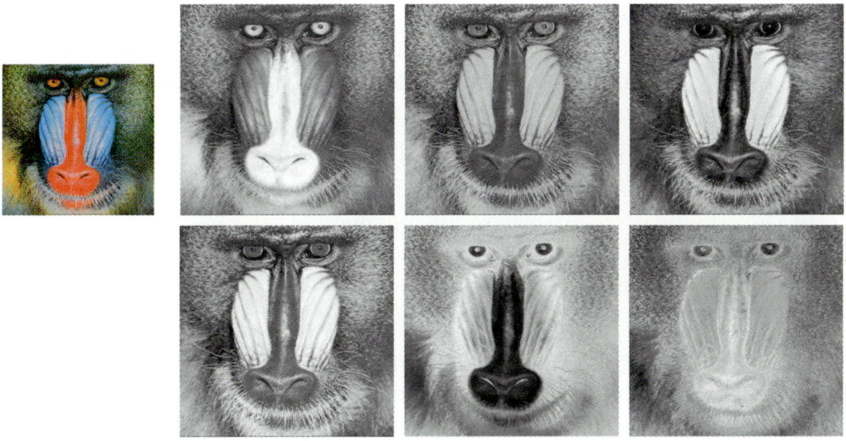

Fig. 4.3. Channel separation - first row: Original collage image; second row: individual RGB channels; third row: eigenchannel images.

colour images are decomposed into separate channels to perform the same processes. However, this gives rise to difficulties in capturing both the inter-channel and spatial properties of the texture and special care is usually necessary. Alternatively, we can decorrelate the image channels using Principal Component Analysis (PCA) and then perform texems analysis in each independent channel separately. We prefer this approach and use it to compare against our full colour texem model introduced later.

Let $\mathbf{c}_i = [r_i, g_i, b_i]^T$ be a colour pixel, $\mathbf{C} = \{\mathbf{c}_i \in \mathcal{R}^3, i = 1, 2, ..., q\}$ be the set of q three dimensional vectors made up of the pixels from the image, and $\bar{\mathbf{c}} = \frac{1}{q}\sum_{\mathbf{c}\in\mathbf{C}} \mathbf{c}$ be the mean vector of $\mathbf{C}$. Then, PCA is performed on the mean-centred colour feature matrix $\mathbf{C}$ to obtain the eigenvectors $E = [e_1, e_2, e_3]$, $e_j \in \mathcal{R}^3$. Singular Value Decomposition can be used to obtain these principal components. The colour feature space determined by these eigenvectors is referred to as the reference eigenspace $\Upsilon_{\bar{\mathbf{c}},E}$, where the colour features are well represented. The image can then be projected onto this reference eigenspace:

$$\mathbf{C}' = \overrightarrow{PCA}(\mathbf{C}, \Upsilon_{\bar{\mathbf{c}},E}) = E^T(\mathbf{C} - \bar{\mathbf{c}}J_{1,q}), \tag{4.7}$$

where $J_{1,q}$ is a $1 \times q$ unit matrix consisting of all 1s. This results in three eigenchannels, in which graylevel texem analysis can be performed separately.

Figure 4.3 shows a comparison of RGB channel separation and PCA eigenchannel decomposition. The R, G, and B channels shown in the second row are highly correlated to each other. Their spatial relationship (texture) within each channel are very similar to each other, i.e. the channels are not sufficiently complimentary. On the other hand, each eigenchannel in the third row exhibits its own characteristics. For example, the first eigenchannel preserves most of the textural information while the last eigenchannel maintains the ambient emphasis of the image. Later in Sec. 4.3, we demonstrate the benefit of decorrelating image channels in novelty detection.

4.2.2.2. *Full colour model*

By decomposing the colour image and analysing image channels individually, the inter-channel and intra-channel spatial interactions are not taken into account. To facilitate such interactions, we use a different formulation for texem representation and consequently change the inference procedure so that no vectorisation of image patches is required and colour images do not need to be transformed into separate channels. Contrary to the way graylevel texems were developed, where each texem was represented by a single multivariate Gaussian function, for colour texems we assume that pixels are statistically independent in each texem with Gaussian distribution at each pixel position in the texem. This is similar to the way the image epitome is generated by Jojic *et al.*[13] Thus, the probability of patch $\mathbf{Z}_i$ given the kth texem can be formulated as a joint probability assuming neighbouring pixels are statistically conditionally independent, i.e.:

$$p(\mathbf{Z}_i|\mathbf{m}_k) = p(\mathbf{Z}_i|\boldsymbol{\mu}_k, \boldsymbol{\omega}_k) = \prod_{j \in S} \mathcal{N}(\mathbf{Z}_{j,i}; \boldsymbol{\mu}_{j,k}, \boldsymbol{\omega}_{j,k}), \tag{4.8}$$

where S is the pixel patch grid, $\mathcal{N}(\mathbf{Z}_{j,i}; \boldsymbol{\mu}_{j,k}, \boldsymbol{\omega}_{j,k})$ is a Gaussian distribution over $Z_{j,i}$, and $\boldsymbol{\mu}_{j,k}$ and $\boldsymbol{\omega}_{j,k}$ denote mean and covariance at the jth pixel in the kth texem. Similarly to Eq. (4.2) but using the component probability function in Eq. (4.8), we assume the following probabilistic mixture model:

$$p(\mathbf{Z}_i|\Theta) = \sum_{k=1}^{K} p(\mathbf{Z}_i|\mathbf{m}_k, \Theta)\boldsymbol{\alpha}_k, \tag{4.9}$$

where the parameters are $\Theta = \{\boldsymbol{\alpha}_k, \boldsymbol{\mu}_k, \boldsymbol{\omega}_k\}_{k=1}^{K}$ and can be determined by optimising the data log-likelihood given by

$$\log p(\mathbf{Z}|K, \Theta) = \sum_{i=1}^{P} \log \left(\sum_{k=1}^{K} p(\mathbf{Z}_i|\mathbf{m}_k, \Theta)\boldsymbol{\alpha}_k \right). \tag{4.10}$$

Fig. 4.4. Eight 7 × 7 texems extracted from the image in Fig. 4.3. Each texem $\mathbf{m}$ is defined by mean values (first row), $\boldsymbol{\mu} = [\boldsymbol{\mu}_1, \boldsymbol{\mu}_2, ..., \boldsymbol{\mu}_S]$, and corresponding variance images (second row), $\boldsymbol{\omega} = [\boldsymbol{\omega}_1, \boldsymbol{\omega}_2, ..., \boldsymbol{\omega}_S]$, i.e. $\mathbf{m} = \{\boldsymbol{\mu}, \boldsymbol{\omega}\}$. Note, $\boldsymbol{\mu}_j$ is a 3×1 colour vector, and $\boldsymbol{\omega}_j$ is a 3×3 matrix characterising the covariance in the colour space. Each element $\boldsymbol{\omega}_j$ in $\boldsymbol{\omega}$ is visualised using total variance of $\boldsymbol{\omega}_j$, i.e. $\sum \text{diag}(\boldsymbol{\omega}_j)$.

The EM technique can be used again to find the maximum likelihood estimate:

$$\hat{\Theta} = \arg\max \log(\mathcal{L}(\Theta|\mathbf{Z})) = \arg\max_{\Theta} \log p(\mathbf{Z}|K, \Theta)\,. \tag{4.11}$$

The new estimates, denoted by $\hat{\boldsymbol{\alpha}}_k$, $\hat{\boldsymbol{\mu}}_k$, and $\hat{\boldsymbol{\omega}}_k$, are updated during the EM iterations:

$$\begin{aligned}
\hat{\boldsymbol{\alpha}}_k &= \frac{1}{P}\sum_{i=1}^{P} p(\mathbf{m}_k|\mathbf{Z}_i, \Theta^{(t)})\,,\\
\hat{\boldsymbol{\mu}}_k &= \{\hat{\boldsymbol{\mu}}_{j,k}\}_{j\in S}\,,\\
\hat{\boldsymbol{\omega}}_k &= \{\hat{\boldsymbol{\omega}}_{j,k}\}_{j\in S}\,,\\
\hat{\boldsymbol{\mu}}_{j,k} &= \frac{\sum_{i=1}^{P} \mathbf{Z}_{j,i}\, p(\mathbf{m}_k|\mathbf{Z}_i, \Theta^{(t)})}{\sum_{i=1}^{P} p(\mathbf{m}_k|\mathbf{Z}_i, \Theta^{(t)})}\,,\\
\hat{\boldsymbol{\omega}}_{j,k} &= \frac{\sum_{i=1}^{P} (\mathbf{Z}_{j,i} - \hat{\boldsymbol{\mu}}_{j,k})(\mathbf{Z}_{j,i} - \hat{\boldsymbol{\mu}}_{j,k})^T p(\mathbf{m}_k|\mathbf{Z}_i, \Theta^{(t)})}{\sum_{i=1}^{P} p(\mathbf{m}_k|\mathbf{Z}_i, \Theta^{(t)})}\,,
\end{aligned} \tag{4.12}$$

where

$$p(\mathbf{m}_k|\mathbf{Z}_i, \Theta^{(t)}) = \frac{p(\mathbf{Z}_i|\mathbf{m}_k, \Theta^{(t)})\boldsymbol{\alpha}_k}{\sum_{k=1}^{K} p(\mathbf{Z}_i|\mathbf{m}_k, \Theta^{(t)})\boldsymbol{\alpha}_k}\,. \tag{4.13}$$

The iteration continues till the values stabilise. Various sizes of texems can be used and they can overlap to ensure they capture sufficient textural characteristics. We can see that when the texem reduces to a single pixel size, Eq. (4.12) becomes Gaussian mixture modelling based on pixel colours.

Figure 4.4 illustrates eight 7×7 texems extracted from the Baboon image in Fig. 4.3. They are arranged according to their descending order of *priors*

$\boldsymbol{\alpha}_k$. We may treat each prior, $\boldsymbol{\alpha}_k$, as a measurement of the contribution from each texem. The image then can be viewed as a superposition of various sizes of image patches taken from the means of the texems, a linear combination, with added variations at each pixel position governed by the corresponding variances.

4.2.3. *Multiscale texems*

To capture sufficient textural properties, texems can be from as small as 3×3 to larger sizes such as 21×21. However, the dimension of the space patches $\mathbf{Z}$ are transformed into will increase dramatically as the dimension of the patch size increases. This means that a very large number of samples and high computational costs are needed in order to accurately estimate the probability density functions in very high dimensional spaces,[18] forcing the procurement of a large number of training samples.

Instead of generating variable-size texems, fixed size texems can be learnt in multiscale. This will result in (multiscale) texems with a small size, e.g. 5×5. Besides computational efficiency, exploiting information at multiscale offers other advantages over single-scale approaches. Characterising a pixel based on local neighbourhood pixels can be more effectively achieved by examining various neighbourhood relationships. The corresponding neighbourhood at coarser scale obviously offers larger spatial interactions. Also, processing at multiscale ensures the capture of the optimal resolution, which is often data dependent. We shall investigate two different approaches for texems analysis in multiscale.

4.2.3.1. *Texems in separate scales*

First, we learn small fixed size texems in separate scales of a Gaussian pyramid. Let us denote $\mathbf{I}^{(n)}$ as the nth level image of the pyramid, $\mathbf{Z}^{(n)}$ as all the image patches extracted from $\mathbf{I}^{(n)}$, l as the total number of levels, and $S^{\downarrow}$ as the down-sampling operator. We then have

$$\mathbf{I}^{(n+1)} = S^{\downarrow} G_\sigma(\mathbf{I}^{(n)}), \qquad \forall n, n = 1, 2, ..., l-1\,, \tag{4.14}$$

where G_σ denotes the Gaussian convolution. The finest scale layer is the original image, $\mathbf{I}^{(1)} = \mathbf{I}$. We then extract multiscale texems from the image pyramid using the method presented in the previous section. Similarly, let $\mathbf{m}^{(n)}$ denote the nth level of multiscale texems and $\Theta^{(n)}$ the parameters associated at the same level.

During the EM process, the stabilised estimation of a coarser level is used as the initial estimation for the finer level, i.e.

$$\hat{\Theta}^{(n,t=0)} = \Theta^{(n+1)}, \tag{4.15}$$

which hastens the convergence and achieves a more accurate estimation.

4.2.3.2. *Multiscale texems using branch partitioning*

Starting from the pyramid layout described above, each pixel in the finest level can trace its parent pixel back to the coarsest level forming a unique route or branch. Take the full colour texem for example, the conditional independence assumption amongst pixels within the local neighbourhood shown in Eq. (4.8) makes the parameter estimation tractable. Here, we assume pixels *in the same branch* are conditionally independent, i.e.

$$p(\mathbf{Z}_i|\mathbf{m}_k) = p(\mathbf{Z}_i|\boldsymbol{\mu}_k, \boldsymbol{\omega}_k) = \prod_{n=1}^{l} \mathcal{N}(\mathbf{Z}_i^{(n)}; \boldsymbol{\mu}_k^{(n)}, \boldsymbol{\omega}_k^{(n)}), \tag{4.16}$$

where $\mathbf{Z}_i$ here is a branch of pixels, and $\mathbf{Z}_i^{(n)}$, $\boldsymbol{\mu}_k^{(n)}$, and $\boldsymbol{\omega}_k^{(n)}$ are the colour pixel at level n in ith branch, mean at level n of kth texem, and variance at level n of kth texem, respectively. This is essentially the same form as Eq. (4.8), hence, we can still use the EM procedure described previously to derive the texems. However, the image is not partitioned into patches, but rather laid out in multiscale first and then separated into branches, i.e pixels are collected across scales, instead of from its neighbours.

4.2.4. *Comments*

The texem model is motivated from the observation that in random texture surfaces of the same family, the pattern may appear to be different in textural manifestation from one sample to another, however, the visual impression and homogeneity remains consistent. This suggests that the random pattern can be described with a few textural primitives.

In the texem model, the image is assumed to be a superposition of patches with various sizes and even various shapes. The variation at each pixel position in the construction of the image is embedded in each texem. Thus, it can be viewed as a two-layer *generative* statistical model. The image $\mathbf{I}$, in the first layer, is generated from a collection of texems $\mathcal{M}$ in the second layer, i.e. $\mathcal{M} \rightarrow \mathbf{I}$. In deriving the texem representations from an image or a set of images, a bottom-up learning process can be used as presented in this chapter. Figure 4.2 illustrates the two-layer structure and the bottom-up learning procedure.

Relationship to Textons - Both the texem and the texton models characterise textural images by using micro-structures. Textons were first formally introduced by Julesz[19] as fundamental image structures, such as elongated blobs, bars, crosses, and terminators, and were considered as atoms of pre-attentive human visual perception. Zhu *et al.*[20] define textons using the superposition of a number of image bases, such as Laplacian of Gaussians and Gabors, selected from an over-complete dictionary. However, the texem model is significantly different from the texton model in that (i) it relies directly on subimage patches instead of using base functions, and (ii) it is an implicit, rather than an explicit, representation of primitives. The design of a bank of base functions to obtain sensible textons is non-trivial and likely to be application dependent. Much effort is needed to explicitly extract visual primitives (textons), such as blobs, but in the proposed model, each texem is an encapsulation of texture primitive(s). Not using base functions also allows texems more flexibility to deal with multi-spectral images.

4.3. Novelty Detection

In this section, we show an application of the texem model to defect detection on ceramic tile surfaces exhibiting rich and random texture patterns.

Visual surface inspection tasks are concerned with identifying regions that deviate from defect-free samples according to certain criteria, e.g. pattern regularity or colour. Machine vision techniques are now regularly used in detecting such defects or imperfections on a variety of surfaces, such as textile, ceramics tiles, wood, steel, silicon wafers, paper, meat, leather, and even curved surfaces, e.g. Refs. 16 and 21–23. Generally, this detection process should be viewed as different to texture segmentation, which is concerned with splitting an image into homogeneous regions. Neither the defect-free regions nor the defective regions have to be texturally uniform. For example, a surface may contain totally different types of defects which are likely to have different textural properties. On the other hand, a defect-free sample should be processed without the need to perform "segmentation", no matter how irregular and unstationary the texture.

In an application such as ceramic tile production, the images under inspection may appear different from one surface to another due to the random texture patterns involved. However, the visual impression of the same product line remains consistent. In other words, there exist textural primitives that impose consistency within the product line. Figure 4.1 shows three example tile images from the same class (or production run) decorated with a marble texture. Each tile has different features on its surface, but they all still exhibit a consistent visual impression. One may collect enough samples to cover the range of variations and this approach has been widely used in texture classification and defect detection, e.g. for textile defects.[24] It usually requires a large number of non-defective samples and lengthy training stages; not necessarily practical in a factory environment. Additionally, defects are usually unpredictable.

Instead of the traditional classification approach, we learn texems, in an unsupervised fashion, from a very small number of training samples. The texems encapsulate the texture or visual primitives. As the images of the same (tile) product contain the same textural elements, the texems can be used to examine the same source similarity, and detect any deviations from the norm as defects.

4.3.1. *Unsupervised training*

Texems lend themselves well to performing unsupervised training and testing for novelty detection. This is achieved by automatically determining the threshold of statistical texture variation of defect-free samples at each resolution level. For training, a small number of defect free samples (e.g. 4 or 5 only) are arranged within the multiscale framework, and patches with the same texem size are extracted. The probability of a patch $\mathbf{Z}_i^{(n)}$ belonging to texems in the corresponding n^{th} scale is:

$$p(\mathbf{Z}_i^{(n)}|\Theta^{(n)}) = \sum_{k=1}^{K^{(n)}} p(\mathbf{Z}_i^{(n)}|\mathbf{m}_k^{(n)}, \Theta^{(n)})\boldsymbol{\alpha}_k^{(n)}, \tag{4.17}$$

where $\Theta^{(n)}$ represents the parameter set for level n, $\mathbf{m}_k^{(n)}$ is the kth texem at the nth image pyramid level, and $p(\mathbf{Z}_i^{(n)}|\mathbf{m}_k^{(n)}, \Theta^{(n)})$ is a product of Gaussian distributions shown in Eq. (4.9) with parameters associated to texem set $\boldsymbol{\mathcal{M}}$. Based on this probability function, we then define a novelty score function as the negative log likelihood:

$$\mathcal{V}(\mathbf{Z}_i^{(n)}|\Theta^{(n)}) = -\log p(\mathbf{Z}_i^{(n)}|\Theta^{(n)}). \tag{4.18}$$

The lower the novelty score, the more likely the patch belongs to the same family and vice versa. Thus, it can be viewed as a same source similarity measurement. The distribution of the scores for all the patches $\mathbf{Z}^{(n)}$ at level n of the pyramid forms a 1D novelty score space which is not necessarily a simple Gaussian distribution. In order to find the upper bound of the novelty score space of defect-free patches (or the lower bound of data likelihood), K-means clustering is performed in this space to approximately model the space. The cluster with the maximum mean is the component of the novelty score distribution at the boundary between good and defective textures. This component is characterised by mean $u^{(n)}$ and standard deviation $\sigma^{(n)}$. This K-means scheme replaces the single Gaussian distribution assumption in the novelty score space, which is commonly adopted in a parametric classifier in novelty detection, e.g. Ref. 25 and for which the correct parameter selection is critical. Instead, dividing the novelty score space and finding the critical component, here called the boundary component, can effectively lower the parameter sensitivity. The value of K should be generally small (we empirically fixed it at 5). It is also notable that a single Gaussian classifier is a special case of the above scheme, i.e. when $K = 1$. The maximum novelty score (or the minimum data likelihood), $\Lambda^{(n)}$ of a patch $\mathbf{Z}_i^{(n)}$ at level n across the training images is then established as:

$$\Lambda^{(n)} = u^{(n)} + \lambda\sigma^{(n)}, \tag{4.19}$$

where λ is a simple constant. This completes the training stage in which, with only a few defect-free images, we determine the texems and an automatic threshold for marking new image patches as good or defective.

4.3.2. *Novelty detection and defect localisation*

In the testing stage, the image under inspection is again layered into a multiscale framework and patches at each pixel position $\mathbf{x}$ at each level n are examined against the learnt texems. The probability for each patch and its novelty score are then computed using Eqs. (4.17) and (4.18) and compared to the maximum novelty score, determined by $\Lambda^{(n)}$, at the corresponding level. Let $Q^{(n)}(\mathbf{x})$ be the novelty score map at the nth resolution level. Then, the potential defect map, $\mathcal{D}^{(n)}(\mathbf{x})$, at level n is:

$$\mathcal{D}^{(n)}(\mathbf{x}) = \begin{cases} 0 & \text{if } Q^{(n)}(\mathbf{x}) \leq \Lambda^{(n)} \\ Q^{(n)}(\mathbf{x}) - \Lambda^{(n)} & \text{otherwise}, \end{cases} \tag{4.20}$$

$\mathcal{D}^{(n)}(\mathbf{x})$ indicates the probability of there being a defect. Next, the information coming from all the resolution levels must be consolidated to build the certainty of the defect at position $\mathbf{x}$. We follow a framework[22] which combines information from different levels of a multiscale pyramid and reduces false alarms. It assumes that a defect must appear in at least two adjacent resolution levels for it to be certified as such. Using a logical AND, implemented through the geometric mean of every pair of adjacent levels, we initially obtain a set of combined maps as:

$$\mathcal{D}^{(n,n+1)}(\mathbf{x}) = [\mathcal{D}^{(n)}(\mathbf{x})\mathcal{D}^{(n+1)}(\mathbf{x})]^{1/2} . \tag{4.21}$$

Note each $\mathcal{D}^{(n+1)}(\mathbf{x})$ is scaled up to be the same size as $\mathcal{D}^{(n)}(\mathbf{x})$. This operation reduces false alarms and yet preserves most of the defective areas. Next, the resulting $\mathcal{D}^{(1,2)}(\mathbf{x})$, $\mathcal{D}^{(2,3)}(\mathbf{x})$, ..., $\mathcal{D}^{(l-1,l)}(\mathbf{x})$ maps are combined in a logical OR, as the arithmetic mean, to provide

$$\mathcal{D}(\mathbf{x}) = \frac{1}{l-1}\sum_{n=1}^{l-1} \mathcal{D}^{(n,n+1)}(\mathbf{x}) , \tag{4.22}$$

where $\mathcal{D}(\mathbf{x})$ is the final consolidated map of (the joint contribution of) all the defects across all resolution scales of the test image.

The multiscale, unsupervised training, and novelty detection stages are applied in a similar fashion as described above in the cases of graylevel and full colour model texem methods. In the separate channel colour approaches (i.e. before and after decorrelation) the final defective maps from each channel are ultimately combined.

4.3.3. *Experimental results*

The texem model is initially applied to the detection of defects on ceramic tiles. We do not evaluate the quality of the localised defects found (against a groundtruth) since the defects in our data set are difficult to manually localise. However, whole tile classification rates, based on overall "defective" and "defect-free" labelling by factory-floor experts is presented. In order to evaluate texems, the result of experiments on texture collages made from textures in the MIT VisTex texture database[26] is outlined. A comparative study of three different approaches to texem analysis on colour images and a Gabor filter bank based method is given.

4.3.3.1. *Ceramic tile application*

We applied the proposed *full colour texem model* to a variety of randomly textured tile data sets with different types of defects including physical damage, pin holes, textural imperfections, and many more. The 256×256

test samples were pre-processed to assure homogeneous luminance, spatially and temporally. In the experiments, only five defect-free samples were used to extract the texems and to determine the upper bound of the novelty scores $\Lambda^{(n)}$. The number of texems at each resolution level were empirically set to 12, and the size of each texem was 5×5 pixels. The number of multiscale levels was $l = 4$. These parameters were fixed throughout our experiments on a variety of random texture tile prints.

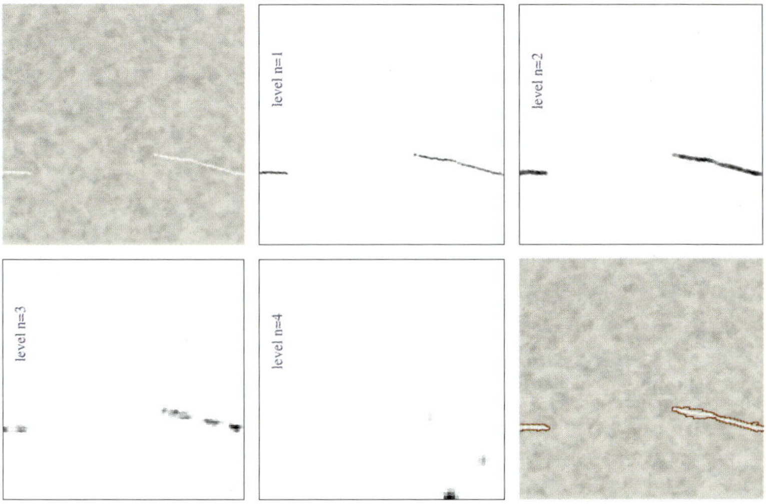

Fig. 4.5. Localising textural defects - from top left to bottom right: original defective tile image, detected defective regions at different levels $n = 1, 2, 3, 4$, and the final defective region superimposed on the original image.

Figure 4.5 shows a random texture example with defective regions introduced by physical damage. The potentially defective regions detected at each resolution level n, $n = 1, ..., 4$, are marked on the corresponding images in Fig. 4.5. It can be seen that the texems show good sensitivity to the defective region at different scales. As the resolution progresses from coarse to fine, additional evidence for the defective region is gathered. The final image shows the defect superimposed on the original image. As mentioned earlier, the defect fusion process can eliminate false alarms, e.g. see the extraneous false alarm regions in level $n = 4$ which disappear after the operations in Eqs. (4.21) and (4.22).

More examples of different random textures are shown in Fig. 4.6. In each family of patterns, the textures are varying but have the same visual

Fig. 4.6. Defect localisation (different textures) - The first row shows example images from three different tile families with different chromato-textural properties. Defects shown in the next row, from left to right, include print error, surface bumps, and thin cracks. The third row shows another three images from three different tile families. Defects shown in the last row, from left to right, include cracks and print errors.

impression. In each case the proposed method could find structural and chromatic defects of various shapes and sizes.

Figure 4.7 shows three examples when using *graylevel* texems. Various defects, such as print errors, bumps, and broken corner, are successfully

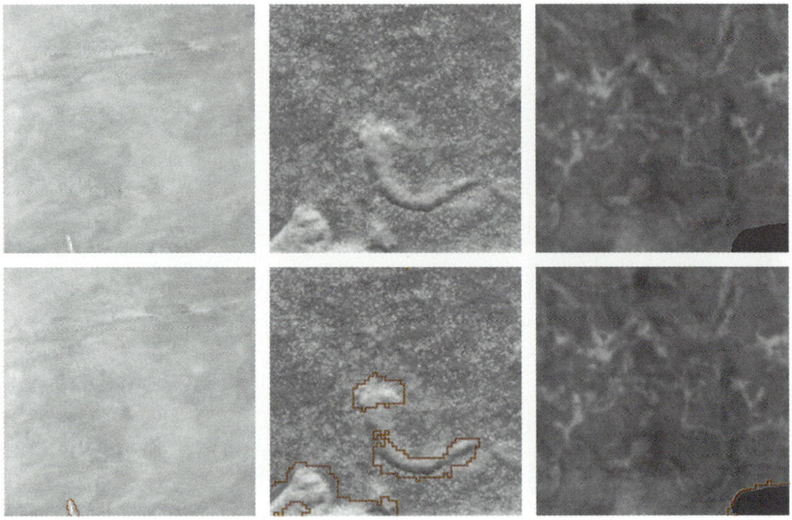

Fig. 4.7. Graylevel texems defect localisation.

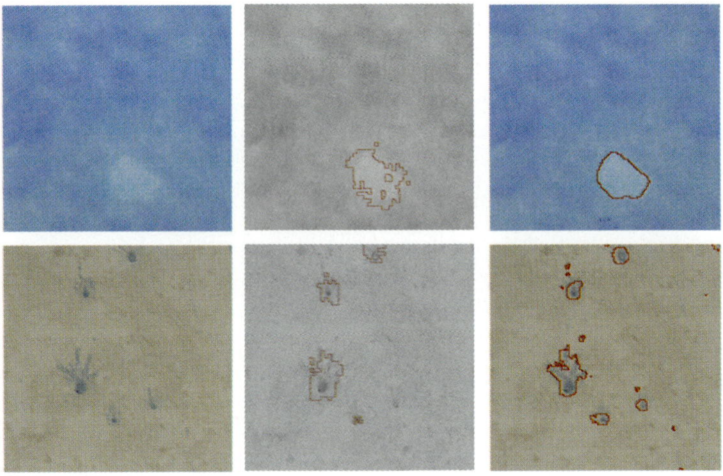

Fig. 4.8. Defect localisation comparison - left column: original texture with print errors, middle column: results using graylevel texems, right column: results using colour texems.

detected. Graylevel texems were found adequate for most defect detection tasks where defects were still reasonably visible after converting from colour to gray scale. However, colour texems were found to be more powerful in localising defects and better discriminants in cases involving chromatic defects. Two examples are compared in Fig. 4.8. The first shows a tile image with a defective region, which is not only slightly brighter but also less saturated in blue. The colour texem model achieved better results in localising the defect than the graylevel one. The second row in Fig. 4.8 demonstrates a different type of defect which clearly possesses a different hue from the background texture. The colour texems found more affected regions, more accurately.

The full colour texem model was tested on 1018 tile samples from ten different families of tiles consisting of 561 defect-free samples and 457 defective samples. It obtained a defect detection accuracy rate of 91.1%, with sensitivity at 92.6% and specificity at 89.8%. The graylevel texem method was tested on 1512 graylevel tile images from eight different families of tiles consisting of 453 defect-free samples and 1059 defective samples. It obtained an overall accuracy rate of 92.7%, with sensitivity at 95.9% specificity at 89.5%. We compare the performance of graylevel and colour texem models on the same dataset in later experiments.

As patches are extracted from each pixel position at each resolution level, a typical *training stage* involves examining a very large number of patches. For the graylevel texem model, this takes around 7 minutes, on a 2.8GHz Pentium 4 Processor running Linux with 1GB RAM, to learn the texems in multiscale and to determine the thresholds for novelty detection. The testing stage then requires around 12 seconds to inspect one tile image. The full colour texem model is computationally more expensive and can be more than 10 times slower. However, this can be reduced to the same order as the graylevel version by performing window-based, rather than pixel-based, examination at the training and testing stages.

4.3.3.2. *Evaluation using VisTex collages*

For performance evaluation, 28 image collages were generated (see some in Fig. 4.10) from textures in VisTex.[26] In each case the background is the learnt texture for which colour texems are produced and the foreground (disk, square, triangle, and rhombus) is treated as the novelty to be detected. This is not a texture segmentation exercise, but rather defect segmentation. The textures used were selected to be particularly similar in nature in the foreground and the background, e.g. see the collages in the first or third columns of Fig. 4.10. We use *specificity* for how accurately defect-free samples were classified, *sensitivity* for how accurately defective samples were classified, and *accuracy* as the correct classification rate of all samples:

$$\begin{cases} spec. = \frac{N_t \cap N_g}{N_g} \times 100\% \\ sens. = \frac{P_t \cap P_g}{P_g} \times 100\% \\ accu. = \frac{N_t \cap N_g + P_t \cap P_g}{N_g + P_g} \times 100\% \end{cases} \quad (4.23)$$

where P is the number of defective samples, N is the number of defect-free samples, and the subscripts t and g denote the results by testing and groundtruth respectively. The foreground is set to occupy 50% of the whole image to allow the sensitivity and specificity measures have equal weights.

We first compare the two different channel separation schemes in each case using graylevel texem analysis in the individual channels. For the RGB channel separation scheme, defects detected in each channel were then combined to form the final defect map. For the eigenchannel separation scheme, the reference eigenspace from training images was first derived. As the patterns on each image within the same texture family can still be different, hence the individually derived principal components can also differ from one image to another. Furthermore, defective regions can affect the principal components resulting in different eigenspace responses from different training samples. Thus, instead of performing PCA on each training image separately, a single eigenspace was generated from several training images, resulting in a reference eigenspace in which defect-free samples are represented. Then, all new, previously unseen images under inspection were projected onto this eigenspace such that the transformed channels share the same principal components. Once we obtain the reference eigenspace, $\Upsilon_{\bar{c},E}$, defect detection and localisation are performed in each of the three corresponding channels by examining the local context using the graylevel texem model, the same process as used in RGB channel separation scheme. Figure 4.9 shows a comparison of direct RGB channel separation and PCA based channel separation. The eigenchannels are clearly more differentiating.

Experimental results on the colour collages showed that the PCA based method achieved a significant improvement over the correlated RGB channels with an overall accuracy of 84.7% compared to 79.1% (see Table 4.1).

Fig. 4.9. Channel separation - first row: Original collage image; second row: individual RGB channels; third row: eigenchannel images.

Graylevel texem analysis in image eigenchannels appear to be a plausible approach to perform colour analysis with relatively economic computational complexity. However, the full colour texem model, which models inter-channel and intra-channel interactions simultaneously, improved the performance to an overall detection accuracy of 90.9%, 91.2% sensitivity and 90.6% specificity. Example segmentations (without any post-processing) of all the methods are shown in the last three rows of Fig. 4.10.

We also compared the proposed method against a non-filtering method using LBPs[15] and a Gabor filtering based novelty detection method.[22] The LBP coefficients were extracted from each RGB colour band. The estimation of the range of coefficient distributions for defect-free samples and the novelty detection procedures were the same as that described in Sec. 4.3.2. We found that LBP performs very poorly, but a more sophisticated clas-

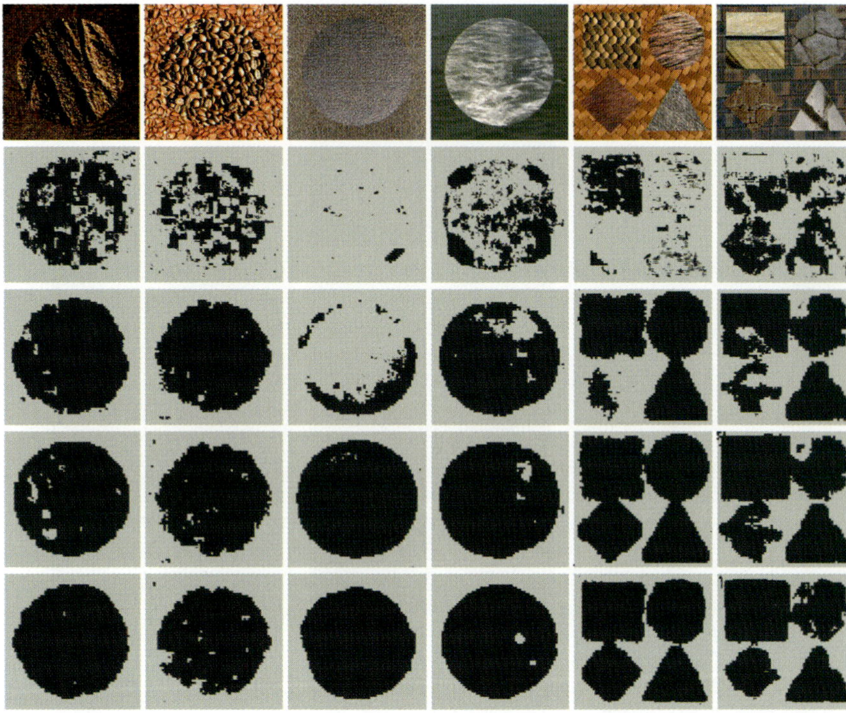

Fig. 4.10. Collage samples made up of materials such as foods, fabric, sand, metal, water, and novelty detection results without any post-processing. Rows from top: original images, Escofet *et al.*'s method, graylevel texems directly in RGB channels, graylevel texems in PCA decorrelated RGB eigenchannels, full colour texem model.

sifier may improve the performance. Gabor filters have been widely used in defect detection, see Refs. 22 and 23 as typical examples. The work by Escofet et al.,[22] referred to here as Escofet's method, is the most comparable to ours, as it is (a) performed in a novelty detection framework and (b) uses the same defect fusion scheme across the scales. Thus, following Escofet's method to perform novelty detection on the synthetic image collages, the images were filtered through a set of 16 Gabor filters, comprising four orientations and four scales. The texture features were extracted from filtering responses. Feature distributions of defect-free samples were then used for novelty detection. The same logical process was used to combine defect candidates across the scales. An overall detection accuracy of 71.5% was obtained by Escofet's method; a result significantly lower than texems (see Table 4.2). Example results are shown in the second row of Fig. 4.10.

Table 4.1. Novelty detection comparison: graylevel texems in image RGB channels and image eigenchannels (values are %s).

No.	RGB channels			Eigenchannels		
	spec.	sens.	accu.	spec.	sens.	accu.
1	81.7	100	90.7	82.0	100	90.9
2	80.7	100	90.2	80.8	100	90.3
3	87.6	99.9	93.7	82.4	100	91.1
4	94.3	97.2	95.7	93.9	95.7	94.8
5	87.3	30.7	59.3	77.9	99.6	88.6
6	76.6	100	88.2	77.8	100	88.8
7	96.0	93.4	94.7	90.1	98.6	94.3
8	87.8	97.7	92.7	85.6	95.3	90.4
9	85.5	52.0	68.9	76.1	100	87.9
10	92.2	25.2	59.1	77.8	99.2	88.4
11	89.1	33.6	61.6	80.3	97.2	88.6
12	82.5	88.4	85.4	79.5	97.7	88.5
13	93.5	47.8	70.9	93.0	49.0	71.2
14	80.9	99.9	90.3	81.1	100	90.5
15	98.7	55.3	77.2	98.3	74.8	86.7
16	84.5	78.1	81.3	86.5	92.7	89.6
17	75.1	60.8	67.9	62.3	87.9	73.8
18	64.9	69.5	67.2	60.9	91.9	74.8
19	75.1	60.0	67.5	57.0	87.4	72.2
20	83.9	91.8	87.8	85.4	90.0	87.7
21	78.6	97.3	87.8	88.4	98.4	93.4
22	88.5	49.8	69.4	79.5	76.3	77.9
23	98.2	44.5	71.6	96.6	34.8	66.0
24	60.6	69.8	65.2	64.5	86.8	75.7
25	58.7	100	79.4	64.8	99.9	82.3
26	84.1	91.6	87.9	76.5	94.2	85.3
27	73.2	87.8	80.5	64.7	99.9	82.3
28	74.5	88.3	81.4	65.7	94.6	80.1
Overall	82.7	75.4	**79.1**	78.9	90.8	**84.7**

There are two important parameters in the texem model for novelty detection, the size of texems and the number of the texems. In theory, the size of the texems is arbitrary. Thus, it can easily cover all the necessary spatial frequency range. However, for the sake of computational simplicity, a window size of 5×5 or 7×7 across all scales generally suffices. The number of texems can be automatically determined using model order selection methods, such as MDL, though they are usually computationally expensive. We used 12 texems in each scale for over 1000 tile images and collages and found reasonable, consistent performance for novelty detection.

Table 4.2. Novelty detection comparison: Escofet's method and the full colour texem model (values are %s).

No.	Escofet's Method			Colour Texems		
	spec.	sens.	accu.	spec.	sens.	accu.
1	95.6	82.7	89.2	91.9	99.9	95.9
2	96.9	83.7	90.3	84.4	100	92.1
3	96.1	61.5	79.0	91.1	99.8	95.4
4	98.0	53.1	75.8	97.0	92.9	95.0
5	98.8	1.5	50.7	92.1	98.8	95.4
6	96.6	70.0	83.4	96.3	98.6	97.4
7	98.9	26.8	63.2	98.6	79.4	89.0
8	91.4	74.4	83.0	89.6	99.8	94.7
9	90.8	49.0	70.1	86.4	100	93.1
10	94.3	7.2	51.2	92.8	99.6	96.2
11	94.6	8.6	52.1	96.3	90.8	93.6
12	86.9	44.0	65.7	88.4	98.8	93.5
13	96.8	71.0	84.0	91.0	91.9	91.5
14	90.7	95.2	93.0	82.5	100	91.1
15	98.4	27.2	63.2	96.5	76.3	86.5
16	95.5	43.0	69.3	96.3	71.2	83.8
17	80.0	56.5	68.2	83.5	98.7	91.1
18	73.9	60.4	67.2	83.9	96.5	90.2
19	84.9	52.0	68.4	90.4	71.3	80.9
20	94.4	52.0	73.2	95.1	88.8	91.9
21	94.0	48.9	71.6	95.8	75.9	85.9
22	95.8	23.4	60.0	92.2	72.0	82.2
23	97.1	35.1	66.5	93.6	67.8	80.9
24	89.4	46.4	67.9	81.6	98.1	89.8
25	82.6	92.9	87.7	88.3	100	93.9
26	94.5	55.3	74.9	94.3	92.2	93.2
27	93.9	36.5	65.2	85.9	98.9	92.4
28	81.2	55.3	68.3	82.0	95.2	88.6
Overall	92.2	50.5	**71.5**	90.6	91.2	**90.9**

4.4. Colour Image Segmentation

Clearly each patch from an image has a measurable relationship with each texem according to the *posteriori*, $p(\mathbf{m}_k|\mathbf{Z}_i, \Theta)$, which can be conveniently obtained using Bayes' rule in Eq. (4.13). Thus, every texem can be viewed as an individual textural class component, and the *posteriori* can be regarded as the component likelihood with which each pixel in the image can be labelled. Based on this, we present two different multiscale approaches to carry out segmentation. The first, interscale post-fusion, performs segmentation at each level separately and then updates the label probabilities from coarser to finer levels. The second, branch partitioning, simplifies the procedure by learning the texems across the scales to gain efficiency.

4.4.1. *Segmentation with interscale post-fusion*

For segmentation, each pixel needs to be assigned a class label, $c = \{1, 2, ..., K\}$. At each scale n, there is a random field of class labels, $C^{(n)}$. The probability of a particular image patch, $\mathbf{Z}_i^{(n)}$, belonging to a texem (class), $c = k, \mathbf{m}_k^{(n)}$, is determined by the *posteriori* probability, $p(c = k, \mathbf{m}_k^{(n)}|\mathbf{Z}_i^{(n)}, \Theta^{(n)})$, simplified as $p(c^{(n)}|\mathbf{Z}_i^{(n)})$, given by:

$$p(c^{(n)}|\mathbf{Z}_i^{(n)}) = \frac{p(\mathbf{Z}_i^{(n)}|\mathbf{m}_k^{(n)})\boldsymbol{\alpha}_k^{(n)}}{\sum_{k=1}^{K} p(\mathbf{Z}_i^{(n)}|\mathbf{m}_k^{(n)})\boldsymbol{\alpha}_k^{(n)}}, \tag{4.24}$$

which is equivalent to the stabilised solution of Eq. (4.13). The class probability at given pixel location $(x^{(n)}, y^{(n)})$ at scale n then can be estimated as $p(c^{(n)}|(x^{(n)}, y^{(n)})) = p(c^{(n)}|\mathbf{Z}_i^{(n)})$. Thus, this labelling assignment procedure initially partitions the image in each individual scale. As the image is laid hierarchically, there is inherited relationship among parent and children pixels. Their labels should also reflect this relationship. Next, building on this initial labelling, the partitions across all the scales are fused together to produce the final segmentation map.

The class labels $c^{(n)}$ are assumed conditionally independent given the labelling in the coarser scale $c^{(n+1)}$. Thus, each label field $C^{(n)}$ is assumed only dependent on the previous coarser scale label field $C^{(n+1)}$. This offers efficient computational processing, while preserving the complex spatial dependencies in the segmentation. The label field $C^{(n)}$ becomes a Markov chain structure in the scale variable n:

$$p(c^{(n)}|c^{(>n)}) = p(c^{(n)}|c^{(n+1)}), \tag{4.25}$$

where $c^{(>n)} = \{c^{(i)}\}_{i=n+1}^{l}$ are the class labels at all coarser scales greater than the nth, and $p(c^{(l)}|c^{(l+1)}) = p(c^{(l)})$ as l is the coarsest scale. The coarsest scale segmentation is directly based on the initial labelling.

A quadtree structure for the multiscale label fields is used, and $c^{(l)}$ only contains a single pixel, although a more sophisticated context model can be used to achieve better interaction between child and parent nodes, e.g. a pyramid graph model.[27] The transition probability $p(c^{(n)}|c^{(n+1)})$ can be efficiently calculated numerically using a lookup table. The label assignments at each scale are then updated, from coarsest to the finest, according to the joint probability of the data probability and the transition probability:

$$\begin{cases} \hat{c}^{(l)} = \arg\max_{c^{(l)}} \log p(c^{(l)}|(x^{(l)}, y^{(l)})), \\ \hat{c}^{(n)} = \arg\max_{c^{(n)}} \{\log p(c^{(n)}|(x^{(n)}, y^{(n)})) + \log p(c^{(n)}|c^{(n+1)})\} \quad \forall n < l. \end{cases} \tag{4.26}$$

The segmented regions will be smooth and small isolated holes are filled.

4.4.2. *Segmentation using branch partitioning*

As discussed earlier in Sec. 4.2.3, an alternative multiscale approach can be used by partitioning the multiscale image into branches based on hierarchical dependency. By assuming that pixels within the same branch are conditionally independent to each other, we can directly learn multiscale colour texems using Eq. (4.16). The class labels then can be directly obtained without performing interscale fusion by evaluating the component likelihood using Bayes' rule: $p(c|\mathbf{Z}_i) = p(\mathbf{m}_k|\mathbf{Z}_i, \Theta)$, where $\mathbf{Z}_i$ is a branch of pixels. The label assignment for $\mathbf{Z}_i$ is then according to:

$$\hat{c} = \arg\max_{c} p(c|\mathbf{Z}_i)\,. \tag{4.27}$$

Thus, we simplify the approach presented in Sec. 4.4.1 by avoiding the inter-scale fusion after labelling each scale.

4.4.3. *Texem grouping for multimodal texture*

A textural region may contain multiple visual elements and display complex patterns. A single texem might not be able to fully represent such textural regions, hence, several texems can be grouped together to jointly represent "multimodal" texture regions. Here, we use a simple but effective method proposed by Manduchi[28] to group texems. The basic strategy is to group some of the texems based on their spatial coherence. The grouping process simply takes the form:

$$\hat{p}(\mathbf{Z}_i|c) = \frac{1}{\hat{\beta}_c} \sum_{k \in G_c} p(\mathbf{Z}_i|\mathbf{m}_k)\alpha_k, \qquad \hat{\beta}_c = \sum_{k \in G_c} \alpha_k\,, \tag{4.28}$$

where G_c is the group of texems that are combined together to form a new cluster c which labels the different texture classes, and $\hat{\beta}_c$ is the *priori* for new cluster c. The mixture model can thus be reformulated as:

$$p(\mathbf{Z}_i|\Theta) = \sum_{c=1}^{\hat{K}} \hat{p}(\mathbf{Z}_i|\mathbf{m}_k)\hat{\beta}_c\,, \tag{4.29}$$

where $\hat{K}$ is the desired number of texture regions. Equation (4.29) shows that pixel i in the centre of patch $\mathbf{Z}_i$ will be assigned to the texture cluster c which maximises $\hat{p}(\mathbf{Z}_i|c)\hat{\beta}_c$:

$$c = \arg\max_c \hat{p}(\mathbf{Z}_i|c)\hat{\beta}_c = \arg\max_c \sum_{k\in G_c} p(\mathbf{Z}_i|\mathbf{m}_k)\alpha_k\,. \tag{4.30}$$

The grouping in Eq. (4.29) is carried out based on the assumption that the *posteriori* probabilities of grouped texems are typically spatially correlated. The process should minimise the decrease of model descriptiveness, D, which is defined as:[28]

$$D = \sum_{j=1}^{K} D_j\,, \qquad D_j = \int p(\mathbf{Z}_i|\mathbf{m}_j)p(\mathbf{m}_j|\mathbf{Z}_i)d\mathbf{Z}_i = \frac{E[p(\mathbf{m}_j|\mathbf{Z}_i)^2]}{\alpha_j}\,, \tag{4.31}$$

where $E[.]$ is the expectation computed with respect to $p(\mathbf{Z}_i)$. In other words, the compacted model should retain as much descriptiveness as possible. This is known as the Maximum Description Criterion (MDC). The descriptiveness decreases drastically when well separated texem components are grouped together, but decreases very slowly when spatially correlated texem component distributions merge together. Thus, the texem grouping should search for smallest change in descriptiveness, ΔD. It can be carried out by greedily grouping two texem components, $\mathbf{m}_a$ and $\mathbf{m}_b$, at a time with minimum ΔD_{ab}:

$$\Delta D_{ab} = \frac{\alpha_b D_a + \alpha_a D_b}{\alpha_a + \alpha_b} - \frac{2E[p(\mathbf{m}_a|\mathbf{Z}_i)p(\mathbf{m}_b|\mathbf{Z}_i)]}{\alpha_a + \alpha_b}\,. \tag{4.32}$$

We can see that the first term in Eq. (4.32) is the maximum possible descriptiveness loss when grouping two texems, and the second term in Eq. (4.32) is the normalised cross correlation between the two texem component distributions. Since one texture region may contain different texem components that are significantly different to each other, it is beneficial to smooth the *posteriori* as proposed by Manduchi[28] such that a pixel that originally has high probability to just one texem component will be softly assigned to a number of components that belong to the same "multimodal" texture. After grouping, the final segmentation map is obtained according to Eq. (4.30).

Fig. 4.11. Testing on synthetic images - first row: original image collages, second row: groundtruth segmentations, third row: JSEG results, fourth row: results of the proposed method using interscale post-fusion, last row: results of the proposed method using branch partitioning.

4.4.4. *Experimental results*

Here, we present experimental results using colour texem based image segmentation with a brief comparison with the well-known JSEG technique.[29]

Figure 4.11 shows example results on five different texture collages with the original image in the first row, groundtruth segmentations in the second row, the JSEG result in the third row, the proposed interscale post-fusion method in the fourth row, and the proposed branch partition method in the final row. The two proposed schemes have similar performance, while

Fig. 4.12. An example of the interscale post-fusion method followed by texem grouping - first row: original image and its segmentation result, second row: initial labelling of 5 texem classes for each scale, third row: updated labelling after grouping 5 texems into 3, fourth row: results of interscale fusion.

JSEG tends to over-segment which partially arises due to the lack of prior knowledge of number of texture regions.

Figure 4.12 focuses on the interscale post-fusion technique followed by texem grouping. The original image and the final segmentation are shown at the top. The second row shows the initial labelling of 5 texem classes for each pyramid level. The texems are grouped to 3 classes as seen in the third row. Interscale fusion is then performed and shown in the last row. Note there is no fusion in the fourth (coarsest) scale.

Three real image examples are given in Fig. 4.13. For each image, we show the original images, its JSEG segmentation and the results of the two proposed segmentation methods. The interscale post-fusion method produced finer borders but is a slower technique.

The results shown demonstrate that the two proposed methods are more able in modelling textural variations than JSEG and are less prone to over-segmentation. However, it is noted that JSEG does not require the number

Fig. 4.13. Testing on real images - first column: original images, second column: JSEG results, third column: results of the proposed method using interscale post-fusion, fourth column: results of the proposed method using branch partitioning.

of regions as prior knowledge. On the other hand, texem based segmentation provides a useful description for each region and a measurable relationship between them. The number of texture regions may be automatically determined using model-order selection methods, such as MDL. The post-fusion and branch partition schemes achieved comparable results, while the branch partition method is faster. However, a more thorough comparison is necessary to draw complete conclusions.

4.5. Conclusions

In this chapter, we presented a two-layer generative model, called texems, to represent and analyse textures. The texems are textural primitives that are learnt across scales and can characterise a family of images with similar visual appearance. We demonstrated their derivation for graylevel and colour images using two different mixture models with different computational complexities. PCA based data factorisation was advocated while channel decorrelation was necessary. However, by decomposing the colour image and analysing eigenchannels individually, the inter-channel interactions were not taken into account. The full colour texem model was found most powerful in generalising colour textures.

Two applications of the texem model were presented. The first was to perform defect localisation in a novelty detection framework. The method required only a few defect free samples for unsupervised training to detect defects in random colour textures. Multiscale analysis was also used to reduce the computational costs and to localise the defects more accurately. It was evaluated on both synthetic image collages and a large number of tile images with various types of physical, chromatic, and textural defects. The comparative study showed texem based local contextual analysis significantly outperformed a filter bank method and the LBP based texture features in novelty detection. Also, it revealed that incorporating interspectral information was beneficial, particularly when defects were chromatic in nature. The ceramic tile test data was collected from several different sources and had different chromato-textural characteristics. This showed that the proposed work was robust to variations arising from the sources. However, better accuracy comes at a price. The colour texems can be 10 times slower than the grayscale texems at the learning stage. They were also much slower than the Gabor filtering based method but had fewer parameters to tune. The computational cost, however, can be drastically reduced by performing window-based, instead of pixel based, examination at the training and testing stages. Also, there are methods available, such as Ref. 30, to compute the Gaussian function, which is a major part of the computation, much more efficiently. The results also demonstrate that the graylevel texem is also a plausible approach to perform colour analysis with relatively economic computational complexity.

The second application was to segment colour images using multiscale colour texems. As a mixture model was used to derive the colour texems, it was natural to classify image patches based on posterior probabilities. Thus, an initial segmentation of the image in multiscale was obtained by directly using the posteriors. In order to fuse the segmentation from different scales together, the quadtree context model was used to interpolate the label structure, from which the transition probability was derived. Thus, the final segmentation was obtained by top-down interscale fusion. An alternative multiscale approach using the hierarchical dependency among multiscale pixels was proposed. This resulted in a simplified image segmentation without interscale post fusion. Additionally, a texem grouping method was presented to segment multi-modal textures where a texture region contained multiple textural elements. The proposed methods were briefly compared against JSEG algorithm with some promising results.

Acknowledgement

This research work was funded by the EC project G1RD-CT-2002-00783 MONOTONE, and X. Xie was partially funded by ORSAS UK.

References

1. X. Xie and M. Mirmehdi, TEXEMS: Texture exemplars for defect detection on random textured surfaces, *IEEE Transactions on Pattern Analysis and Machine Intelligence*, Vol. 29, No. 8, pp. 1454–1464 (2007).
2. T. Caelli and D. Reye, On the classification of image regions by colour, texture and shape, *Pattern Recognition.* **26**(4), 461–470, (1993).
3. R. Picard and T. Minka, Vision texture for annotation, *Multimedia System.* **3**, 3–14, (1995).
4. M. Dubuisson-Jolly and G. A., Color and texture fusion: Application to aerial image segmentation and GIS updating, *Image and Vision Computing.* **18**, 823–832, (2000).
5. A. Monadjemi, B. Thomas, and M. Mirmehdi. Speed v. accuracy for high resolution colour texture classification. In *British Machine Vision Conference*, pp. 143–152, (2002).
6. S. Liapis, E. Sifakis, and G. Tziritas, Colour and texture segmentation using wavelet frame analysis, deterministic relaxation, and fast marching algorithms, *Journal of Visual Communication and Image Representation.* **15**(1), 1–26, (2004).
7. A. Rosenfeld, C. Wang, and A. Wu, Multispectral texture, *IEEE Transactions on Systems, Man, and Cybernetics.* **12**(1), 79–84, (1982).
8. D. Panjwani and G. Healey, Markov random field models for unsupervised segmentation of textured color images, *IEEE Transactions on Pattern Analysis and Machine Intelligence.* **17**(10), 939–954, (1995).
9. B. Thai and G. Healey, Modeling and classifying symmetries using a multiscale opponent color representation, *IEEE Transactions on Pattern Analysis and Machine Intelligence.* **20**(11), 1224–1235, (1998).
10. M. Mirmehdi and M. Petrou, Segmentation of color textures, *IEEE Transactions on Pattern Analysis and Machine Intelligence.* **22**(2), 142–159, (2000).
11. J. Bennett and A. Khotanzad, Multispectral random field models for synthesis and analysis of color images, *IEEE Transactions on Pattern Analysis and Machine Intelligence.* **20**(3), 327–332, (1998).
12. C. Palm, Color texture classification by integrative co-occurrence matrices, *Pattern Recognition.* **37**(5), 965–976, (2004).
13. N. Jojic, B. Frey, and A. Kannan. Epitomic analysis of appearance and shape. In *IEEE International Conference on Computer Vision*, pp. 34–42, (2003).

14. M. Varma and A. Zisserman. Texture classification: Are filter banks necessary? In *IEEE Conference on Computer Vision and Pattern Recognition*, pp. 691–698, (2003).
15. T. Ojala, M. Pietikäinen, and T. Mäenpää, Multiresolution gray-scale and rotation invariant texture classification with local binary patterns, *IEEE Transactions on Pattern Analysis and Machine Intelligence*. **24**(7), 971–987, (2002).
16. F. Cohen, Z. Fan, and S. Attali, Automated inspection of textile fabrics using textural models, *IEEE Transactions on Pattern Analysis and Machine Intelligence*. **13**(8), 803–809, (1991).
17. X. Xie and M. Mirmehdi. Texture exemplars for defect detection on random textures. In *International Conference on Advances in Pattern Recognition*, pp. 404–413, (2005).
18. B. Silverman, *Density Estimation for Statistics and Data Analysis*. (Chapman and Hall, 1986).
19. B. Julesz, Textons, the element of texture perception and their interactions, *Nature*. **290**, 91–97, (1981).
20. S. Zhu, C. Guo, Y. Wang, and Z. Xu, What are textons?, *International Journal of Computer Vision*. **62**(1-2), 121–143, (2005).
21. C. Boukouvalas, J. Kittler, R. Marik, and M. Petrou, Automatic color grading of ceramic tiles using machine vision, *IEEE Transactions on Industrial Electronics*. **44**(1), 132–135, (1997).
22. J. Escofet, R. Navarro, M. Millán, and J. Pladellorens, Detection of local defects in textile webs using Gabor filters, *Optical Engineering*. **37**(8), 2297–2307, (1998).
23. A. Kumar and G. Pang, Defect detection in textured materials using Gabor filters, *IEEE Transactions on Industry Applications*. **38**(2), 425–440, (2002).
24. A. Kumar, Neural network based detection of local textile defects, *Pattern Recognition*. **36**, 1645–1659, (2003).
25. A. Monadjemi, M. Mirmehdi, and B. Thomas. Restructured eigenfilter matching for novelty detection in random textures. In *British Machine Vision Conference*, pp. 637–646, (2004).
26. MIT Media Lab. VisTex texture database, (1995). URL `http://vismod.media.mit.edu/vismod/imagery/VisionTexture/vistex.html`.
27. H. Cheng and C. Bouman, Multiscale bayesian segmentation using a trainable context model, *IEEE Transactions on Image Processing*. **10**(4), 511–525, (2001).
28. R. Manduchi. Mixture models and the segmentation of multimodal textures. In *IEEE Conference on Computer Vision and Pattern Recognition*, pp. 98–104, (2000).
29. Y. Deng and B. Manjunath, Unsupervised segmentation of color-texture regions in images and video, *IEEE Transactions on Pattern Analysis and Machine Intelligence*. **23**(8), 800–810, (2001).
30. L. Greengard and J. Strain, The fast Gauss transform, *SIAM Journal of Scientific Computing*. **2**, 79–94, (1991).

Chapter 5

Colour Texture Analysis

Paul F. Whelan and Ovidiu Ghita

Vision Systems Group, School of Electronic Engineering
Dublin City University, Dublin, Ireland
E-mail: paul.whelan@dcu.ie & ghitao@eeng.dcu.ie

This chapter presents a novel and generic framework for image segmentation using a compound image descriptor that encompasses both colour and texture information in an adaptive fashion. The developed image segmentation method extracts the texture information using low-level image descriptors (such as the Local Binary Patterns (LBP)) and colour information by using colour space partitioning. The main advantage of this approach is the analysis of the textured images at a micro-level using the local distribution of the LBP values, and in the colour domain by analysing the local colour distribution obtained after colour segmentation. The use of the colour and texture information separately has proven to be inappropriate for natural images as they are generally heterogeneous with respect to colour and texture characteristics. Thus, the main problem is to use the colour and texture information in a joint descriptor that can adapt to the local properties of the image under analysis. We will review existing approaches to colour and texture analysis as well as illustrating how our approach can be successfully applied to a range of applications including the segmentation of natural images, medical imaging and product inspection.

5.1. Introduction

Image segmentation is one of the most important tasks in image analysis and computer vision[1,2,3,4]. The aim of image segmentation algorithms is to partition the input image into a number of disjoint regions with similar properties. Texture and colour are two such image properties that have received significant interest from research community[1,3,5,6], with prior research generally focusing on examining colour and texture features as separate entities rather than a unified image descriptor. This is motivated by the fact that although innately related, the inclusion of colour and texture features in a coherent image segmentation framework has proven to be more difficult that initially anticipated.

5.1.1. *Texture analysis*

Texture is an important property of digital images, although image texture does not have a formal definition it can be regarded as a function of the variation of pixel intensities which form repeated patterns[6,7]. This fundamental image property has been the subject of significant research and is generally divided into four major categories: statistical, model-based, signal processing and structural[2,5,6,8], with specific focus on statistical and signal processing (e.g. multi-channel Gabor filtering) methods. One key conclusion from previous research[5,6] is the fact that the filtering-based approaches can adapt better than statistical methods to local disturbances in texture and illumination.

Statistical measures analyse the spatial distribution of the pixels using features extracted from first and second–order histograms[6,8]. Two of the most investigated statistical methods are the gray-level differences[9] and co-occurrence matrices[7]. These methods performed well when applied to synthetic images but their performance is relatively modest when applied to natural images unless these images are defined by uniform textures. It is useful to note that these methods appear to be used more often for texture classification rather than texture-based segmentation. Generally these techniques are considered as the base of evaluation for more sophisticated texture analysis techniques and since their introduction these methods have been further advanced. Some notable statistical techniques include the work of Kovalev and Petrou[10], Elfadel and Picard[11] and Varma and Zisserman[12].

Signal processing methods have been investigated more recently. With these techniques the image is typically filtered with a bank of filters of differing scales and orientations in order to capture the frequency changes[13,14,15,16,17,18]. Early signal processing methods attempted to analyse the image texture in the Fourier domain, but these approaches were clearly outperformed by techniques that analyse the texture using multi-channel narrow band Gabor filters. This approach was firstly introduced by Bovik et al[13] when they used quadrature Gabor filters to segment images defined by oriented textures. They conclude that in order to segment an image the spectral difference sampled by narrow-band filters is sufficient to discriminate between adjacent textured image regions. This approach was further advanced by Randen and Husoy[18] while noting that image filtering with a bank of Gabor filters or filters derived from a wavelet transform[19,20] is computationally demanding. In their paper they propose the methodology to compute optimized filters for texture discrimination and examine the performance of these filters with respect to algorithmic complexity/feature separation on a number of test images. They conclude that the complicated design required in calculating the optimized filters is justified since the overall filter-based segmentation scheme will require a smaller number of filters than the standard implementation that uses Gabor filters. A range of signal processing based texture segmentation techniques have been proposed, for more details the reader can consult the reviews by Tuceryan and Jain[6], Materka and Strzelecki[8] and Chellappa et al[5].

5.1.2. *Colour analysis*

Colour is another important characteristic of digital images which has naturally received interest from the research community. This is motivated by advances in imaging and processing technologies and the proliferation of colour cameras. Colour has been used in the development of algorithms that have been applied to many applications including object recognition[21,22], skin detection[23], image retrieval[24,25,26] and product inspection[27,28]. Many of the existing colour segmentation techniques are based on simple colour partitioning (clustering) techniques and their performance is appropriate only if the colour information is locally homogenous.

Colour segmentation algorithms can be divided into three categories, namely, pixel-based colour segmentation techniques, area based segmentation techniques and physics based segmentation techniques[3,29,30]. The pixel-based colour segmentation techniques are constructed on the assumption that colour is a constant property in the image to be analysed and the segmentation task can be viewed as the process of grouping the pixels in different clusters that satisfy a colour uniformity criteria. According to Skarbek and Koschan[30] the pixel based colour segmentation techniques can be further divided into two main categories: histogram-thresholding segmentation and colour clustering techniques. The histogram-based segmentation techniques attempt to identify the peaks in the colour histogram[21,27,31,32,33] and in general provide a coarse segmentation that is usually the input for more sophisticated techniques. Clustering techniques have been widely applied in practice to perform image segmentation[34]. Common clustering-based algorithms include K-means[35,36,37], fuzzy C-means[35,38], mean shift[39] and Expectation-Maximization[40,41]. In their standard form the performance of these algorithms have been shown to be limited since the clustering process does not take into consideration the spatial relationship between the pixels in the image. To address this limitation Pappas[37] has generalized the standard K-means algorithm to enforce the spatial coherence during the cluster assignment process. This algorithm was initially applied to greyscale images and was later generalized by Chen et al[42]. Area based segmentation techniques are defined by the region growing and split and merge colour segmentation schemes[30,43,44,45,46]. As indicated in the review by Lucchese and Mitra[3] the common characteristic of these methods is the fact that they start with an inhomogeneous partition of the image and they agglomerate the initial partitions into disjoint image regions with uniform characteristics until a homogeneity criteria is upheld. Area-based approaches are the most investigated segmentation schemes, due in part to the fact that the main advantage of these techniques over pixel-based methods is that the spatial coherence between adjacent pixels is enforced during the segmentation process. In this regard, notable contributions are represented by the work of Panjwani and Healey[47], Tremeau and Borel[46], Celenk[34], Cheng and Sun[44], Deng and Manjunath[48], Shafarenko et al[32] and Moghaddamzadeh and Bourbakis[45]. For a complete evaluation of these colour segmentation techniques refer to the reviews by Skarbek and

Koschan[30], Lucchese and Mitra[3] and Cheng et al[29]. The third category of colour segmentation approaches is represented by the physics-based segmentation techniques and their aim is to alleviate the problems generated by uneven illumination, highlights and shadows which generally lead to over-segmentation[49,50,51]. Typically these methods require a significant amount of a-priori knowledge about the illumination model and the reflecting properties of the objects that define the scene. These algorithms are not generic and their application is restricted to scenes defined by a small number of objects with known shapes and reflecting properties.

5.1.3. *Colour-texture analysis*

The colour segmentation techniques mentioned previously are generally application driven, whereas more sophisticated algorithms attempt to analyze the local homogeneity using complex image descriptors that include the colour and texture information. The use of colour and texture information collectively has strong links with the human perception and the development of an advanced unified colour-texture descriptor may provide improved discrimination over viewing texture and colour features independently. Although the motivation to use colour and texture information jointly in the segmentation process is clear, how best to combine these features in a colour-texture mathematical descriptor is still an open issue. To address this problem a number of researchers augmented the textural features with statistical chrominance features[25,52,53]. Although simple, this approach produced far superior results than texture only algorithms and in addition the extra computational cost required by the calculation of colour features is negligible when compared with the computational overhead associated with the extraction of textural features. In this regard, Mirmehdi and Petrou[54] proposed a colour-texture segmentation approach where the image segmentation is defined as a probabilistic process embedded in a multiresolution approach. In other words, they blurred the image to be analysed at different scale levels using multiband smoothing algorithms and they isolated the core colour clusters using the K-means algorithm, which in turn guided the segmentation process from blurred to focused images. The experimental results indicate that their algorithm is able to produce accurate image segmentation even in cases when it has been applied to images with poorly defined regions. A related approach is proposed by Hoang et al[55] where they applied a bank of Gabor filters on each channel of an image represented in the wavelength-Fourier space. Since the resulting data has large dimensionality (each pixel is represented by a 60 dimensional feature vector) they applied Principal Component Analysis (PCA) to reduce the dimension of the feature space. The reduced feature space was clustered using a K-means algorithm, followed by the application of a cluster merging procedure. The main novelty of this algorithm is the application of the standard multiband filtering approach to colour images and the reported results indicate that the representation of colour-texture in the wavelength-Fourier space proved to be accurate in capturing texture statistics. Deng and Manjunath[48] proposed a different colour-texture segmentation method that is divided into two main computational stages. In the first stage the colours are quantized into a reduced number of classes while in the second stage a spatial segmentation is performed based on texture composition. They argue that decoupling the colour similarity from spatial distribution was beneficial since it is difficult to analyse the similarity of the colours and their distributions at the same time. Tan and Kittler[33] developed an image segmentation algorithm where the texture and colour information are used as separate attributes within the segmentation process. In their approach the texture information is extracted by the application of a local linear transform while the colour information is defined by the six colour features derived from the colour histogram. The use of colour and texture information as separate channels in the segmentation process proved to be opportune and this approach has been adopted by many researchers. Building on this, the paper by Pietikainen et al[31] evaluates the performance of a joint colour Local Binary Patterns (LBP) operator against the performance of the 3D histograms calculated in the Ohta colour space. They conclude that the colour information sampled by the proposed 3D histograms is more powerful then the texture information sampled by the joint LBP distribution. This approach has been further advanced by Liapis and Tziritas[24] where they developed a colour-texture approach used for image retrieval. In their implementation they extracted the texture features using the Discrete Wavelet Frames analysis while the colour feature were extracted using 2D histograms calculated from chromaticity components of the images converted in the CIE Lab colour space.

In this chapter we detail the development of a novel colour texture segmentation technique (referred to as CTex) where the colour and texture information are combined adaptively in a composite image descriptor. In this regard the texture information is extracted using the LBP method and the colour information by using an Expectation-Maximization (EM) space partitioning technique. The colour and texture features are evaluated in a flexible split and merge framework were the contribution of colour and texture is adaptively modified based on the local colour uniformity. The resulting colour segmentation algorithm is modular (i.e. it can be used in conjunction with any texture and colour descriptors) and has been applied to a large number of colour images including synthetic, natural, medical and industrial images. The resulting image segmentation scheme is unsupervised and generic and the experimental data indicates that the developed algorithm is able to produce accurate segmentation.

5.2. Algorithm Overview

The main computational components of the image segmentation algorithm detailed in this chapter are illustrated in Fig. 5.1. The first step of the algorithm extracts the texture features using the Local Binary Patterns method as detailed by Ojala[56]. The colour feature extraction is performed in several steps. In order to improve the local colour uniformity and increase the robustness to changes in illumination the input colour image is subjected to anisotropic diffusion-based filtering. An additional step is represented by the extraction of the dominant colours that are used for initialization of the EM algorithm that is applied to perform the colour segmentation. From the LBP/C image and the colour segmented image, our algorithm calculates two types of local distributions, namely the colour and texture distributions that are used as input features in a highly adaptive split and merge architecture. The output of the split and merge algorithm has a blocky structure and to improve the segmentation result obtained after merging the algorithm applies a pixelwise procedure that exchanges the pixels situated at the boundaries between various regions using the colour information computed by the EM algorithm.

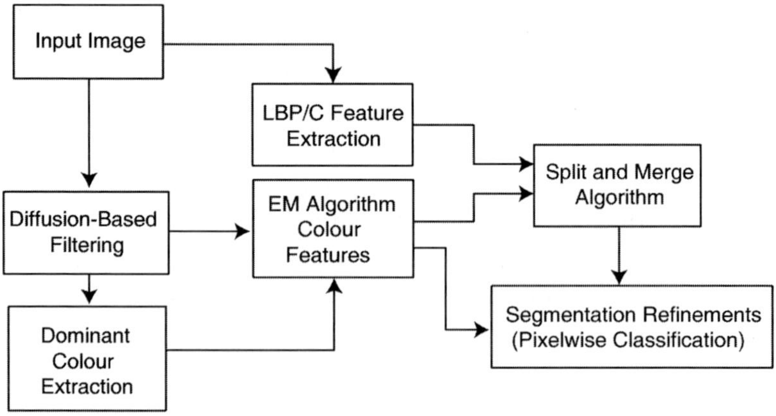

Fig. 5.1. Overview of the CTex colour-texture segmentation algorithm.

5.3. Extraction of Colour-Texture Features

As indicated in Section 5.1 there are a number of possible approaches for extracting texture features from a given input image, the most relevant approaches either calculate statistics from co-occurrence[7] matrices or attempt to analyze the interactions between spectral bands calculated using multi-channel filtering[13,15,17]. In general, texture is a local attribute in the image and ideally the texture features need to be calculated within a small image area. But in practice the texture features are typically calculated for relatively large image blocks in order to be statistically relevant. The Local Binary Patterns (LBP) concept developed by Ojala et al[57] attempts to decompose the texture into small texture units and the texture features are defined by the distribution (histogram) of the LBP values calculated for each pixel in the region under analysis. These LBP distributions are powerful texture descriptors since they can be used to discriminate textures in the input image irrespective of their size (the dissimilarity between two or more textures can be determined by using a histogram intersection metric). An LBP texture unit is represented in a 3 × 3 neighbourhood which generates 2^8 possible standard texture units. In this regard, the LBP texture unit is obtained by applying a simple threshold operation with respect to the central pixel of the 3 × 3 neighbourhood.

$$T = t(s(g_0 - g_c),\ldots,s(g_{P-1} - g_c))$$
$$s(x) = \begin{cases} 1 & x \geq 0 \\ 0 & x < 0 \end{cases} \quad (5.1)$$

where T is the texture unit, g_c is the grey value of the central pixel, g_P are the pixels adjacent to the central pixel in the 3 × 3 neighbourhood and s defines the threshold operation. For a 3 × 3 neighbourhood the value of P is 9. The LBP value for the tested pixel is calculated using the following relationship:

$$LBP = \sum_{i=1}^{P-1} s(g_i - g_c) * 2^i \quad (5.2)$$

where $s(g_i - g_c)$ is the value of the thresholding operation illustrated in equation (5.1). As the LBP values do not measure the greyscale variation, the LBP is generally used in conjunction with a contrast measure, referred to as LBP/C. For our implementation this contrast measure is the normalized difference between the grey levels of the pixels with a LBP value of 1 and the pixels with a grey level 0 contained in the texture unit. The distribution of the LBP/C of the image represents the texture spectrum. The LBP/C distribution can be defined as a 2D histogram of size *256* × *b*, where the *b* defines the number of bins required to sample the contrast measure (Fig. 5.2). In practice the contrast measure is sampled in 8 or 16 bins (experimentally it has been observed that best results are obtained when $b = 8$).

As mentioned previously the LBP texture descriptor has good discriminative power (see Fig. 5.2 where the LBP distributions for different textures are illustrated) but the main problem associated with LBP/C texture descriptors is the fact that they are not invariant to rotation and scale (see Fig. 5.3). However the sensitivity to texture rotation can be an advantageous property for some applications such as the inspection of wood parquetry, while for other applications such as the image retrieval it can be a considerable drawback. Ojala et al[57] have addressed this in the development of a multiresolution rotationally invariant LBP descriptor.

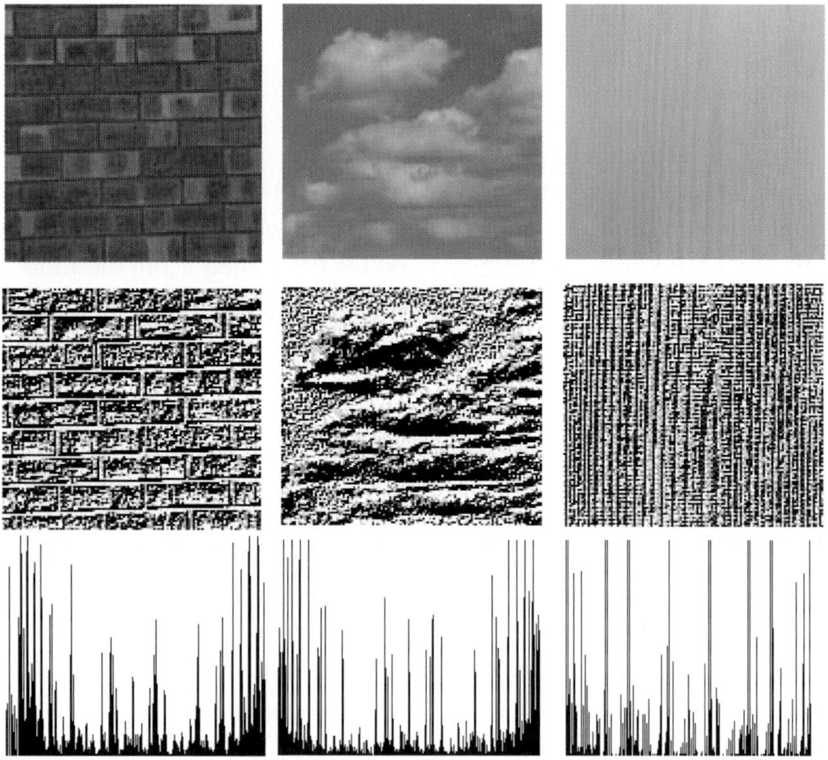

Fig. 5.2. The LBP distributions associated with different textures. First row – Original images (brick, clouds and wood from the VisTex database[66]). Second row – LBP images. Third row – LBP distributions (horizontal axis: LBP value, vertical axis: the number of elements in each bin).

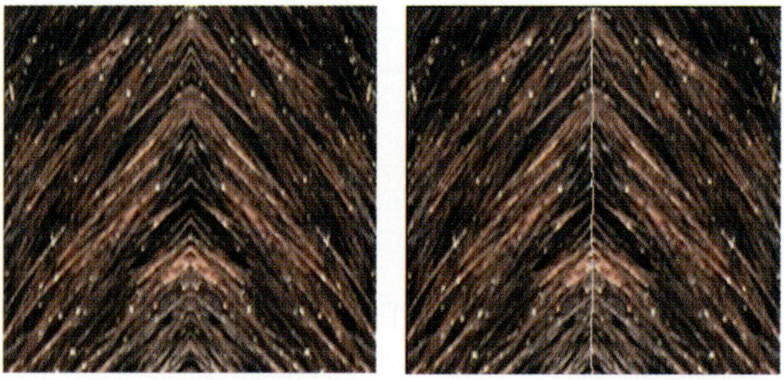

(a) (b)

Fig. 5.3. Segmentation of a test image that demonstrates the LBP/C texture descriptors sensitivity to texture rotation. (a) Original image defined by two regions with similar texture and different orientations (from the VisTex database[66]). (b) Colour-texture segmentation result.

5.3.1. *Diffusion-based filtering*

In order to improve the local colour homogeneity and eliminate the spurious regions caused by image noise we have applied an anisotropic diffusion-based filtering to smooth the input image (as originally developed by Perona and Malik[58]). Standard smoothing techniques based on local averaging or Gaussian weighted spatial operators[59] reduce the level of noise but this is obtained at the expense of poor feature preservation (i.e. suppression of narrow details in the image). To avoid this undesired effect in our implementation we have developed a filtering strategy based on anisotropic diffusion where smoothing is performed at intra regions and suppressed at region boundaries[41,58,60]. This non-linear smoothing procedure can be defined in terms of the derivative of the flux function:

$$u_t = div(D(|\nabla u|)\nabla u) \tag{5.3}$$

where u is the input data, D represents the diffusion function and t indicates the iteration step. The smoothing strategy described in equation (5.3) can be implemented using an iterative discrete formulation as follows:

$$I_{x,y}^{t+1} = I_{x,y}^{t} + \lambda \sum_{j=1}^{4} [D(\nabla_j I)\nabla_j I] \tag{5.4}$$

$$D(\nabla I) = e^{-\left(\frac{\nabla I}{k}\right)^2} \in (0,1] \tag{5.5}$$

where $\nabla_j I$ is the gradient operator defined in a 4-connected neighbourhood, λ is the contrast operator that is set in the range $0 < \lambda < 0.16$ and k is the diffusion parameter that controls the smoothing level. It should be noted that in cases where the gradient has high values, $D(\nabla I) \to 0$, the smoothing process is halted.

5.3.2. *Expectation-maximization (EM) algorithm*

The EM algorithm is the key component of the colour feature extraction. The EM algorithm is implemented using an iterative framework that attempts to calculate the maximum likelihood between the input data and a number of Gaussian distributions (Gaussian Mixture Models – GMM)[40,41]. The main advantage of this probabilistic strategy over rigid clustering algorithms such as K-means is its ability to better handle the uncertainties during the mixture assignment process. Assuming that we try to approximate the data using M mixtures, the mixture density estimator can be calculated using the following expression:

$$p(x \mid \Phi) = \sum_{i=1}^{M} \alpha_i p_i(x \mid \Phi_i) \tag{5.6}$$

where $x = [x_1, \ldots, x_k]$ is a k–dimensional vector, α_i is the mixing parameter for each GMM and $\Phi_i = \{\sigma_i, m_i\}$. The values σ_i, m_i are the standard deviation and the mean of the mixture. The function p_i is the Gaussian distribution and is defined as follows:

$$p_i(x \mid \Phi_i) = \frac{1}{\sqrt{2\pi}\sigma_i} e^{-\frac{\|x-m_i\|^2}{2\sigma_i^2}}, \quad \sum_{i=0}^{M} \alpha_i = 1 \tag{5.7}$$

The algorithm consists of two steps, the expectation and maximization step. The expectation step (E-step) is represented by the expected log-likelihood function for the complete data as follows:

$$Q(\Phi, \Phi(t)) = E[\log p(X, Y \mid \Phi) \mid X, \Phi(t)] \tag{5.8}$$

where Φ(t) are the current parameters and Φ are the new parameters that optimize the increase of *Q*. The *M*-step is applied to maximize the result obtained from the *E*-step.

$$\Phi(t+1) = \arg\max_{\Phi} Q(\Phi \mid \Phi(t)) \text{ and}$$
$$Q(\Phi(t+1), \Phi(t)) \geq Q(\Phi, \Phi(t)) \tag{5.9}$$

The *E* and *M* steps are applied iteratively until the increase of the log-likelihood function is smaller than a threshold value. The updates for GMMs can be calculated as follows:

$$\alpha_i(t+1) = \frac{\sum_{j=1}^{N} p(i \mid x_j, \Phi(t))}{N} \tag{5.10}$$

$$m_i(t+1) = \frac{\sum_{j=1}^{N} x_j\, p(i \mid x_j, \Phi(t))}{\sum_{j=1}^{N} p(i \mid x_j, \Phi(t))} \tag{5.11}$$

$$\sigma_i(t+1) = \frac{\sum_{j=1}^{N} p(i \mid x_j, \Phi(t)) \left\| x_j - m_i(t+1) \right\|^2}{\sum_{j=1}^{N} p(i \mid x_j, \Phi(t))} \tag{5.12}$$

where $$p(i \mid x_j, \Phi) = \frac{\alpha_i p_i(x_j \mid \Phi_i)}{\sum_{k=1}^{M} \alpha_k p_k(x_j \mid \Phi_K)}.$$

The EM algorithm is a powerful space partitioning technique but its main weakness is its sensitivity to the starting condition (i.e. the initialization of the mixtures Φ_i). The most common procedure to initialize the algorithm consists of a process that selects the means of the mixture by picking randomly data points from input image. This initialization procedure is far from optimal and may force the algorithm to converge to local minima. Another disadvantage of the random initialization procedure is the fact that the space partitioning algorithm may produce different results when executed with the same input data. To alleviate this problem a large number of algorithms have been developed to address the initialization of space partitioning techniques[41,61,62].

5.3.3. *EM initialization using colour quantization*

The solution we have adopted to initialize the parameters for mixtures $\Phi_i = \{\sigma_i, m_i\}$, $i = 1...M$ with the dominant colours from the input image, consists of extracting the peaks from the colour histogram calculated after the application of colour quantization. For this implementation we applied linear colour quantization[63,64] by linearly re-sampling the number of colours on each colour axis. The dominant colours contained in the image represented in the colour space C are extracted by selecting the peaks from the colour histogram as follows:

$$P_j = \arg\max_C(ColorHistogram), \quad \text{j} = 1, \ldots, \text{M} \tag{5.13}$$

Experimentally it has been observed that the EM initialization is optimal when the quantization levels are set to low values between 2 to 8 colours for each component (i.e. the quantized colour image will have $8 \times 8 \times 8$ colours – 3 bits per each colour axis – if the quantization level is set to 8). This is motivated by the fact that for low quantization levels the colour histogram is densely populated and the peaks in the histogram are statistically relevant. The efficiency of this quantization procedure is illustrated in Fig. 5.4 where we illustrate the differences between initializing the EM algorithm using the more traditional random procedure and our approach (see Ilea and Whelan[41] for more details).

5.4. Image Segmentation Algorithm

The image segmentation method used in our implementation is based on a split and merge algorithm[65] that adaptively evaluates the colour and texture information. The first step of the algorithm recursively splits the image hierarchically into four sub-blocks using the texture information extracted using the Local Binary Patterns/Contrast (LBP/C) method[53,56,57]. The splitting decision evaluates the uniformity factor of the region under analysis that is sampled using the Kolmogorov-Smirnov Metric (MKS). The Kolmogorov-Smirnov metric is a non-parametric test that is employed to evaluate the similarity between two distributions as follows:

$$MKS(s,m) = \sum_{i=0}^{n} \left| \frac{H_s(i)}{n_s} - \frac{H_m(i)}{n_m} \right| \tag{5.14}$$

where n represents the number of bins in the sample and model distributions (H_s and H_m), n_s and n_m are the number of elements in the sample and model distributions. We have adopted the MKS similarity measure in preference to other statistical metrics (such as the G-statistic or χ^2 test) as the MKS measure is normalized and its result is bounded.

To evaluate the texture uniformity within the region in question, the pairwise similarity values of the four sub-blocks are calculated and the ratio between the highest and lowest similarity values are compared with a threshold value (split threshold).

$$U = \frac{MKS_{\max}}{MKS_{\min}} \tag{5.15}$$

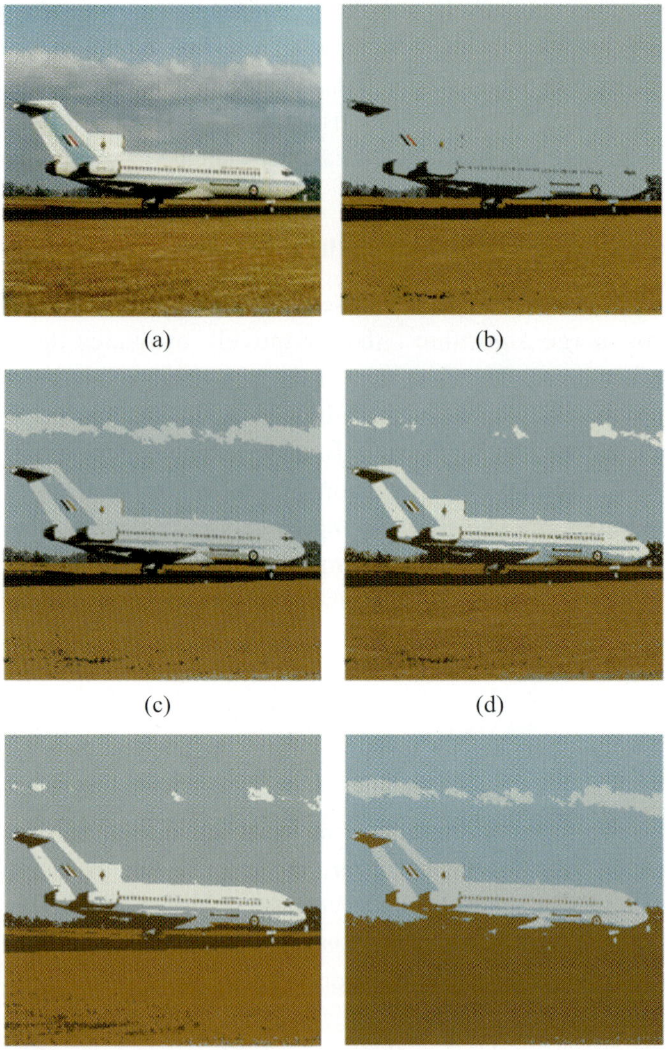

(a) (b)

(c) (d)

(e) (f)

Fig. 5.4. EM colour segmentation. (a) Original image[71]. (b) Colour segmentation using random initialization (best result). (c–f) Colour segmentation using colour quantization. (c) Quantization level 4. (d) Quantization level 8. (e) Quantization level 16. (f) Quantization level 64.

The region is split if the ratio U is higher than the split threshold. The split process continues until the uniformity level imposed by the split threshold (S_{th}) is upheld or the block size is smaller than a predefined size value (for this implementation the smallest block size has been set to 16×16 or 32×32 based on the size of the input image). During the splitting process two distributions are computed for each region resulting after the split process, the LBP/C distribution that defines the texture and the distribution of the colour labels computed using the colour segmentation algorithm previously outlined. The processing steps required by the split phase of the algorithm are illustrated in Fig. 5.5.

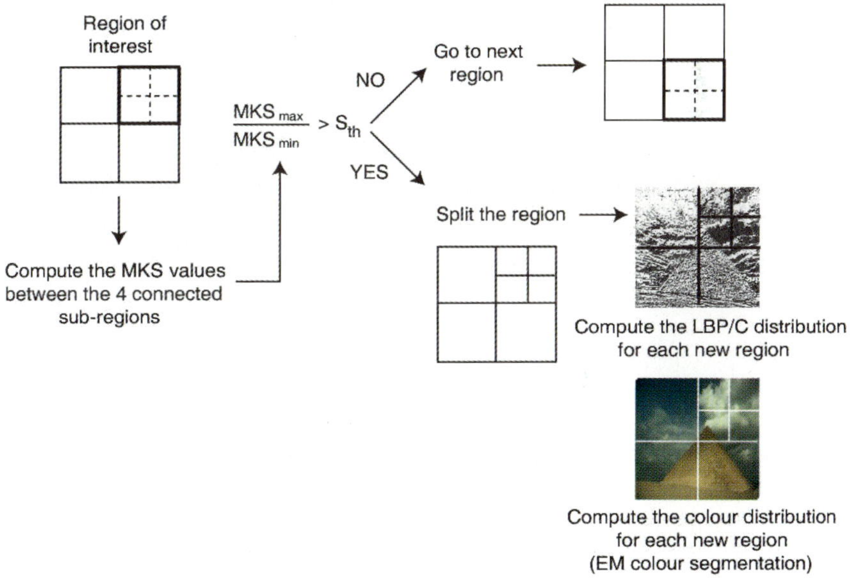

Fig. 5.5. The split phase of the CTex image segmentation algorithm.

The second step of the image segmentation algorithm applies an agglomerative merging procedure on the image resulting after splitting in order to join the adjacent regions that have similar colour-texture characteristics. This procedure calculates the merging importance (MI) between all adjacent regions resulting from the split process and the adjacent regions with the smallest MI value are merged. Since the MI values sample the colour-texture characteristics for each region, for this implementation we developed a novel merging scheme[41] that is able to locally adapt to the image content (texture and colour information) by evaluating the uniformity of the colour distribution. In this regard, if the colour distribution is homogenous (i.e. it is defined by one dominant colour) the weights w_1 and w_2 in equation (5.16) are adjusted to give the colour distribution more importance. Conversely, if the colour distribution is heterogeneous the texture will have more importance. The calculation of the weights employed to compute the MI values for merging process (see equation 5.16) is illustrated in equations (5.17 and 5.18).

$$MI(r_1, r_2) = w_1 * MKS(TD_1, TD_2) + w_2 * MKS(CD_1, CD_2) \tag{5.16}$$

where r_1, r_2 represent the adjacent regions under evaluation, w_1 and w_2 are the weights for texture and colour distributions respectively, MKS defines the Kolmogorov-Smirnov Metric, TD_i is the texture distribution for region i and CD_i is the colour distribution for region i. The weights w_1 and w_2 are calculated as follows:

$$K_i = \frac{\arg\max_C (CD_i)}{N_i}, \; K_i \in (0,1] \text{ and } i = 1,2 \tag{5.17}$$

where $\arg\max_C (CD_i)$ is the bin with the maximum number of elements in the distribution CD_i, N_i is the total number of elements in the distribution CD_i and C is the colour space.

$$w_2 = \frac{\sum_{i=1}^{2} K_i}{2} \quad \text{and} \quad w_1 = 1 - w_2 \tag{5.18}$$

where w_1 and w_2 are the texture and colour weights employed in equation (5.16). The merging process is iteratively applied until the minimum value for MI is higher than a pre-defined merge threshold (i.e. $MI_{min} > M_{th}$), see Fig. 5.6.

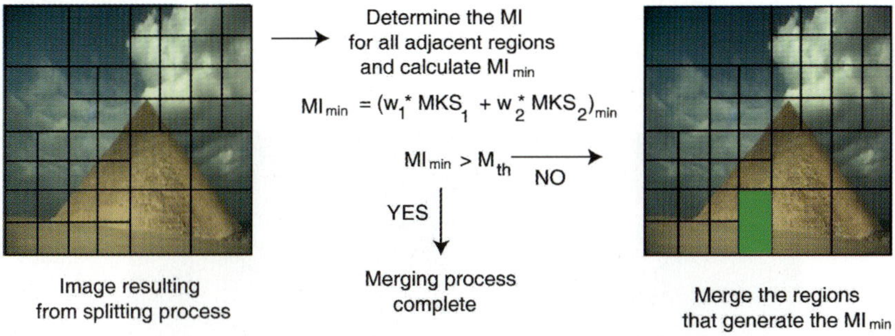

Fig. 5.6. The merge phase of the image segmentation algorithm (the adjacent regions with the smallest MI value are merged and are highlighted in the right hand side image).

The resulting image after the application of the merging process has a blocky structure since the regions resulting from the splitting process are rectangular. To compensate for this issue the last step of the algorithm applies a pixelwise procedure that exchanges the pixels situated at the boundaries between adjacent regions using the colour information computed from the colour segmentation algorithm previously outlined. This procedure calculates for each pixel situated on the border the colour distribution within an 11×11 window and the algorithm evaluates the MKS value between this distribution and the distributions of the regions which are 4-connected with the pixel under evaluation. The pixel is re-labelled (i.e. assigned to a different region) if the smallest MKS value is obtained between the distribution of the pixel and the distribution of the region that has a different label than the pixel under evaluation. This procedure is repeated iteratively until the minimum MKS value obtained for border pixels is higher than the merge threshold (M_{th}) to assure that the border refinement procedure does not move into regions defined by different colour characteristics. We have evaluated the pixelwise procedure for different window sizes and this experimentation indicates that window sizes of 11×11 and 15×15 provided optimal performance. For small window sizes the colour distribution became sparse and the borders between the image regions are irregular. Typical results achieved after the application of the pixelwise procedure are illustrated in Figs. 5.7 and 5.8. Figure 5.8d illustrates the limitation of the LBP/C texture operator when dealing with randomly oriented textures (see the segmentation around the border between the rock and the sky).

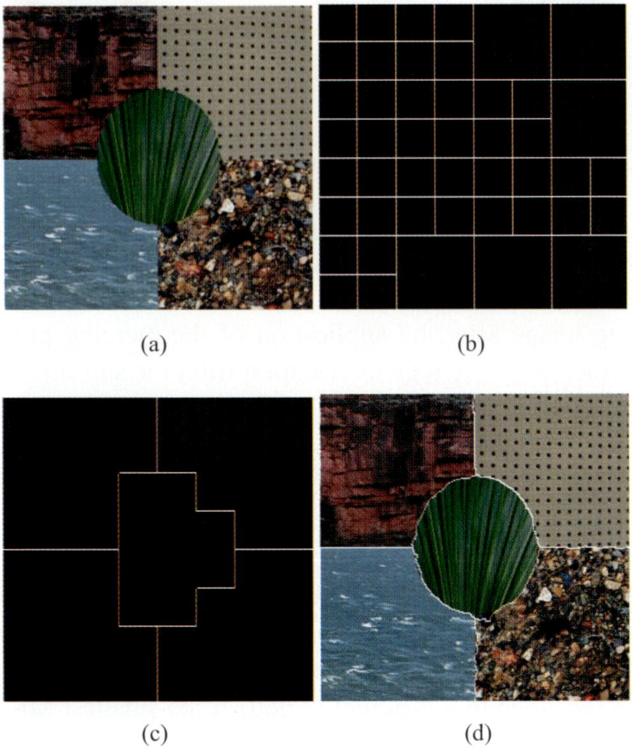

Fig. 5.7. Image segmentation process. (a) Original image. (b) Image resulting from splitting (block size 32 × 32). (c) Image resulting from merging. (d) Final segmentation after the application of the pixelwise procedure.

5.5. Experimental Results

The experiments were conducted on synthetic colour mosaic images (using textures from VisTex database[66]), natural and medical images. In order to examine the contribution of the colour and texture information in the segmentation process the split and merge parameters were set to the values that return the minimum segmentation error. The other key parameter is the diffusion parameter k and its influence on the performance of the algorithm will be examined in detail.

(a) (b) (c) (d)

Fig. 5.8. Image segmentation process. (a) Original image[56]. (b) Image resulting from splitting (block size 16×16). (c) Image resulting from merging. (d) Final segmentation after the application of the pixelwise procedure.

5.5.1. *Segmentation of synthetic images*

As the ground truth data associated with natural images is difficult to extract and is influenced by the subjectivity of the human operator, the efficiency of this algorithm is evaluated on mosaic images created using various VisTex reference textures. In our tests we have used 15 images where the VisTex textures were arranged in different patterns and a number of representative images are illustrated in Fig. 5.9. Since the split and merge algorithm would be favoured if we perform the analysis on test images with rectangular regions, in our experiments we have also included images with complex structures where the borders between different regions are irregular.

Fig. 5.9. Some of the VisTex images used in our experiments. (From top to bottom and left to right: Image 3, Image 9, Image 10, Image 11, Image 13 and Image 5)

An important issue for our research is to evaluate the influence of the colour and texture information in the segmentation process. In this regard, we have examined the performance of the algorithm in cases where texture alone, colour alone and colour-texture information is used in the segmentation process.

The experimental results are illustrated in Table 5.1 and it can be observed that texture and colour alone results are generally inferior to results obtained when texture and colour local distributions are used in the segmentation process. The balance between the texture and colour is performed by the weights w_1 and w_2 in equation (5.16) and to obtain the texture and colour alone segmentations these parameters were overridden with manual settings (i.e. $w_1 = 1$, $w_2 = 0$ for texture alone segmentation and $w_1 = 0$, $w_2 = 1$ for colour alone segmentation). When the colour and texture distributions were used in a compound image descriptor these parameters were computed automatically using the expressions illustrated in equations (5.17) and (5.18). For all experiments the initial number of mixtures (GMMs) are set to 10 ($M = 10$). The inclusion of colour and texture in a compound image descriptor proved to improve the overall segmentation results. The contribution of colour to the segmentation process will be more evident when the algorithm is applied to natural images where the textures are more heterogeneous than those in the test images defined by VisTex textures.

Table 5.1. Performance of our CTex colour-texture segmentation algorithm when applied to VisTex mosaic images (% error given).

Image Index	Texture-only (%)	Colour-only (%)	Colour-Texture (%)
Image 1	0.33	2.49	0.45
Image 2	0.98	2.08	1.77
Image 3	5.47	2.10	0.88
Image 4	4.31	4.94	1.81
Image 5	8.77	4.30	3.17
Image 6	4.70	5.11	4.06
Image 7	33.55	2.52	6.57
Image 8	1.82	5.25	2.07
Image 9	18.47	1.15	0.50
Image 10	3.63	2.07	1.89
Image 11	33.73	2.52	1.81
Image 12	5.25	2.77	2.29
Image 13	40.56	4.39	3.87
Image 14	3.18	0.58	0.75
Image 15	2.60	1.94	1.94
Overall:	11.15	2.97	2.25

The segmentation results reported in Table 5.1 were obtained in the condition that the split and merge parameters are set to arbitrary values to obtain best results. From these parameters the split threshold has a lesser importance since the result from the split phase does not need to be optimized. In our experiments we have used large values for this parameter that assure almost a uniform splitting of the input image and as a result the split threshold has a marginal influence on the performance of the algorithm. The merge threshold has a strong impact on the final results and experimentally it has been determined that this threshold parameter should be set to values in the range (0.6-1.0) depending on the complexity of the input image (the merge threshold should be set to lower values when the input image is heterogeneous (complex) with respect to colour and texture information). The optimal value for this parameter can be determined by using the algorithm in a supervised scheme by indicating the final number of regions that should result from the merging stage. A typical example that illustrates the influence of the merge threshold on the final segmented result is illustrated in Fig. 5.10.

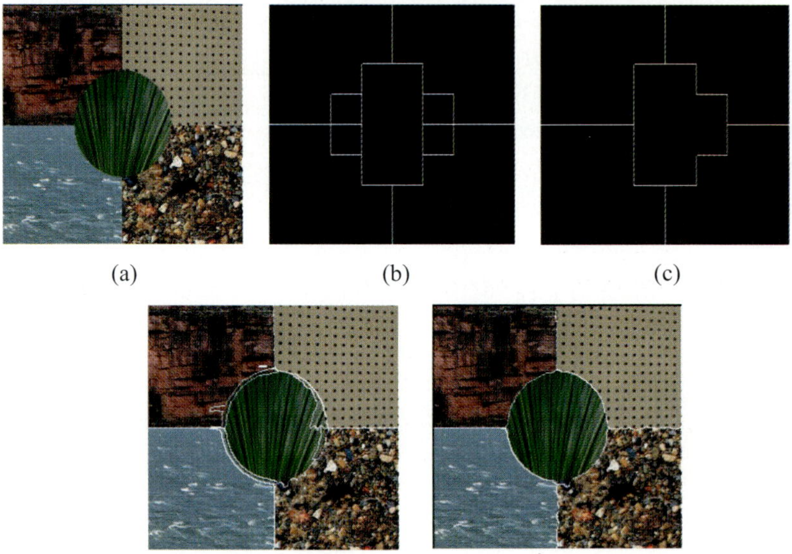

(a) (b) (c)

(d) (e)

Fig. 5.10. Example outlining the influence of the merge threshold. (a) Original image. (b) The image resulting from the merge stage ($M_{th} = 0.8$). (c) The image resulting from the merge stage ($M_{th} = 1.0$). (d) The final segmentation result after pixelwise classification ($M_{th} = 0.8$). (e) The final segmentation result after pixelwise classification ($M_{th} = 1.0$).

It can be observed that even for non-optimal settings for the merge threshold the algorithm achieves accurate segmentation. The effect of the sub-optimal setting for the merge threshold will generate extra regions in the image resulting from the merge stage and since these regions do not exhibit strong colour-texture characteristics they will have a thin long structure around the adjacent regions in the final segmentation results. These regions can be easily identified and re-assigned to the bordering regions with similar colour-texture characteristics. When the segmentation algorithm was tested on synthetic mosaic images the experimental data indicates that the algorithm has a good stability with respect to the diffusion parameter k and the benefit of using pronounced smoothing becomes evident when the image segmentation scheme is applied to noisy and low-resolution images. The influence of this parameter will be examined when we discuss the performance of the colour-texture segmentation scheme on natural and medical images.

5.5.2. *Segmentation of natural images*

The second set of experiments was dedicated to the examination of the performance of the CTex algorithm when applied to natural images. We applied the algorithm on a range of natural images and images with low signal to noise ratio (Figs. 5.11 to 5.13).

Fig. 5.11. Segmentation results when the algorithm has been applied to natural images (Berkley[67] and Caltech[71] databases).

The segmentation results obtained from natural images are consistent with the results reported in Table 5.1 where the most accurate segmentation is obtained when the colour and texture are used in a joint image descriptor. This can be observed in Fig. 5.12 where are illustrated the segmentation results obtained for cases where texture and colour information are used alone and when colour and texture distributions are used as joint features in the image segmentation process.

Fig. 5.12. Segmentation results. (First column) Texture only segmentation. (Second column) Colour only segmentation. (Third column) Colour-texture segmentation.

The diffusion filtering parameter k was also examined. The diffusion filtering scheme was applied to reduce the image noise, thus improving local colour homogeneity. Clearly this helps the image segmentation, especially when applied to images with uneven illumination and image noise. The level of smoothing in equation (5.5) is controlled by the parameter k (smoothing is more pronounced for high values of k). In order to assess the influence of this parameter we have applied the colour-texture segmentation scheme to low resolution and noisy images. The effect of the diffusion filtering on the colour-segmented result is illustrated in Fig. 5.13 where the original image "rock in the sea" is corrupted with Gaussian noise (standard deviation = 20 grayscale levels for each component of the RGB colour space).

(a) (b) (c)

(d) (e)

Fig. 5.13. Effect of the diffusion filtering on the segmentation results. (a) Noisy image corrupted with Gaussian noise (Oulu database[56,47,72,73]). (b) Image resulting from EM algorithm – no filtering. (c) Image resulting from EM algorithm – diffusion filtering $k = 30$. (d) Colour-texture segmentation – no filtering. (e) Colour-texture segmentation – diffusion filtering $k = 30$.

One particular advantage of our colour-texture segmentation technique is the fact that it is unsupervised and it can be easily applied to practical applications including the segmentation of medical images and product inspection. To complete our discussion on colour texture we will detail two case studies, namely the identification of skin cancer lesions[36] and the detection of visual faults on the surface of painted slates[28].

5.5.3 *Segmentation of medical images*

Skin cancer is one of the most common types of cancer and it is typically caused by excessive exposure to the sun radiation[68], but it can be cured in more than 90% of the cases if it is detected in its early stages. Current clinical practice involves a range of simple measurements performed on the lesion border (e.g. **A**symmetry, **B**order irregularity, **C**olour variation and lesion **D**iameter (also known as the ABCD parameters)). The evaluation of these parameters is carried out by manually annotating the melanoma images. This is not only time consuming but it is subjective and often non reproducible process. Thus an important aim is the development of an automated technique that is able to robustly and reliably segment skin cancer lesions in medical images[36,68,70]. The segmentation of skin cancer images it is a difficult task due to the colour variation associated within both the skin lesion and healthy tissue. In order to determine the accuracy of the developed algorithm the ground truth was constructed by manually tracing the skin cancer lesion outline and comparing it with the results returned by our colour-texture image segmentation algorithm (see Fig. 5.14). Additional details and experimental results are provided in Ilea and Whelan[36].

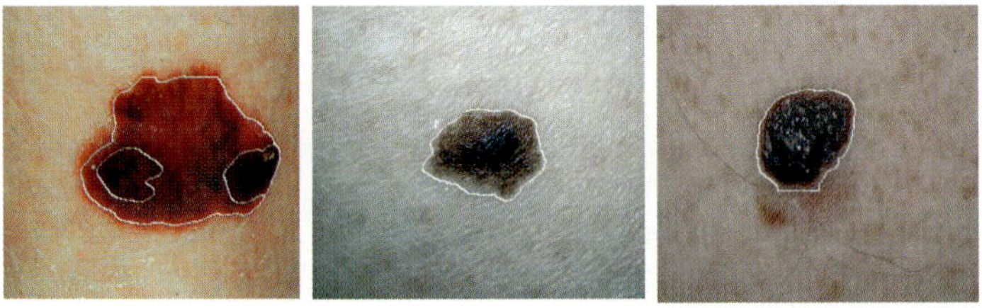

(a) (b) (c)

Fig. 5.14. Segmentation of skin cancer lesion images (original images (b) & (c) courtesy of: © <Eric Ehrsam, MD >, Dermatlas; http://www.dermatlas.org).

5.5.4. *Detection of visual faults on painted slates*

Roof slates are cement composite rectangular slabs which are typically painted in dark colours with a high gloss finish. While their primary function is to prevent water ingress to the buildings they have also a decorative role. Although slate manufacturing is a highly automated process, currently the slates are inspected manually as they emerge via a conveyor from the paint process line. Our aim was to develop an automated quality/process control system capable of grading the painted slates. The visual defects present on the surface of the slates can be roughly categorized into substrate and paint defects. Paint defects include no paint, insufficient paint, paint droplets, efflorescence, paint debris and orange peel. Substrate defects include template marks, incomplete slate formation, lumps, and depressions. The size of these defects ranges from 1 mm^2 to hundreds of mm^2 (see Fig. 5.15 for some representative defects).

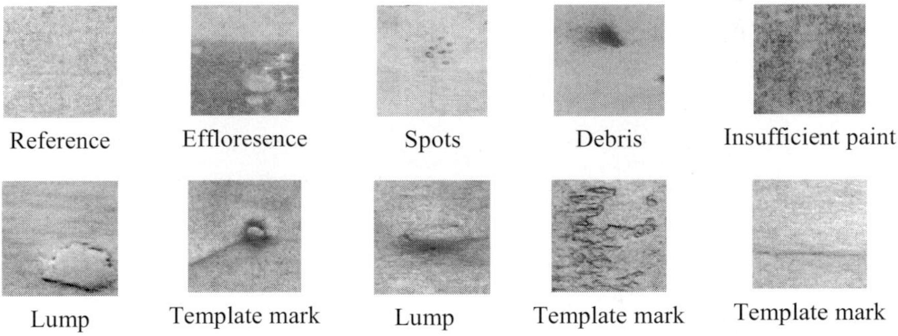

Fig. 5.15. Typical paint and substrate defects found on the slate surface.

The colour-texture image segmentation algorithm detailed in this chapter is a key component of the developed slate inspection system (see Ghita et al. [28] for details). In this implementation for computational purposes the EM algorithm has been replaced with a standard K-means algorithm to extract the colour information. The inspection system has been tested on 235 slates (112 reference-defect free slates and 123 defective slates) where the classification of defective slates and defect-free slates was performed by an experienced operator based on a visual examination. A detailed performance characterization of the developed inspection system is depicted in Table 5.2. Figure 5.16 illustrates the identification of visual defects (paint and substrate) on several representative defective slates.

Table 5.2. Performance of our colour-texture based slate inspection system.

Slate type	Quantity	Fail	Pass	Accuracy
Reference	112	2	110	98.21 %
Defective	123	123	0	100 %
Total	235			99.14 %

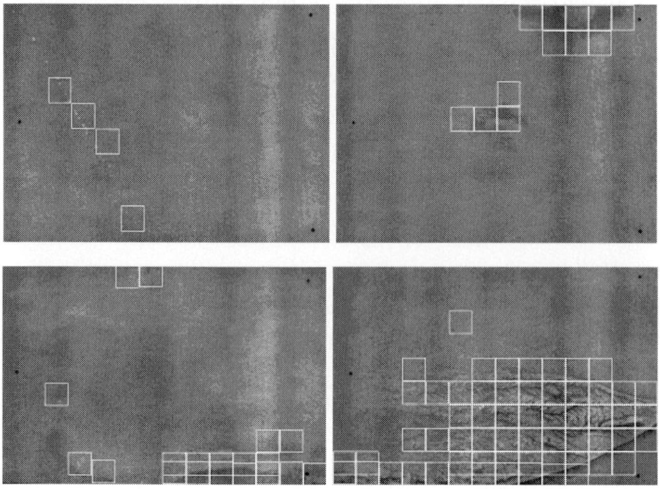

Fig. 5.16. Identification of visual defects on painted slates.

5.6. Conclusions

In this chapter we have detailed the implementation of a new methodology for colour-texture segmentation. The main contribution of this work is the development of a novel image descriptor that encompasses the colour and texture information in an adaptive fashion. The developed image segmentation algorithm is modular and can be easily adapted to accommodate any texture and colour feature extraction techniques. The colour-texture segmentation scheme has been quantitatively evaluated on complex test images and the experimental results indicate that the adaptive inclusion of texture and colour produces superior results that in cases where the colour and texture information were used in separation. The CTex algorithm detailed in this chapter has been successfully applied to the segmentation of natural, medical and industrial images.

Acknowledgements

We would like to acknowledge the contribution of current and former members of the Vision Systems Group, namely Dana Elena Ilea for the development of the EM colour clustering algorithm and segmentation of medical images, Dr. Padmapryia Nammalwar for the development of the split and merge image segmentation framework and Tim Carew for his work in the development of the slate inspection system. This work has been supported in part by Science Foundation Ireland (SFI) and Enterprise Ireland (EI).

References

1. K.S. Fu and J.K. Mui, A survey on image segmentation, *Pattern Recognition*, 13, p. 3-16 (1981).
2. R.M. Haralick and L.G. Shapiro, *Computer and Robot Vision*, Addison-Wesley Publishing Company (1993).
3. L. Lucchese and S.K. Mitra, Color image segmentation: A state-of-the-art survey, in Proc. of the *Indian National Science Academy*, vol. 67A, no. 2, p. 207-221, New Delhi, India (2001).
4. Y.J. Zhang, A survey on evaluation methods for image segmentation, *Pattern Recognition*, 29(8), p. 1335-1346 (1996).
5. R. Chellappa, R.L. Kashyap and B.S. Manjunath, *Model based texture segmentation and classification*, in The Handbook of Pattern Recognition and Computer Vision, C.H. Chen, L.F. Pau and P.S.P Wang (Editors) World Scientific Publishing (1998).
6. M. Tuceryan and A.K. Jain, *Texture analysis*, in The Handbook of Pattern Recognition and Computer Vision, C.H. Chen, L.F. Pau and P.S.P Wang (eds.) World Scientific Publishing (1998).
7. R.M. Haralick, Statistical and structural approaches to texture, in *Proc of IEEE*, 67, p. 786-804 (1979).
8. A. Materka and M. Strzelecki, Texture analysis methods – A review, *Technical Report*, University of Lodz, Cost B11 Report (1998).
9. J.S. Wezska, C.R. Dyer, A. Rosenfeld, A comparative study of texture measures for terrain classification, *IEEE Transactions on Systems, Man and Cybernetics*, 6(4), p. 269-285 (1976).
10. V.A. Kovalev and M. Petrou, Multidimensional co-occurrence matrices for object recognition and matching. *CVGIP: Graphical Model and Image Processing*, 58(3), p. 187-197 (1996).
11. I.M. Elfadel and R.W. Picard, Gibbs random fields, cooccurrences and texture modeling, *IEEE Transactions on Pattern Analysis and Machine Intelligence*, 16(1), p. 24-37 (1994).
12. M. Varma and A. Zisserman, Unifying statistical texture classification frameworks, *Image and Vision Computing*, 22, p. 1175-1183 (2004).

13. A.C. Bovik, M. Clark and W.S. Geisler, Multichannel texture analysis using localized spatial filters, *IEEE Transactions on Pattern Analysis and Machine Intelligence*, 12(1), p. 55-73 (1990).
14. A.C. Bovik, Analysis of multichannel narrow band filters for image texture segmentation, *IEEE Transactions on Signal Processing*, 39, p. 2025-2043 (1991).
15. J.M. Coggins and A.K. Jain, A spatial filtering approach to texture analysis, *Pattern Recognition Letters*, 3, p. 195-203 (1985).
16. A.K. Jain and F. Farrokhnia, Unsupervised texture segmentation using Gabor filtering, *Pattern Recognition*, 33, p. 1167-1186 (1991).
17. T. Randen and J.H. Husoy, Filtering for texture classification: A comparative study, *IEEE Transactions on Pattern Analysis and Machine Intelligence*, 21(4), p. 291-310 (1999).
18. T. Randen and J.H. Husoy, Texture segmentation using filters with optimized energy separation, *IEEE Transactions on Image Processing*, 8(4), p. 571-582 (1999).
19. C. Lu, P. Chung, and C. Chen, Unsupervised texture segmentation via wavelet transform, *Pattern Recognition*, 30(5), p. 729-742 (1997).
20. S. Mallat, Multifrequency channel decomposition of images and wavelet models, *IEEE Transactions on Acoustic, Speech and Signal Processing*, 37(12), p. 2091-2110 (1989).
21. B. Schiele and J.L. Crowley, Object recognition using multidimensional receptive field histograms, in Proc of the *4th European Conference on Computer Vision* (ECCV 96), Cambridge, UK (1996).
22. M. Swain and D. Ballard, Color indexing, *International Journal of Computer Vision*, 7(1), p. 11-32 (1991).
23. M.J. Jones and J.M. Rehg, Statistical color models with application to skin detection, *International Journal of Computer Vision*, 46(1), p. 81-96 (2002).
24. S. Liapis and G. Tziritas, Colour and texture image retrieval using chromaticity histograms and wavelet frames, *IEEE Transactions on Multimedia*, 6(5), p. 676-686 (2004).
25. A. Mojsilovic, J. Hu and R.J. Safranek, Perceptually based color texture features and metrics for image database retrieval, in Proc. of the *IEEE International Conference on Image Processing* (ICIP'99), Kobe, Japan (1999).
26. C.H. Yao and S.Y. Chen, Retrieval of translated, rotated and scaled color textures, *Pattern Recognition*, 36, p. 913-929 (2002).
27. C. Boukouvalas, J. Kittler, R. Marik and M. Petrou, Color grading of randomly textured ceramic tiles using color histograms, *IEEE Transactions on Industrial Electronics*, 46(1), p. 219-226 (1999).
28. O. Ghita, P.F. Whelan, T. Carew and P. Nammalwar, Quality grading of painted slates using texture analysis, *Computers in Industry*, 56(8-9), p. 802-815 (2005).
29. H.D. Cheng, X.H. Jiang, Y. Sun and J.L. Wang, Color image segmentation: Advances & prospects, *Pattern Recognition*, 34(12) p. 2259-2281, (2001).
30. W. Skarbek and A Koschan, Color image segmentation – A survey, *Technical Report*, University of Berlin (1994).

31. M. Pietikainen, T. Maenpaa and J. Viertola, Color texture classification with color histograms and local binary patterns, in Proc. of the *2nd International Workshop on Texture Analysis and Synthesis*, Copenhagen, Denmark, p. 109-112 (2002).
32. L. Shafarenko, M. Petrou and J. Kittler, Automatic watershed segmentation of randomly textured color images, *IEEE Transactions on Image Processing*, 6(11), p. 1530-1544 (1997).
33. T.S.C. Tan and J. Kittler, Colour texture analysis using colour histogram, *IEE Proceedings - Vision, Image, and Signal Processing*, 141(6), p. 403-412 (1994).
34. M. Celenk, A color clustering technique for image segmentation, *Graphical Models and Image Processing*, 52(3), p. 145-170 (1990).
35. R.O. Duda, P.E. Hart and D.E. Stork, *Pattern classification*, Wiley Interscience, 2nd Edition (2000).
36. D.E. Ilea and P.F. Whelan, Automatic segmentation of skin cancer images using adaptive color clustering, in Proc. of the *China-Ireland International Conference on Information and Communications Technologies* (CIICT 06), Hangzhou, China (2006).
37. T.N. Pappas, An adaptive clustering algorithm for image segmentation, *IEEE Transactions on Image Processing*, 14(4), p. 901-914 (1992).
38. R.L. Cannon, J.V. Dave and J.C. Bezdek, Efficient implementation of the fuzzy c-means clustering algorithms, *IEEE Transactions on Pattern Analysis and Machine Intelligence*, 8(2), p. 249-255 (1996).
39. D. Comaniciu and P. Meer, Mean shift: A robust approach toward feature space analysis, *IEEE Transactions on Pattern Analysis and Machine Intelligence*, 24(5), p. 603-619 (2002).
40. J.A. Blimes, A gentle tutorial of the EM algorithm and its application to parameter estimation for Gaussian Mixed and Hidden Markov Models, *Technical Report*, University of California, Berkely, TR-97-021 (1998).
41. D.E. Ilea and P.F. Whelan, Color image segmentation using a self-initializing EM algorithm, in Proc. of the *International Conference on Visualization, Imaging and Image Processing* (VIIP 2006), Palma de Mallorca, Spain (2006).
42. J. Chen, T.N. Pappas, A. Mojsilovic, and B.E. Rogowitz, Image segmentation by spatially adaptive color and texture features, in *Proc.* of *International Conference on Image Processing* (ICIP 03), 3, Barcelona, Spain, p. 777-780 (2003).
43. J. Freixenet, X. Munoz, J. Marti and X. Llado, Color texture segmentation by region-boundary cooperation, in *European Conference on Computer Vision* (ECCV), Lecture Notes in Computer Science (LNCS 3022), Prague (2004).
44. H.D. Cheng and Y. Sun, A hierarchical approach to color image segmentation using homogeneity, *IEEE Transactions on Image Processing*, 9(12), p. 2071-2082 (2000).
45. A. Moghaddamzadeh and N. Bourbakis, A fuzzy region growing approach for segmentation of color images, *Pattern Recognition*, 30(6), p. 867-881 (1997).
46. A. Tremeau and N. Borel, A region growing and merging algorithm to color segmentation, *Pattern Recognition*, 30(7), p. 1191-1203 (1997).
47. D.K. Panjwani and G. Healey, Markov Random Field Models for unsupervised segmentation of textured color images, *IEEE Transactions on Pattern Analysis and Machine Intelligence*, 17(10), p. 939-954 (1995).

48. Y. Deng and B.S. Manjunath, Unsupervised segmentation of color-texture regions in images and video, *IEEE Transactions on Pattern Analysis and Machine Intelligence*, 23(8), p. 800-810 (2001).
49. G. Healey, Using color for geometry-insensitive segmentation, *Optical Society of America*, 22(1), p. 920-937 (1989).
50. G. Healey, Segmenting images using normalized color, *IEEE Transactions on Systems, Man and Cybernetics*, 22(1), p. 64-73 (1992).
51. S.A. Shafer, Using color to separate reflection components, *Color Research and Applications*, 10(4), p. 210-218 (1985).
52. A. Drimbarean and P.F. Whelan, Experiments in colour texture analysis, *Pattern Recognition Letters*, 22, p. 1161-1167 (2001).
53. P. Nammalwar, O. Ghita and P.F. Whelan, Experimentation on the use of chromaticity features, Local Binary Pattern and Discrete Cosine Transform in colour texture analysis, in Proc. of the *13'th Scandinavian Conference on Image Analysis* (SCIA), Goteborg, Sweden, p. 186-192 (2003).
54. M. Mirmehdi and M. Petrou, Segmentation of color textures, *IEEE Transactions on Pattern Analysis and Machine Intelligence*, 22(2), p. 142-159 (2000).
55. M.A. Hoang, J.M. Geusebroek and A.W. Smeulders, Color texture measurement and segmentation, *Signal Processing*, 85(2), p. 265-275 (2005).
56. T. Ojala and M. Pietikainen, Unsupervised texture segmentation using feature distributions, *Pattern Recognition*, 32(3), p. 477-486 (1999). See also University of Oulu Texture Database: http://www.outex.oulu.fi/temp/
57. T. Ojala, M. Pietikainen and T. Maenpaa, Multiresolution gray-scale and rotation invariant texture classification with Local Binary Patterns, *IEEE Transactions on Pattern Analysis and Machine Intelligence*, 24(7), p. 971-987 (2002).
58. P. Perona and J. Malik, Scale-space and edge detection using anisotropic diffusion, *IEEE Transactions on Pattern Analysis and Machine Intelligence*, 12(7), p. 629-639 (1990).
59. M. Sonka, V. Hlavac and R. Boyle, *Image processing, analysis and machine vision*, 2nd edition, PWS Boston (1998).
60. J. Weickert, *Anisotropic diffusion in image processing*, Teubner Verlag, Stuttgart (1998).
61. S. Khan and A. Ahmad, Cluster center initialization algorithm for K-means clustering, *Pattern Recognition Letters*, 25(11), p. 1293-1302 (2004).
62. J.M. Pena, J.A. Lozano and P. Larranaga, An empirical comparison of four initialization methods for the K-Means algorithm, *Pattern Recognition Letters*, 20(10), p. 1027-1040 (1999).
63. J. Puzicha, M. Held, J. Ketterer, J.M. Buhmann and D. Fellner, On spatial quantization of color images, *IEEE Transactions on Image Processing*, 9(4), p. 666-682 (2000).
64. X. Wu, Efficient statistical computations for optimal color quantization, Graphics Gems 2, Academic Press (1991).
65. P. Nammalwar, O. Ghita and P.F. Whelan, Integration of feature distributions for colour texture segmentation, in Proc. of the *17th International Conference on Pattern Recognition* (ICPR), Cambridge, UK, p. 716-719 (2004).

66. Vision Texture (VisTex) Database, Massachusetts Institute of Technology, Media Lab, http://vismod.media.mit.edu/vismod/imagery/VisionTexture/vistex.html
67. D. Martin and C. Fowlkes and D. Tal and J. Malik, A Database of Human Segmented Natural Images and its Application to Evaluating Segmentation Algorithms and Measuring Ecological Statistics, Proc. 8th *Int'l Conf. Computer Vision*, Vol. p.416-423 (2001). See also the Berkley Segmentation Dataset and Benchmark Database: www.eecs.berkeley.edu/Research/Projects/CS/vision/bsds/
68. NIH Consensus Conference. Diagnosis and treatment of early melanoma, *JAMA* 268, p. 1314-1319 (1992).
69. Dermatology Image Atlas: http://www.dermatlas.org
70. L. Xu, M. Jackowski, A. Goshtasby, D. Roseman, S. Bines, C. Yu, A. Dhawan and A. Huntley, Segmentation of skin cancer images, *Image and Vision Computing*, 17, p. 65-74 (1999).
71. Caltech Image Database. http://www.vision.caltech.edu/archive.html
72. P.P. Ohanian and& R.C. Dubes, Performance evaluation for four classes of textural features. *Pattern Recognition* 25:819-833 (1992).
73. A.K. Jain and K. Karu, Learning texture description masks. *IEEE Transactions on Pattern Analysis and Machine Intelligence* 18:195-205 (1996).

Chapter 6

3D Texture Analysis

Mike Chantler[†] and Maria Petrou[‡]

[†] *Texture Lab*
School of Mathematical and Computer Sciences
Heriot-Watt University, Edinburgh EH14 4AS
http://www.macs.hw.ac.uk/texturelab/

[‡] *Communications and Signal Processing Group*
Electrical and Electronic Engineering Department,
Imperial College, London SW7 2AZ, UK
E-mail: maria.petrou@imperial.ac.uk

This chapter deals with the analysis of 3D surface texture. A model of the surface-to-image function is developed. This theory shows that sidelighting acts as a directional filter of the surface height function. Thus the directionality and power of image texture is a function of the illuminant's slant and tilt angles.

The theory is extended to common texture features such as those of Gabor and Laws to show that their behaviours follow that of simple harmonic motion. Variation of illuminant's tilt causes class centres to describe a trajectory on a hyper-ellipse, while changes in slant cause the hyper-ellipse to grow or shrink. Thus it is not surprising that classifiers trained under one set of illumination conditions will fail under another.

Finally we develop a classifier that exploits a simplified version of this theory. Given a single image of a surface texture taken under unknown illumination conditions our classifier will return both the estimated illumination direction and the class assignment.

6.1. Introduction

Texture classification normally involves three processes (Figure 6.1).

(1) the subject must be illuminated and its image acquired;
(2) feature generators are applied to the digitized image to produce a set

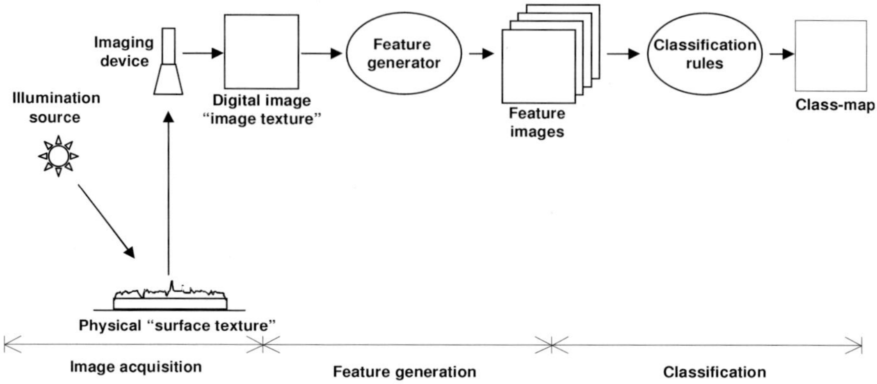

Fig. 6.1. Texture classification.

of feature images or statistics;

(3) a set of classification rules (for instance, a set of statistically derived discriminant functions or a support vector machine) are applied to classify the image.

If this process is applied locally, then the image may be segmented into different texture classes and the output will be a class-map. Alternatively, if the statistics are aggregated across the full image, then a single (image-wide) classification is provided. The former is appropriate for the segmentation and classification of non-stationary textures, while the latter is appropriate for the classification of stationary textures.[1]

Since the late seventies there has been a vast quantity of work published particularly on the last two processes (feature generation and classification) and excellent surveys have been provided by several researchers.[1–5] The comparison of these techniques has been facilitated by the adoption of the Brodatz album[6] as the *de facto* test set of *image textures*.

While this resource allowed the performance of texture classification schemes to be advanced to nearly flawless operation, it did not enable researchers to separate out the effects of imaging conditions from the intrinsic characteristics of the *surface textures* themselves. (See Figure 6.2 for an example of the effect of illumination variation on image texture.)

It was not until the mid-nineties that researchers started to investigate the influence of the image acquisition stage and particularly the effect of illumination on image texture. Chantler showed that variation in illu-

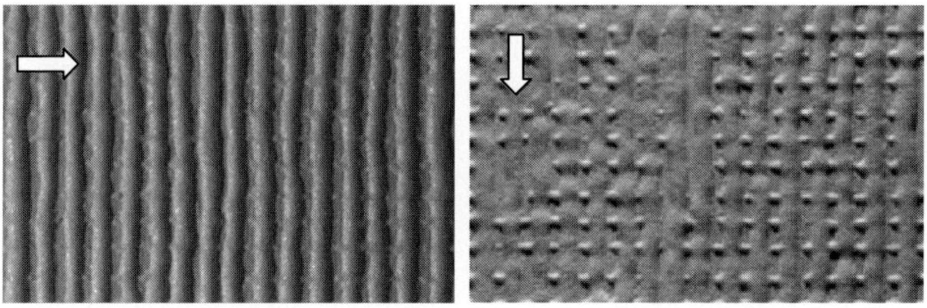

Fig. 6.2. The dramatic effect that variation in illumination conditions can have on *image texture* is shown above. A single surface sample has been imaged using two different lighting directions (illumination direction indicated by arrows.)

mination conditions adversely affected classification performance.[7] Dana et al. established the Columbia-Utrecht database of real world surface textures which was used to investigate bidirectional texture functions.[8] Later they developed histogram[9,10] and correlation models[11] of these textures. Leung and Malik[12,13] Cula and Dana[14] and Varma and Zisserman[15,16] all developed classification schemes using filter banks and 3D 'textons' for the purposes of illumination and viewpoint invariant classification, and many others have since used this database to develop classification schemes that are robust to changes in imaging conditions.

The emphasis of this chapter however, is different from the empirical approaches discussed above as it develops and exploits a theory of feature behaviour derived from first principles.

In the next section an image model of surface texture is developed[7] based upon Kube and Pentland's model of the effect of illumination direction on images of fractal surfaces.[17] Section 6.3 extends this to cover feature behaviour, and it is this theory that is used in Section 6.6 to develop a novel classifier that simultaneously estimates lighting direction and classifies surface texture.[18,19] The simple model of Section 6.3 is generalised in Section 6.4 by relaxing some of its restrictive assumptions, while Section 6.5 compares the predictions made by the simple and the full model in terms of feature behaviour prediction.

6.2. The Effect of Illumination on Images of Surface Texture

This section presents a simple model of the image of an illuminated three-dimensional surface texture. It is based on theory developed by Kube and Pentland[17] and further developed by Chantler.[7] It expresses the power spectrum of the image in terms of the surface texture's height spectrum and its illumination vector.

6.2.1. *A model of image texture as a function of illumination direction*

The model is developed by expressing Lambert's law in terms of partial derivatives of the surface height function, linearising the result, and applying it in the frequency domain to give an expression for the discrete Fourier transform of the image as a function of the slant and tilt of the illumination vector. The major assumptions are:

(1) the surface is Lambertian and of uniform albedo;
(2) the illumination originates from a collimated source;
(3) the camera projection is orthographic;
(4) shadowing and occlusions are not significant; and
(5) surface slope angles are low.

Given these assumptions, the image may be simply expressed using Lambert's cosine law:

$$i(x, y) = \mathbf{l} \cdot \mathbf{n}(x, y) \tag{6.1}$$

where:

- $i(x, y)$ is the radiant intensity measured at each point (x, y) on the surface;
- $\mathbf{l}$ is the illumination vector scaled by the illumination's intensity and the surface albedo; and
- $\mathbf{n}(x, y)$ is the surface normal function;

Given the geometry defined in Figure 6.3 we may express Equation (6.1) in terms the illumination's slant (σ) and tilt (τ) angles and the surface's partial derivatives, to give:

$$i(x, y) = \frac{-\cos(\tau)\sin(\sigma)p(x, y) - \sin(\tau)\sin(\sigma)q(x, y) + \cos(\sigma)}{\sqrt{p^2(x, y) + q^2(x, y) + 1}} \tag{6.2}$$

where:

- $p(x, y)$ is the partial derivative of the surface height function in the x direction, and
- $q(x, y)$ is the partial derivative of the surface height function in the y direction.

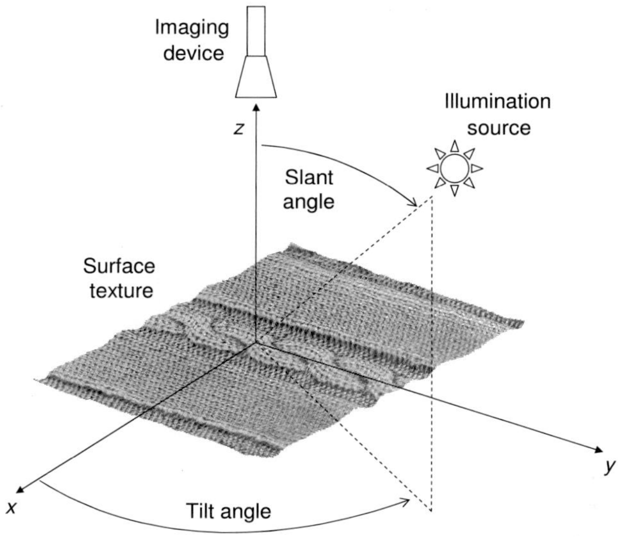

Fig. 6.3. Definition of illumination slant and tilt angles.

For p and $q \ll 1$ we can use a truncated Maclaurin series to linearise this equation:

$$i(x, y) = -\cos(\tau)\sin(\sigma)p(x, y) - \sin(\tau)\sin(\sigma)q(x, y) + \cos(\sigma)$$

Transforming the above into the frequency domain and discarding the mean term (which is not normally used in texture classification) we obtain:

$$\begin{aligned}\mathcal{I}(u, v) &= [-\cos(\tau)\sin(\sigma)\, i\, u - \sin(\tau)\sin(\sigma)\, i\, v]\mathcal{H}(u, v) \\ &= [-\cos(\tau)\sin(\sigma)\, i\,\omega\, \cos(\theta) - \sin(\tau)\sin(\sigma)\, i\,\omega\, \sin(\theta)]\mathcal{H}(u, v)\end{aligned} \tag{6.3}$$

where:

$\mathcal{I}(u, v)$	is the discrete Fourier transform (DFT) of $i(x, y)$;
$\mathcal{H}(u, v)$	is the DFT of the surface height function;
(u, v)	are Cartesian coordinates of the DFT basis functions, and
(ω, θ)	are the corresponding polar coordinates.

Combining the trigonometric functions produces a more concise form:

$$\mathcal{I}(u, v) = -i\,\omega\, \sin(\sigma)\cos(\theta - \tau)\mathcal{H}(u, v) \tag{6.4}$$

Equation 6.4 is essentially the **imaging model** developed by Kube and Pentland[17] generalised to surfaces of low slope angle and expressed using more intuitive trigonometric terms.

6.2.2. *Implications of the imaging model*

In the context of this chapter the most important features of Equation 6.4 are the $\cos(\theta - \tau)$ and $\sin(\sigma)$ factors.

The latter provides an overall scaling of image texture: increasing the slant angle to near grazing incidence increases the variance of the signal while reducing the mean component ($\cos(\sigma)$). The result is that the 'texture' in the image is emphasised and this corresponds to our normal experience of viewing a surface texture that has been illuminated from the side. On the other hand, reducing the slant angle so that the illumination is at the zenith of the surface (near the camera axis) has the opposite effect. The mean value is at a maximum and the variance of the image texture is reduced which has the effect of 'washing out' the image and making the texture difficult to discern. These slant induced effects can be alleviated to a certain extent by normalising the image to a given mean and variance and this is a common pre-processing step in texture analysis.

However, the $\cos(\theta - \tau)$ factor shows that imaging with side-lighting also acts as a directional filter as illustrated by Figure 6.4.

This figure shows two images of an *isotropic* surface texture; only the illumination's tilt angle (τ) has been changed between the two photographs. The associated polar-plots clearly show the directional filtering effect of side-lighting. The data shown in the left plot closely follow the predicted $|\cos(\theta - \tau)|$[a] function and reach a maximum at $\theta = 0°$. Similarly for the $\tau = 90°$ plot, except that this time the maximum directional response is at $\theta = \pm 90°$.

This directional effect cannot be removed by simple normalisation and if ignored can cause significant misclassification when the tilt angle is changed between training and classification sessions.[7] It is possible to perform compensating filtering to alleviate this phenomenon, but this tends to produce rather brittle classifiers.[20]

What is needed, therefore, is a more principled examination of the behaviour of common classification schemes and their texture features.

[a]Note that a $|\cos(\theta - \tau)|$ factor is used because the plots are of Fourier *magnitude*.

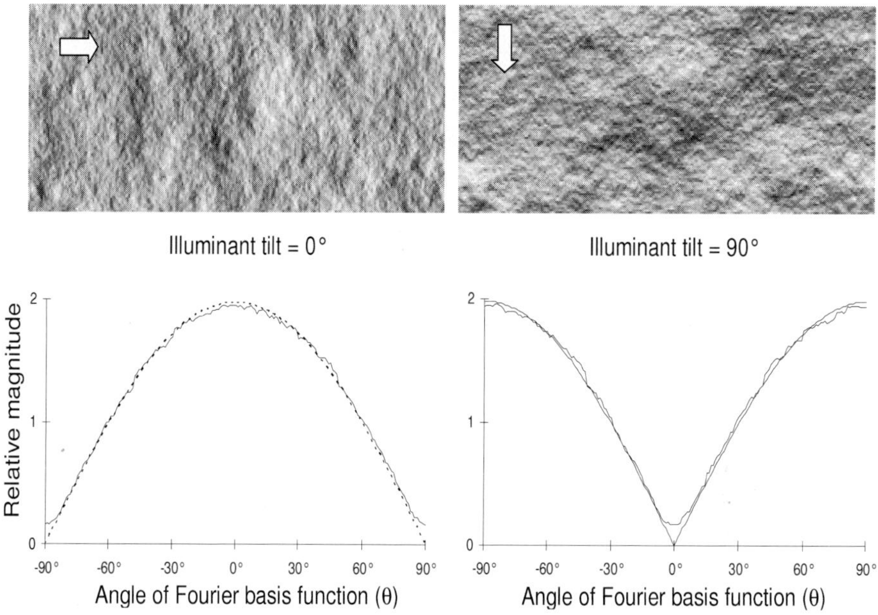

Fig. 6.4. The effect of varying illumination direction on the directionality of image texture. The images show an isotropic fractal surface imaged at $\tau = 0°$ and $\tau = 90°$. The graphs show the magnitude polar-plots of their Fourier transforms together with best fit $|\cos(\theta - \tau)|$ functions.

6.3. The Behaviour of Texture Filters to Changes in Illumination Direction

The preceding section provided a model (equation 6.4) of the *image acquisition* stage of the texture classification process as shown in Figure 6.1. This section extends that theory to the *feature generation* stage.

As previously discussed, there has been a vast amount of literature published over the last three decades on texture feature design and performance. Here we shall restrict our examination to one very common class of feature: that produced by linear filtering followed by variance estimation. These features include Laws masks, ring/wedge filters, Gabor filter banks, wavelets, quadrature mirror filters, eigenfilters, linear predictors, optimized finite impulse response filters, the *con* statistic of co-occurrence matrices and many more.[5]

The common structure of these features is the FRF (filter-rectify-filter) hypothesis of early processing in the human visual system (see Figure 6.5).

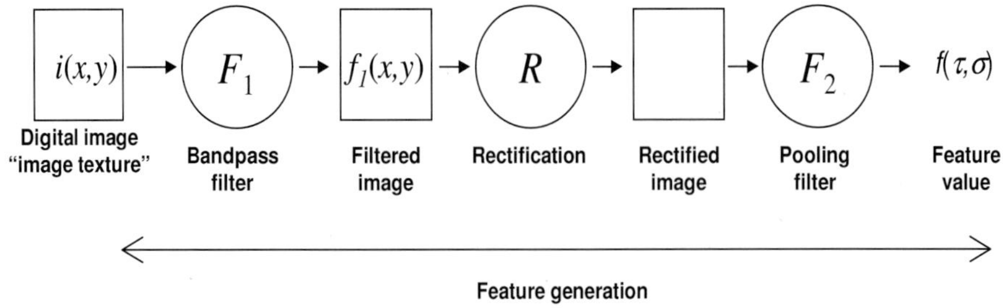

Fig. 6.5. The 'FRF' structure common to many texture features.

This is commonly known as the *back pocket model* in psychophysics, because 'it has become the default model that researchers in that field routinely "pull from their back pocket" to attempt to make sense of new texture segregation results'.[21] The first filter (F_1) is commonly thought of as a bandpass function (e.g. Gabor). There is however, one major difference between the common psychophysics and computer vision implementations of the second filter. In psychophysics, F_2 is often thought of as another (albeit of lower frequency) bandpass filter. In contrast, in computer vision, F_2 is more often implemented as a pooling (or averaging) filter, and when this is coupled with an R stage, that is a *square* function, the result is effectively a local variance estimator (assuming a zero mean F_1).

6.3.1. *A model of texture feature behaviour*

For simplicity we shall assume that we are performing image-wide classification (i.e. we expect the query and training images to be stationary and contain texture of a single class) and that we are aggregating the content of each feature image to provide one scalar value per image, per feature. Furthermore, we shall assume that the R stage of the feature is a simple *squaring* function.

Exploiting Parseval's theorem, the output of each feature may, therefore, be represented by:

$$f(\tau,\sigma) = \sum_{x,y} (f_1(x,y))^2 = \frac{1}{NM} \sum_{u,v} |\mathcal{F}_1(u,v)\mathcal{I}(u,v)|^2 \qquad (6.5)$$

where:

$f(\tau,\sigma)$ is the feature value (dependent on the illumination conditions);
$f_1(x,y)$ is the output of the first filter;

$\mathcal{F}_1(u,v)$ is the transfer function of the first linear filter stage F_1, and
$N \times M$ is the size of the DFT $\mathcal{I}(u,v)$.

Substituting in the linear imaging model (Equation 6.4) gives:

$$f(\tau,\sigma) = \frac{1}{NM}\sum_{u,v} |\mathcal{F}_1(u,v)|^2 \omega^2 \sin^2(\sigma)\cos^2(\theta-\tau) H(u,v) \tag{6.6}$$

where:

$H(u,v) = |\mathcal{H}(u,v)|^2$ is the power spectrum of the surface height function.

Using $\cos^2(x) = (1+\cos(2x))/2$ and $\cos(x-y) = \cos(x)\cos(y)+\sin(x)\sin(y)$ gives:

$$\begin{aligned} f(\tau,\sigma) = \frac{1}{2NM}\sum_{u,v} &|\mathcal{F}_1(u,v)|^2 \omega^2 \sin^2(\sigma)[1+\cos(2\theta)\cos(2\tau) \\ &+ \sin(2\theta)\sin(2\tau)]H(u,v) \end{aligned} \tag{6.7}$$

Hence:

$$f(\tau,\sigma) = \sin^2(\sigma)(a + b\cos(2\tau) + c\sin(2\tau)) \tag{6.8}$$

and:

$$f(\tau,\sigma) = \sin^2(\sigma)(a + d\cos(2\tau + \phi)) \tag{6.9}$$

Equation 6.9 is our **simple feature model**. It describes how a feature behaves under changes in illuminant tilt and slant. Parameters a, b, c and d are all constant with respect to the illumination conditions (i.e. none is a function of either τ or σ) and these are specified below:

$$a = \frac{1}{2NM}\sum_{u,v} |\mathcal{F}_1(u,v)|^2 \omega^2 H(u,v)$$

$$b = \frac{1}{2NM}\sum_{u,v} |\mathcal{F}_1(u,v)|^2 \omega^2 H(u,v)\cos(2\theta)$$

$$c = \frac{1}{2NM}\sum_{u,v} |\mathcal{F}_1(u,v)|^2 \omega^2 H(u,v)\sin(2\theta)$$

$$d \equiv \sqrt{b^2+c^2}, \qquad \sin(\phi) \equiv \frac{c}{d}, \qquad \cos(\phi) \equiv \frac{b}{d}$$

Thus, the feature model (Equation 6.9) predicts that the output of a texture feature based on a linear filter is proportional to $\sin^2(\sigma)$ and is also a sinusoidal function of illuminant tilt[b] with a period π radians (that is it has two periods, and therefore two maxima, for every complete revolution of the light source about the camera axis).

6.3.2. *Assessing the feature model's tilt angle prediction*

The most important implication of the feature model for texture classification is its tilt response:

$$tilt(\tau) = (a + d\cos(2\tau + \phi)) \tag{6.10}$$

as the slant response ($\sin^2(\sigma)$) may in principle be removed using image normalisation (as discussed in Section 6.2.2).

We investigated the tilt characteristics of eight features using thirty real surface textures. Many 512×512 eight-bit monochrome images were obtained from thirty surfaces using illuminant tilt angles between $0°$ and $180°$, incremented in either $10°$ or $15°$ steps. The slant angle used for these images was $45°$. In addition, six of the surfaces were also captured as above but using a $60°$ slant. Sample images of this dataset are available in Chantler et al.[22] These were processed with eight different texture features (Laws and Gabor). The resulting 324 tilt responses were each assessed to see how closely they followed a sinusoidal function of 2τ. The deviation from the best fit solutions were measured using their mean squared error.

6.3.2.1. *Texture features — details*

While the R and F_2 stages of all features were identical (squaring and pooling over the whole image) the F_1 stage differed. Six Gabor filters[23] were used because of their popularity in the literature. We use the notation $typeF\Omega A\Theta$ to denote the F_1 stage of a Gabor with a centre frequency of Ω cycles per image-width, a direction of Θ degrees, and of *type* complex or real. Five complex Gabor filters (comF25A0, comF25A45, comF25A90, comF25A135, comF50A45) alongside one real Gabor filter (realF25A45) were used.

We also used two Laws filters[24] due to their simplicity, effectiveness, and the fact that they were one of the first sets of filters to be used for texture classification. Laws investigated the performance of a number of filters, all

[b]In the case that both the surface and the filter are isotropic, the response will degenerate to a sinusoid of zero amplitude. That is, the filter output will be independent of τ.

derived in the first instance from three simple one-dimensional FIR filters:

$L3 = (1, 2, 1) \implies$ "level detection"
$E3 = (-1, 0, 1) \implies$ "edge detection"
$S3 = (-1, 2, -1) \implies$ "spot detection"

He obtained 5×5 and larger filters by convolving and transposing these 1×3 masks. The two we used were $E5L5$ and $L5E5$:

$$E5L5 = E5^T * L5 = (E3*E3)^T * (L3*L3) = \begin{bmatrix} -1 & -4 & -6 & -4 & -1 \\ -2 & -8 & -12 & -8 & -2 \\ 0 & 0 & 0 & 0 & 0 \\ 2 & 8 & 12 & 8 & 2 \\ 1 & 4 & 6 & 4 & 1 \end{bmatrix}$$

The $L5E5$ mask is simply the transpose of $E5L5$. These provided the F_1 stages of the two features. The R and F_2 stages were as described above.

6.3.2.2. *Results of tilt-response investigation*

Figure 6.6 shows the histogram of the mean square error values alongside the median, upper and lower quartile values. In order to provide an insight into what these error values mean, we selected twelve sample plots for display: the four closest to the median error value, the four closest to the

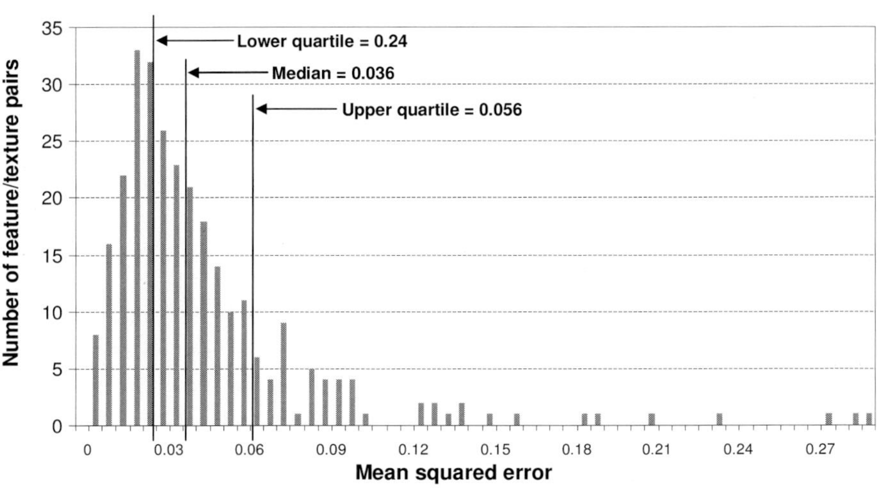

Fig. 6.6. Histogram of mean squared error of the fit of sinusoidal functions to feature data (see figures 6.7 and 6.8).

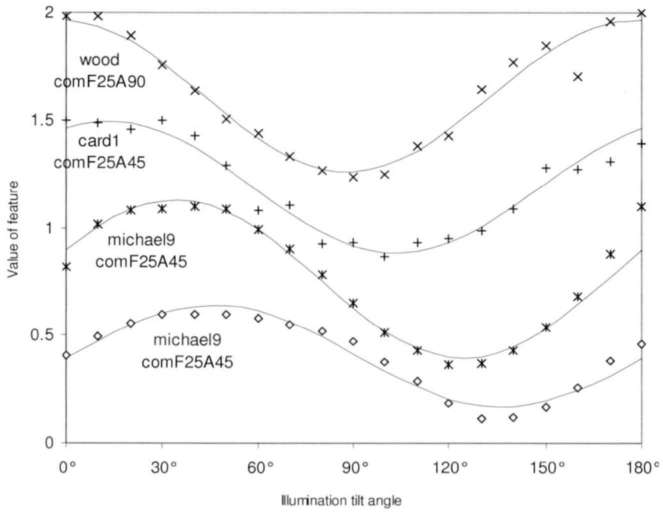

Fig. 6.7. Four datasets with error metrics closest to the **median error** of 0.036. Each plot shows how one output of one feature varies when it is repeatedly applied to the same physical texture sample, but under different illuminant tilt angles (τ). For instance, the top plot shows the results of applying feature comF25A90 to texture *wood* for 19 illumination conditions. Discrete points indicate measured output and the curves show the best-fit sinusoids of period 2τ.

lower quartile error value and the four closest to the upper quartile. These are shown in Figures 6.7 and 6.8.

What is evident from these results is that even filter/texture combinations with 'poor' error metrics follow the sinusoidal behaviour quite closely. This is all the more surprising considering how many of our textures significantly violate the 'no shadow' and 'low slope angle' assumptions.[25]

6.4. Model Generalisation

The analysis performed in the previous section is done in the frequency domain and so it cannot distinguish between changes due to changes in illumination direction and changes caused by variable surface albedo. That is why the asumption of uniform albedo was necessary. By working directly in the spatial domain, however, we may do without such a restrictive assumption. In addition, the model used in the previous section was linearised under the assumption of small values of p and q. In this section we relax both these assumptions.

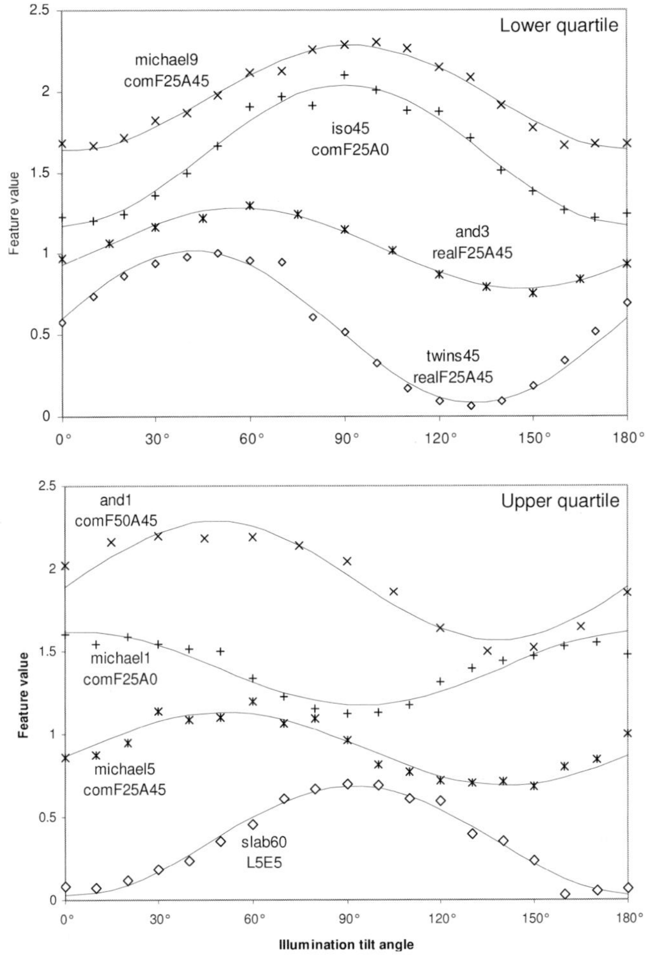

Fig. 6.8. The eight datasets closest to the upper and lower quartiles.

Further, in this section, instead of using the surface height function, we describe a surface in terms of generalised normals which incorporate both derivatives of surface height and surface albedo, and we consider the behaviour of linear filtering features in the spatial domain instead of in the frequency domain. This allows us to relax restrictions of the previous methods: the proposed model accommodates for rougher surfaces as well as albedo variations. We show that the tilt response may be described as a mixture of single and double argument sine waves, and that the form of the illumination tilt response for any linear filter may be predicted from a set of cross-correlation matrices of surface normals (up to a positive correction term which appears due to image errors and artifacts such as shadows and highlights). More details can be found in Refs. 26 and 27.

We assume that the surface is parallel to the image plane, so its global normal is collinear with z. We assume that a Lambertian 3D textured surface may be represented by a set of small flat patches, each patch corresponding to an image pixel. We characterise the mth patch by a *generalised normal*, which is a vector $\mathbf{N}_m \equiv \rho_m \mathbf{n}_m$, where ρ_m is the Lambertian albedo of the patch, and $\mathbf{n}_m$ is its normal. Such a description allows us to use albedo and surface patch orientation simultaneously.

We illuminate the surface in turn by Q illumination sources with illumination vectors $\mathbf{L}^q = \lambda^q \mathbf{l}^q$, where $\mathbf{l}^q$ is the direction and λ^q is the intensity of the qth light source, $q = 1, \ldots, Q$. The image intensity at the mth pixel of the surface under the qth illuminant, therefore, is given by

$$I_m^q = \lambda^q \, \rho_m (\mathbf{l}^q)^T \mathbf{n}_m = (\mathbf{L}^q)^T \mathbf{N}_m \tag{6.11}$$

We stack all Q photometric equations corresponding to the same position within the image to obtain a linear system of equations

$$\mathbf{I}_m = L\mathbf{N}_m \tag{6.12}$$

where L is the illumination matrix: $L = (\mathbf{L}^1, \ldots, \mathbf{L}^Q)^T$. This system has a straightforward solution provided there are at least 3 linearly independent illuminants in the configuration:

$$\mathbf{N}_m = [L]^{-1}\mathbf{I}_m$$

where $[L]^{-1} = (L^T L)^{-1} L^T$ is the left inverse of L. If $Q = 3$, the left inverse becomes the inverse of L.

In what follows we assume that all the normals of the training surfaces are calculated from a photometric set. This means that we have at our disposal a vector field, from which various statistical parameters may be derived. In this section, like in the previous one, we consider second-order statistics calculated from the joint distribution of particular neighbours of the field of normals.

We consider the response of a linear filter applied to an image as a random variable r, instantiated by the responses at different positions within the image. The energy estimation of the filtered image in the frequency domain corresponds to the variance estimation of r in the spatial domain as well (Parseval's theorem). The random variable r is in fact a linear combination of a collection of M random variables which constitute a neighbourhood in an image, defined by the filter's support. Consider a particular filter mask. We enumerate its elements to get a vector $\mathbf{F} : M \times 1$, and also enumerate the pixels within the neighbourhood in the same way to obtain an intensity vector $\mathbf{I}$. The filter response of this neighbourhood to the filter is:

$$r = \mathbf{F}^T\mathbf{I} \tag{6.13}$$

Particular image neighbourhoods instantiate random vector $\mathbf{I}$, whereas their filter responses instantiate random variable r.

We define a texture feature f as the variance of random variable r calculated across the image:

$$f \equiv \sigma_r^2 = \mathcal{E}\{(r - \mathcal{E}\{r\})^2\} \tag{6.14}$$

Let us consider the part of the surface itself, which corresponds to a neighbourhood of the image. We enumerate the surface patches which it comprises in the same way as the corresponding pixel values of the image neighbourhood. The generalised normals of these patches make up a matrix $N \equiv (\mathbf{N}_1, \mathbf{N}_2, \ldots, \mathbf{N}_M)$ so that for some deterministic illumination vector $\mathbf{L}$, we calculate the image pixel values as:

$$\mathbf{I} = N^T\mathbf{L} \tag{6.15}$$

Again, the $3 \times M$ matrix N may be thought of as a random matrix, which is instantiated by particular areas of the surface in question. Then the random filter response r may be expressed in terms of the extended surface normals N of the neighbourhood

$$r = \mathbf{F}^T N^T \mathbf{L} \tag{6.16}$$

where both $\mathbf{F}$ and $\mathbf{L}$ are deterministic, and N is random.

To find how texture feature $f \equiv \sigma_r^2$ depends on the illumination, let us consider a *surface response vector* $\mathbf{R} \equiv N\mathbf{F}$ so that:

$$r = \mathbf{R}^T\mathbf{L} \tag{6.17}$$

It is easy to show that the variance of the linear combination may be expressed in terms of the coefficients and the covariance matrix of the comprising variables. For a linear combination $y = \mathbf{A}^T\mathbf{X}$ of random variables $\mathbf{X} = (x_1, \ldots, x_n)^T$ the variance of y may be expressed as

$$\sigma_y^2 = \mathbf{A}^T\Sigma_X\mathbf{A} \tag{6.18}$$

where Σ_X is the covariance matrix of $\mathbf{X}$. Then we immediately obtain from (6.18) and (6.17)

$$f = \mathbf{L}^T \Phi \mathbf{L} \tag{6.19}$$

where Φ is the covariance matrix of $\mathbf{R}$. Covariance matrix Φ is deterministic since we have already applied averaging. It represents the statistical properties of the surface response to a particular filter. Each combination of filter and surface type define their own matrix. Furthermore, each component f_k of feature vector $\mathbf{D}$, calculated for some bank of K filters $\{\mathbf{F}_k\}$ of size M, has the above form, and $\mathbf{D}$ may be computed from the known illumination and a set of matrices Φ_k.

The above analysis amounts to exchanging the order of the linear operations of filtering and rendering. Each component of random vector $\mathbf{R}$ is the filter response of one of the components of the generalised normal (imagine each component as an image so that the generalised normal field is a stack of three such images). Instead of rendering an image from a normal field and then filtering it, we filter the normal field and apply the rendering operation to the resulting vector. Note, however, that rendering is a linear operation only for Lambertian surfaces in the absence of shadows: both highlights and shadows disturb the linearity.

6.4.1. *Matrix Φ and surface normals correlation*

Let us now turn our attention to the structure of matrix Φ. The ij-th element of matrix Φ is the covariance of surface response components R_i and R_j. Consider, for example, the ith component R_i. It is a linear combination of random variables N_{im}, $m = 1, \ldots, M$, where N_{im} is the ith component of the generalised normal at the mth position within the neighbourhood. All generalised normals are drawn from the same distribution and have the same mean. Let us denote the mean generalised normal by $\bar{\mathbf{N}}$. To simplify the calculation, we introduce an unbiased set of normals $\hat{\mathbf{N}}_m \equiv \mathbf{N}_m - \bar{\mathbf{N}}$. Let us also consider a matrix S_{ij} such that its mn-th element is the covariance between the ith component of the normal at the mth position within the neighbourhood and the jth component at the nth position:

$$\begin{aligned} S_{ij}[mn] = \text{cov}\{N_{im}, N_{jn}\} &= \mathcal{E}\left\{(N_{im} - \bar{N}_i)(N_{jn} - \bar{N}_j)\right\} \\ &= \mathcal{E}\left\{\hat{N}_{im}\hat{N}_{jn}\right\} \end{aligned} \tag{6.20}$$

The ij-th element of Φ is by definition:

$$\begin{aligned}\phi_{ij} &\equiv \mathcal{E}\left\{(R_i - \bar{R}_i)(R_j - \bar{R}_j)\right\} \\ &= \mathcal{E}\left\{\sum_{m=1}^{M} F_m \hat{N}_{im} \sum_{n=1}^{M} F_n \hat{N}_{jn}\right\} = \sum_{m=1}^{M}\sum_{n=1}^{M} F_m F_n \mathcal{E}\left\{\hat{N}_{im}\hat{N}_{jn}\right\} = \mathbf{F}^T S_{ij} \mathbf{F}\end{aligned} \tag{6.21}$$

Note that while matrices S_{ij} are not necessarily symmetric, the following is true: $S_{ij} = S_{ji}^T$. Therefore we need only six matrices instead of nine to cover all possible combinations of i and j.

Equation 6.21 separates the statistical properties of the surface from the filter. The six $M \times M$ matrices S_{ij} fully capture the behaviour of a texture feature for any linear filter defined by a vector of size M. These matrices may be used for surface characterisation.

6.5. Texture Features under Changing Illumination Direction

Equation 6.19 describes how texture features respond to the changing illumination direction and intensity.

Let us represent the illumination vector as a function of illumination intensity λ, slant angle σ, and tilt angle τ:

$$\mathbf{L} = \lambda\left(\cos\tau\cos\sigma, \sin\tau\cos\sigma, \sin\sigma\right)^T$$

Then we may express the texture feature f as a function of λ, σ, and τ:

$$\begin{aligned}f(\lambda,\sigma,\tau) &= \lambda^2\left[\phi_{11}\cos^2\tau\cos^2\sigma + \phi_{22}\sin^2\tau\cos^2\sigma + \phi_{33}\sin^2\sigma\right. \\ &\quad + 2\phi_{12}\cos\tau\sin\tau\cos^2\sigma + 2\phi_{13}\cos\tau\cos\sigma\sin\sigma \\ &\quad \left.+ 2\phi_{23}\sin\tau\cos\sigma\sin\sigma\right] \\ &= \lambda^2\left[\cos^2\sigma(\phi_{11}\cos^2\tau + 2\phi_{12}\cos\tau\sin\tau + \phi_{22}\sin^2\tau)\right. \\ &\quad \left.+ 2\cos\sigma\sin\sigma(\phi_{13}\cos\tau + \phi_{23}\sin\tau) + \phi_{33}\sin^2\sigma\right]\end{aligned} \tag{6.22}$$

From the above it is obvious that the dependence of texture features on the intensity of the illumination is a scaling factor of the intensity squared.

Dependence on the tilt angle of the illumination From (6.22) we deduce that:

$$\begin{aligned}f(\lambda,\sigma,\tau) &= A_\tau\cos^2\tau + B_\tau\cos\tau\sin\tau + C_\tau\sin^2\tau + D_\tau\cos\tau + E_\tau\sin\tau + F_\tau \\ &= \mathcal{A}_\tau\sin(2\tau+\alpha) + \mathcal{B}_\tau\sin(\tau+\beta) + \mathcal{C}_\tau\end{aligned} \tag{6.23}$$

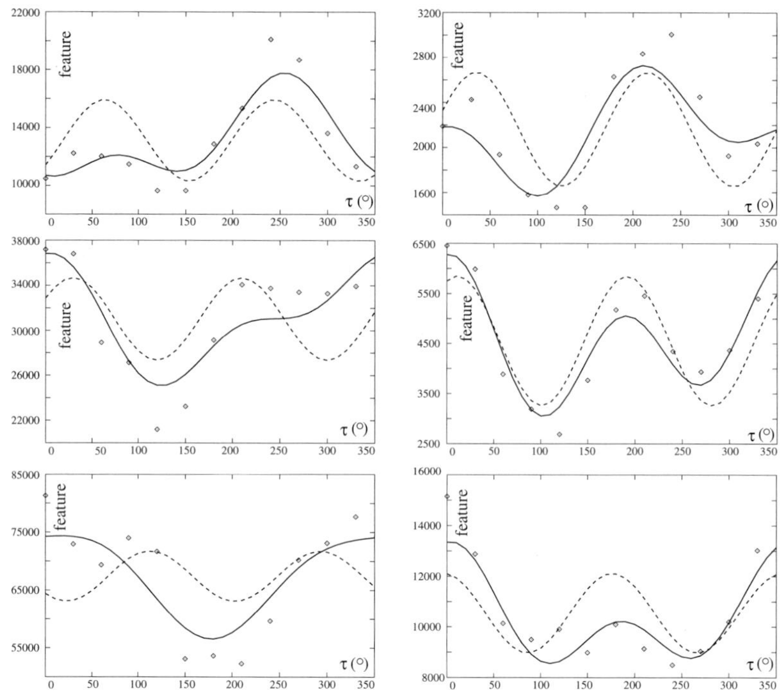

Fig. 6.9. Texture features as functions of tilt for surfaces *aab*, *aam* and *aas*, of the Photex database,[28] from top to bottom, and Laws filters E5E5 and E5S5, from left to right, respectively. Solid line: behaviour predicted by the generalised model; dashed line: behaviour predicted by the simple model; points: experimental data.

where coefficients $\mathcal{A}_\tau$, $\mathcal{B}_\tau$ and $\mathcal{C}_\tau$ are all functions of σ and λ:

$$\mathcal{A}_\tau(\sigma, \lambda, \Phi) = \lambda^2 \cos^2 \sigma \sqrt{\phi_{12}^2 + \left(\frac{\phi_{11} - \phi_{12}}{2}\right)^2} \tag{6.24}$$

$$\mathcal{B}_\tau(\sigma, \lambda, \Phi) = \lambda^2 \; 2 \cos\sigma \sin\sigma \sqrt{\phi_{13}^2 + \phi_{23}^2} \tag{6.25}$$

$$\mathcal{C}_\tau(\sigma, \lambda, \Phi) = \lambda^2 \left[\cos^2 \sigma \frac{\phi_{11} - \phi_{22}}{2} + \sin^2 \sigma \phi_{33}\right] \tag{6.26}$$

$$\alpha(\Phi) = \arctan \frac{\phi_{11} - \phi_{22}}{2\phi_{12}} \tag{6.27}$$

$$\beta(\Phi) = \arctan \frac{\phi_{13}}{\phi_{23}} \tag{6.28}$$

In other words, the texture features depend on tilt through a linear combination of sines of single and double arguments.

In the general case the form of such a function is rather complex, and very much depends on the particular form of matrix Φ as well as on the slant angle of the illumination. To illustrate the variety of these functions, Fig. 6.9 shows the tilt response of three surfaces to Laws' filters E5E5 and E5S5 with $\sigma = 45°$.

Dependence on the slant angle of the illumination In a similar way it is easy to see that the textural features depend on the slant angle of the illumination as a sine of a double argument:

$$\begin{aligned} f(\lambda, \sigma, \tau) &= A_\sigma \cos^2 \sigma + B_\sigma \cos \sigma \sin \sigma + C_\sigma \sin^2 \sigma \\ &= \mathcal{A}_\sigma \sin(2\sigma + \gamma) + \mathcal{B}_\sigma \end{aligned} \tag{6.29}$$

where coefficients $\mathcal{A}_\sigma$ and $\mathcal{B}_\sigma$, are functions of τ and λ, and the phase γ is a function of τ:

$$\mathcal{A}_\sigma(\tau, \lambda, \Phi) = \lambda^2 \sqrt{y^2 + \left(\frac{x - \phi_{33}}{2}\right)^2} \tag{6.30}$$

$$\mathcal{B}_\sigma(\tau, \lambda, \Phi) = \lambda^2 \frac{x + \phi_{33}}{2} \tag{6.31}$$

$$\gamma(\tau, \Phi) = \arctan \frac{x - \phi_{33}}{y} \tag{6.32}$$

where

$$x(\tau, \Phi) \equiv \phi_{11} \cos^2 \tau + 2\phi_{12} \cos \tau \sin \tau + \phi_{22} \sin^2 \tau \tag{6.33}$$

$$y(\tau, \Phi) \equiv \phi_{13} \cos \tau + \phi_{23} \sin \tau \tag{6.34}$$

6.5.1. *The simple model as a special case of the generalised model*

In this section we show that under the assumptions of Section 6.2.1, the generalised model given by Equation 6.22 reduces to the simple model of Section 6.3, given by Equation 6.9.

The frequency domain approach in Section 6.3 describes the surface as a height function $H(x, y)$, thus the 3D textures with albedo variation have to be excluded. Without loss of generality, we assume the albedo to be

1 across the surface. Then the local surface normals can be expressed in terms of the partial derivatives of the height function

$$\mathbf{N} \equiv \mathbf{n} = \frac{(-p, -q, 1)^T}{\sqrt{p^2 + q^2 + 1}} \tag{6.35}$$

where $p \equiv \frac{\partial}{\partial x} H(x, y)$, and $q \equiv \frac{\partial}{\partial y} H(x, y)$.

In order to linearise (6.35), we assume that $|p|, |q| \ll 1$. This means that the vertical component of the surface normal is assumed fixed, and the (random) normal in the mth position within the neighbourhood is $\mathbf{N}_m \approx (-p_m, -q_m, 1)$.

Let us consider the mn-th element of the description matrix S_{13}:

$$S_{13}[mn] = cov\{N_{1m}, N_{3n}\} = cov\{-p_m, 1\} = 0, \tag{6.36}$$

since the covariance between a random variable and a constant is 0. Therefore, matrix S_{13} consists entirely of zeros. Similarly, it can be shown that matrices S_{23} and S_{33} also consist of zeros.

Then for any filter $\mathbf{F}$ the corresponding elements of matrix Φ will also be zeros:

$$\phi_{ij} = \mathbf{F}^T S_{ij} \mathbf{F} = 0 \qquad \text{for } \{ij\} = \{13\}, \{23\}, \{33\}$$

Therefore, the surface response matrix Φ has the form:

$$\Phi = \begin{bmatrix} \phi_{11} & \phi_{12} & 0 \\ \phi_{12} & \phi_{22} & 0 \\ 0 & 0 & 0 \end{bmatrix} \tag{6.37}$$

In this case, the contribution from the sine and cosine terms of a single argument in 6.23 disappears, and we are left with the sine term of double tilt angle as predicted by Equation 6.9.

6.6. Classifying Textures while Estimating Illumination Conditions

This section exploits the simple feature model (Equation 6.9) to develop a texture classifier that is not only robust to illumination variation but that can also provide an estimate of the lighting conditions under which the query texture was captured. For application of the general model (Equation 6.22) to texture classification and illumination direction detection, the reader is referred to Ref. 27.

Most texture classifiers use more than one feature measure and these multiple feature measures are normally collected together into a single feature vector:

$$\mathbf{f} = [f_1, f_2, f_3 \ldots, f_i]^T \tag{6.38}$$

So, before describing the classification system itself, we shall first investigate the behaviour of multidimensional feature vectors to changes in illumination direction in order to give some insight into the necessary form of the decision rules.

6.6.1. *Behaviour in a multi-dimensional feature space as a function of illumination direction*

For illustrative purposes we consider the behavior of a 2D feature vector as a function of tilt(τ) and slant(σ).

$$\mathbf{f} = [f_1, f_2]^T \tag{6.39}$$

If the feature vector is derived from a set of images of one texture class captured under a variety of illumination vectors, the results can be plotted in a two-dimensional (f_1, f_2) feature space. Applying the simple feature model (Equation 6.9) to each dimension, we obtain:

$$f_1(\tau, \sigma) = \sin^2(\sigma)(a_1 + d_1 \cos(2\tau + \phi_1))$$

$$f_2(\tau, \sigma) = \sin^2(\sigma)(a_2 + d_2 \cos(2\tau + \phi_2))$$

Changes of the illuminant slant (σ), therefore, simply scale the 2D scatter plot. However, variation of tilt causes a more complex behaviour. Since the frequency of the two cosines is the same, the two equations provide two simple harmonic motion components. Therefore, the trajectory in (f_1, f_2) space as a function of tilt is in general an ellipse.

There are two special cases. If the surface is isotropic and the two filters are identical except for a difference in direction of 90°, the mean values and the oscillation amplitudes of the two features are the same and the phase difference becomes 180°. Thus, the scatter plot for an isotropic texture and two identical but orthogonal filters is a straight line.

If the surface is isotropic and the two filters are identical except for a difference in direction of 45°, the mean values and the oscillation amplitudes of the two features are again the same but the phase difference is now 90°. In this case the scatter plot is a circle.

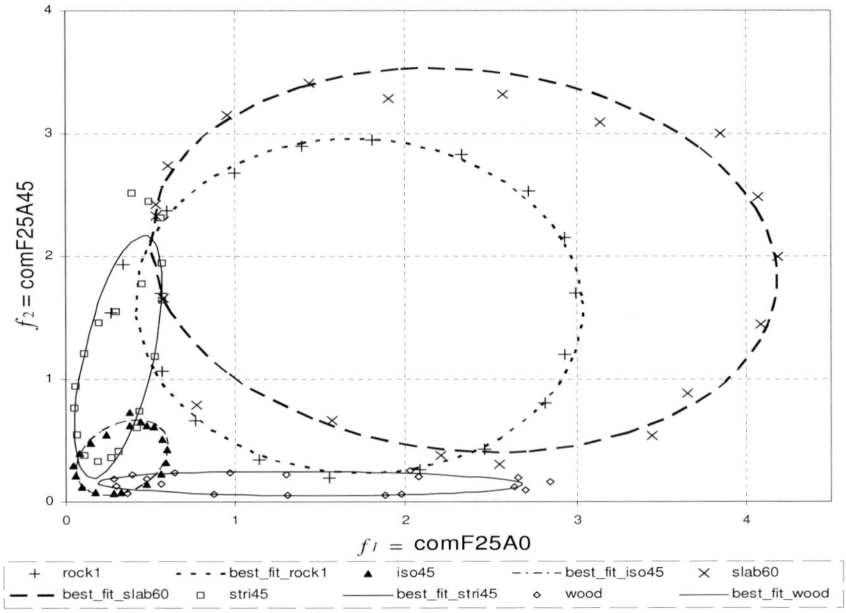

Fig. 6.10. The behaviour of five textures in the comF25A0/comF25A45 feature space alongside their best fitted ellipses. Changing tilt causes a texture class's feature vector $\mathbf{f} = (f_1, f_2)$ to move round the corresponding ellipse. Changing slant causes an overall scaling of the graph. Each ellipse corresponds to a single texture. Each point corresponds to a different value of illuminant tilt. All points on the same ellipse correspond to the same surface.

The line and the circle are the two special cases of all possible curves. In the general case of two or more filters, the result is an ellipse or a trajectory on a super-ellipse.

Figure 6.10 shows the behaviour of two Gabor filters as a function of illuminant tilt, for five real textures. It clearly shows the elliptical behaviour of the cluster means.

6.6.2. *A probabilistic model of feature behaviour*

In practice, a feature vector's actual behaviour ($\mathbf{f}(\tau, \sigma)$) will differ from the ideal predicted by the simple feature model (as shown in Figure 6.10) for a variety of reasons, the majority being associated with violation of the model's assumptions such as that caused by self-shadowing. We collectively model all of these discrepancies as a zero mean, Gausian distribution with standard deviation s.

We can now express the relationship between the feature and lighting direction for a given texture class k in probabilistic terms:

$$p_k(f_i|\tau,\sigma) = \frac{1}{s_i\sqrt{2\pi}}\exp\left[-\frac{[f_i - \sin^2(\sigma)(a_i + b_i\cos(2\tau) + c_i\sin(2\tau))]^2}{2s_i^2}\right] \tag{6.40}$$

where $p_k(f_i|\tau,\sigma)$ is the probability of the event of feature i having value f_i occurring, given that the texture k is lit from (τ,σ).

The feature vector, $\mathbf{f}$, is composed of i features. Assuming these are independent, the joint probability density function is:

$$P_k(\mathbf{f}|\tau,\sigma) = \prod_i \frac{1}{s_i\sqrt{2\pi}}\exp\left[-\frac{[f_i - \sin^2(\sigma)(a_i + b_i\cos(2\tau) + c_i\sin(2\tau))]^2}{2s_i^2}\right] \tag{6.41}$$

Thus, our probabilistic model of the behaviour of an i-dimensional feature vector $\mathbf{f}$ requires the estimation of $4i$ parameters (i.e. i sets of a_i, b_i, c_i and s_i) for each of K texture training classes.

6.6.3. *Classification*

From the 2D scatter diagram (Figure 6.10) it is obvious that linear and higher order classifiers are likely to experience difficulty in dealing with this classification problem. We have, therefore, chosen to exploit the hyper-elliptical model of feature behaviour described above.

The easiest way of understanding the classifier is to consider the 2D case (Figure 6.10). In this system a query texture's feature vector ($\mathbf{f}_q$) is represented as a single point on the scatter diagram. The classification task, therefore, becomes one of finding the point on each class ellipse which is closest (in the probabilistic sense) to $\mathbf{f}_q$. The distances to these points, weighted by class variances, provide class likelihoods. The query texture is assigned to the class with the largest likelihood over all lighting conditions (τ,σ).

The classifier is trained by estimating K elliptical probabilistic models (Equation 6.41) i.e. one for each texture class. Each texture class must be imaged under at least four (preferably more) different illumination directions and features calculated from these images. In this work, we use twelve images at two slant angles to estimate the parameter values of the model.[c]

When presented with a feature vector $\mathbf{f}_q$ from a query image, the classifier uses these (K) models to identify the most likely lighting direction and texture class.

The probability that a query texture having feature vector $\mathbf{f}_q$ has been illuminated from (τ, σ) and is of class k can be related to Equation 6.41 using Bayes' theorem:

$$P_k(\tau, \sigma|\mathbf{f}_q) = \frac{P_k(\mathbf{f}_q|\tau, \sigma)P_k(\tau, \sigma)}{P_k(\mathbf{f}_q)} \tag{6.42}$$

Now, assuming all lighting directions are, *a priori*, equally likely, $P(\tau, \sigma)$ is constant and because we are only interested in the *relative* probabilities of the values of σ and τ at a given $\mathbf{f}_q$, we may replace $P_k(\mathbf{f}_q)$ with a constant, i.e.

$$P_k(\tau, \sigma|\mathbf{f}_q) = \alpha P_k(\mathbf{f}_q|\tau, \sigma) \tag{6.43}$$

The most likely direction of the light source, $\hat{\tau_k}$, $\hat{\sigma_k}$ for each texture class k is estimated by *maximising* the likelihood function of that texture.

$$(\hat{\tau_k}, \hat{\sigma_k}) = \arg\max_{(\tau,\sigma)} P_k(\mathbf{f}_q|\tau, \sigma) \tag{6.44}$$

To find the maximum we take logarithms:

$$\ln P_k(\mathbf{f}_q|\tau, \sigma) = \ln \prod_i \left(\frac{1}{s_i\sqrt{2\pi}} \right) + \sum_i \frac{[f_i + \sin^2(\sigma)(a_i + b_i \cos(2\tau) + c_i \sin(2\tau))]^2}{2s_i^2} \tag{6.45}$$

Then we work out the partial derivatives with respect to τ and σ and equate both to zero. The trigonometric terms are simplified by substituting $x = \sin^2(\sigma)$ and $y = \cos(2\tau)$ and the two resulting equations are solved to provide a 12th order polynomial in x. This is straight forward but results in a long series of expressions that are not provided here (a full treatment

[c]Note that it is not necessary for the training images representing a class to come from the same *surface instantiation* i.e. they may be from different parts of the same surface type, but the *relative* illumination vectors must be known.

may be obtained from Ref. 25). The resulting multiple solutions are tested to obtain the values of $\hat{\tau_k}$ and $\hat{\sigma_k}$ that maximise 6.45 for each candidate class (k).

We now have a series of K competing hypotheses about the class of the sample and the direction it was lit from. Again, we are interested only in relative probabilities. If we assume the classes are, initially, equally likely, the most likely class may be identified by finding the highest class probability, i.e. by evaluating:

$$\hat{k} = \arg\max_k P_k(\mathbf{f}_q|\hat{\tau_k}, \hat{\sigma_k}) \tag{6.46}$$

6.6.4. *Summary of classification process*

Training

Obtain images: Capture multiple images of each of the K surface texture classes under a variety of (recorded) illumination directions. Note that these images do not need to be spatially registered with one another.

Calculate feature vectors: Apply the i feature generators to produce an i-dimensional feature vector $\mathbf{f}$ for each image.

Estimate the class models: Use these feature vectors $\mathbf{f}$ (and their associated illumination directions) to estimate the $4i$ (a_i, b_i, c_i, s_i) parameters for each of the K texture class models.

Classification

Calculate query feature vector: Calculate $\mathbf{f}_q = [f_1, f_2....f_i]$ from the query image (note that the illumination directions do not have to be known).

Calculate the maximum likelihoods: Use the optimisation procedure described above and the feature vector $\mathbf{f}_q$, to find the illumination directions $(\hat{\tau_k}, \hat{\sigma_k})$ that maximise the loglikelihood (Equation 6.45) for each of the K candidate texture classes.

Classify: Assign the unknown texture to class $\hat{k}$ with the largest of the log-likelihoods P_k found in the previous step.

Output: The selected texture class $\hat{k}$ together with the estimate of the illumination angles for that class $(\hat{\tau_k}, \hat{\sigma_k})$ are returned as the classifier's output. The value of the corresponding probability $P_{\hat{k}}(\mathbf{f}_q|\hat{\tau_k}, \hat{\sigma_k})$ can be returned as the confidence in the classification result.

6.6.5. *Experiments*

For evaluation we used $K = 25$ surface textures. A set of 12-bit 512×512 monochrome images of each sample was captured at slant angles (σ) of 45° and 60° and tilt angles (τ) of 30° increments. Half were used for training and half kept for testing.

A set of 12 Gabor filters provided the feature sets. These filters were combined into *banks* as shown in the table below.

Table 6.1. Tilt and slant experiment: Gabor filter bank configurations.

filter	Gabor filter bank						
	12	10	8	6	4	3	2
comF20A0	X	X	X	X	X	X	X
comF20A45	X	X	X				
comF20A90	X	X	X	X	X	X	X
comF20A135	X	X	X				
comF30A0	X						
comF30A45	X	X	X	X	X	X	
comF30A90	X						
comF30A135	X	X	X	X	X		
comF40A0	X	X	X	X			
comF40A45	X	X					
comF40A90	X	X	X	X			
comF40A135	X	X					

6.6.5.1. *Tilt and slant classification results*

The classifier was assessed both in terms of its ability to estimate the illumination angles and its ability to perform classification.

The accuracy of tilt estimation is shown in Figure 6.11 (top). 76% of the estimates were within 5° of the correct value and 82% were within 10°. Only one texture sample was more than 20° in error.

The accuracy of slant estimation is shown in Figure 6.11 (bottom). There are several points to note regarding this. First, two training slants, separated by 15° were used. 26% of the tests were more than 7.5° in error. Second, estimation from 45° was significantly more accurate than the estimation from 60° (52% of samples have less than 2° of error for the 45° case, compared with only 4% for the 60°case). Third, the image samples that perform poorly for tilt estimation correspond to those that perform badly for slant estimation—these tend to be drawn from the AD* and AF* sets (repeating primitives and fabrics) both of which experience significant shadowing. The last two points suggest that the prime source of

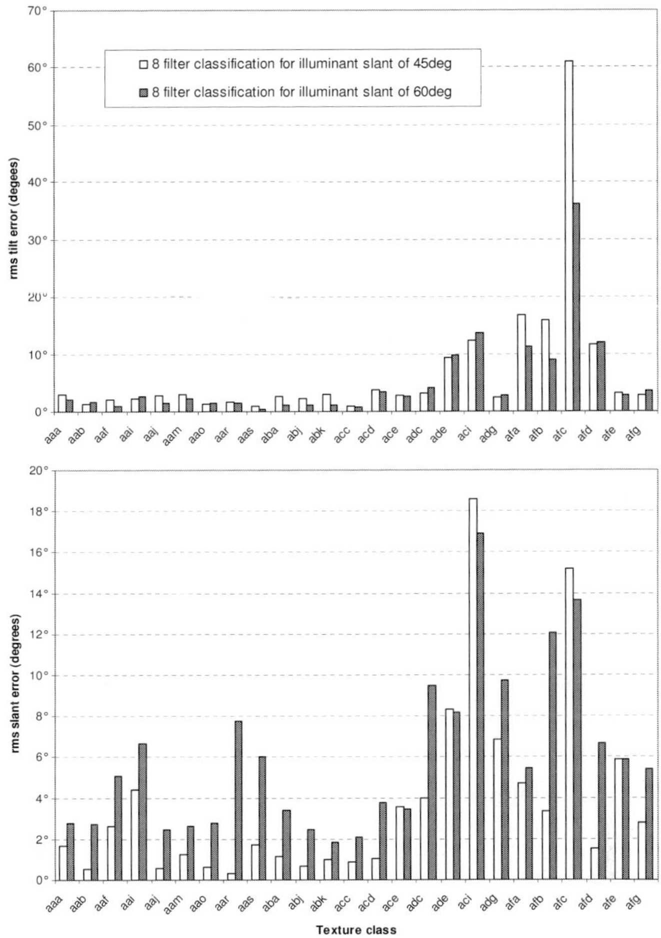

Fig. 6.11. Tilt and slant experiment: root mean square tilt error (top) and rms slant error (bottom).

inaccuracy is shadowing. How to deal with shadows and highlights in the context of photometric stereo is described in detail in Ref. 29.

The second, more important criterion for the classifier is classification accuracy. We applied 6 feature sets composed of between 3 and 12 Gabor filters to the dataset, i.e. 25 samples lit from 24 different directions. The overall error rate is shown in Figure 6.12. The most effective feature vector, composed of 10 features, gave a 98% classification rate. Increasing the number of features gave a small increase in the error rate and also led to

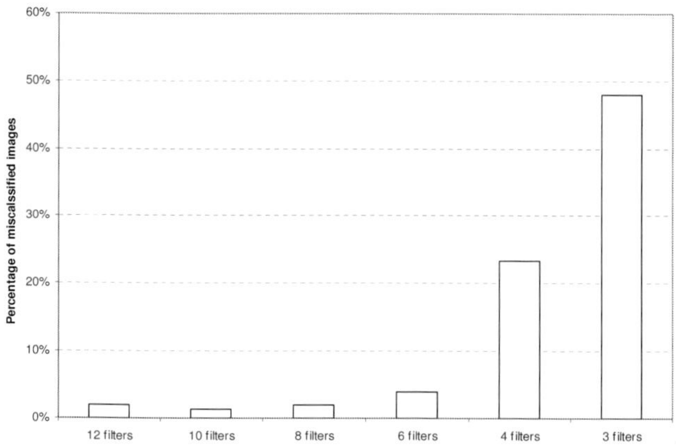

Fig. 6.12. Tilt and slant experiment: classification errors.

problems in obtaining numerical solutions to the polynomial. Reducing the number of features increased the error rate — with the most significant increase occurring for sets of less than 6 features.

6.7. Conclusions

In this chapter:

(1) we presented imaging models for surface texture characterisation, and showed how linear texture features may be expressed as functions of the lighting tilt and slant angles;
(2) we used the simplified version of this new theory to develop a novel classifier that can classify surface textures and *simultaneously* estimate the illumination conditions.

The first point above is the most significant. The models are general to a large class of conventional texture features and they explain, from first principles, why these features are trigonometric functions of the illumination conditions.

Hence, given better *a priori* information (i.e. the model) it should be possible to build a variety of improved applications ranging from illuminant estimators through to classifiers and segmentation tools.

We applied the simplified feature model to the texture classification process and found that, despite the many assumptions that we made during its derivation, it represents the behaviour of the Gabor and Laws features surprisingly well. Admittedly the test set was limited to images taken of thirty surface textures and contained no really specular surfaces. However, shadowing, local illumination effects, and albedo variation are clearly evident in many of our images. We therefore feel that, with the exception of highly specular surfaces, this model has proven to be robust to violation of many of the initial assumptions.

This has allowed us to develop a reliable classifier that simultaneously estimates the direction of the illumination while performing the classification task. Tests with a separate set of twenty-five sample textures have shown that the system is capable of reliably classifying a range of surface texture while accurately resolving the illumination's tilt angle, and to a lesser extent its slant angle.

Acknowledgements

The authors would like to thank Michael Schmidt, Andreas Penirsche, Svetlana Barsky and Ged McGunnigle for their help in this work and acknowledge that a substantial part of it was funded by EPSRC.

References

1. M. Petrou and P. Garcia Sevilla, *Image Processing: Dealing with texture.* (John Wiley, ISBN-13: 978-0-470-02628-1, 2006).
2. R. Haralick, Statistical and structural approaches to texture, *Proceedings of the IEEE.* **67**(5), 786–804 (May, 1979).
3. L. Van Gool, P. Dewaele, and A. Oosterlinck, Texture analysis anno 1983, *CVGIP.* **29**, 336–357, (1985).
4. T. Reed and J. Hans du Buf, A review of recent texture segmentation and feature extraction techniques, *CVGIP.* **57**(3), 359–372 (May, 1993).
5. T. Randen and J. Husoy, Filtering for texture classification: A comparative study, *IEEE Trans. on Pattern Analysis and Machine Intelligence.* **21**(4), 291–310 (April, 1999).
6. P. Brodatz, *Textures: a photographic album for artists and designers.* (Dover, New York, 1966).
7. M. Chantler, Why illuminant direction is fundamental to texture analysis, *IEE Proc. Vision, Image and Signal Processing.* **142**(4), 199–206 (August, 1995).
8. K. Dana, S. Nayar, B. van Ginneken, and J. Koenderink. Reflectance and texture of real-world surfaces. In *Proceedings of IEEE Conference on Computer Vision and Pattern Recognition*, pp. 151–157, (1997).
9. K. Dana and S. Nayar. Histogram model for 3d textures. In *Proceedings of*

IEEE Conference on Computer Vision and Pattern Recognition, pp. 618–624, (1998).
10. B. van Ginneken, J. Koenderink, and K. Dana, Texture histograms as a function of irradiation and viewing direction, *International Journal of Computer Vision.* **31**(2/3), 169–184 (April, 1999).
11. K. Dana and S. Nayar. Correlation model for 3d texture. In *Proceedings of ICCV99: IEEE International Conference on Computer Vision*, pp. 1061–1067, (1999).
12. T. Leung and J. Malik. Recognizing surfaces using three-dimensional textons. In *Proceedings of ICCV99: IEEE International Conference on Computer Vision*, pp. 1010–1017, (1999).
13. T. Leung and J. Malik, Representing and recognizing the visual appearance of materials using three-dimensional textons, *International Journal of Computer Vision.* **43**(1), 29–44 (June, 2001).
14. C. O.G. and D. K.J. Recognition methods for 3d textured surfaces. In *Proceedings of SPIE, San Jose* (January, 2001).
15. M. Varma and A. Zisserman. Classifying materials from images: to cluster or not to cluster? In *Texture2002: The 2nd international workshop on texture analysis and synthesis, 1 June 2002, Copenhagen*, pp. 139–144, (2002).
16. M. Varma and A. Zisserman. Classifying images of materials: Achieving viewpoint and illumination independence. In *ECCV2002, European Conference on Computer Vision*, pp. 255–271, (2002).
17. P. Kube and A. Pentland, On the imaging of fractal surfaces, *IEEE Trans. on Pattern Analysis and Machine Intelligence.* **10**(5), 704–707 (September, 1988).
18. A. Penirschke, M. Chantler, and M. Petrou. Illuminant rotation invariant classification of 3d surface textures using lissajous's ellipses. In *TEXTURE 2002, The 2nd International Workshop on Texture Analysis and Synthesis*, pp. 103–107, (2002).
19. M. Chantler, M. Petrou, A. Penirschke, M. Schmidt, and G. McGunnigle, Classifying surface texture while simultaneously estimating illumination, *International Journal of Computer Vision.* **62**, 83–96, (2005).
20. M. Chantler. *The effect of variation in illuminant direction on texture classification.* PhD thesis, Department of Computing and Electrical Engineering, Heriot Watt University, Scotland, (1994).
21. M. Landy and I. Oruc, Properties of second-order spatial frequency channels, *Vision Research.* **42**(19), 2311–2329 (September, 2002).
22. M. Chantler, M. Schmidt, M. Petrou, and G. McGunnigle. The effect of illuminant rotation on texture filters: Lissajous's ellipses. In *ECCV2002, European Conference on Computer Vision*, vol. III, pp. 289–303, (2002).
23. A. Jain and F. Farrokhnia, Unsupervised texture segmentation using gabor filters, *Pattern Recognition.* **24**(12), 1167–1186 (December, 1991).
24. K. Laws. *Textured Image Segmentation.* PhD thesis, Electrical Engineering, University of Southern California, (1980).
25. A. Penirschke, *Illumination Invariant Classification of 3D Surface Textures.*

Number RM/02/4, (Department of Computing and Electrical Engineering Heriot Watt University, 2002).
26. S. Barsky. *Surface Shape and Color Reconstruction Using Photometric Stereo.* PhD thesis, School of Electronics and Physical Science, Univ. of Surrey, U.K., (2003).
27. S. Barsky and M. Petrou, Surface texture using photometric stereo data: classification and direction of illumination detection, *Journal of Mathematical Imaging and Vision*, **29**, 185–204.
28. http://www.macs.hw.ac.uk/texturelab/database/Photex/index.htm.
29. S. Barsky and M. Petrou, The 4-source photometric stereo technique for 3-dimensional surfaces in the presence of highlights and shadows, *IEEE Transactions on Pattern Anaysis and Machine Intelligence.* **25**(10), 1239–1252 (2003).

Chapter 7

Shape, Surface Roughness and Human Perception

Sylvia C. Pont and Jan J. Koenderink
Helmholtz Institute, Department of Physics and Astronomy, Utrecht University, Princetonplein 5, 3584 CC Utrecht, the Netherlands

3D Image texture due to the illumination of rough surfaces provides cues about the light field and the surface geometry on the meso and on the macro scales. We discuss 3D texture models, their application in the computer vision domain, and psychophysical studies. Global, histogram-based cues such as the "texture contrast function" allow for simple robust inferences with regard to the light field and to the surface structure of 3D objects. If one additionally takes the spatial structure of the image texture into account, it is possible to calculate local estimates of surface geometry and the local illumination orientation. The local illumination orientation can be estimated within a few degrees for rendered Gaussian as well as real surfaces, algorithmically and by human observers. Using such local estimates of illumination orientation, we can determine the global structure of the "illuminance flow" for 3D objects. The illuminance flow is a robust indicator of the light field and thus reveals global structure in a scene. It is an important prerequisite for many subsequent inferences from the image such as shape from shading.

7.1. 3D Texture and Photomorphometry

We study the structure of 3D image texture (or simply "3D texture"). 3D texture is image texture due to the illumination of rough surfaces. The illumination of corrugated surfaces causes shading, shadowing, interreflections and occlusion effects on the micro scale. Such 3D textures depend strongly on the viewing direction and on the illumination conditions, see figure 7.1. The upper half of the figure shows a subset of a Bidirectional Texture function (BTF; see Dana *et al.*[13]) of plaster from the CUReT database.[12] This database contains BTFs of 256 photographs each and

BRDFs (Bidirectional Reflectance Distribution Function[49]) of more than 60 natural surfaces, and is widely used in texture research. Note that due to qualitative differences the textures cannot be "texture mapped",[17] in contradistinction to 2D "wallpaper" type of textures. The lower part of figure 7.1 shows a golf ball (left) and a golf ball painted matte white (right), illuminated with a collimated light source (lower half images) or a hemispherical diffuse source (upper half images) from the Utrecht Oranges database.[55] From the shadowing and shading effects it is visually evident that the illumination comes from the left and that the illumination is much more diffuse in the upper case than in the lower case. The texture due to the dimples in the balls clearly differs from point to point over the surface of the ball. This is caused by the variation of the illumination and viewing angles. For spherical pits in a surface it is possible to derive analytical solutions for the reflectance for the locally matte,[35] specular[53] and glossy cases.[60] As far as we know, this is the only geometry for which the problem has been solved in an exact way. This problem can be solved because the interreflections and shadowing effects are local, that is to say confined to the pit. Typically, the interreflections and shadowing effects will not be local, rendering the problem impossible to solve analytically. Therefore, we need a statistical approach for typical surfaces. In the rest of this chapter we will only treat such statistical approaches.

The image structure is determined by the object's shape, surface structure, reflectance properties, and by the light field. Evidently, this provides us with cues about the object's shape, surface structure, reflectance properties, and about the light field. This so-called inverse problem is heavily underdetermined and therefore suffers from many ambiguities. Figure 7.2 illustrates just a few of such ambiguities: the illumination directions for the two textures differ by 180° though they seem to be similar, due to the so-called convex-concave ambiguity[61] (illustrated in the two images and schemes at the lower left). The so-called bas-relief ambiguity[5] also applies. This is illustrated in the lower right images: if the relief decreases while the illumination is lowered the result will be a similar image except for an albedo transformation. Many authors described such ambiguities, though the full formal treatment of appearance metamery still forms a challenging problem. These basic cue ambiguities are of fundamental importance in studies of human vision, unfortunately they are rarely taken into account. Of course these problems apply to a much broader range of applications and not to 3D texture analysis only. "Photomorphometry" refers to any method that purports to derive 3D–shape information from 2D–images of

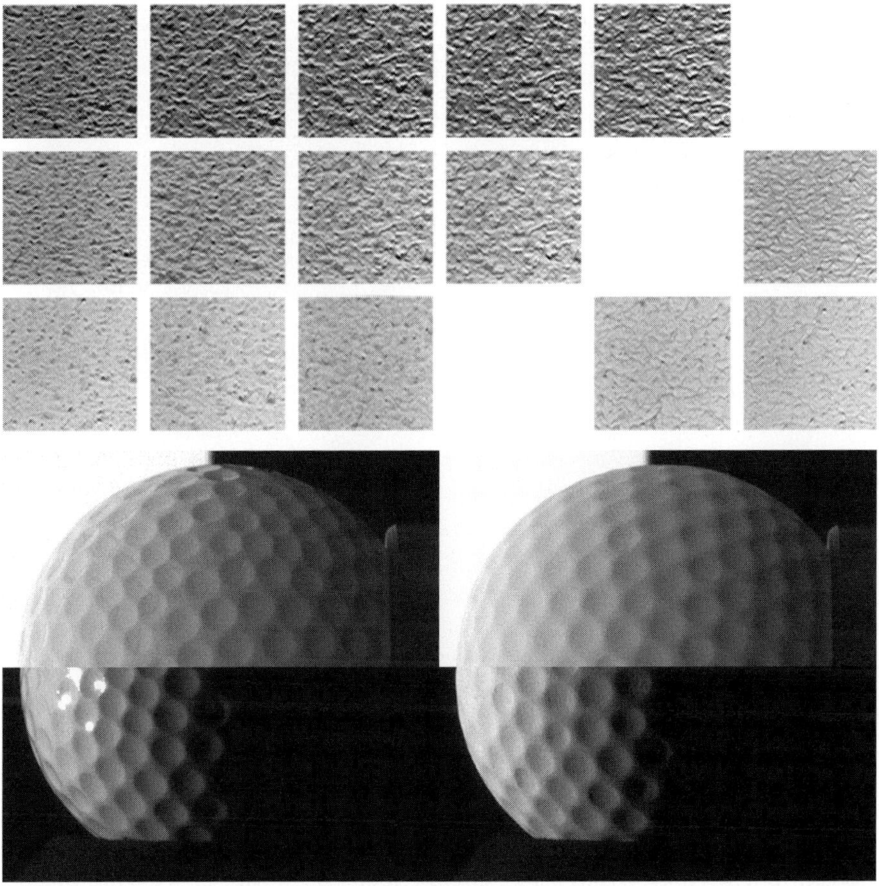

Fig. 7.1. 3D textures depend strongly on the viewing direction and on the illumination conditions. Here we show plasterwork for various illumination elevation (from below to above: 11.25°, 33.75°, 56.25° with respect to the surface normal) and viewing angles (from left to right: −56.25°, −33.75°, −11.25°, 11.25°, 33.75°, 56.25°) and a golf ball in collimated (lower half images) and hemispherical diffuse illumination (upper half images), left a non-painted glossy ball and right a ball painted matte white.

3D–objects. Especially when the image is due to irradiation with some unknown beam of radiation the problem is very hard.

In this chapter we focus on 3D texture models, their application in computer vision and psychophysics. Psychophysical research into 3D texture is still in its childhood, in contradistinction to the literature about "wallpaper" type of textures (see for instance the review by Landy and Graham[42]).

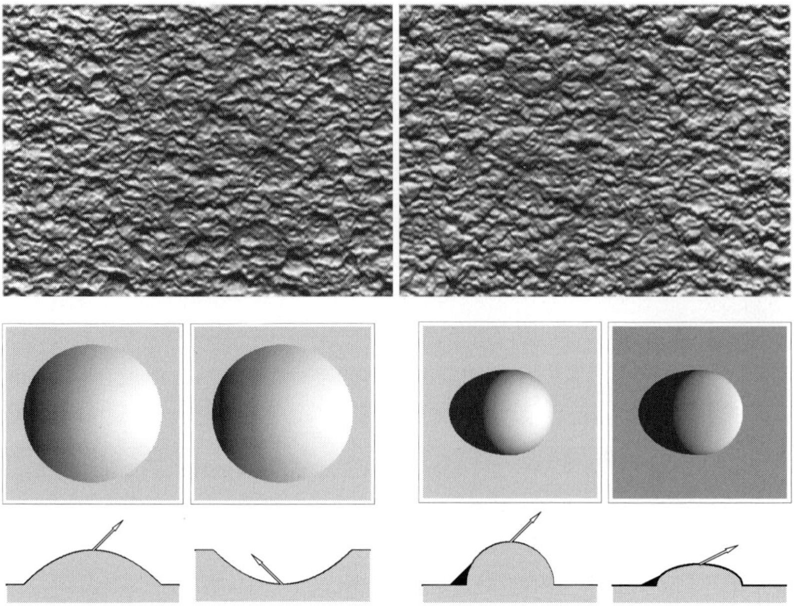

Fig. 7.2. An image of plaster and the same image rotated by 180°. For most observers the illumination seems to be from above in both cases. This ambiguity is due to the convex-concave ambiguity which is illustrated in the lower left scheme. Judgments of the illumination direction and of the relief from 3D textures also suffer from the bas-relief ambiguity, which is illustrated in the lower right pictures.

Most results for wallpaper textures cannot simply be applied to 3D texture perception, because 3D texture is dependent on both the viewing and illumination geometries (wallpaper textures can be mapped using the foreshortening transformation, but 3D textures cannot, see figure 7.1). The perception of 3D texture is closely related to the interpretation of scenes in general. The interpretation of scenes involves situational awareness, represented by (chrono-)geometrical and light-field frameworks.[21,47] Cues which globally specify the light-field framework in natural scenes are 3D texture gradients,[21] shading, shadowing, atmospheric perspective, etcetera.

This chapter is divided in three sections. In each section we discuss physics-based models, image analysis, and perception research. In the first of the three sections, we treat *histogram-based properties.* In the second section examples are given of how the *spatial structure of 3D texture* provides cues about the material and about the light field. In the third section we discuss the *global structure of 3D texture gradients* over 3D objects. This provides additional cues about the material properties, the light field and the object shape.

7.2. Histogram-Based Properties

The simplest measures of texture are based on the distributions of radiance, which can be studied via the histograms of pixel values in image textures (because generally the radiance values correspond monotonically with the pixel values). We ignore color. From pixel gray value histograms one may derive simple measures such as the average gray value, the variance of gray values, percentiles (for instance the 5% and 95% percentiles, as robust measures of minimum and maximum values for natural textures), and the texture contrast. Such measures vary systematically as a function of illumination and viewing angles. In the next subsection we discuss the most simple micro facet model which explains variations of mean and extremum radiance values of 3D textures and of the texture contrast. This Bidirectional Texture Contrast Function (BTCF[58]) can be used to do semi-quantitative estimates with regard to surface roughness. The measurement of texture contrast is about the simplest analysis that makes sense. The next "step up" would be to specify the histogram-modes, that is the global structure of histograms.

7.2.1. *Image analysis of histogram-based properties*

The appearance of rough locally matte material, for instance plasterwork or wrinkled paper, is almost uniquely defined by the illumination direction. Such materials locally scatter light in a diffuse manner, that is, almost Lambertian, such that the viewing angle becomes (almost) irrelevant. Lambert's surface attitude effect,[41] dating from the 18^{th}c. states that, if $\boldsymbol{n}$ denotes the outward surface normal, and $\boldsymbol{i}$ the direction towards the light source (both assumed to be unit vectors), then the surface irradiance caused by the incident beam is proportional to the inner product $\boldsymbol{n}\cdot\boldsymbol{i}$. Thus the image intensity at any point is proportional with the cosine of the obliquity of the incident beam at the corresponding surface location. More specifically, for a surface albedo $\varrho(u,v)$ (where $\{u,v\}$ denote parameters on the surface), and radiance of the incident beam N one has

$$I(u,v) = \frac{\varrho(u,v)N}{\pi}\,(\boldsymbol{n}(u,v)\cdot\boldsymbol{i}),$$

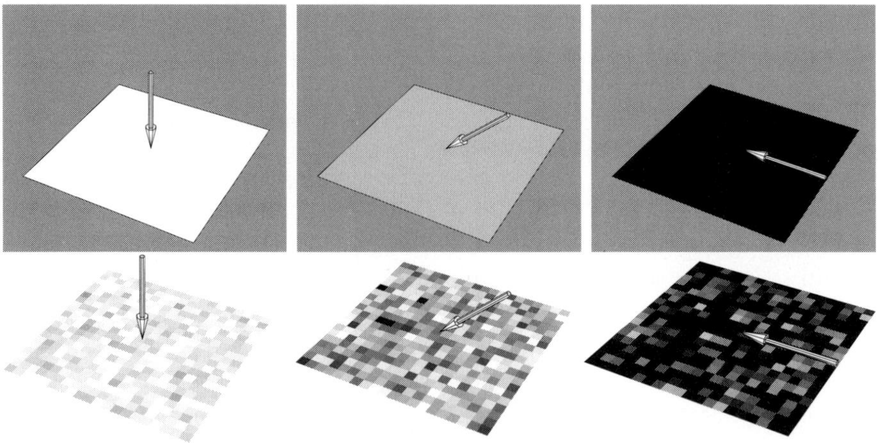

Fig. 7.3. The top row illustrates Lambert's attitude effect, commonly known as "shading". The bottom row shows what will be observed if the surface is rough on the microscale. (Here we deployed "bump mapping" for a Gaussian random normal deviation field.) The statistical structure of the texture yields an "observable" that is not less salient or relevant than the conventional shading.

where $I(u, v)$ denotes the image intensity at the location in the image corresponding to the surface location $\{u, v\}$. Conventionally one assumes $\varrho(u, v) = \varrho_0$, a constant (often even $\varrho_0 = 1$).

In this setting it is evidently only the *normal* component $\boldsymbol{i}_\perp = (\boldsymbol{n} \cdot \boldsymbol{i})\, \boldsymbol{n}$ of the direction of the incident beam with respect to the local surface that is (at least partially) *observable* through the "shading".

Cursory examination of actual photographs reveals that this is perhaps a bit too much of an "idealization". Most surfaces are *rough on the micro-scale*, which is to say that the fluctuations of the surface normal on finer than some fiducial scale are considered due to "roughness" and not to "shape", that is surface relief. Such roughness can be observed to lead to image "texture" which depends mainly on the *tangential* component $\boldsymbol{i}_\| = \boldsymbol{i}_\perp - \boldsymbol{i}$ of the direction of incidence. (See figure 7.3.) The contrast "explodes" near the terminator of the attached shadow (see figure 7.1), an effect that can frequently be observed in natural scenes and is well known to visual artists.[1,30]

This effect can be described using a simple micro facet model.[58] We assume a range of slants of micro facets at any point of the sphere centered on the fiducial slant (the local attitude on the global object) and extending to an amount $\Delta\theta$ (the maximum local attitude due to 3D surface corrugations) on either side. A more realistic model, using a statistical model of the surface, allows calculation of the full histogram of radiance at the eye or camera. Such a more realistic model[3] yields essentially the same results as the most simple model presented later. The main effects are due to the fact that the local facet normals differ in slant from the fiducial slant. The major features of the 3D texture contrast can be understood from a classical "bump mapping" approach (see figure 7.3); a description that only recognizes the statistics of the orientations of surface micro facets, disregarding the height distribution completely.

A contrast measure is essentially a measure that captures the relative width of the histogram. There are some distinct notions of contrast in common use, and each has its uses. We used the following contrast definiton: the difference of the maximum and minimum irradiance divided by twice the fiducial irradiance. For real textures we deal with the 5% ("minimum"), 95% ("maximum") and 50% (median radiance) levels, which are robust measures required for natural images. The median radiance may often be used as an estimate of the fiducial radiance, but it may well be biased, especially near the terminator.

For collimated beams such as direct sunlight vignetting is all or none: one hemisphere is in total darkness (the "body shadow"), see figure 7.1. The illuminated hemisphere has a radiance distribution $\cos\theta$ where θ is the angle from the pole facing the source, according to the surface attitude effect (Lambert's Law[41]). The theory is illustrated in figure 7.4, for the case of a collimated beam and of a diffuse beam. The maximum / minimum irradiances will be $\cos(\theta \pm \Delta\theta)$ (the dashed lines in figure 7.4). The contrast monotonically increases from the illuminated pole to the terminator, actually explodes near the terminator. Note that the contrast curves extend into the shadow regions up to angles of $\Delta\theta$, because we only reckoned with attitude distributions, not height distributions.

For diffuse beams (for instance an overcast sky or an infinite luminous pane at one side of the scene) vignetting is gradual, see figure 7.1 the upper half images of the golf balls. For a hemispherically diffuse beam the irradiance of a sphere is proportional with $(1+\cos\theta)/2 = \cos(\theta/2)\times\cos(\theta/2)$ (with θ the angle from the pole that faces the source). Although the first expression is the conventional one,[17] the terms have no physical meaning. In the second expression one factor is due to the fact that a surface facet is typically only illuminated by part of the source, the other parts being occluded by the object itself (vignetting) and the other factor is due to the fact that the surface facet will be at an oblique attitude with respect to

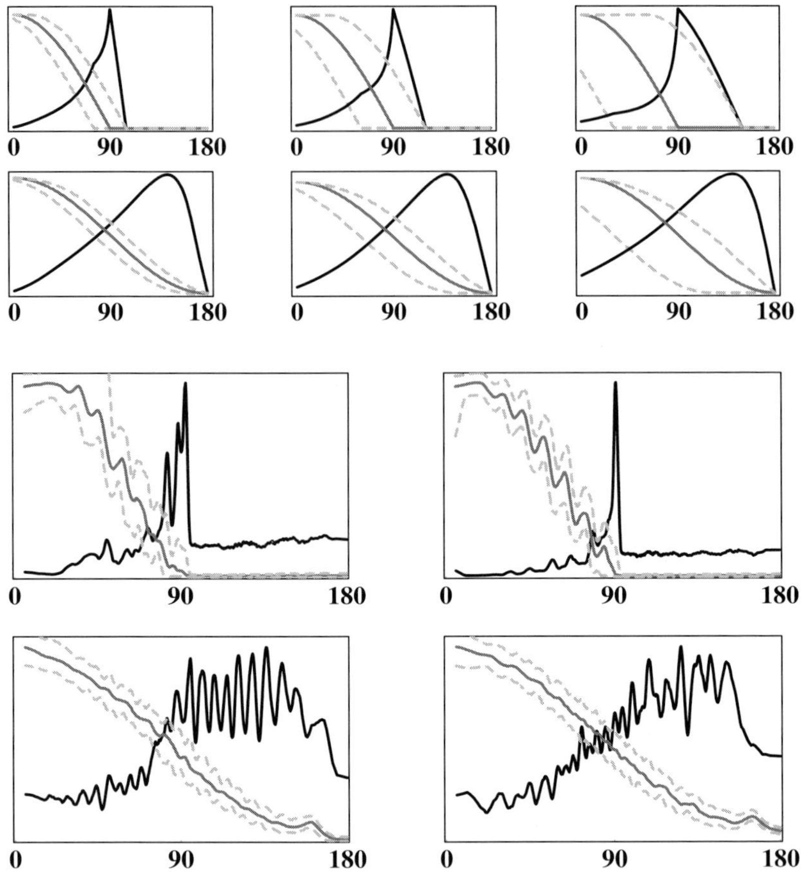

Fig. 7.4. The top array illustrates the BTCF model theoretically, the lower array empirically, for the golf balls in figure 7.1. In each array, the upper rows show data for the collimated case and the lower row for the diffusely illuminated case. The columns for the theoretical plots represent data for $\Delta\theta = 15°, 30°, 60°$. The fiducial radiance is plotted in dark gray, the minimum and maximum radiance in dashed light gray, and the contrast in black curves. For the theoretical plots we assumed an ambient level of 1% (note that the contrast maximum will be arbitrarily large when the ambient light level is low). We scaled all curves such that they cover the maximum range in the graphs. The wiggles in the empirical curves reflect the dimples in the golf balls.

the effective source direction. The maximum / minimum irradiances are $\cos(\theta/2)\cos(\theta/2 \pm \Delta\theta)$, so the contrast monotonically increases from $1/4$ at $\theta = 0$ to infinity at $\theta = \pi$, see figure 7.4.

From observation of the texture histograms we are able to estimate some overall measures of the slope distribution (for details and empirical data see Ref. 58). For collimated illumination an estimate of the range of orientations of surface microfacets orientations can be obtained in several independent ways. An estimation of the effective heights of surface protrusions can be found from the distance from the terminator at which parts of the surface that are in the cast shadow region still manage to catch a part of the incident beam.

Such comparatively crude, but very robust measures suffice to obtain quite reasonable estimates of the main features of 3D texture (the spread of surface normals about the average). These observations allow one to guesstimate the BRDF. Reflectance distribution models[3,23,33,51] depend on only a few parameters, the spread of slopes of microfacets being the most important. Thus more precise shape from shading inferences are possible when the 3D texture information is taken into account, because these inferences depend upon knowledge of the (usually unknown) BRDF of the surface. The Bidirectional Texture Contrast Function might be a good start in a bootstrap procedure for inverse rendering and BRDF guesstimation. The resulting functions can be finetuned on the basis of more detailed estimates such as the exact shape of the histograms, and other types of measures based on the spatial structure of 3D texture (see next section).

The width of a specular patch on a globally curved object is a direct measure of the angular spread of normals (global curvature and spread of the illumination assumed known) and the patchiness is a direct measure for the width of the height autocorrelation function.[46] Thus the structure and width of the specularity and the nature of the 3D texture are closely related and any inference concerning surface micro structure should regard both.

Analysis of the exact shapes of the histograms of BTFs shows that the histograms generally consist of one or more modes which vary (or even (dis-)appear) as a function of the viewing and illumination geometry. In figure 7.5 the "rough plastic" (sample 4) BTF subset from the Curet database[12] is shown with the same format as the BTF in figure 7.1 (but rotated 90°), together with its –smoothed– histograms and an analysis of the histogram modes. The black bars are shown in the centres of the modes, with a height equal to half the maximum value of the mode and a width equal to an eighth of the width of the mode. We chose this sample, because the modal structure contains the three most common modes observed for materials in the Curet database. These modes are easy to trace to image texture properties, and, moreover, easy to name, with reference

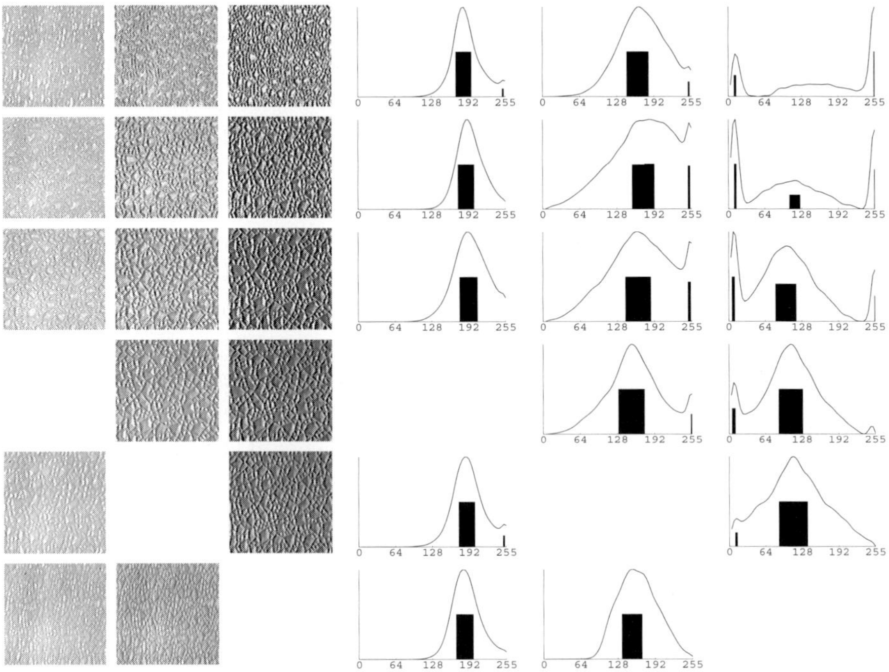

Fig. 7.5. A BTF subset of rough plastic and the corresponding histograms, plus an analysis of the modal structure of the histograms. The format of the BTF is the same as for figure 7.1, but rotated 90°.

to the optical effects which cause them: the shadow mode (the small peak at the very left), the highlight mode (the small peak at the very right) and the broad middle mode which might be called a "diffuse mode". For different materials, these modes were observed in different combinations and for different angles.

However, this categorization does not apply to all common materials. For example, sometimes more than three modes are observed and sometimes a single narrow mode which cannot be attributed to one of the former optical effects. In order to handle such cases one needs to take the specific physical effects[7] into account. Examples of such an analysis include the backscattering mode,[35,53] the split specular mode[54] and the surface scattering mode.[36]

7.2.2. *Perception and 3D texture histogram-based cues*

Research into 3D texture perception is still in its childhood and the few studies which we are aware of present a rather fragmentary picture. With regard to perception and 3D histogram-based cues one should keep in mind that the human visual system effectively signals relative luminance differences (for instance image contrast), not absolute luminance values.

Ho *et al.*[26] investigated "roughness" perception for computer generated locally Lambertian facetted textures, which looked similar to wrinkled paper and which were illuminated by a point light source plus an ambient component. The scenes were rendered from two different viewpoints and viewed binocularly. They varied the relief of the surface and the angle of the (point) light source with regard to the virtual surface between 50° and 70° from the tangent plane. The textures were presented in pairs, for which observers had to judge which of the two textures appeared to be "rougher". All observers judged surfaces to be rougher for more shallow illumination. The addition of objects whose shading, cast shadows, and specular highlights provided cues about the light field did not improve performance. They found that histogram-based properties of the textures, namely the texture contrast, the standard deviation of the luminance, the mean luminance, and the proportion of the texture in shadow (or "black-shot"[43]) accounted for a substantial amount of the observers systematic deviations from roughness constancy with changes in lighting condition. A similar result was found in subsequent studies,[27] in which they investigated the effects of viewing direction for fixed illumination direction. Thus, histogram-based 3D texture properties affect relief perception, which consequently is dependent on viewing and illumination directions (even though veridical disparity cues were available).

Several authors[22,63] noticed that histograms of white and black rough surfaces look qualitatively different (e.g. have different shapes) and that humans seem to be able to discriminate images of white and black rough surfaces (even if the average image gray level is equalized). In order to test these observations they used images of opaque real rough surfaces, for which subjects had to estimate the albedo. They found that the perceived albedo is indeed quite robust to changes in mean texture luminance or surround luminance, which they called self-anchoring. Black, shiny surfaces tended to self-anchor better than others. Moreover, they found that manipulating the statistics of the textures strongly affected the perceived albedo. Although they did not test it formally, they found that such changes went hand in hand with a strongly affected perceived local reflectance (e.g. specular to diffuse). These results clearly suggest that human observers are sensitive to other modal properties of the histogram besides the shadow mode.

7.3. The Spatial Structure of 3D Texture

In the section about histogram-based properties we showed how comparatively crude, but very robust measures suffice to obtain quite reasonable estimates of the main features of surface roughness and that human observers actually use such cues. However, it is not just the histogram that is of relevance; it is easy to construct two rough surfaces that give rise to the same histogram, but different spatial structures. The simplest observation of the spatial structure of the texture allows inferences concerning the width of the autocorrelation function of heights or the width of a typical surface modulation. The distribution of the heights themselves can only indirectly be inferred from the width of the autocorrelation function and the spread of normals.

The spatial structure of 3D image textures, as well as their histograms, varies systematically as a function of viewing and illumination of the rough surface, and is of course dependent on the surface geometry and surface reflectance. In the next subsection we will discuss how the second order statistical properties of 3D textures depend on illumination and viewing directions, and, moreover, how the illumination orientation can be estimated on the basis of the second order statistics.

7.3.1. *Image analysis of the spatial structure of 3D texture*

For isotropic random rough surfaces the image textures can be anisotropic owing to oblique illumination. This anisotropy can be picked up by local differential operators[11] (see also Chapter 6 by Chantler and Petrou). It is possible to model this for Lambertian Gaussian random surfaces.[6,38,45,64] The simplest case involves a frontoparallel plane (see figure 7.6). In this case it can be shown that the direction of the largest eigenvalue of either of the "structure tensors" $\langle \boldsymbol{g} \cdot \boldsymbol{g}^{\dagger} \rangle$ or $\langle \boldsymbol{H} \cdot \boldsymbol{H}^{\dagger} \rangle$ lies in the plane of incidence, where $\boldsymbol{g}(x,y)$ denotes the depth gradient $\nabla z(x,y)$, $\boldsymbol{H}$ the depth Hessian $\nabla\nabla z(x,y)$ and the operator $\langle \cdots \rangle$ denotes a local spatial average at a scale coarser than the "micro–scale".[38] In other words, on the basis of the second order statistics it is possible to estimate the orientation of the irradiance. Note that these estimates are subject to the convex-concave and bas-relief

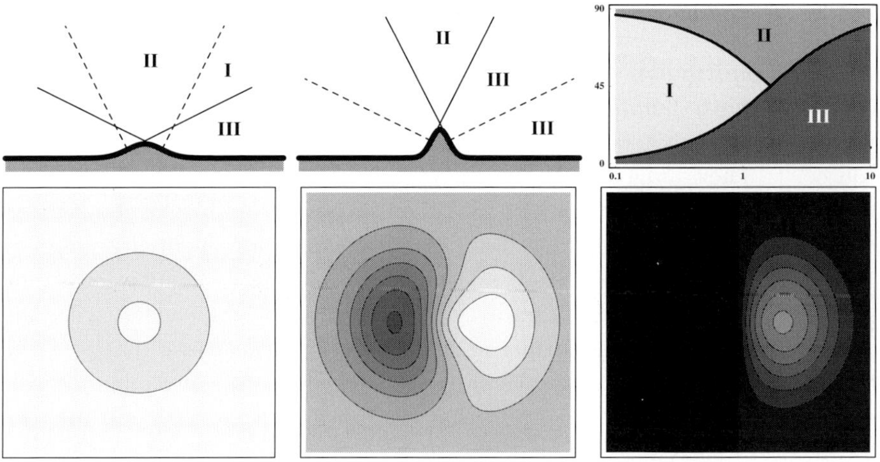

Fig. 7.6. The shading regimes for a Gaussian hill on a plane. I: second order shading; II: first order shading; III: shadowing. The upper row shows the cases of low relief (left) and high relief (middle) and the regimes as a function of illuminant obliquety (vertical) and height of the hill (horizontal, logarithmic scale). The true shading regime applies only to low relief and intermediary obliqueties. The lower row shows the Gaussian hill of low relief in normal view in the second order shading regime (left), the first order shading regime (center) and the shadow regime (right).

ambiguities, see figure 7.2. The direction of the local plane of incidence has thus to be considered an additional "observable".

Although the assumptions of our simple second order model appear rather restrictive, empirical data shows that this "irradiance flow" can be detected reliably for virtually any isotropic random roughness. For textures of the Curet database[12] (surfaces that are not Gaussian, with BRDFs which are far from Lambertian, and with local vignetting and interreflections present) we recovered the irradiance orientation with an accuracy of a few degrees.

In natural scenes one hardly ever views surfaces from the exact normal direction. So, an important extension of the theory is the case of oblique viewing, for which the inferences of the irradiance orientation will deviate from the veridical value in a systematic way. If only perspective foreshortening is taken into account we predict that the irradiance orientation can be recovered up to viewing angles of 55°, but for larger angles there are no unique solutions on the basis of this model.[59]

7.3.2. *Perception and the spatial structure of 3D texture*

The data on irradiance orientation estimation for the Curet database were compared with human performance in a psychophysical experiment in which human subjects judged both the azimuth and the elevation of the source.[37] They judged the azimuth within approximately 15°, except for the fact that they made random 180° flips (expected because of the convex-concave ambiguity) and showed a slight preference for "light from above" settings. The source elevation settings were almost at chance level (the bas-relief ambiguity). So, these results were in good agreement with the data of the model in the former section, which based the estimates of the irradiance orientation on the second order statistics of local luminance gradients. This agreement suggests that the underlying mechanism may be located very early in the visual stream.

In another experiment in which human subjects had to perform the same task for rendered Gaussian surfaces, the results were similar in the shading regime (no shadows).[40] But, interestingly, in the shadow-dominated regime (see figure 7.6) they did not make random 180° flips and the elevations of the source were also judged with remarkable accuracy. The latter result was probably due to the statistical homogeneity of the stimulus set, and likely cues are the ones mentioned in the section about histogram-based properties (fraction of shadowed surface, average pixel value, variance and contrast). The cue which observers used to avoid the convex-concave confusions has not been identified yet. Possible candidates might be the difference between cast and body shadow edges and the asymmetric shapes of shadows.

7.4. The Global Structure of 3D Texture of Illuminated 3D Objects

The last "step up" will be made in this section: we will discuss one example of the use of the global structure of 3D texture gradients over illuminated 3D objects. In the previous section we showed how the irradiance orientation can be estimated from the second order statistical properties of 3D textures. Here we discuss an intuitive example of how such estimates can be used in "shape from shading". With regard to perception studies of the global structure of 3D texture we will discuss consequences of these considerations rather than psychophysics as such, because the latter are not available.

7.4.1. *Image analysis of the global structure of 3D texture over 3D objects*

Consider the field of directions defined by the intersections of the local planes of incidence with the surface. This field of the *tangential* components of the direction of the incident beam we call the "surface illuminance flow".[56] It is formally structured as the (viscous) flow of water over a geographical landscape.[34] Its projection in the image will be called the "image illuminance flow". We represent it as a field of unit vectors in the image plane and we assume it to be *observable*. This is certainly the case for frontoparallel surfaces of low relief, covered with an isotropic roughness, and predicted[59] to be applicable up to viewing angles of 55° (a topic still under –empirical– study).

It might be objected that the image irradiance flow is only "observable" at some *finite scale*, because the definition of (either one of the) structure tensors involves local averaging. This is obviously the case, but exactly the same objection applies to the classical "shading". If there is image texture due to roughness (essentially a decision to limit the analysis to a certain range of scales), then the local "image intensity" has to be defined as a local average too. In fact, no real "observable" can truly be a "point property", any measurement implies a choice of scale.[16] Thus it makes sense to accept the choice of scale as a fact of life and to consider both the "shading" and the "flow" as proper observables. One then needs to study the SFS problem in this augmented setting. So far this has not been attempted in the literature, we offer an analysis in this chapter.

In accordance with the bulk of the literature we focus on cases where the irradiating beam may be assumed uniform and homogeneous and the objects opaque, with Lambertian surfaces (completely diffusely scattering surfaces). This is the situation that is closely approximated by the setting of the academic artist drawing from (usually classical) plaster casts.[4] In the visual arts one speaks of "shading" or "chiaroscuro", in computer science of "shading" (the "forward" problem considered in computer graphics) and Shape From Shading[28] ("SFS", the "inverse" problem considered in computer vision).

The forward problem has been important to artists since classical antiquety. Relevant literature is due to Leonardo,[44] Alberti,[2] on to the 19^{th}c.'s treatises on academic practice. The scientific literature starts with Bouguer,[8] Lambert,[41] and Gershun.[20] The inverse problem was only implicit for centuries, after all, art was produced in order to evoke certain responses from customers. The explicit, scientific era only starts in the 20thc. with the astronomer van Diggelen's work.[14] Van Diggelen proposed to compute the lunar relief from photometric data (microdensitometer traces of photographs). A good selection of the early "Shape From Shading" work in "computer vision" can be found in the book by Horn.[28]

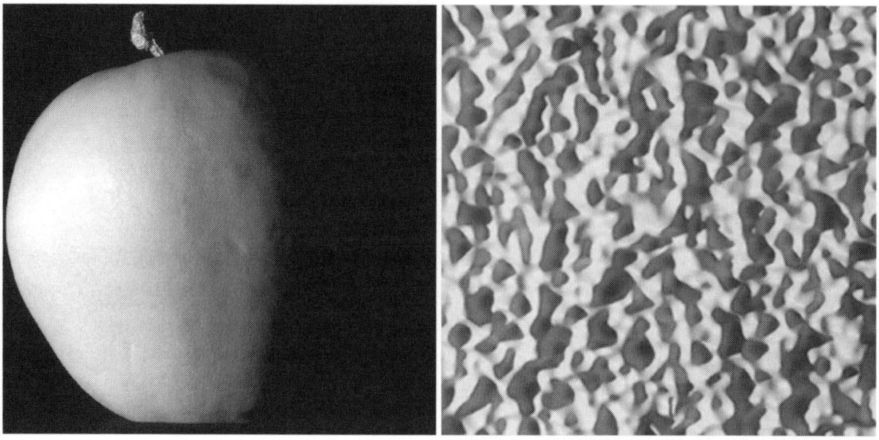

Fig. 7.7. An apple and a Gaussian surface, both illuminated with a collimated beam.

The general SFS problem has never been solved, the set of possible solutions is too large to describe explicitly.[5] The problem is usually cut down to size through the introduction of additional constraints. The most common assumption is that the direction of the incident beam is known. In quite a few cases it is even assumed to coincide with the viewing direction, therewith changing the problem markedly.

In cases where the global layout of the scene (especially the occluding contours) is visible, the direction of illumination is easily seen[52] (for instance the moon or the apple in figure 7.7). In cases one sees only part of a surface, it may be next to impossible to infer the illumination direction (for instance a uniform patch in the visual field may be due to a uniform surface illuminated by a uniform beam from an arbitrary direction). In the latter case the direction of illumination is only revealed by the 3D texture (for instance the Gaussian surface in figure 7.7 or the plaster wall in figure 7.8).

In computer vision one deals almost exclusively with "full solutions", ignoring either partial solutions, or mere qualitative deductions from photometric data. One of the few exceptions (because very "robust" against relaxation of various assumptions) is the fact that a large class of stationary points of the surface irradiance corresponds to parabolic points of the surface (surface inflection points). The latter property is a differential topological (thus qualitative), rather than analytic result. The SFS problem is very "ill posed" and most algorithms (often implicitly) use surface integrability conditions to impose sorely needed additional constraints. As a result one has no purely local, algebraic algorithms. Typical solutions are of a global type and impose various (often *ad hoc*) boundary conditions on the solution of partial differential equations.[19]

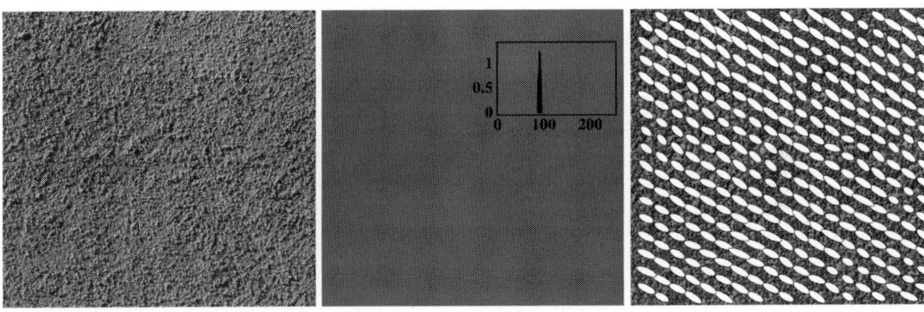

Fig. 7.8. Left: Region of interest taken from a photograph of a facade, showing a piece of a plaster wall in sunlight; Center: The local average is approximately constant, this is also evident from the inset showing the histogram of pixel values; Right: The structure tensor reveals a uniform image illuminance flow; the orientations of the ellipses represent the local illuminance orientation estimates and the areas of the ellipses represent the confidence levels of those estimates. Since both the contrast gradient and the gradient of the flow are zero this is a degenerate situation from a photomorphometric perspective. It corresponds to a planar surface. Any plane transverse to the viewing direction is an equally good explanation of the photometric structure.

That one may not expect unique solutions for the SFS problem is shown easily enough by the numerous examples of different reliefs (3–D surfaces in object space) that—though indeed distinct reliefs—nevertheless yield identical images. In some settings the transformations of relief may be combined with transformations of the distribution of surface albedo.[5] These "image–equivalent surfaces" are the orbits under certain groups of "ambiguity transformations". Both discrete and continuous groups of ambiguity transformations have been identified. The complete group has never (to the best of our knowledge) been outlined though. Moreover, most of the classical SFS algorithms yield some specific default result without any attempt to construct the complete (or at least a more complete) set of solutions at all. Computer vision algorithms that run into multiple solutions use a variety of *post hoc* methods (*e.g.*, Bayesian estimation on the basis of various *ad hoc* priors[18]) in order to arrive at some "best" (or at least acceptable) specific solution.

One very common method in artistic practice is to think of relief as a broad ribbon along the "flow of light". (See figure 7.9.) This allows an especially simple and convenient way of "shading" as one darkens the ribbon as it turns away from the flow.[10,24,25,29,50]

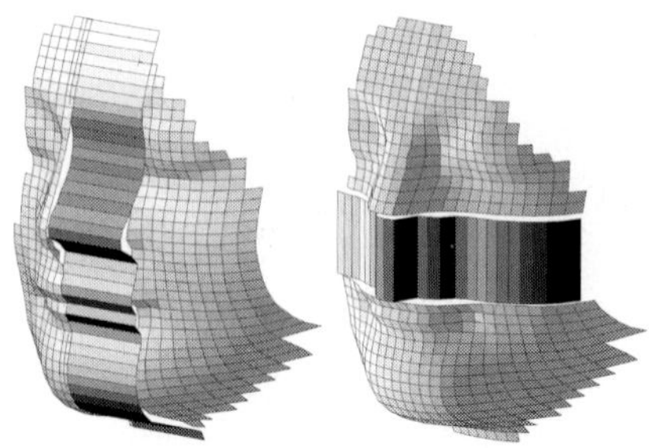

Fig. 7.9. Two examples of the method of ribbons along the flow of light.

Such practices suggest (at least) two important principles. One is that it might make sense to use a multiple scale approach[62] in which structures at finer scales are described *relative* to structures at coarser scales. The other principle is that *the relief can be foliated in terms of surface ribbons along the flow lines*, thus decreasing the dimensionality of the problem.

Here we concentrate throughout on "true shading", that is on the first order shading regime, see figure 7.6. Thus we consider low relief and neither frontal, nor striking illumination. Although these considerations are indeed of *fundamental importance* in photomorphometry one rarely (if ever) sees them mentioned explicitly in the literature. In this chapter we consider one simple approach to photomorphometry: The method involves "contrast integration along flow strips". This method closely resembles the artistic praxis of shading by means of (imaginary) "ribbons". It is a simple and effective method that assumes that the flow field is known at least approximately, and that assumes a number of initial guesses to settle the ambiguities.

Consider a strip of surface cut out along a flow line of the surface irradiance flow as in figure 7.9. In artistic praxis one avoids geodesic curvature and twist,[32] thus considers only "normally curved" strips. For such strips the shading gradient simply follows curvature. Because strips are only infinitesimally extended in the binormal direction, one may also shade by curvature in the general case. However, in doing that one evidently sacrifices surface integrity when one does so for parallel strips treated independently. The twist of the strip indicates how the shading of contiguous strips is related.

A very simple (and very coarse!) method of photomorphometry is obtained under the following simplifying assumptions that approach the standard "ribbon" method of academic drawing (but of course in reverse!) rather closely:

— we assume low relief on a fiducial frontoparallel plane;
— we assume that the plane of incidence is known, thus the flow is a uniform field of known direction;
— we assume that the relief along some curve transverse to the flow is known;
— we assume that the initial slants of the ribbons along this tranverse flow is known too.

Then we simply integrate the image intensity contrast

$$C(s) = \frac{I(s) - I(0)}{I(0)},$$

along the flow lines, starting at the transverse curve ($s = 0$). For instance, let the x–direction be the flow direction, and let the strip $y = 0$ be "magically given". Then the depth is obtained as

$$z(x) = z_0(0, y) + x z_x(0, y) + \cot\vartheta \int_0^x C(x)\, dx.$$

Here ϑ is the obliquity, which is in general unknown. Any guess will yield the same relief modulo a depth scaling though (the bas–relief ambiguity). The depth offset is irrelevant, but the linear term is clearly of importance. For a single strip it represents the "additive planes" ambiguity, if one attempts to glue strips together to fuse into a surface one has to make sure that the additive planes "mesh" somehow. A stable method to do so assumes that the depth is "magically" given on a closed curve, the boundary of the region for which we attempt to find the relief, then the initial slope (z_x) can be estimated as the slope of the chord in the flow direction.

The curves obtained in this way will describe a surface if the contrast is a smooth field and the initial conditions along the transverse curve are smooth too. The resulting surface will depend on the assumptions of course. In order to obtain at least somewhat reasonable results the flow direction will have to be at least approximately correct. The choice of obliquity is almost irrelevant (at least to a human observer's presentations) because it merely affects the depth of relief. The initial conditions along the transverse curve can be varied in order to obtain a relief that is credible given the initial expectations. Crude as such a method might be, it typically leads to reasonable results very easily. It may well be that this pretty much exhausts what human observers generically do in case no contour information is available. The method has the advantage of being very robust (for instance against nonlinear transformations of the intensity dimension) and flexible, *e.g.*, it is easy to change the scale or to deal with missing data.

By way of an example we use an informal snapshot of a footprint on the beach. We orient it by eye such that the direction of illumination appears to be horizontal, and we simply integrate along the horizontal directions. Although the flow estimate is as rough as can be (in figure 7.10 we show flow estimates which are clearly different from a uniform, horizontal field in detail), the result of this simple computation are very encouraging though (see figure 7.11).

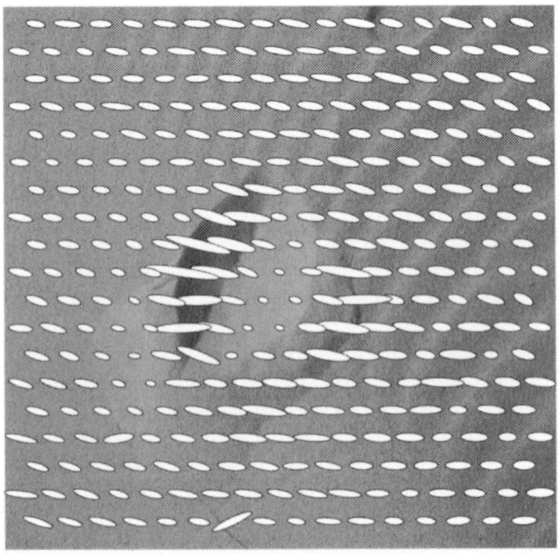

Fig. 7.10. Result of an image illuminance flow calculation (based on the gradient structure tensor) for a photograph of a footprint on the beach. The orientations of the ellipses represent the local illuminance orientation estimates and the areas of the ellipses represent the confidence levels of those estimates. The flow is roughly (but not quite) uniform.

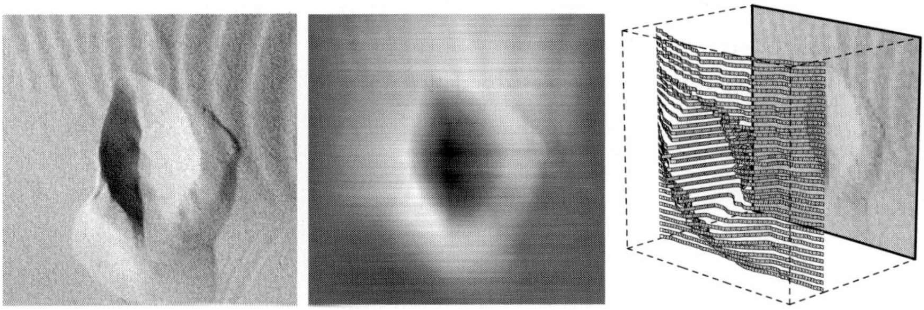

Fig. 7.11. Result of strip integration along horizontal strips. The resulting relief estimate looks promising. We have no ground truth in this case, but we know that the algorithm is exact in the correct setting. Left: The image; Center: Computed depth map (darker is deeper); Right: Another representation of the computed relief.

7.4.2. *Global structure and perception*

The "shading cue" has been studied for over a century for the case of human perception[31,39,48] (psychophysics). It has often been the case that human perceptual abilities have been looked at as "proofs of principle" in computer vision research. Even after decades of research in computer vision human performance still sets the standard in many cases of practical interest.

There exist a number of facts in human psychophysics that are immediately relevant to the photomorphometric problem.

One important fact is that human observers are keenly sensitive to image illuminance flow,[37] see the former section. Observers detect the *orientation* (direction *modulo* 180°) of the image illuminance flow to within a few degrees. They are less sensitive to obliqueness, but in non–planar objects they are immediately aware of the obliqueness *variations* (due to local surface attitude variations) due to the modulations of texture contrast (not just due to shading).

Another important fact is that human observers can indeed use pure shading (the case of smooth surfaces, *i.e.*, in the absence of texture) as a shape cue. However, they are dependent on complementary cues (*e.g.*, contour) to deploy the shading cue effectively,[15] evidently because of the large group of ambiguity transformations in the case the flow direction is not specified.

It is not known whether human observers are able to use the shading and image illuminance flow cues as complementary structures, at least there are no formal psychophysical data on the issue. Informal observations suggest that human observers use the cue pair very effectively though. This is strongly suggested by reports from photographers that sharp rendering of texture contrast due to surface roughness greatly improves the sense of three–dimensionality in photographs, especially in highly directional light fields.[1]

The human observer is not subject to ambiguity in the sense that *presentations* (the momentary optical awareness, prior to "perceptions" in a cognitive sense) are never ambiguous.[9] Of course the presentations may fluctuate over time, also in the case of invariant optical structure at the cornea. In this sense the human "SFS solutions" (if there can be said to exist such entities) are unique and never multivalued.

7.5. Conclusions

In this chapter we discussed physics-based 3D texture models, their application in the computer-vision domain, and some related psychophysical studies. Surprisingly simple models that describe global histogram-based cues, such as the bidirectional texture contrast function, were shown to allow for robust inferences with regard to the light field and to the surface roughness of 3D objects. Few psychophysical papers study 3D texture, in contradistinction to 2D wallpaper type of textures. Nevertheless, those studies confirm that human observers actually use such simple histogram-based cues for roughness, albedo and reflectance judgments.

The spatial structure of the image texture provides additional cues with regard to the surface geometry and the illuminance flow. A useful result for the computer vision domain is the finding that the illumination orientation can be estimated robustly on the basis of the second order statistics of the image textures. Furthermore, the good agreement of the algorithmical estimates with the judgments by human observers suggests that the underlying mechanism may be located very early in the visual stream. Next to being a very interesting result in itself, consider this a good example of the surplus-value of interdisciplinary research.

The global structure of the illuminance flow over rough 3D objects is an important prerequisite for many subsequent inferences from the image such as shape from shading. We gave a simple example of how image intensity contrast integration along flow lines can be used for photomorphometry. There is no formal psychophysical data on the question whether human observers are able to use shading and illuminance flow cues as complementary structures. Thus, many challenging questions remain to be answered with regard to the modal structure of 3D texture histograms, the spatial structure of 3D texture, and certainly with regard to its global structure over 3D objects.

Acknowledgments

Sylvia Pont was supported by the Netherlands Organisation for Scientific Research (NWO). This work was sponsored via the European program Visiontrain contract number MRTNCT2004005439.

References

1. Adams, A., The Print. Bulfinch: New York, 1995.
2. Alberti, L. B., Della Pittura. Thomas Ventorium: Basle, 1540.
3. Ashikhmin, M., Premoze, S., Shirley, P.: A microfacet-based BRDF generator. Proceedings ACM SIGGRAPH, New Orleans, 2000, 65–74
4. Baxandall, M., Shadows and enlightenment. Yale University Press: New Haven, 1997.
5. Belhumeur, P. N., Kriegman, D. J., Yuille, A. L., The bas–relief ambiguity. International Journal of Computer Vision 35, 33–44, 1999.
6. Berry, M. V., Hannay, J. H., Umbilic points on gaussian random surfaces. J.Phys.A: Math.Gen., 10(11), 1809–1821, 1977.
7. Born, M., Wolf, E.: *Principles of Optics.* Cambridge University Press, Cambridge, 1998
8. Bouguer, P., Traié dOptique sur la Gradation de la Lumière: ouvrage posthume... publié par M. lAbbé de la Caille... pour servir de Suite aux Mémoires de lAcadémie Royale des Sciences, H. L. Guerin & L. F. Delatour: Paris, 1760.
9. Brentano, F., Psychologie vom empirisichen Standpunkt. Leipzig, 1874.
10. Bridgman, G. B., Bridgman's life drawing. Dover: New York, 1971.
11. Chantler, M., Schmidt M., Petrou M., McGunnigle G.: The effect of illuminant rotation on texture filters: Lissajous's Ellipses. Proceedings ECCV, Copenhagen, 2002, 289–303.
12. Curet: *Columbia–Utrecht Reflectance and Texture Database.* `http://www.cs.columbia.edu/CAVE/curet`
13. Dana, K.J., Ginneken, B. van: Reflectance and texture of real-world surfaces. Proceedings IEEE Computer Science Conference on Computer Vision and pattern Recognition, 1977.
14. Diggelen, J. van, A photometric investigation of the slopes and heights of the ranges of hills in the Maria of the moon. Bull.Atron.Inst.Netherlands 11, 1951.
15. Erens, R. G. F., Kappers, A. M. L., Koenderink, J. J., Estimating the gradient direction of a luminance ramp. Vision Research 33, 1639–1643, 1993.

16. Florack L. M. J., The Structure of Scalar Images. Computational Imaging and Vision Series, Kluwer Academic Publishers: Dordrecht, 1996.
17. Foley, J. D., Dam, A. van, Feiner, S. K. and Hughes, J. F.: *Computer Graphics, Principles and Practice.* Addison–Wesley Publishing Company, Reading, Massachusetts, 1990
18. Freeman, W. T.: Exploiting the generic viewpoint assumption. International Journal Computer Vision, 20 (3), 243–261, 1996.
19. Frankot, R. T., Chellappa, R., A method for enforcing integrability in shape from shading algorithms. IEEE Pami–10, 439–451, 1988.
20. Gershun, A.: The Light Field. Transl. by P. Moon and G. Timoshenko. J.Math.Phys. **18(51)**, 1939.
21. Gibson, J.: *The perception of the visual world.* Houghton Mifflin Company, Boston, 1950.
22. Gilchrist, A.: The perception of surface blacks and whites. Scientific American 240 112–123, 1979.
23. Ginneken, B.van, Stavridi M., Koenderink J.J.: Diffuse and specular reflection from rough surfaces. Applied Optics **37(1)**, 130–139, 1998.
24. Hale, N. C., Abstraction in art and nature. Watson–Guptill: New York, 1972.
25. Hamm, J., Drawing the head and figure. Perigee Books: New Yor, 1963.
26. Ho, Y.-X., Landy, M. S., Maloney, L. T., How direction of illumination affects visually perceived surface roughness. Journal of Vision, 6, 634–648, 2006.
27. Ho, Y.-X., Landy, M. S., Maloney, L. T., The effect of viewpoint on visually perceived surface roughness in binocularly viewed scenes. Journal of Vision, 6(6), Abstract 262, 262a, 2006.
28. Horn, B. K. P., Brooks, M. J.: Shape from Shading. The M.I.T. Press, Cambridge Massachusetts, 1989
29. Jacobs, T. S., Drawing with an open mind. Watson–Guptil: New York, 1986.
30. Jacobs, T. S.: *Light for the Artist.* Watson–Guptill Publications, New York, 1988
31. Kardos, L., Ding und Schatten. Zeitschrift für Psychologie, Erg. bd 23, 1934.
32. Koenderink, J. J.: *Solid Shape* The MIT Press, Cambridge, Massachusetts, 1990.
33. Koenderink, J. J., Doorn, A. J. van: Illuminance texture due to surface mesostructure. J.Opt.Soc.Am. A **13(3)**, 452–463, 1996.
34. Koenderink, J. J., Doorn, A. J. van, The structure of relief. Advances in Imaging and Electron Physics, P. W. Hawkes (ed.), Vol. 103, 65–150, 1998.
35. Koenderink, J. J., Doorn, A. J. van, Dana, K. J., Nayar, S.: Bidirectional reflection distribution function of thoroughly pitted surfaces. International Journal of Computer Vision **31** (2/3), 129–144, 1999.
36. Koenderink, J. J., Pont, S. C.: The secret of velvety skin. Machine Vision and Applications; Special Issue on Human Modeling, Analysis and Synthesis 14, 260–268, 2003.
37. Koenderink, J. J., Doorn, A. J. van, Kappers, A. M. L., Pas S. F. te, Pont S. C.: Illumination Direction from texture shading. Journal of the Optical Society of America A, 20(6), 987–995, 2003.

38. Koenderink, J. J., Pont, S. C., Irradiation direction from texture. Journal of the Optical Society of America A20(10), 1875–1882, 2003.
39. Koenderink, J. J., Doorn, A. J. van, Shape and shading. In: The visual neurosciences, L. M. Chalupa, J. S. Werner (eds.), The M.I.T. Press, Cambridge, Mass., 1090–1105, 2003.
40. Koenderink, J. J., Doorn, A. J. van, Pont, S. C.: Light direction from shad(ow)ed random Gaussian surfaces. Perception 33, 1405–1420, 2004.
41. Lambert, J. H.: *Photometria Sive de Mensure de Gradibus Luminis, Colorum et Umbræ*. Eberhard Klett, Augsburg, 1760
42. Landy M. S., Graham N., Visual perception of texture, In Chalupa, L. M. & Werner, J. S. (Eds.), The Visual Neurosciences (pp. 1106-1118). Cambridge, MA: MIT Press.
43. Landy M. S., Chubb C., Balckshot: an unexpected dimension of human sensitivity to contrast. Journal of Vision 3(9), Abstract 60, 60a, 2003.
44. Leonardo da Vinci, Treatise on Painting. Editio Princeps, 1651.
45. Longuet–Higgins, M. S., The statistical analysis of a random, moving surface. Phil.Trans.R.Soc.Lond. A, 249(966), 321–387, 1957.
46. Lu, R.: *Ecological Optics of Materials*. Ph.D. thesis Utrecht University, 2000
47. Marr, D., Vision: A Computational Investigation into the Human Representation and Processing of Visual Information, Freeman: New York, 1982.
48. Metzger, W., Gesetze des Sehens. Waldemar Kramer: Frankfurt, 1975.
49. Nicodemus, F. E, Richmond, J. C., Hsia, J. J.: *Geometrical Considerations and Nomenclature for Reflectance*. Natl.Bur.Stand., (U.S.), Monogr. 160, 1977
50. Nicolaides, K., The natural way to draw. Houghton Mifflin,: Boston, 1941.
51. Nayar, S. K., Oren, M.: Visual appearance of matte surfaces. Science **267**, (1995), 1153–1156
52. Pentland, A. P.: Local shading analysis IEEE TPAMI 6, 170–187 1984.
53. Pont, S. C., Koenderink, J. J.: BRDF of specular surfaces with hemispherical pits. Journal of the Optical Society of America A, 19(2), 2456-2466, 2002.
54. Pont, S. C., Koenderink, J. J.: Split off-specular reflection and surface scattering from woven materials. Applied Optics IP, 42(8), 1526-1533, 2002.
55. Pont, S. C., Koenderink, J. J.: The Utrecht Oranges Set. Technical report and database; database available on request. 2003.
56. Pont, S. C., Koenderink, J. J., Illuminance flow. In: Computer analysis of images and Patterns, N. Petkov, M. A. Westenberg (eds.), Springer: Berlin, 90–97, 2003.
57. Pont, S.C., Koenderink, J.J.: Surface illuminance flow. Proceedings Second International Symposium on 3D Data Processing Visualization and Transmission, Aloimonos Y., Taubin G. (Eds.). 2004.
58. Pont, S. C., Koenderink, J. J.: Bidirectional Texture Contrast Function. International Journal of Computer Vision, 62(1/2), special issue: Texture Synthesis and Analysis, 17–34, 2005.
59. Pont, S. C., Koenderink, J. J.: Irradiation orientation from obliquely viewed texture. In: O.F. Olsen et al. (Eds.): DSSCV 2005, LNCS 3753, pp. 205–210. Springer-Verlag Berlin Heidelberg. 2005.

60. Pont, S. C., Koenderink, J. J.: Reflectance from locally glossy thoroughly pitted surfaces. Computer Vision and Image Understanding, 98, 211-222, 2005.
61. Ramachandran, V. S.: Perceiving shape from shading. The perceptual world: Readings from Scientific American magazine. I. Rock. New York, NY, US, W. H. Freeman & Co, Publishers. 127–138, 1990.
62. Ron, G., Peleg, S., Multiresolution Shape From Shading. IEEE, 350–355, 1989.
63. Sharan L., Li Y., Adelson E. H., Image statistics for surface reflectance estimation. Journal of Vision, 6(6), Abstract 101, 101a, 2006.
64. Varma, M., Zisserman, A., Estimating illumination direction from textured images. CVPR (1), 179-186, 2004.

Chapter 8

Texture for Appearance Models in Computer Vision and Graphics

Oana G. Cula[†] and Kristin J. Dana[‡]

[†]*Johnson & Johnson, Skillman, New Jersey, USA*

[‡]*Rutgers University, Piscataway, New Jersey, USA*

Appearance modeling is fundamental to the goals of computer vision and computer graphics. Traditionally, appearance was modeled with simple shading models (e.g. Lambertian or specular) applied to known or estimated surface geometry. However, real world surfaces such as hair, skin, fur, gravel, scratched or weathered surfaces, are difficult to model with this approach for a variety of reasons. In some cases it's not practical to obtain geometry because the variation is so complex and fine-scale. The geometric detail is not resolved with laser scanning devices or with stereo vision. Simple reflectance models assume that all light is reflected from the point where it hits the surface, i.e. no light is transmitted into the surface. But in many real surfaces, a portion of the light incident on one surface point is scattered beneath the surface and exits at other surface points. This subsurface scattering causes difficulties in accurately modeling a surface such as frosted glass or skin with a simple geometry plus shading model. So even when a precise geometric profile is attainable, applying a pointwise shading model is not sufficient. Because of these issues, image-based modeling has become a popular alternative to modeling with geometry and point-wise shading.

Real world surfaces are often textured with a variation in color (as in a paisley print or leopard spots) or a fine-scale surface height variation (e.g. crumpled paper, rough plaster, sand). Surface texture complicates appearance prediction because local shading, shadowing, foreshortening and occlusions change the observed appearance when lighting or viewing directions have changed. As an example, consider a globally planar surface of wrinkled leather where large local shadows appear when the surface is obliquely illuminated and disappear when the surface is frontally illuminated. Accounting for the variation of appearance due to changes in imaging parameters is a key issue in developing accurate models. The terms BRDF and BTF have been used to describe surface appearance. The BRDF (bidirectional reflectance distribution function) describes surface reflectance as a function of viewing and illumination angles. Since surface reflectance varies spatially for textured surfaces, the BTF was introduced to add a spatial variation. More specifically, the bidirectional texture function (BTF) is observed image texture as a function of viewing and illumination directions. In this chapter, topics in BRDF and BTF modeling for vision and graphics are presented. Two methods for recognition are described in detail: (1) bidirectional feature histograms and (2) symbolic primitives that are more useful for recognizing subtle differences in texture.

8.1. Introduction

The visual appearance of an object or person, is a seemingly simple concept. In everyday life, we see the visual appearance of objects, surfaces and scenes. We remember what we see, and store some type of cognitive representation of the visual world around us. So what are the important attributes of appearance? Size, shape and color are clearly at the top of the list. But for accurate computational descriptions of appearance, as needed for recognition and rendering algorithms, attributes of size, shape and color are not sufficient. The need for a more comprehensive description of appearance is the motivation behind the study and appreciation of texture. The scenes and surfaces of our world are filled with textures: rocks, sand, trees, skin, velvet, burlap, foliage, screen, crystals. In this chapter, we concentrate on textured objects or surfaces which have a fine-scale geometric variation as depicted in Figure 8.1. By fine-scale, we mean geometric details (height changes) that are small compared to the viewing distance and are typically hard to measure such as fine-scale wrinkles in leather, venation of leaves, fibers of textiles, fuzziness of a peach, weave of a fabric, and roughness of plaster. These textures have also been termed relief textures or 3D textures and can be accompanied by color variations.

In natural environments, most surfaces exhibit some amount of fine-scale geometry (tactile texture) or roughness. Because of this non-smooth surface geometry, appearance is affected by local occlusion, shadowing and foreshortening, as shown in Figure 8.2. Here, the rough surface of the plaster is viewed under different surface tilts and light source directions, so appearance changes significantly. More examples are shown in Figure 8.3 which shows hair and fabric texture. Figure 8.4 shows an interesting demonstration of unwrapping the texture of a ball to visualize the constituent image. This unwrapped texture image is the result of an operation that is essentially the inverse of texture mapping. With texture mapping,

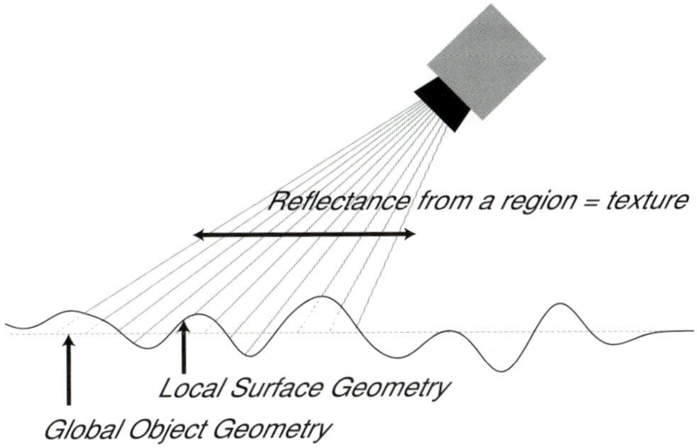

Fig. 8.1. Surface appearance or texture is the reflected light in a spatial region. We are interested in the case when the local geometry is not smooth and has some roughness. In general this fine-scale geometry is difficult to measure or model so image-based modeling techniques are useful.

Fig. 8.2. Four images of the same rough plaster surface. As the surface tilt and illumination direction varies, surface appearance changes.

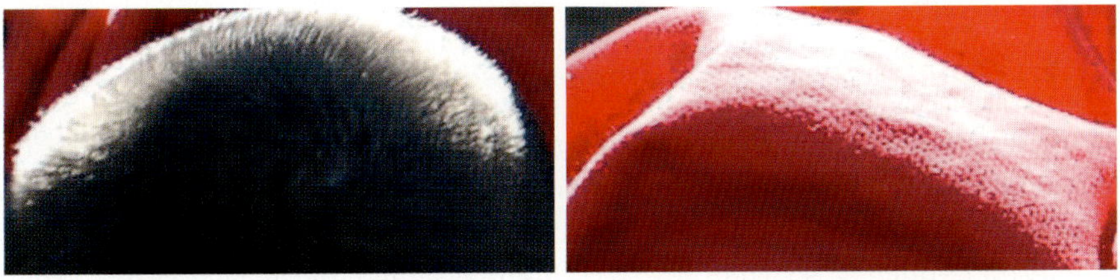

Fig. 8.3. Complexities of real surfaces. (Left) Hair in sunlight. (Right) Fabric texture.

a single image is mapped onto the geometry of the ball. The unwrapping requires multiple stages and knowledge of the object geometry and camera parameters. The important point for the purposes of this discussion is that the unwrapped image is not uniform in appearance. The lighting and viewpoint variations around the ball cause a change in appearance of

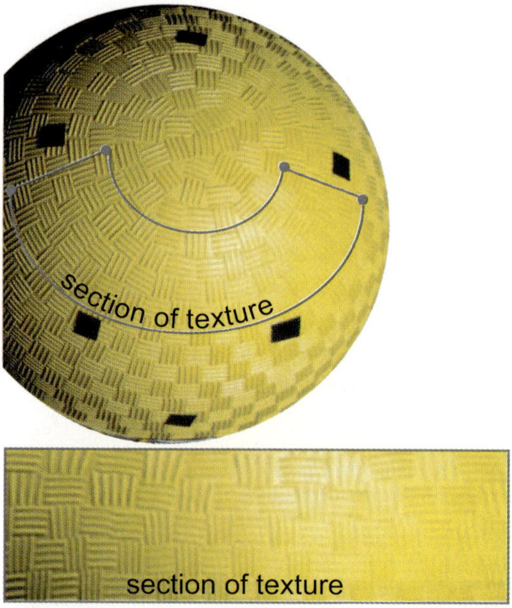

Fig. 8.4. Unwrapped texture of a ball. Since the ball geometry is known, the section of the image can be unwrapped (inverse of texture mapping) and the local appearance of the texture section is shown. Notice that local foreshortening, shadowing and occlusions change across the texture because of the differences in global surface orientation and illumination direction.

the fine-scale texture. Therefore instead a single texture image, cannot sufficiently capture appearance.

8.1.1. *Geometry-based vs. image-based*

Knowing that a single image is not sufficient to capture appearance, the pertinent question is: what additional information is needed? There are essentially two options. The first is geometry-based: measure fine-scale geometry explicitly so that an extremely detailed mesh is created. The second option is image-based: sample the space of imaging parameters, i.e. choose a finite set of illumination and viewing directions, and record the image of the surface. In general, the geometry-based approach is not favored for several reasons. First, fine-scale geometry is often very hard to measure. Consider the hair texture of Figure 8.3, a laser scanner or stereo method would have great difficulty because of the large amount of occlusions. Consider also the very fine details on skin texture such as individual pores. Each scanning system has a finite resolution so there is an inevitable loss of detail. Also, the translucency of materials such as skin make scanning very difficult. Laser scanners work best for white opaque objects that do not exhibit internal light scattering.

But even if we could measure the fine-scale geometry perfectly, geometry is not appearance. In order to render the object the reflectance must be known. A typical computer graphics shader uses very simple shading models that are only an approximation of the actual reflectance. For highly accurate modeling, the bidirectional reflectance distribution function (BRDF) for the surface material is needed. The BRDF gives the surface reflectance for any combination of viewing direction and incident illumination direction. Additionally, many real world surfaces are not spatially homogeneous, so the BRDF changes across the surface. To measure the BRDF at each point, the reflectance is measured from all exitance angles and for all incident angles. But for a rough surface, some angles are occluded by the neighbors, i.e. the peaks and valleys of the surface create occlusions making a pointwise BRDF is difficult to measure.

Additionally, BRDF models assume that all light is reflected from the point where it hits the surface, i.e. no light is transmitted into the surface. But in many real surfaces, a portion of the light incident on one surface point is scattered beneath the surface and exits at other surface points.[1,2] This subsurface scattering causes difficulties in accurately modeling a surface such as frosted glass or skin with a simple geometry plus shading model. So even when a precise geometric profile is attainable, applying a pointwise shading model is not sufficient. Because of these issues, image-based modeling has become a popular alternative to modeling with geometry and point-wise shading. The BTF (bidirectional texture function) is the nomenclature introduced in[3,4] for an image-based characterization of texture appearance.

8.2. BRDF and BTF: A Historical Perspective

The BRDF has been a standard term in computer vision for decades. It's formal definition is the ratio of the radiance exiting a surface point to the irradiance incident on the surface point. Informally it's the ratio of the amount of input light to the output light. The units of the BRDF can seem formidable at first glance, *watts per steridian per meter*^{2} . To parse the units, consider that the amount of input light is the light power in watts measured per unit area, so input light has the units watts per meter^2. The

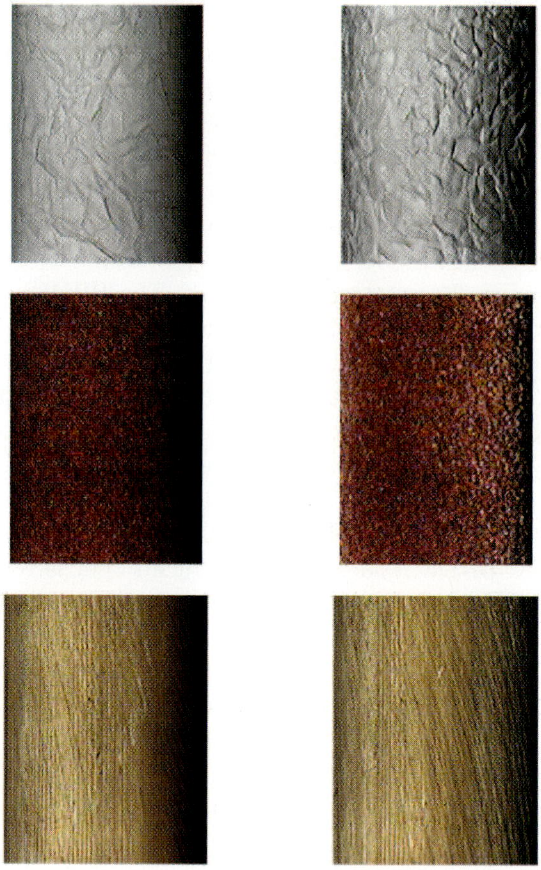

Fig. 8.5. Comparison of standard texture mapping and BTF mapping. (Left) standard texture mapping. (Right) BTF texture mapping. Images from Ref. 4.

amount of output light is slightly more complicated. The total output light is watts per meter^2 but it radiates in many directions. For the BRDF we are interested in the amount of output light in a particular direction. The units of the solid angle in a particular direction are steridians. Hence, the output light is measured in watts per meter^2, per steridian. The BRDF was first defined by Nicodemus in 1970.[5] Since it is a function of viewing and illumination angles it can be expressed as $f(\theta_i, \phi_i, \theta_v, \phi_v)$.

Real world surfaces typically do not have a uniform BRDF due to both surface markings and surface texture. The bidirectional texture function (BTF) extends the BRDF in order to characterize surfaces reflectance that varies spatially. The early concept of BTF was introduced with the Columbia-Utrecht Texture and Reflectance (CUReT) database in 1996[3,4] and used for numerous texture modeling and recognition studies. The BTF is expressed as $f(x, y, \theta_i, \phi_i, \theta_v, \phi_v)$, but there is an important subtlety in the definition. As discussed, in 8.1, the BTF is not simply the BRDF at each surface point. The BTF concept is best expressed when considering a flat piece of rough material. Instead of modeling the exact fine-scale surface geometry and then applying a measured BRDF on the bumpy mesh, we assume the geometry is locally flat and that appearance changes with viewing and illumination direction. The model ignores the fine-scale geometry when defining viewpoint and illumination directions. That is, the imaging directions are defined with respect to the reference plane. Appearance is captured by obtaining images from multiple viewing and illumination directions. The fine-scale shadowing, occlusions, shading and foreshortening that affect the pixel intensities of the recorded images become part of the appearance model, explicitly, without regard for the height profile of the surface. In effect, the fine-scale geometric variations and any additional color variations are modeled as a spatially varying BRDF $f(x, y, \theta_i, \phi_i, \theta_v, \phi_v)$. Specifically, the reflectance at each point is not a typical reflectance function but instead contains the nonlinearities of the shadowing and occlusions of fine-scale geometry. A surface point at x, y may be shadowed as the illumination direction changes from θ_i to $\theta_i + \delta$ for some small angle δ, causing an abrupt change in the BTF $f(x, y, \theta_i, \phi_i, \theta_v, \phi_v)$ to near zero reflectance.

Of course, the BTF extends to non-flat surfaces as well. The conceptual model is that the object can be characterized by a geometric mesh that is "texture-mapped" not with a single image but with a BTF. Typical texture mapping maps each point of the 3D vertex into a 2D texture image parameterized by the texture coordinates u, v which vary from 0 to 1. But recall that a single image is not sufficient for authentic replications of appearance. Instead the imaging parameters for that vertex must be part of the mapping. That is, the vertex in object space is mapped to $f(u, v, I, V)$ which is the BTF with standard texture coordinates (u,v). Here the vector I is used for the illumination direction instead of the polar and azimuth angles (θ_i, ϕ_i). Similarly the viewing direction is specified by V. A BTF sample is an image $f(x, y, I, V)$ with the x, y coordinates which are now scaled to u, v coordinates which vary from 0 to 1. A comparison of the appearance of standard texture mapping and BTF mapping for simple cylinders is shown in Figure 8.5.

Ongoing research seeks to address the following important questions: 1) How many samples are necessary to appropriately capture appearance? Since the space of parameters is a 4 dimensional space with variations of illumination and viewing angles, even a sparse sampling of the space gives a large number of images. For example, 30 illumination angles and 30 viewing angles for each illumination direction is 900 images. 2) Where should the samples be positioned in the space of imaging parameters to best represent the surface? Should the viewing and illumination angles chosen be a uniform sampling of the imaging space? Are there some directions that should be sampled more densely? 3) How can in-between samples be obtained, i.e. how to interpolate a full continuous BTF from the finite number of measured samples.

One of the difficulties in answering these questions is that the answer depends on the surface itself. In an empirical study of a set from the Curet database,[6] it was shown that a very important sample for recognizing the surface was the sample which was viewed at a 45 degree angle from the global surface normal and illuminated from the opposite 45 degree angle. This empirical result is consistent with intuition because shadows and occlusions accentuate details but too many shadows obscure the surface. Another important issue in evaluating the effectiveness of the BTF is to consider the perceptual issues in replacing geometry with texture. An important contribution in this area is the work of Ref. 7.

8.3. Recent Developments in BTF Measurements and Models

Surface appearance has been a popular topic in computer vision and computer graphics in the last decade. The research can be categorized into the following topics: (1) recognition, (2) representation, (3) rendering and (4) measurement.

Recognition methods have been developed which learn the appearance of textured surface through a training stage using example images from surfaces with varying imaging parameters, i.e. varying illumination and viewing directions. The 3D texton method,[8,9] uses textons from registered training images to build an appearance vector which is the observed appearance under multiple imaging parameters. Histograms of appearance vectors characterize the texture and can be used to recognize novel image sets under the same imaging parameters. The bidirectional feature histogram (BFH) method[6,10,11] uses an image texton vocabulary from arbitrary unregistered input images. Once the image texton library is learned, histograms of texton labels characterize surfaces. Histograms from multiple images using different imaging parameters characterize surface appearance under multiple viewing and illumination This model is used for recognizing a surface using a single image under unknown imaging parameters that was not part of the training set. More details of the BFH recognition method are provided in Section 8.4.1. Another method which uses histograms of learned image features is Ref. 12, and this method clusters using rotationally invariance filter responses in order to learn local image features.

Representations for surface BTF's are computational models built from measurements that can be used to synthesize appearance from novel viewing and illumination directions. These representations provide a means of interpolating between samples and storing surface information in a concise format. Representations methods that have been employed thus far for BTF's include principal components analysis (PCA),[13–16] spherical harmonics,[17] basis functions of recovered BRDF's,[18] tensor factorization,[19] and steerable basis textures.[20]

Rendering BTF's in an efficient manner for realistic surface appearance in graphics has received significant attention in the literature. Early pioneering work included view dependent texture in image-based rendering of architecture.[21] More recent work on texture rendering that enables efficient BTF rendering includes.[22–26] A variation of BTF rendering which models surface geometry as a displacement mapping includes.[27–29]

Measurements of surface appearance are particularly important in creating models for recognition, rendering and representations. Sampling the appearance space is the first step to most of the current example-based methods. In addition to the Curet database, there have been several more recent texture databases including the Bonn BTF database,[30,31] Oulu Texture Database,[32] and the Heriot-Watt Photex database.[33] The Photex database has the advantage of having registered data amenable to photometric stereo. The latest in texture databases characterizing the time varying aspect of surface appearance including surfaces whose appearance changes as the dry (wood paint), decay (fruit), and corrode (metals).[34]

Specialized devices are needed to measure appearance. The measurement apparatus is often a gonioreflectometer with lighting and cameras at multiple positions over a hemisphere or dome.[35,36] For object or face appearance, dome-based imaging apparatus is necessary. However, texture surfaces can often be characterized by a small locally flat sample that make smaller devices a reasonable option. The fundamental difficulty in changing the imaging parameters to obtain appearance measurements has led to several novel devices to measure texture appearance. These include a texture camera,[37,38] kaleidoscope for BTF measurements,[39] and a photometric stereo desktop scanner.[40]

Measurements of surface appearance have been incorporated in digital archiving work in order to create an accurate digital representation of the appearance of historical sites and artwork, Important work in this area include digitizing the Florentine Pieta[41,42] and the digital Michelangelo project.[43] In these projects the goal is to measure both global shape and local surface appearance. The main goal is a digital representation that can simulate the physical presence of the archived object.

Some of the fascinating papers in the literature on appearance are those that explain specific phenomena in real world surfaces. Models have been developed for weathered materials,[44] the appearance of finished wood,[45] velvet,[46,47] granite,[48] and plant leaves.[49] These models consider the physics of the surface and how light interacts at the material boundaries to create an accuarate prediction of appearance. The specific methods demonstrate the complexities and the variety of natural surfaces.

Modeling texture appearance with images instead of geometry has a consistent foundation with general image-based rendering approaches in graphics,[50–54] and appearance-based modeling in vision.[55–59] Image-based rendering caused a convergence of computer graphics and computer vision. Prior work in graphics concentrated on modeling object geometry and applying shading models. Image-based rendering allowed rendering without ever knowing the object geometry. Similarly, with the BTF, rendering is done with no knowledge of the surface geometry.

8.4. Appearance Models for Recognition

In this section we detail one method for recognition based on texture appearance called the bidirectional feature histogram. This method is but one of many modeling and recognition papers in the field. However, it has the advantage that the actual viewing and illumination parameters do not have to be known for the test and for the training images. Application of the model in recognizing skin texutres is discussed in Section 8.5.

8.4.1. *Bidirectional feature histogram*

One model for the BTF is the Bidirectional Feature Histogram.[10] A statistical representation is a useful tool for modeling texture for recognition purposes. The standard framework for texture recognition consists of a primitive and a statistical distribution (histogram) of this primitive over space. So how does one account for changes with imaging parameters (view/illumination direction)? Either the primitive or the statistical distribution should be a function of the imaging parameters. Using this framework, the comparison of our approach with the 3D texton method[9] is straightforward. The 3D texton method uses a primitive that is a function of imaging parameters, while our method uses a statistical distribution that is a function of imaging parameters. In our approach the histogram of features representing the texture appearance is called bidirectional because it is a function of viewing and illumination directions. The advantage of our approach is that we don't have to align the images obtained under different imaging parameters.

The primitive used in our BTF model is obtained as follows. We start by taking a large set of surfaces, filter these surfaces by oriented multiscale filters and then cluster the output. The hypothesis is that locally there are a finite number of intensity configurations so the filter outputs will form clusters (representing canonical structures like bumps, edges, grooves pits). The clustering of filter outputs are textons. A particular texture sample is processed using several images obtained under different imaging parameters (i.e. different light source directions and camera directions). The local structures are given a texton label from an image texton library (set up in preprocessing). For each image, the texton histograms are computed. Because these histograms are a function of two directions (light source and viewing direction), they're called bidirectional feature histograms or BFH. The recognition is done in two stages: (1) a training stage where a BFH is created for each class using example images and (2) a classification stage. In the classification stage we only need a single image and the light and camera direction is unknown and arbitrary. Therefore we can train with one set of imaging conditions but recognize under a completely different set of imaging conditions.

Within a texture image there are generic structures such as edges, bumps and ridges. Figure 8.6 illustrates the pre-processing step of constructing the image texton library. We use a multiresolution filter bank F, with size denoted by $3 \times f$, and consisting of oriented derivatives of

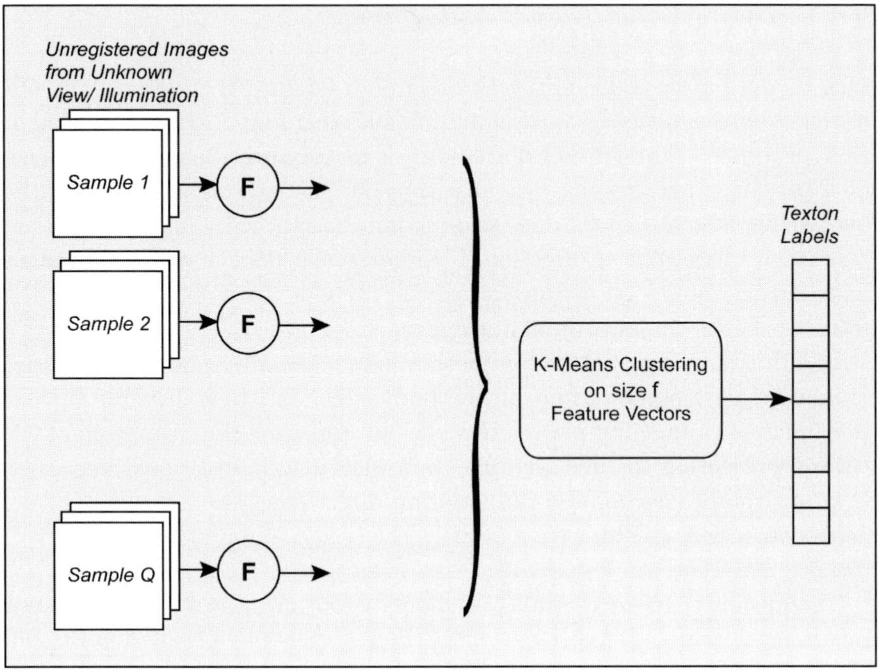

Fig. 8.6. Creation of the image texton library. The set of q unregistered texture images from the BTF of each of the Q samples are filtered with the filter bank F consisting of $3 \times f$ filters, i.e. f filters for each of the three scales. The filter responses for each pixel are concatenated over scale to form feature vectors of size f. The feature space is clustered via k-means to determine the collection of key features, i.e. the image texton library.

Gaussian filters and center surround derivatives of Gaussian filters on three scales as in Ref. 9. Each pixel of a texture image is characterized by a set of three multi-dimensional feature vectors obtained by concatenating the corresponding filter responses over scale. K-means clustering is used on these concatenated filter outputs to get image textons. By using a large set of images in creating the set of image textons, the resulting library is generic enough to represent the local features in novel texture images that were not used in creating the library.

The histogram of image textons is used to encode the global distribution of the local structural attribute over the texture image. This representation, denoted by $H(l)$, is a discrete function of the labels l induced by the image texton library, and it is computed as described in Figure 8.7. Each texture image is filtered using the same filter bank F as the one used for

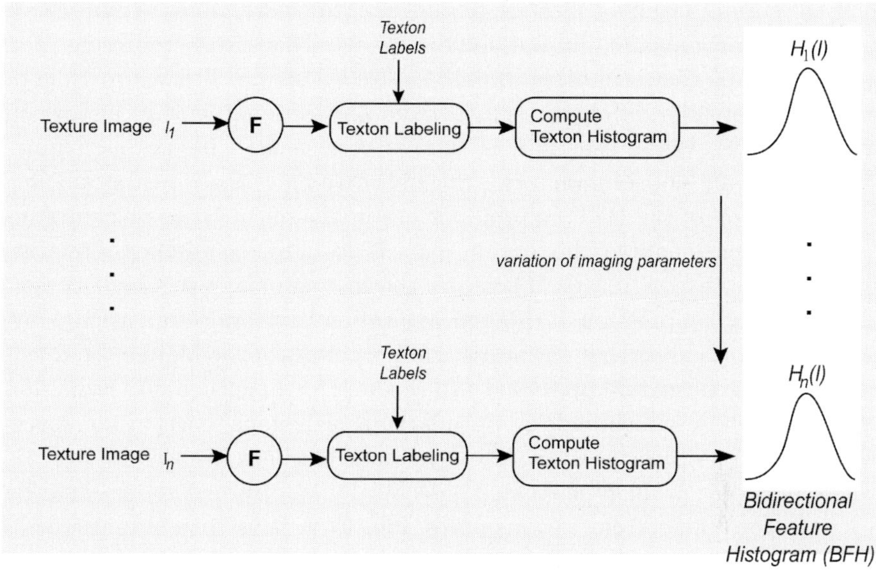

Fig. 8.7. 3D texture representation. Each texture image I_j, $j = 1 \ldots n$, is filtered with filter bank F, and filter responses for each pixel are concatenated over scale to form feature vectors. The feature vectors are projected onto the space spanned by the elements of the image texton library, then labeled by determining the closest texton. The distributions of labels over the images are approximated by the texton histograms $H_j(l)$, $j = 1 \ldots n$. The set of texton histograms, as a function of the imaging parameters, forms the 3D texture representation, referred to as the bidirectional feature histogram (BFH).

creating the texton library. Each pixel within the texture image is represented by a multidimensional feature vector obtained by concatenating the corresponding filter responses over scale. In the feature space populated by both the feature vectors and the image textons, each feature vector is labeled by determining the closest image texton. The spatial distribution of the representative local structural features over the image is approximated by computing the texton histogram. Given the complex height variation of the 3D textured sample, the texture image is strongly influenced by both the viewing direction and the illumination direction under which the image is captured. Accordingly, the corresponding image texton histogram is a function of the imaging conditions.

Note that in our approach, neither the image texton nor the texton histogram encode the change in local appearance of texture with the imaging conditions. These quantities are local to a single texture image. We represent the surface using a collection of image texton histograms, acquired as a function of viewing and illumination directions. This surface representation is described by the term *bidirectional feature histogram.* It is worthwhile to explicitly note the difference between the bidirectional feature histogram and the BTF. While the BTF is the set of measured images as a function of viewing and illumination, the bidirectional feature histogram is a representation of the BTF suitable for use in classification or recognition.

The dimensionality of histogram space is given by the number of textons in the image texton library. Therefore the histogram space is high dimensional, and a compression of this representation to a lower-dimensional one is suitable, providing that the statistical properties of the bidirectional feature histograms are still preserved. To accomplish dimensionality reduction we employ PCA, which finds an optimal new orthogonal basis in the space, while best describing the data. This approach has been inspired by Ref. 57, where a similar problem is treated, specifically an object is represented by set of images taken from various poses, and PCA is used to obtain a compact lower-dimensional representation.

In the classification stage, the subset of testing texture images is disjoint from the subset used for training. Again, each image is filtered by F, the resulting feature vectors are projected in the image texton space and labeled according to the texton library. The texton distribution over the texture image is approximated by the texton histogram. The classification is based on a single novel texture image, and it is accomplished by projecting the corresponding texton histogram onto the universal eigenspace created during training, and by determining the closest point in the eigenspace. The 3D texture sample corresponding to the manifold onto which the closest point lies is reported as the surface class of the testing texture image.

8.5. Application: Human Skin Texture Recognition

8.5.1. *Hand texture recognition*

Many texture recognition experiments are done with textures from very distint classes, like many of the textures of the CUReT database. However, it is particularly interesting to show recognition of textured surfaces that are not very different in composition. An illustrative example is the recognition of different samples of skin texture. Human skin has fine-scale details as shown in Figure 8.8 including skin glyphs, skin imperfections, skin dryness, scars, etc. These images are from the Rutgers Skin Texture Database.[11]

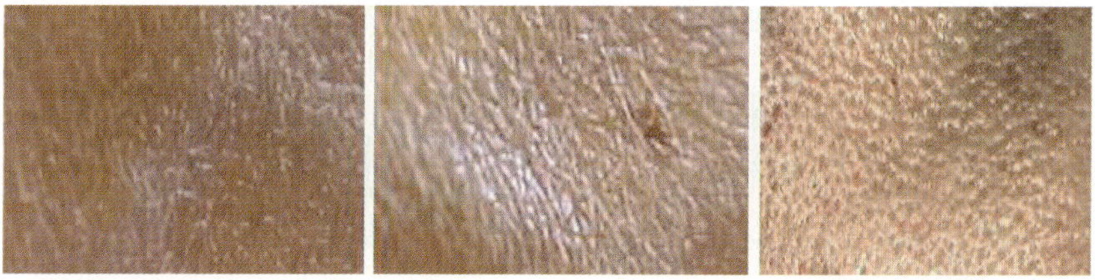

Fig. 8.8. Examples of skin texture showing fine-scale geometric detail.

Consider the task of recognizing which section of the hand is depicted in a particular skin texture image. Different regions of the hand have distinct textural features, although the distinction is more subtle than with other textured surfaces, e.g pebbles vs. grass. We summarize a simple experiment for hand texture recognition that was described in more detail in Ref. 11. For this experiment, the bidirectional feature histogram model is used. The skin regions correspond to three distinct regions of a finger: bottom segment on palm side, fingertip, and bottom segment on the back of the hand, as illustrated in Figure 8.9. Test images are from two subjects: for subject 1 both the index and middle fingers of left hand have been imaged, for subject 2 the index finger of left hand has been measured. For each of 9 combinations of finger region, finger type and subject, 30 images are captured, corresponding to 3 camera poses, and 10 light source positions for each camera pose. As a result the dataset for the hand texture experiments contains 270 skin texture images. Figure 8.10 illustrates few examples of texture images in this dataset. During preprocessing each image is converted to gray scale, and is manually segmented to isolate the largest approximately planar skin surface used in the experiments.

For constructing the image texton library, we consider a set of skin texture images from all three classes, however only from index finger of subject 1. This reduced subset of images is used because we assume that the representative features for a texture surface are generic. This assumption is particularly applicable to skin textures, given the local structural similarities between various skin texture classes.

Each texture image is filtered by employing a filter bank consisting of 18 oriented Gaussian derivative filters with six orientations corresponding to three distinct scales as in Ref. 8. The filter outputs corresponding to a certain scale are grouped to form six-dimensional feature vectors. The resulting three sets of feature vectors are used each to populate a feature space, where clustering via k-means is performed to determine the repre-

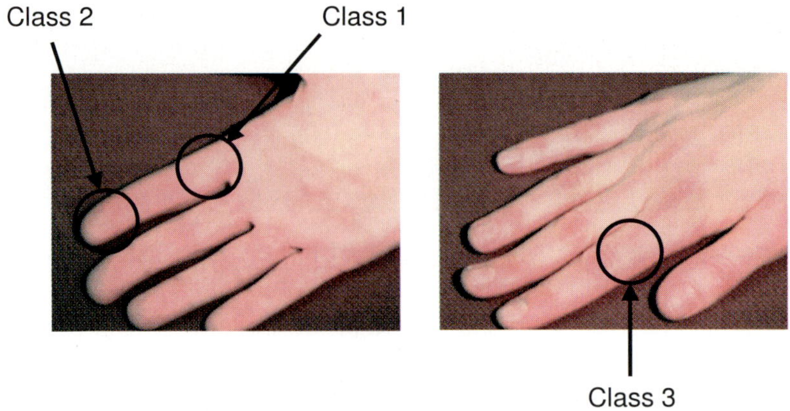

Fig. 8.9. Illustration of the hand locations imaged during the experiments described in Section 8.5.1.

sentatives among the population. We empirically choose to employ in our experiments a texton library consisting of 50 textons for each scale.

During the first set of experiments, the training and testing image sets for each class are disjoint, corresponding to different imaging conditions or being obtained from different surfaces belonging to the same class (e.g. fingertip surface from different fingers). For each of the classes we consider all available data, that is, each texture class is characterized by 90 images. We vary the size of the training set for each class from 45 to 60, and, consequently the test set size is varied from 45 to 30. For a fixed dimensionality of the universal eigenspace, i.e. 30, the profiles of individual recognition rates for each class, as well as the profile of the global recognition rate indexed by the size of the training set are illustrated in Figure 8.11 (a). As the training set for each class is enlarged, the recognition rate improves, attaining the value 100% for the case of 60 texture images for training and the rest of 30 for testing. To emphasize the strength of this result consider that the classification is based on either: a single texture image captured under different imaging conditions than the training set; or a single texture image captured under the same imaging conditions, but from a different skin surface. The variation of recognition rate as a function of the dimensionality of the universal eigenspace, when the size of the training set is fixed to 60, is depicted in Figure 8.11 (b). As expected, the performance improves as the dimensionality of the universal eigenspace is increased.

In training and testing, images are from spatially disjoint image regions. We divide each skin texture image into two non-overlapping subimages,

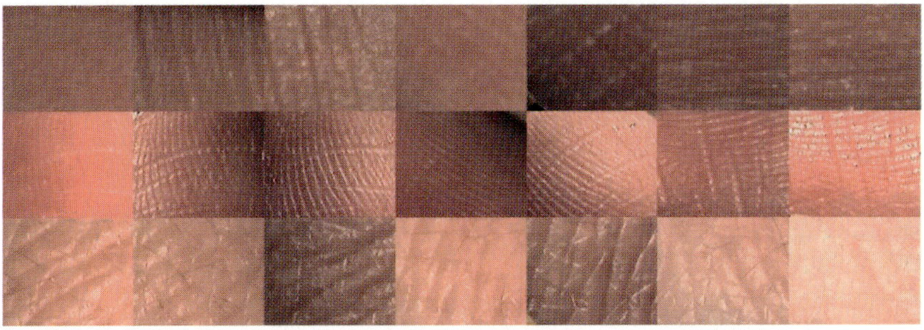

(a)

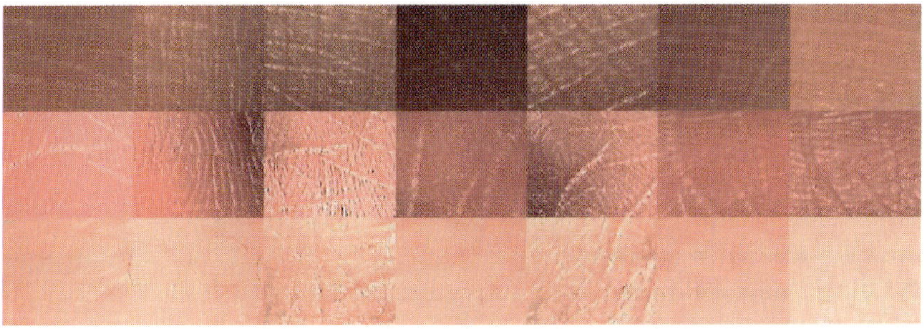

(b)

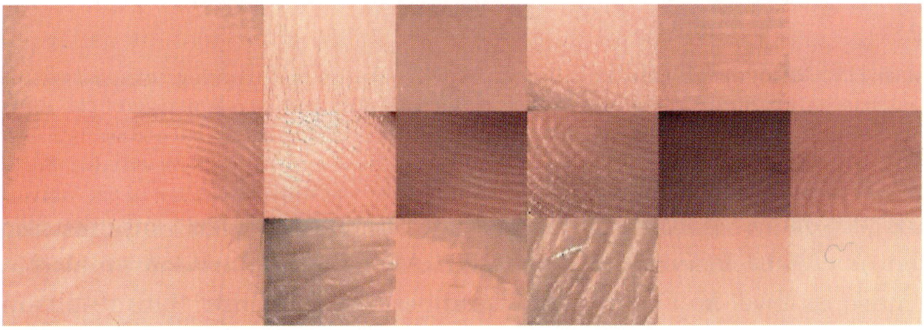

(c)

Fig. 8.10. Examples of hand skin texture images for each location, and for each of the three fingers imaged during our experiments. In each of the pictures first row depicts skin texture corresponding to class 1 (bottom segment, palm side), second row presents texture images from class 2 (fingertip), and third row consists of texture images from class 3 (bottom segment, back of palm). In (a) images are obtained from index finger of subject 1, in (b) from middle finger of subject 1, and in (c) from index finger of subject 2.

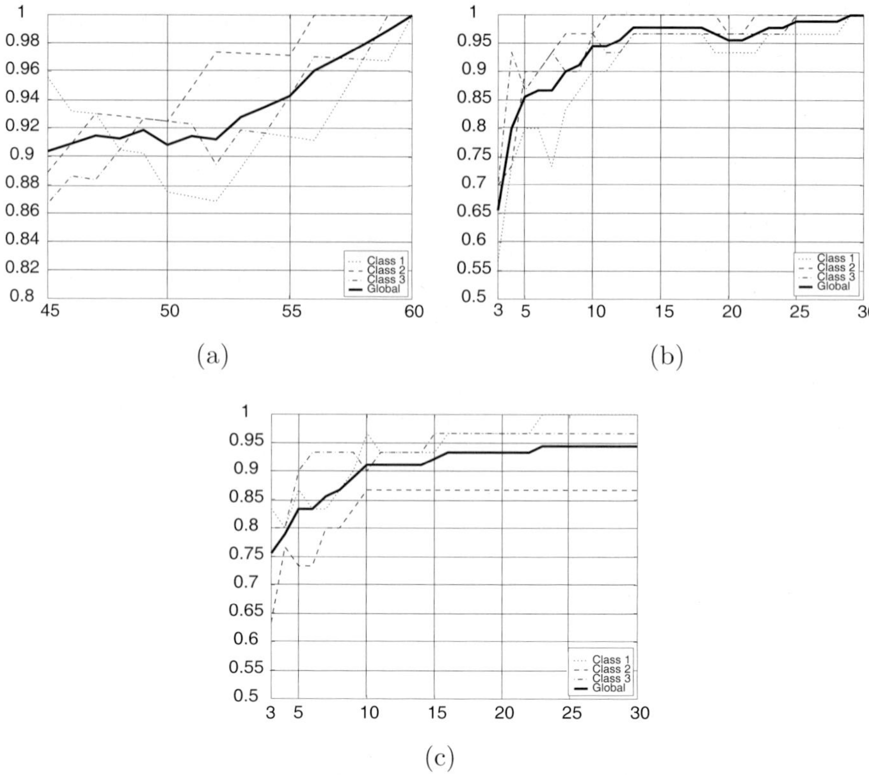

Fig. 8.11. Recognition rate as a function of the size of the training set (a) (when dimensionality of the universal eigenspace is fixed to 30), and as a function of the dimensionality of the universal eigenspace (b) (when the training set of each class has cardinality 60), both corresponding to first set of recognition experiments reported in Section 8.5.1. (c) Profile of recognition rate as a function of the dimensionality of the universal eigenspace, corresponding to second recognition experiment, described in Section 8.5.1.

denoted as lower half subimage, and upper half subimage. This results in a set of 60 texture subimages, two for each of the 30 combinations of imaging parameters. For this experiment we consider data obtained from index finger of subject 1. The training set is constructed by alternatively choosing lower half and upper half subimages, which correspond to all 30 imaging conditions. The testing set is the complement of training set relative to the set of 60 subimages for each class. The recognition rate indexed by the dimensionality of the universal eigenspace is plotted in Figure 8.11 (c). For the case of a 30-dimensional eigenspace, the global recognition rate is about 95%, when for class 1 is attained a recognition rate of 100%, class 3 is classified with an error smaller than 4%, and for class 2 the recognition rate is about 87%. Class 2 is the most problematic to be classified, due in part to the non-planarity of the fingertip.

8.6. Image Texton Alternative

Although the image texton method works well when inter-class separation is large, there are several drawbacks to this approach. Clustering the feature vectors (filter outputs) in a high dimensional space is difficult and the results are highly dependent on the prechosen number of clusters. Furthermore, pixels which have very different filter responses are often part of the same perceptual texture primitive.

Consider the texture primitive needed to characterize structure in a textured region such as skin pores (see Figure 8.8). For this task, the local geometric arrangement of intensity edges is important. However, the exact magnitude of the edge pixels is not of particular significance. In the clustering approach, two horizontal edges with different gradient magnitude may be given different labels and this negatively affects the quality of the texture classification.

One solution to this issue is a representation that is tuned to common edges regardless of the magnitude of the filter response. Specifically, the index of the filter with the maximal response is retained as the feature for each pixel. The local configuration of these nonlinear features is a simple and useful texture primitive. The dimensionality of the texture primitive depends on the number of pixels in the local configuration and can be kept quite low. No clustering is necessary as the texture primitive is directly defined by the spatial arrangement of maximal response features.

As with the bidirectional feature histograms, Each training image provides a primitive histogram and several training images obtained with different imaging parameters are collected for each texture class. The histograms from all training images for all texture classes are used to create an eigenspace. The primitive histograms from a certain class are projected to points in this eigenspace and represent a sampling of the manifold of points for the appearance of this texture class. In theory, the entire manifold would be obtained by histograms from the continuum of all possible viewing and illumination directions. For recognition, the primitive histograms from novel texture images are projected into the eigenspace and compared with each point in the training set. The class of the nearest K neighbors is the classification result. (In our experiments K is set to 5). Figure 8.12 illustrates the main steps of the recognition method.

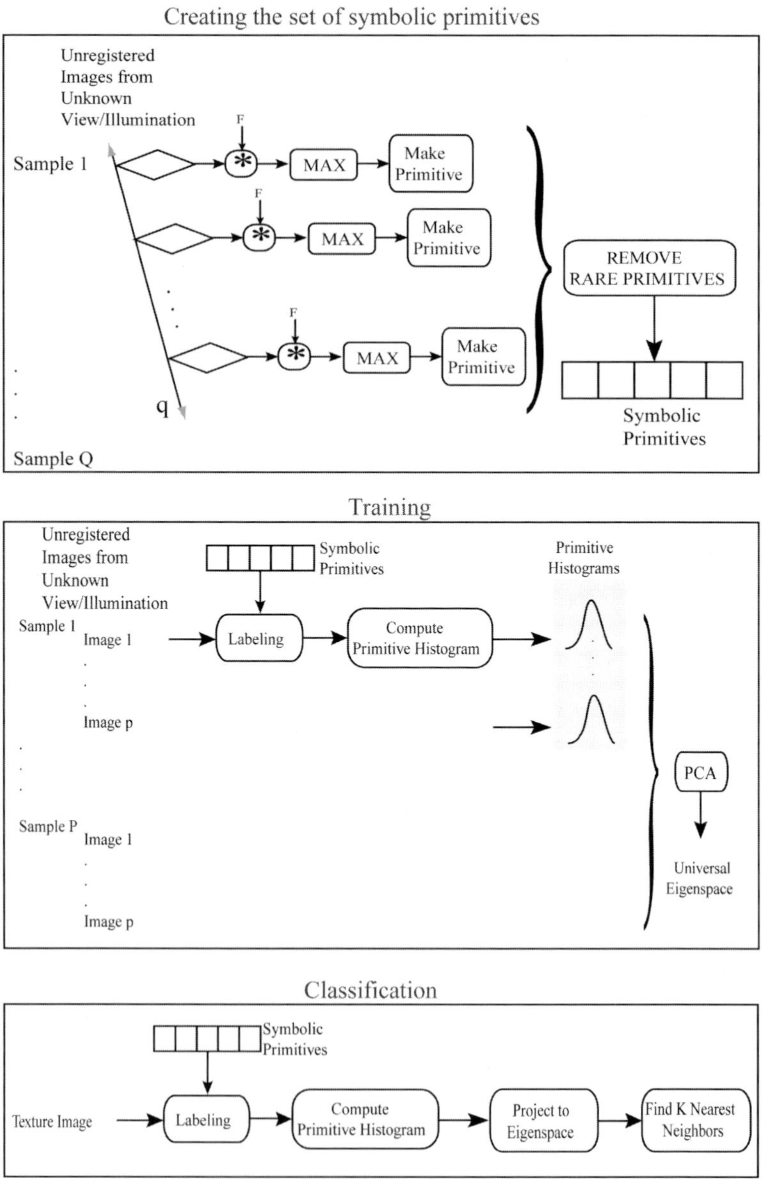

Fig. 8.12. The recognition method based on symbolic primitives. First, a set of representative symbolic primitives is created. During training a skin primitive histogram is created for each image, while the recognition is based on a single novel texture image of unknown imaging conditions.

8.7. Face Texture Recognition

Face recognition has numerous applications for user interfaces and surveillance. Many face recognition systems use overall structure of the face and key facial features such as the configuration and shape of the eyes, nose and mouth. However, fine-scale facial details provide an interesting basis for recognition. Twins will have different skin imperfections and markings. These details that humans may not consciously use in recognition become an additional fingerprint for identification. We summarize the facial recognition experiment in Ref. 11 here.

For face texture recognition, we use features that are the maximal response texture primitive. For this experiment, skin texture images from all 20 subjects are used. The imaged face locations are the forehead, chin, cheek and nose. Each location on each subject is imaged with a set of 32 combinations of imaging angles, therefore the total number of skin images employed during the experiments is 2496 (18 subjects with 4 locations on the face, 2 subjects with 3 locations on the face, 32 imaging conditions per location).

Color is not used as a cue for recognition because we are specifically studying the performance of texture models. The filter bank consists of five filters: 4 oriented Gaussian derivative filters, and one Laplacian of Gaussian filter. These filters are chosen to efficiently identify the local oriented patterns evident in skin structures. The filter bank is illustrated in Figure 8.13 (a). Each filter has size 15x15. Define several types of texture primitives by grouping maximal response indices corresponding to nine neighboring pixels. Specifically, define five types of local configurations, denoted by Pi, i=1...5, and illustrated in Figure 8.13 (b). Featureless regions are assigned a separate index F0, which corresponds to pixels in the image where the filter response are weak, that is, where the maximum filter response is not larger than a threshold. Therefore the texture primitive can be viewed as a string of nine features, where each feature can have values in the set $\{0, ..., 5\}$. A comprehensive set of primitives can be quite extensive, therefore the dimensionality of the primitive histogram can be very large. Hence the need to prune the initial set of primitives to a subset consisting of primitives with high probability of occurrence in the image. Also, this reasoning is consistent with the repetitiveness of the local structure that is characteristic property of texture images.

We construct the set of representative symbolic primitives by using 384 images from 3 randomly selected subjects and for all four locations per

Fig. 8.13. (a) The set of five filters (Fi, i = 1...5) used during the face skin modeling: four oriented Gaussian derivative filters, and one Laplacian of Gaussian derivative filter. (b) The set of five local configurations (Pi, i = 1...5) used for constructing the symbolic primitives.

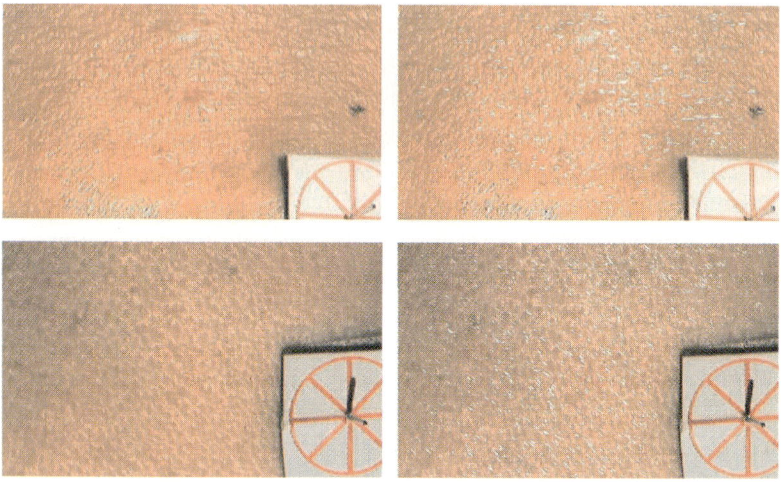

Fig. 8.14. Two instances of images labeled with various texture primitives. The left column illustrates the original images, while the right column presents the image with pixels labeled by certain symbolic primitives (white spots). Specifically, the first row shows pixels in the image labeled by primitives of type P1, where all filters are horizontally oriented; the second row shows images labeled with primitives of type P3, where the filters are oriented at -45°. Notice that indeed the symbolic primitives successfully capture the local structure in the image.

subject. We first construct the set of all symbolic primitives from all 384 skin images, then we eliminate the ones with low probability. The resulting set of representative symbolic primitives is further employed for labeling the images, and consequently to construct the primitive histogram for each image. Figure 8.14 exemplifies five instances of images labeled with various symbolic primitives. The left column illustrates the original images, while the right column presents the images with pixels labeled by certain symbolic primitives (white spots). The first row shows pixels in the image labeled by primitives of type P1, where all filters are horizontally oriented. The second row shows images labeled with primitives of type P3, where the filters are oriented at -45°. Notice that the symbolic primitives successfully capture the local structure in the image.

We use skin images from forehead, cheek, chin and nose to recognize 20 subjects. For each subject, the images are acquired within the same day and do not incorporate changes with aging. A human subject is characterized by a set of 32 texture images for each face location, i.e. 128 images per subject.

Classification is achieved based on a set of four testing images, one for each location (forehead, cheek, chin and nose). Each of the four test images is labeled by a tentative human identification, then the final decision is obtained by taking the majority of classes. The training and testing set are disjoint with respect to imaging parameters (the training images are obtained from different viewing and illumination direction from the test images). Knowledge of the actual viewpoint and illumination direction is never needed in the recognition. In practice this is important because the test (and training images) can be from arbitrary lighting direction and viewpoint which is far more convenient than trying to precisely align the light source and human subject.

To test recognition performance, the number of images in the training set for each subject and location is varied. The remainder of the images is used for the test set. Specifically, the training set is varied from 16 to 26 texture images for each subject and face location, and the final testing is on the remaining four subsets of 16 to 6 texture images per subject and location. The global recognition rate for this experiment reaches 73%. This result suggests that human identification can be aided by including skin texture recognition as a biometric in addition. This experiment uses skin texture alone, which is quite difficult and not typically necessary. In face recognition applications, a combination of recognition based on overall face structure with the addition of facial texture recognition is desirable.

8.8. Summary

Surface appearance is often not well described by geometry and simple shading models, especially when the surface exhibits fine-scale height variation or relief texture. When detailed appearance is needed but geometry/ shading does not provide sufficient accuracy, the bidirectional texture function is an appropriate surface descriptor. Since the BTF is image-based, fine-scale surface geometry is not captured. Effects like shadowing, occlusions and foreshortening are encapsulated as part of an "effective reflectance" when using the BTF. Consequently, the BTF is not the same representation as a BRDF applied to an exact geometric surface profile.

The set of images that comprise a sampled BTF can be used to build texture models such as the bidirectional feature histogram for recognition. Learned vocabularies of local intensity variations, i.e. image textons, are built by clustering feature outputs. An alternative is to look at a local geometric configuration of maximal filter responses. The BTF representation has been used in recognition, rendering and representation of surfaces. Because of the large amount of data required for densely sampling the BTF, efficiency in algorithms and conciseness in representation remains an ongoing research effort.

Acknowledgments

This material is based upon work supported by the National Science Foundation under Grant No. 0092491 and Grant No. 0085864. The unwrapped texture image Figure 8.4 was generated in collaboration with Dongsheng Wang and Dinesh Pai.

References

1. H. W. Jensen, S. R. Marschner, M. Levoy, and P. Hanrahan. A practical model for subsurface light transport. In *Proceedings of SIGGRAPH*, pp. 511–518 (August, 2001). URL `citeseer.ist.psu.edu/jensen01practical.html`.
2. P. Hanrahan and W. Krueger, Reflection from layered surfaces due to subsurface scattering, *Proceedings of SIGGRAPH.* **27**(Annual Conference Series), 165–174, (1993). URL `citeseer.ist.psu.edu/hanrahan93reflection.html`.
3. K. J. Dana, B. van Ginneken, S. K. Nayar, and J. J. Koenderink, Reflectance and texture of real-world surfaces, *Columbia University Technical Report CUCS-048-96* (December. 1996).
4. K. J. Dana, B. van Ginneken, S. K. Nayar, and J. J. Koenderink, Reflectance and texture of real world surfaces, *ACM Transactions on Graphics.* **18**(1), 1–34 (January, 1999).
5. F. E. Nicodemus, Reflectance nomenclature and directional reflectance and emissivity, *Applied Optics.* **9**, 1474–1475, (1970).
6. O. G. Cula and K. J. Dana, Compact representation of bidirectional texture functions, *Proceedings of the IEEE Conference on Computer Vision and Pattern Recognition.* **1**, 1041–1067 (December, 2001).

7. H. Rushmeier, B. Rogowitz, and C. Piatko. Perceptual issues in substituting texture for geometry, (2000). URL `citeseer.ist.psu.edu/rushmeier00perceptual.html`.
8. T. Leung and J. Malik. Recognizing surfaces using three-dimensional textons. In *ICCV '99: Proceedings of the International Conference on Computer Vision-Volume 2*, p. 1010, Washington, DC, USA, (1999). IEEE Computer Society. ISBN 0-7695-0164-8.
9. T. Leung and J. Malik, Representing and recognizing the visual appearance of materials using three-dimensional textons, *Int. J. Comput. Vision.* **43**(1), 29–44, (2001). ISSN 0920-5691. doi: http://dx.doi.org/10.1023/A:1011126920638.
10. O. G. Cula and K. J. Dana, 3D texture recognition using bidirectional feature histograms, *International Journal of Computer Vision.* **59**(1), 33–60 (August, 2004).
11. O. Cula, K. Dana, F. Murphy, and B. Rao, Skin texture modeling, *International Journal of Computer Vision.* **62**(1-2), 97–119 (April-May, 2005).
12. M. Varma and A. Zisserman, Classifying images of materials, *Proceedings of the European Conference on Computer Vision.* pp. 255–271, (2002).
13. K. Nishino, Y. Sato, and K. Ikeuchi, Eigen-texture method: Appearance compression based on 3d model, *Proceedings of the IEEE Conference on Computer Vision and Pattern Recognition.* **1**, 618–624, (1999).
14. A. Zalesny and L. V. Gool, Multiview texture models, *Proceedings of the IEEE Conference on Computer Vision and Pattern Recognition.* **1**, 615–622 (December, 2001).
15. G. Mller, J. Meseth, and R. Klein, Fast environmental lighting for local-pca encoded btfs, *Computer Graphics International.* pp. 198– 205 (June, 2004).
16. J. Dong and M. J. Chantler, Capture and synthesis of 3d surface texture, *International Journal of Computer Vision (VISI).* **62**(1-2), 177–194, (2005).
17. I. Sato, T. Okabe, Y. Sato, and K. Ikeuchi, Appearance sampling for obtaining a set of basis images for variable illumination, *International Conference on Computer Vision.* pp. 800–807 (October, 2003).
18. H. Lensch, J. Kautz, M. Goesele, W. Heidrich, and H. Seidel, Image-based reconstruction of spatial appearance and geometric detail, *ACM Transactions on Graphics.* **22**(2) (April, 2003).
19. M. A. O. Vasilescu and D. Terzopoulos. Tensortextures: multilinear image-based rendering. In *SIGGRAPH '04: ACM SIGGRAPH 2004 Papers*, pp. 336–342, New York, NY, USA, (2004). ACM Press. doi: http://doi.acm.org.proxy.libraries.rutgers.edu/10.1145/1186562.1015725.
20. M. Ashikhmin and P. Shirley, Steerable illumination textures, *ACM Trans. Graph.* **21**(1), 1–19, (2002). ISSN 0730-0301. doi: http://doi.acm.org.proxy.libraries.rutgers.edu/10.1145/504789.504790.
21. P. E. Debevec, C. J. Taylor, and J. Malik. Modeling and rendering architecture from photographs: a hybrid geometry- and image-based approach. In *SIGGRAPH '96: Proceedings of the 23rd annual conference on Computer graphics and interactive techniques*, pp. 11–20, New York, NY, USA, (1996).

ACM Press. ISBN 0-89791-746-4. doi: http://doi.acm.org.proxy.libraries.rutgers.edu/10.1145/237170.237191.

22. B. van Ginneken, J. J. Koenderink, and K. J. Dana, Texture histograms as a function of irradiation and viewing direction, *International Journal of Computer Vision.* **31**(2-3), 169–184, (1999).
23. X. Liu, Y. Yu, and H.-Y. Shum. Synthesizing bidirectional texture functions for real-world surfaces. In *SIGGRAPH '01: Proceedings of the 28th annual conference on Computer graphics and interactive techniques*, pp. 97–106, New York, NY, USA, (2001). ACM Press. ISBN 1-58113-374-X. doi: http://doi.acm.org.proxy.libraries.rutgers.edu/10.1145/383259.383269.
24. W.-C. Ma, S.-H. Chao, Y.-T. Tseng, Y.-Y. Chuang, C.-F. Chang, B.-Y. Chen, and M. Ouhyoung. Level-of-detail representation of bidirectional texture functions for real-time rendering. In *SI3D '05: Proceedings of the 2005 symposium on Interactive 3D graphics and games*, pp. 187–194, New York, NY, USA, (2005). ACM Press. ISBN 1-59593-013-2. doi: http://doi.acm.org.proxy.libraries.rutgers.edu/10.1145/1053427.1053458.
25. X. Tong, J. Zhang, L. Liu, X. Wang, B. Guo, and H.-Y. Shum. Synthesis of bidirectional texture functions on arbitrary surfaces. In *SIGGRAPH '02: Proceedings of the 29th annual conference on Computer graphics and interactive techniques*, pp. 665–672, New York, NY, USA, (2002). ACM Press. ISBN 1-58113-521-1. doi: http://doi.acm.org.proxy.libraries.rutgers.edu/10.1145/566570.566634.
26. T. Malzbender, D. Gelb, and H. Wolters. Polynomial texture maps. In *SIGGRAPH '01: Proceedings of the 28th annual conference on Computer graphics and interactive techniques*, pp. 519–528, New York, NY, USA, (2001). ACM Press. ISBN 1-58113-374-X. doi: http://doi.acm.org.proxy.libraries.rutgers.edu/10.1145/383259.383320.
27. L. Wang, X. Wang, X. Tong, S. Lin, S. Hu, B. Guo, and H. Shum, View-dependent displacement mapping, *ACM SIGGRAPH.* pp. 334–339, (2003).
28. S. Yamazaki, R. Sagawa, H. Kawasaki, K. Ikeuchi, and M. Sakauchi. Projective and view dependent textures: Microfacet billboarding. In *EGRW '02: Proceedings of the 13th Eurographics workshop on Rendering*, pp. 169–180, Aire-la-Ville, Switzerland, Switzerland, (2002). Eurographics Association. ISBN 1-58113-534-3.
29. M. M. Oliveira, G. Bishop, and D. McAllister. Relief texture mapping. In *SIGGRAPH '00: Proceedings of the 27th annual conference on Computer graphics and interactive techniques*, pp. 359–368, New York, NY, USA, (2000). ACM Press/Addison-Wesley Publishing Co. ISBN 1-58113-208-5. doi: http://doi.acm.org.proxy.libraries.rutgers.edu/10.1145/344779.344947.
30. Bonn BTF Database, Bonn BTF database. URL `http://btf.cs.uni-bonn.de`.
31. G. Mller, J. Meseth, M. Sattler, R. Sarlette, and R. Klein, Acquisition, synthesis and rendering of bidirectional texture functions, *Proceedings of Eurographics 2004, State of the Art Reports.* pp. 69–94 (September, 2004).
32. Oulu Texture Database, University of oulu texture database. URL `www.outex.oulu.fi`.

33. Photometric Texture Database, Heriot watt photometric texture database. URL `http://www.macs.hw.ac.uk/texturelab/database/Photex/`.
34. J. Gu, C. Tu, R. Ramamoorthi, P. Belhumeur, W. Matusik, and S. K. Nayar, Time-varying Surface Appearance: Acquisition, Modeling, and Rendering, *SIGGRAPH* (July. 2006).
35. P. Debevec, T. Hawkins, C. Tchou, H. Duiker, W. Sarokin, and M. Sagar, Acquiring the reflectance field of a human face, *Proceedings of SIGGRAPH.* pp. 145–156, (2002).
36. T. Weyrich, W. Matusik, H. Pfister, B. Bickel, C. Donner, C. Tu, J. McAndless, J. Lee, A. Ngan, H. W. Jensen, and M. Gross, Analysis of human faces using a measurement-based skin reflectance model, *ACM Transactions on Graphics (TOG).* **25**, 1013–1024 (July, 2006).
37. K. J. Dana, Brdf/btf measurement device, *International Conference on Computer Vision.* **2**, 460–6 (July, 2001).
38. K. Dana and J. Wang, Device for convenient measurement of spatially varying bidirectional reflectance, *Journal of the Optical Society of America A.* **21**, pp. 1–12 (January, 2004).
39. J. Han and K. Perlin, Measuring bidirectional texture reflectance with a kaliedoscope, *ACM Transactions on Graphics.* **22**(3), 741–748 (July, 2003).
40. M. J. Chantler, 3d surface recovery using a flatbed scanner. URL `http://www.macs.hw.ac.uk/texturelab/scan/texturescan.html`.
41. F. Bernardini, I. Martin, J. Mittleman, H. Rushmeier, and G. Taubin, Building a digital model of michelangelo's florentine pieta, *IEEE Computer Graphics and Applications.* **22**, 59–67 (Jan/Feb, 2002).
42. F. Bernardini, I. Martin, and H. Rushmeier, High quality texture reconstruction, *IEEE Transactions of Vision and Computer Graphics.* **4**(7) (October/November, 2001).
43. M. Levoy, K. Pulli, B. Curless, S. Rusinkiewicz, D. Koller, L. Pereira, M. Ginzton, S. Anderson, J. Davis, J. Ginsberg, J. Shade, and D. Fulk, The digital michelangelo project: 3d scanning of large statues, *Proceedings of SIGGRAPH.* (2000).
44. J. Dorsey and P. Hanrahan, Modeling and rendering of metallic patinas, *Siggraph.* **30**, 387–396, (1996). URL `citeseer.ist.psu.edu/dorsey96modeling.html`.
45. S. R. Marschner, S. H. Westin, A. Arbree, and J. T. Moon. Measuring and modeling the appearance of finished wood. In *SIGGRAPH '05: ACM SIGGRAPH 2005 Papers*, pp. 727–734, New York, NY, USA, (2005). ACM Press. doi: http://doi.acm.org.proxy.libraries.rutgers.edu/10.1145/1186822.1073254.
46. J. Koenderink and S. Pont, The secret of velvety skin, *Mach. Vision Appl.* **14**(4), 260–268, (2003). ISSN 0932-8092. doi: http://dx.doi.org/10.1007/s00138-002-0089-7.
47. R. Lu, J. J. Koenderink, and A. M. L. Kappers, Optical properties (bidirectional reflection distribution functions) of velvet, *Applied Optics.* **37**, 5974–5984, (1998).
48. R. Soulié, S. Mérillou, O. Terraz, and D. Ghazanfarpour, Modeling and

rendering of heterogeneous granular materials: Granite application, *Computer Graphics Forum.* (2006). URL `http://www.msi.unilim.fr/basilic/Publications/2006/SMTG06`. Accepté après révision mineure.
49. L. Wang, W. Wang, J. Dorsey, X. Yang, B. Guo, and H.-Y. Shum. Real-time rendering of plant leaves. In *SIGGRAPH '05: ACM SIGGRAPH 2005 Papers*, pp. 712–719, New York, NY, USA, (2005). ACM Press. doi: http://doi.acm.org.proxy.libraries.rutgers.edu/10.1145/1186822.1073252.
50. S. Chen, Quicktime vr - an image-based approach to virtual environment navigation, *Proceedings of SIGGRAPH.* pp. 29–39 (August, 1995).
51. S. Gortler, R. Grzeszczuk, R. Szeliski, and M. F. Cohen, The lumigraph, *Proceedings of SIGGRAPH.* pp. 43–54, (1996).
52. M. Levoy and P. Hanrahan, Light field rendering, *Proceedings of SIGGRAPH.* pp. 31–42 (August, 1996).
53. L. McMillan and G. Bishop, Plenoptic modeling: An image-based rendering system, *Proceedings of SIGGRAPH.* pp. 39–46 (August, 1995).
54. S. Seitz and C. Dyer, View morphing, *Proceedings of SIGGRAPH.* pp. 21–30 (August, 1996).
55. M. Turk and A. Pentland, Eigenfaces for recognition, *Journal Cognitive Neuro Science.* **3**(1), 71–86, (1991).
56. E. H. Adelson and J. R. Bergen, The plenoptic function and the elements of early vision, *Computational Models of Visual Processing.* pp. 3–20, (1991).
57. H. Murase and S. K. Nayar, Visual learning and recognition of 3-d objects from appearance, *Int. J. Comput. Vision.* **14**(1), 5–24, (1995). ISSN 0920-5691. doi: http://dx.doi.org/10.1007/BF01421486.
58. M. J. Black and A. D. Jepson, Eigentracking: Robust matching and tracking of articulated objects using a view-based representation, *ECCV'96 Fourth European Conference on Computer Vision.* pp. 329–342, (1996).
59. P. N. Belhumeur and D. J. Kriegman, What is the set of images of an object under all possible illumination conditions?, *International Journal of Computer Vision.* **28**(3), 245–260 (March, 1998).

Chapter 9

From Dynamic Texture to Dynamic Shape and Appearance Models

Gianfranco Doretto[†] and Stefano Soatto[‡]
[†] *GE Global Research, Niskayuna, NY 12309*
doretto@research.ge.com

[‡] *University of California, Los Angeles, CA 90095*
soatto@ucla.edu

In this chapter we present a modeling framework for video sequences that exhibit certain temporal regularity properties, intended in a statistical sense. Examples of such sequences include sea-waves, smoke, foliage, talking faces, flags in wind, etcetera. We refer to them as *dynamic textures.* The models we describe are non-linear and designed to capture the joint temporal variability of the appearance and of the shape of the scene, or a portion of it. We discuss the problems of modeling, learning, and synthesis of dynamic textures in the context of time series analysis, system identification theory, and finite element methods. We show that this framework allows inferring models capable of synthesizing infinitely long video sequences of complex dynamic visual phenomena.

9.1. Introduction

In modeling complex visual phenomena one can employ rich models that characterize the global statistics of images, or choose simple classes of models to represent the local statistics of a spatio-temporal "segment," together with the partition of the data into such segments. Each segment could be characterized by certain statistical regularity in space and/or time. The former approach is often pursued in computer graphics, where a global model is necessary to capture effects such as mutual illumination or cast shadows. However, such models are not well suited for inference, since they are far more complex than the data, meaning that from any number of images it is not possible to uniquely recover all the unknowns of a scene. In other words, it is always possible to construct scenes with different *photometry* (material reflectance properties, and light distribution), *geometry* (shape, pose, and viewpoint), and *dynamics* (changes over time of geometry and photometry) that give rise to the same images.[1] For instance, the complex appearance of sea waves can be attributed to a scene with simple reflectance and complex geometry, such as the surface of the sea, or to a scene with simple geometry and simple reflectance but complex illumination, for instance a mirror reflecting the radiance of a complex illumination pattern. The ill-posedness of the visual reconstruction problem can be turned into a well-posed inference problem within the context of a specific task, and one can also use the extra degrees of freedom to the benefit of the application at hand by satisfying some additional optimality criterion (e.g. the minimum description lengthcription length (MDL) principle[2] for compression). This way, even though one cannot infer the "physically correct" model of a scene, one can infer a representation of the scene that can be sufficient to support, for instance, recognition tasks.

In this chapter we survey a series of recent papers that describe statistical models that can explain the measured video signal, predict new measurements, and extrapolate new image data. These models are not models of the scene, but statistical models of the video signal. We put the emphasis on sequences of images that exhibit some form of temporal regularity,[a] such as sequences of fire, smoke, water, foliage, flags or flowers in wind, clouds, talking faces, crowds of waving people, etc., and we refer to them as *dynamic textures*.[4] In statistical terms, we assume that a dynamic texture is a sequence of images, that is a realization from a stationary stochastic process.[b]

In order to capture the visual complexity of dynamic textures we model them in terms of statistical variability from a nominal model. The simplest instance of this approach is to use linear statistical analysis to model the variability of a data set as an affine variety; the "mean" is the nominal model, and a Gaussian density represents linear variability. This is done, for instance, in Eigenfaces[5] where appearance variation is modeled by a Gaussian process, in Active Shape Models[6] where shape variation is represented by a Gaussian Procrustean density,[7] and in *Linear Dynamic Texture Models*,[4,8] where motion is captured by a Gauss-Markov process. Active

[a]The case of sequences that exhibit temporal and spatial regularity is treated in Ref. 3.
[b]A stochastic process is stationary (of order k) if the joint statistics (up to order k) are time-invariant. For instance a process $\{I(t)\}$ is second-order stationary if its mean $\bar{I} \doteq E[I(t)]$ is constant and its covariance $E[(I(t_1) - \bar{I})(I(t_2) - \bar{I})]$ only depends upon $t_2 - t_1$.

Appearance Models (AAM),[6] or linear morphable models,[9] go one step beyond in combining the representation of appearance and shape variation into a conditionally linear model, in the sense that if the shape is known then appearance variation is represented by a Gaussian process, and vice versa. Naturally, one could make the entire program more general and non-linear by "kernelizing" each step of the representation[10] in a straightforward way.[c]

In this chapter we present a more general modeling framework where we model the statistics of data segments that exhibit temporal stationarity using conditionally linear processes for shape, motion and appearance. In other words, rather than modeling only appearance (eigenfaces), only shape (active shape models) or only motion (linear dynamic texture models), using linear statistical techniques, we model all three simultaneously.[d] The result is the *Dynamic Shape and Appearance Model*,[11,12] a richer model that can specialize to the ones we mentioned before. In Section 9.3 we describe a variational formulation of the modeling framework. In Section 9.4 we show how this framework specializes into a model that explicitly accounts for view-point variability in planar scenes, and subsequently specializes into the linear dynamic texture model.[4,8] In Section 9.5 we set up the general learning problem for estimating dynamic shape and appearance models, and briefly discuss the main difficulties that arise from it. In Section 9.6 we reduce the general learning problem to the case of linear dynamic textures, and provide a closed-form solution, where the case of periodic video signals is also treated. In Section 9.7 the linear dynamic texture model is tested on simulation and prediction, showing that even the simplest instance of the model captures a wide range of dynamic textures. The algorithm is simple to implement, efficient to learn and fast to simulate; it allows generating infinitely long sequences from short input sequences, and to control the parameters in the simulation.[13] Section 9.8 describes how view-point variability in planar scenes is inferred and then simulated in a couple of real sequences. Finally, in Section 9.9 we test and simulate the more general dynamic shape and appearance model. We compare it to the linear dynamic texture model, and show significant improvement in both fidelity (RMS error) and complexity (model order). We do not show results on

[c] In principle linear processes can model arbitrary covariance sequences given a high enough order, so the advantage of a non-linear model is to provide lower complexity, at the expense of more costly inference.

[d] Eventually this will have to be integrated into a higher-level spatio-temporal segmentation scheme, but such a high-level model is beyond our scope, and here we concentrate on modeling and learning each segment in isolation.

recognition tasks, and the interested reader can consult[14] for work in this area.

9.2. Related Work

Statistical inference for analyzing and understanding general images has been extensively used for the last two decades. There has been a considerable amount of work in the area of 2D texture analysis, starting with the pioneering work of Julesz,[15] until the more recent statistical models (see Ref. 16 and references therein).

There has been comparatively little work in the specific area of dynamic (or time-varying) textures. The problem has been first addressed by Nelson and Polana,[17] who classify regional activities of a scene characterized by complex, non-rigid motion. Szummer and Picard's work[18] on temporal texture modeling uses the spatio-temporal auto-regressive model, which imposes a neighborhood causality constraint for both spatial and temporal domain. This restricts the range of processes that can be modeled, and does not allow to capture rotation, acceleration and other simple non translational motions. Bar-Joseph et al.[19] uses multi-resolution analysis and tree-merging for the synthesis of 2D textures and extends the idea to dynamic textures by constructing trees using a 3D wavelet transform.

Other related work[20] is used to register nowhere-static sequences of images, and synthesize new sequences. Parallel to these approaches there is the work of Wang and Zhu[21,22] where images are decomposed by computing their primal sketch, or by using a dictionary of Gabor or Fourier bases to represent image elements called "movetons." The model captures the temporal variability of movetons, or the graph describing the sketches. Finally, in Ref. 23 feedback control is used to improve the rendering performance of the linear dynamic texture model we describe in this chapter.

The problem of modeling dynamic textures for the purposes of synthesis has been tackled by the Computer Graphics community as well. The typical approach is to synthesize new video sequences using procedural techniques, entailing clever concatenation or repetition of training image data. The reader is referred to Refs. 24–27 and references therein.

The more general dynamic shape and appearance model is also related to the literature of Active Appearance Models. Unlike traditional AAM's, we do not use "landmarks," and our work follows the lines of the more recent efforts in AAM's, such as the work of Baker et al.[28] and Cootes et al.[29,30]

9.3. Modeling Dynamic Shape and Appearance

In order to characterize the variability of images in response to changes in the geometry (shape), photometry (reflectance, illumination) and dynamics (motion, deformation) of the scene, we need a model of image formation. That is, we need to know how the image is related to the scene and its changes, and indeed what the "scene" *is*. This is no easy feat, because the complexity of the physical world is far superior to the complexity of the images, and therefore one can devise infinitely many models of the scene that yield the same images. Even the wildly simplified physical/phenomenological models commonly used in Computer Graphics are an overkill, because there are ambiguities in reflectance, illumination, shape and motion. In other words, if the physical scene undergoes changes in one of the factors (say shape), the images can be explained away with changes in another factor (say reflectance). In Appendix A we start with a simple physical model commonly used in Computer Graphics and argue that it can be reduced to a far simpler one where the effects of shape, reflectance and illumination are lumped into an "appearance" function, and shape and motion are lumped into a "shape" function, and dynamics is described by the temporal variation of such functions. Instead of modeling the variability of the images through the independent action of the different physical factors, we model it statistically using a conditionally linear process, that describes the variability from the nominal model.

9.3.1. *Image formation model*

In Appendix A we show that, under suitable assumptions, a collection of images $\{I_t(x)\}_{1\leq t\leq \tau}$, $x \in D \subset \mathbb{R}^2$, of a scene made of continuous (not necessarily smooth) surfaces with changing shape, changing reflectance and changing illumination, taken from a moving camera, can be modeled as follows:

$$\begin{cases} I_t(x_t) = \rho_t(x)\ , & x \in \Omega \subset \mathbb{R}^2 \\ x_t = w_t(x)\ , & t = 1, 2, \ldots, \tau \end{cases} \tag{9.1}$$

where $\rho_t : \Omega \subset \mathbb{R}^2 \to \mathbb{R}_+$ is a positive integrable function, which we call *appearance*, and $w_t : \Omega \subset \mathbb{R}^2 \to \mathbb{R}^2$ is a homeomorphism[e] which we call

[e] A homeomorphism is a continuously invertible map, which we also call "warp." Assuming that w_t is a homeomorphism corresponds to assuming that physical changes in the scene do not result in self-occlusions. However, since we aim at using model (9.1) for deriving a statistical model for the variability of the images, we will see that occlusions can

shape. In other words, if we think of an image as a function defined on a domain D, taking values in the range $\mathbb{R}_+$, the domain and range are called shape and appearance respectively, and their changes are called *dynamics*.

9.3.2. *Variability of shape, appearance, and dynamics*

Rather than modeling the variability of the image from physical models of changes of the scene, we are going to learn a statistical model of the variability of the images directly, based on model (9.1). In particular, we are going to assume a very simple model that imposes that changes in shape, appearance and dynamics are conditionally affine. This means that shape is modeled as a Gaussian shape space; given shape, appearance variation is modeled by a Gaussian distribution, and given shape and appearance, motion is modeled by a Gauss-Markov model. Specifically, we assume that

$$w_t(x) = w_0(x) + W(x)s_t \ , \quad x \in \Omega \tag{9.2}$$

where $w_0 : \mathbb{R}^2 \to \mathbb{R}^2$ is a vector-valued function called *nominal warp*, and $W : \mathbb{R}^2 \to \mathbb{R}^{2\times k}$ is a matrix-valued function whose columns are called *principal warps*. The time-varying vector $s_t \in \mathbb{R}^k$ is called the *shape parameter*. Similarly, we assume that

$$\rho_t(x) = \rho_0(x) + P(x)\alpha_t \ , \quad x \in \Omega \tag{9.3}$$

where $\rho_0 : \mathbb{R}^2 \to \mathbb{R}_+$ is called *nominal template*, and the columns of the vector-valued function $P : \mathbb{R}^2 \to \mathbb{R}^{1\times l}$ are the *principal templates*. The time-varying vector $\alpha_t \in \mathbb{R}^l$ is called the *appearance parameter*. The temporal changes of the shape and appearance parameters are modeled by a Gauss-Markov model. This means that there exist matrices $A \in \mathbb{R}^{m\times m}$, $B \in \mathbb{R}^{m\times n}$, $C \in \mathbb{R}^{(k+l)\times m}$, $Q \in \mathbb{R}^{n\times n}$ and a Gaussian process $\{\xi_t \in \mathbb{R}^m\}$ with initial condition ξ_0, driven by $n_t \in \mathbb{R}^n$ such that

$$\begin{cases} \xi_{t+1} = A\xi_t + Bn_t \ , & n_t \overset{IID}{\sim} \mathcal{N}(0, Q) \\ \begin{bmatrix} s_t \\ \alpha_t \end{bmatrix} = \begin{bmatrix} C_1 \\ C_2 \end{bmatrix} \xi_t \ , & \xi_0 \sim \mathcal{N}(\bar{\xi}_0, Q_0) \end{cases} \tag{9.4}$$

where $\{n_t\}$ is a white, zero-mean Gaussian process with covariance Q. For convenience we have broken the matrix C into two blocks, $C_1 \in \mathbb{R}^{k\times m}$ and $C_2 \in \mathbb{R}^{l\times m}$, corresponding to the shape and appearance parameters. Also

be modeled by changes in appearance, and therefore the assumption is not restrictive. Note that, according to (9.1), the image $I_t(x_t)$ is only defined on $x_t \in w_t(\Omega)$, which may be a subset or a superset of D. In the former case, it can be extended to D by regularity, as we describe in this chapter, or by "layering," as described in Refs. 31 and 32.

note that without loss of generality one can lump the effect of B into Q and therefore assume B to be the identity matrix.[33] In addition to modeling the temporal variability in (9.4), another property that differentiates this framework is that in traditional active appearance models the variable x, in (9.2), belongs to $\{x_1, \ldots, x_N\}$, a set of "landmark points," and then it is extended to D in order to perform linear statistical analysis in (9.3). On the other hand, in our model x is defined on the same domain in both equations; the user is not required to define landmarks, and all the shape parameters are estimated during the inference process. Note that the functions ρ_0, P, w_0, and W are not arbitrary and will have to satisfy additional geometric and regularity conditions that we will describe shortly. The complete model of phenomenological image formation can be summarized as follows:

$$\begin{cases} \xi_{t+1} = A\xi_t + n_t \,, \qquad \xi_0 \sim \mathcal{N}(\bar{\xi}_0, Q_0) \,, \quad n_t \overset{IID}{\sim} \mathcal{N}(0, Q) \\ y_t(w_0(x) + W(x)C_1\xi_t) = P(x)C_2\xi_t + \eta_t(x) \,, \quad x \in \Omega \subset \mathbb{R}^2 \end{cases} \tag{9.5}$$

where we assume that only a noisy version of the image $y_t(x) = I_t(x) + \tilde{\eta}_t(x)$ is available on $x \in D$, with noise $\tilde{\eta}_t(x) \overset{IID}{\sim} \mathcal{N}(0, \tilde{R}(x))$. By defining $\eta_t(x) \doteq \rho_0(x) + \tilde{\eta}_t(w_0(x) + W(x)s_t)$, we obtain $\eta_t(x) \overset{IID}{\sim} \mathcal{N}(\rho_0(x), R(x))$, where $R(x) = \tilde{R}(w_0(x) + W(x)s_t)$, and we have absorbed the nominal template as the mean of the noise. We will refer to model (9.5) as the *Dynamic Shape and Appearance (DSA) Model.*

9.4. Specializations of the Model

The model (9.5) can be further simplified or specialized for particular scenarios. For instance, one may want to model changes in the viewpoint explicitly. As we argue in Appendix A, these are ambiguous if the scene is allowed to deform and change reflectance arbitrarily. However, occasionally one may have knowledge that the scene is rigid in the coarse scale, and variability in the images is only due to changes in albedo (or fine-scale shape) and viewpoint, for instance in moving video of a fountain, or foliage.[20] In this case, following the notation of Appendix A, $w_t(x) = \pi(g_t S(x))$. Depending on $\rho_t(x)$, one may have enough information to infer an estimate of camera motion g_t and shape S up to a finite-dimensional group of transformations, sort of an equivalent of "structure from motion" for a dynamic scene.[20] Note that S is an infinite-dimensional unknown, and therefore inference can be posed in a variational framework following the guidelines of Ref. 1.

One simple case where viewpoint variation can be inferred with a simple finite-dimensional model is when the scene is *planar*, so that $\pi(g_t S(x)) = H_t x$ where $H_t \in \mathbb{GL}(3)/\mathbb{R}$ is an homography[f] (a projective transformation) and x is intended in homogeneous coordinates. The model therefore becomes

$$\begin{cases} \xi_{t+1} = A\xi_t + n_t \\ H_{t+1} = F_t H_t + n_{H_t} \\ y_t(H_t x) = P(x)C_2\xi_t + \eta_t(x) \end{cases} \tag{9.6}$$

where $F_t \in \mathbb{R}^{9\times 9}$ is a (possibly) time-varying matrix and n_{H_t} is a driving noise designed to guarantee that H_t remains an homography. Note that since $P(x)$ and C_2 can only be determined as a product, we can substitute them with $C(x) \doteq P(x)C_2$. Moreover, the assumption of a planar scene can be made without loss of generality, since all modeling responsibility for deviations from planarity can be delegated to the appearance $\rho_t(\cdot)$.

Model (9.6) can be further reduced by assuming that not only the scene is planar, but that such a plane is not moving and coincides with the image plane (H_t constant and equal to the identity). This yields

$$\begin{cases} \xi_{t+1} = A\xi_t + n_t \\ y_t(x) = C(x)\xi_t + \eta_t(x) \end{cases} \tag{9.7}$$

where changes in shape are not modeled explicitly and all the modeling responsibility falls on the appearance parameters and principal templates. This is the *Linear Dynamic Texture (LDT) Model*, which is a particular instance of the more general model proposed in Refs. 4 and 8. It is a linear Gauss-Markov model and it is well known that it can capture the second-order properties of a generic stationary stochastic process.[4]

In the next Section 9.5 we will setup the learning problem and sketch the solution for the case of the DSA model (9.5). For a full derivation of the learning procedure, as well as the learning of model (9.6), the interested reader is referred to Refs. 11 and 12.

9.5. Learning Dynamic Shape and Appearance Models

Given a noisy version of a collection of images $\{y_t(x)\}_{1\leq t\leq \tau}$, $x \in D$, learning the model (9.5) amounts to determining the functions $w_0(\cdot)$ (nominal

[f] $\mathbb{GL}(3)$ is the general linear group of invertible 3×3 matrices. Homographies can be represented as invertible matrices up to a scale.[34]

warp), $W(\cdot)$ (principal warps), $\rho_0(\cdot)$ (nominal template), $P(\cdot)$ (principal templates), the dynamic parameters A, C and covariance Q that minimize a discrepancy measure between the data and the model. In formulas we are looking for[g]

$$\begin{cases} \arg\min_{w_0, W, \rho_0, P, A, C, Q} E\left[\int_\Omega |\eta_t(x) - \rho_0(x)|^2 dx + \nu \|n_t\|^2\right] \\ \text{subject to (9.5) and } \int_\Omega P_{\cdot i}(x) P_{\cdot j}(x)\, \mathrm{d}x = \delta_{ij} = \int_\Omega W_{\cdot i}(x) W_{\cdot j}(x)\, \mathrm{d}x \end{cases} \tag{9.8}$$

The last set of constraints, where δ_{ij} denote the Kronecker's delta and $P_{\cdot i}$ and $W_{\cdot i}$ represent the i-th column of P and W respectively, imposes orthogonality of the shape and appearance bases, and could be relaxed under suitable conditions. The cost function comprises a data fidelity term, and another term that accounts for the linear dynamics in (9.5), weighted according to a regularizing constant ν.

Needless to say, solving (9.8) is a tall order. One of the main difficulties is that it entails performing a minimization in an infinite-dimensional space. To avoid this, in Refs. 11 and 12 we reduce the problem using finite-element methods (FEM),[35] which provide with a straightforward way to regularize the unknowns.[h] The result is an alternating minimization procedure that solves (9.8) iteratively with a minimization in a finite-dimensional space.

An important ambiguity that arises in solving (9.8) is related to the shape and appearance state dimensionality k, and l. In fact, one could decide a priori how much image variability should be modeled by the shape, and how much by the appearance. For instance, the linear dynamic texture model implicitly assumes that all the modeling responsibility is delegated to the appearance ($k = 0$). However, in designing an automatic procedure that infers all the unknowns, this is a fundamental problem. In Refs. 11 and 12 we use model complexity as the arbiter that automatically selects model dimensionality, and assigns how modeling responsibility is shared among appearance, shape, and motion.

Since describing the details of the solution of problem (9.8) is outside the scope of this overview chapter, we refer the interested reader to Refs. 11 and 12 to probe further, and the next Section 9.6 will setup and solve the simpler problem of learning linear dynamic texture models.

[g] In principle the domain of integration Ω should also be part of the inference process; for comments on this issue, the reader is referred to Refs. 11 and 12.

[h] Note that for solving problem (9.8) one has to introduce another regularization term, which ensures the shape function $w_t(x)$ to be an homeomorphism, see Refs. 11 and 12 for details.

9.6. Learning Linear Dynamic Texture Models

Given a sequence of noisy images $\{y_t(x)\}_{1\leq t\leq \tau}$, $x \in D$, learning the linear dynamic texture model (9.7) amounts to identifying the model parameters A, $C(x)$, and Q. This is a *system identification problem*,[36] where one has to infer a dynamical model from a time series. The maximum-likelihood formulation of the linear dynamic texture learning problem can be posed as follows:

$$\begin{aligned}&\text{given } y_1(x),\ldots,y_\tau(x), \text{ find}\\ &\hat{A},\hat{C}(x),\hat{Q} = \arg\max_{A,C,Q} \log p(y_1(x),\ldots,y_\tau(x)) \qquad (9.9)\\ &\text{subject to (9.7) and } n_t \overset{IID}{\sim} \mathcal{N}(0,Q).\end{aligned}$$

While we refer the reader to Ref. 4 for a more complete discussion about how to solve problem (9.9), how to set out the learning via prediction error methods, and for a more general definition of the dynamic texture model, here we summarize a number of simplifications that lead us to a simple closed-form procedure.

In (9.9) we have to make assumptions on the class of filters $C(x)$ that relate the image measurements to the state ξ_t. There are many ways in which one can choose them. However, in texture analysis the dimension of the signal is huge (tens of thousands components) and there is a lot of redundancy. Therefore, we view the choice of filters as a dimensionality reduction step and seek for a decomposition of the image in the simple (linear) form $I_t(x) = \sum_{i=1}^{l} \xi_{i,t}\theta_i(x) \doteq C(x)\xi_t$, where $C(x) = [\theta_1(x),\ldots,\theta_l(x)] \in \mathbb{R}^{p\times l}$ and $\{\theta_i\}$ can be an orthonormal basis of L^2, a set of principal components, or a wavelet filter bank, and $p \gg l$, where p is the number of pixels in the image.

The first observation concerning model (9.7) is that the choice of matrices A, $C(x)$, Q is not unique, in the sense that there are infinitely many such matrices that give rise to exactly the same sample paths $y_t(x)$ starting from suitable initial conditions. This is immediately seen by substituting A with TAT^{-1}, $C(x)$ with $C(x)T^{-1}$ and Q with TQT^T, and choosing the initial condition Tx_0, where $T \in \mathbb{GL}(l)$ is any invertible $l \times l$ matrix. In other words, the basis of the state-space is arbitrary, and any given process has *not* a unique model, but an *equivalence class* of models $\mathcal{R} \doteq \{[A] = TAT^{-1}, [C(x)] = C(x)T^{-1}, [Q] = TQT^T, \mid T \in \mathbb{GL}(l)\}$. In order to identify a unique model of the type (9.7) from a sample path $y_t(x)$, it is necessary to choose a representative of each equivalence class: such a representative is called a *canonical model realization*, in the sense that it does not depend on the choice of basis of the state space (because it has been fixed).

While there are many possible choices of canonical models (see for instance Ref. 37), we will make the assumption that $\text{rank}(C(x)) = l$ and choose the canonical model that makes the columns of $C(x)$ orthonormal: $C(x)^T C(x) = I_l$, where I_l is the identity matrix of dimension $l \times l$. As we will see shortly, this assumption results in a unique model that is tailored to the data in the sense of defining a basis of the state space such that its covariance is asymptotically diagonal (see Equation (9.14)).

With the above simplifications one may use *subspace identification* techniques[36] to learn model parameters in closed-form in the maximum-likelihood sense, for instance with the well known N4SID algorithm.[33] Unfortunately this is not possible. In fact, given the dimensionality of our data, the requirements in terms of computation and memory storage of standard system identification techniques are far beyond the capabilities of the current state of the art workstations. For this reason, following Ref. 4, we describe a closed-form sub-optimal solution of the learning problem, that takes few seconds to run on a current low-end PC when $p = 170 \times 110$ and $\tau = 120$.

9.6.1. *Closed-form solution*

Let $Y_1^\tau \doteq [y_1, \ldots, y_\tau] \in \mathbb{R}^{p\times\tau}$ with $\tau > l$, and similarly for $\Xi_1^\tau \doteq [\xi_1, \ldots, \xi_\tau] \in \mathbb{R}^{l\times\tau}$ and $N_1^\tau \doteq [\eta_1, \ldots, \eta_\tau] \in \mathbb{R}^{p\times\tau}$, and notice that

$$Y_1^\tau = C\Xi_1^\tau + N_1^\tau \ . \tag{9.10}$$

Now let $Y_1^\tau = U\Sigma V^T$; $U \in \mathbb{R}^{p\times l}$; $U^T U = I_l$; $V \in \mathbb{R}^{\tau\times l}$, $V^T V = I_l$ be the singular value decomposition (SVD)[38] with $\Sigma = \text{diag}\{\sigma_1, \ldots, \sigma_l\}$, and $\{\sigma_i\}$ be the singular values, and consider the problem of finding the best estimate of C in the sense of Frobenius: $\hat{C}_\tau, \hat{\Xi}_\tau = \arg\min_{C,\Xi_1^\tau} \|N_1^\tau\|_F$ subject to (9.10). It follows immediately from the fixed rank approximation property of the SVD[38] that the unique solution is given by

$$\hat{C}_\tau = U \ , \quad \hat{\Xi}_\tau = \Sigma V^T \ , \tag{9.11}$$

$\hat{A}$ can be determined uniquely, again in the sense of Frobenius, by solving the following linear problem:

$$\hat{A}_\tau = \arg\min_A \|\Xi_1^\tau - A\Xi_0^{\tau-1}\|_F \ , \tag{9.12}$$

where $\Xi_0^{\tau-1} \doteq [\xi_0, \ldots, \xi_{\tau-1}] \in \mathbb{R}^{l\times\tau}$ which is trivially done in closed-form using the state estimated from (9.11):

$$\hat{A}_\tau = \Sigma V^T D_1 V (V^T D_2 V)^{-1} \Sigma^{-1} , \tag{9.13}$$

where $D_1 = \begin{bmatrix} 0 & 0 \\ I_{\tau-1} & 0 \end{bmatrix}$ and $D_2 = \begin{bmatrix} I_{\tau-1} & 0 \\ 0 & 0 \end{bmatrix}$. Notice that $\hat{C}_\tau$ is uniquely determined up to a change of sign of the components of C and ξ. Also note that

$$E[\hat{\xi}_t \hat{\xi}_t^T] \equiv \lim_{\tau\to\infty} \frac{1}{\tau} \sum_{k=1}^{\tau} \hat{\xi}_{t+k} \hat{\xi}_{t+k}^T = \Sigma V^T V \Sigma = \Sigma^2 , \tag{9.14}$$

which is diagonal as mentioned in the first part of Section 9.6. Finally, the sample input noise covariance Q can be estimated from

$$\hat{Q}_\tau = \frac{1}{\tau} \sum_{i=1}^{\tau} \hat{n}_i \hat{n}_i^T , \tag{9.15}$$

where $\hat{n}_t \doteq \hat{\xi}_{t+1} - \hat{A}_\tau \hat{\xi}_t$. Should $\hat{Q}$ not be full rank, its dimensionality can be further reduced by computing the SVD $\hat{Q} = U_Q \Sigma_Q U_Q^T$ where $\Sigma_Q = \mathrm{diag}\{\sigma_{Q,1}, \ldots, \sigma_{Q,n_v}\}$ with $n_v \leq l$, and one can set $n_t \doteq B v_t$, with $v_t \sim \mathcal{N}(0, I_{n_v})$, and $\hat{B}$ such that $\hat{B}\hat{B}^T = \hat{Q}$.

In the algorithm above we have assumed that the order of the model l was given. In practice, this needs to be inferred from the data. Following Ref. 4, one can determine the model order from the singular values $\sigma_1, \sigma_2, \ldots$, by choosing l as the cutoff where the singular values drop below a threshold. If the singular values are normalized according to their total energy,[11,12] the threshold assumes relative meaning and can be consistently used to learn and compare different models. A threshold can also be imposed on the difference between adjacent singular values.

9.6.2. *Learning periodic dynamic textures*

The linear dynamic texture model (9.7) is suitable for dynamic visual processes that are periodic signals over time. This can be achieved if $Q = 0$, which means that the model is not excited by driving noise, and all the eigenvalues of A (the poles of the linear dynamical system) are located on the unit circle of the complex plane. In order to learn a model of this kind one can use a slight variation of the procedure highlighted in Section 9.6.1.[39] In fact, in estimating A one has to take into account the eigenvalue property, which means that A has to be orthogonal. Adding this constraint

Fig. 9.1. **Escalator.** Example of a dynamic texture that is a periodic signal. Top row: samples from the original sequence (120 training images of 168×112 pixels). Bottom row: extrapolated samples (using $l = 21$ components). The original data set comes from the MIT Temporal Texture database.[18] (From Doretto.[39])

transforms problem (9.12) into a Procrustes problem,[38] which can still be solved in closed-form. More precisely, if the SVD of $\Xi_1^\tau \Xi_0^{\tau-1^T}$ is given by $U_A \Sigma_A V_A^T$, one can estimate A as

$$\hat{A}_\tau = \arg \min_{\{A | A^T A = I_n\}} \| \Xi_1^\tau - A \Xi_0^{\tau-1} \|_F = U_A V_A^T \ . \tag{9.16}$$

The top row of Figure 9.1 shows a video sequence of an escalator, which is a periodic signal. The bottom row shows some synthesized frames. The reader may observe that the quality of the synthesized frames makes them indistinguishable from the original ones. Figure 9.2 instead, shows that all the eigenvalues of the matrix $\hat{A}$ lie on the unit circle of the complex plane.

9.7. Validation of the Linear Dynamic Texture Model

One of the most compelling validations for a dynamic texture model is to simulate it to evaluate to what extent the synthesis captures the essential perceptual features of the original data. Given a typical training sequence of about one hundred frames, using the procedure described in Section 9.6.1 one can learn model parameters in a few seconds, and then synthesize a potentially infinite number of new images by simulating the linear dynamic texture (LDT) model (9.7). To generate a new image one needs to draw a sample n_t from a Gaussian distribution with covariance Q, update the state $\xi_{t+1} = A\xi_t + n_t$, and compute the image $I_t = C\xi_t$. This can be done in real time.

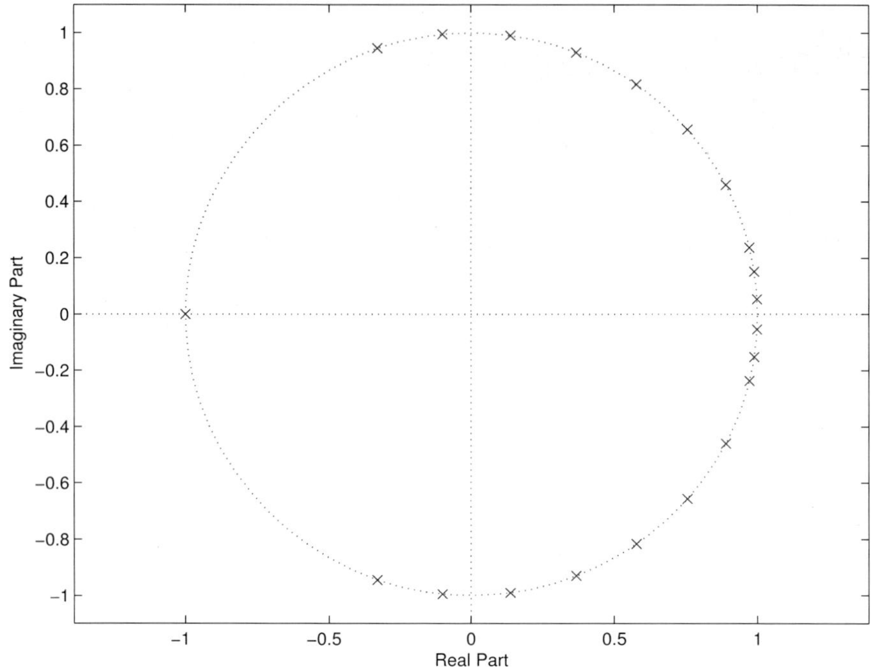

Fig. 9.2. Plot of the complex plane with the eigenvalues of $\hat{A}$ for the escalator sequence (from Doretto[39]).

Even though the result is best shown in movies,[i] Figure 9.3 and Figure 9.4 provide some examples of the kind of output that one can get. They show that even the simple model (9.7), which captures only the second-order temporal statistics of a video sequence, is able to capture most of the perceptual features of sequences of images of natural phenomena, such as fire, smoke, water, flowers or foliage in wind, etc. In particular, here the dimension of the state was set to $l = 50$, and ξ_0 was drawn from a zero-mean Gaussian distribution with covariance inferred from the estimated state $\hat{\Xi}_1^\tau$. In Figure 9.3, the training sequences were borrowed from the MIT Temporal Texture database,[18] the length of these sequences ranges from $\tau = 100$ to $\tau = 150$ frames, and the synthesized sequences are 300 frames long. In Figure 9.4, the training sets are color sequences that were captured by the authors except for the fire sequence that comes from the

[i]The interested reader is invited to visit the website `http://vision.ucla.edu/~doretto/` for demos on dynamic texture synthesis.

Fig. 9.3. Top row: **Fountain** ($\tau = 100$, $p = 150 \times 90$), **Plastic** ($\tau = 119$, $p = 190 \times 148$). Bottom row: **River** ($\tau = 120$, $p = 170 \times 115$), **Smoke** ($\tau = 150$, $p = 170 \times 115$). For every sequence: Two samples from the original sequence (top row), and two samples from a synthesized sequence (bottom row) (from Doretto et al.,[4] © 2003 Springer-Verlag).

Artbeats Digital Film Library.[j] The length of the sequences is $\tau = 150$ frames, the frames are 320×220 pixels, and the synthesized sequences are 300 frames long.

An important question is how long should the input sequence be in order to capture the dynamics of the process. To answer this question experimentally, for a fixed state dimension, we consider the prediction error as a function of the length τ, of the input (training) sequence. This means that for each length τ, we predict the frame $\tau + 1$ (not part of the training set) and compute the prediction error per pixel in gray levels. We do so many times in order to infer the statistics of the prediction error, i.e. mean and variance at each τ. Using one criterion for learning (the procedure in Section 9.6.1), and another one for validation (prediction error) is informative for challenging the model. Figure 9.5 shows an error-bar plot including mean and standard deviation of the prediction error per pixel for

[j] `http://www.artbeats.com`

Fig. 9.4. Color examples. Top row: **Fire** ($\tau = 150$, $p = 360 \times 243$), **Fountain** ($\tau = 150$, $p = 320 \times 220$). Bottom row: **Ocean** ($\tau = 150$, $p = 320 \times 220$), **Water** ($\tau = 150$, $p = 320 \times 220$). For every sequence: Two samples from the original sequence (top row), and two samples from a synthesized sequence (bottom row) (from Doretto et al.,[4] © 2003 Springer-Verlag).

the steam sequence. The average error decreases and becomes stable after approximately 70 frames. The plot of Figure 9.5 validates *a-posteriori* the model (9.7) inferred with the procedure described in Section 9.6.1. Other dynamic textures have similar prediction error plots.[4]

9.8. Simulation of Viewpoint Variability

We tested model (9.6) with two sequences that we call pool and waterfall. The former has 170, and the latter 130 color frames of 350×240 pixels. The shape state dimension was set to $k = 8$, whereas the appearance state dimension was learnt with a relative cutoff threshold $\gamma_\rho = 0.01$, giving $l = 34$ for the pool sequence, and $l = 42$ for the waterfall sequence. The interested reader is referred to Refs. 11 and 12 for details on learning model (9.6). Figure 9.6 illustrates the generation of the appearance domain Ω of the two sequences as the intersection of the original image domain D mapped according to the inverse of the estimated homographies $\{H_i\}$. Figure 9.7

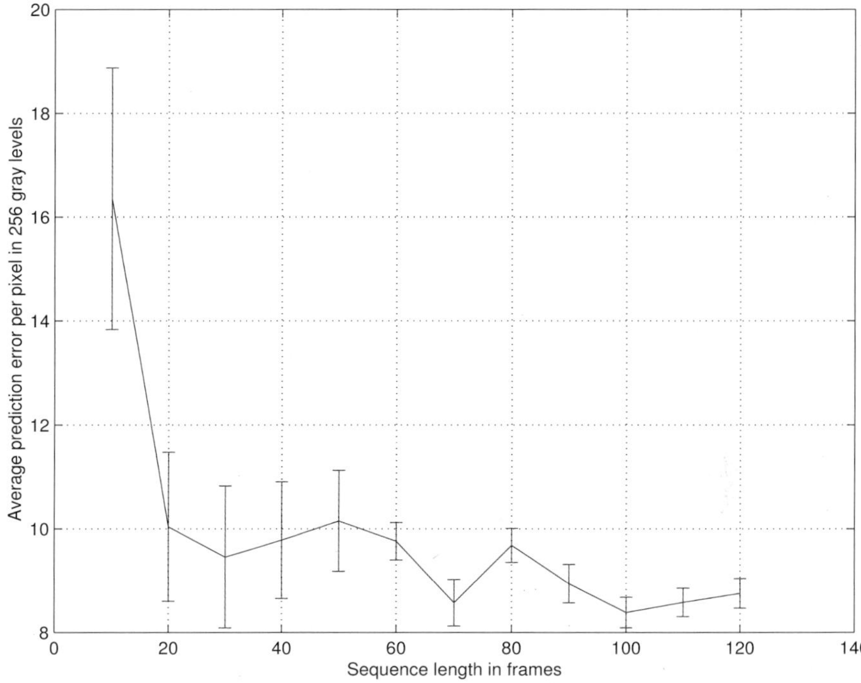

Fig. 9.5. Error-bar plot of the average prediction error and standard deviation (for 100 trials) per pixel (expressed in gray levels with a range of $[0, 255]$), as a function of the length of the steam training sequence. The state dimension is set to $l = 20$ (from Doretto et al.,[4] © 2003 Springer-Verlag).

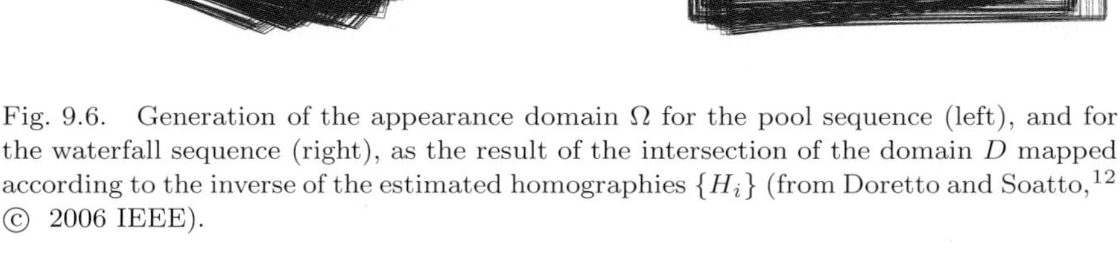

Fig. 9.6. Generation of the appearance domain Ω for the pool sequence (left), and for the waterfall sequence (right), as the result of the intersection of the domain D mapped according to the inverse of the estimated homographies $\{H_i\}$ (from Doretto and Soatto,[12] © 2006 IEEE).

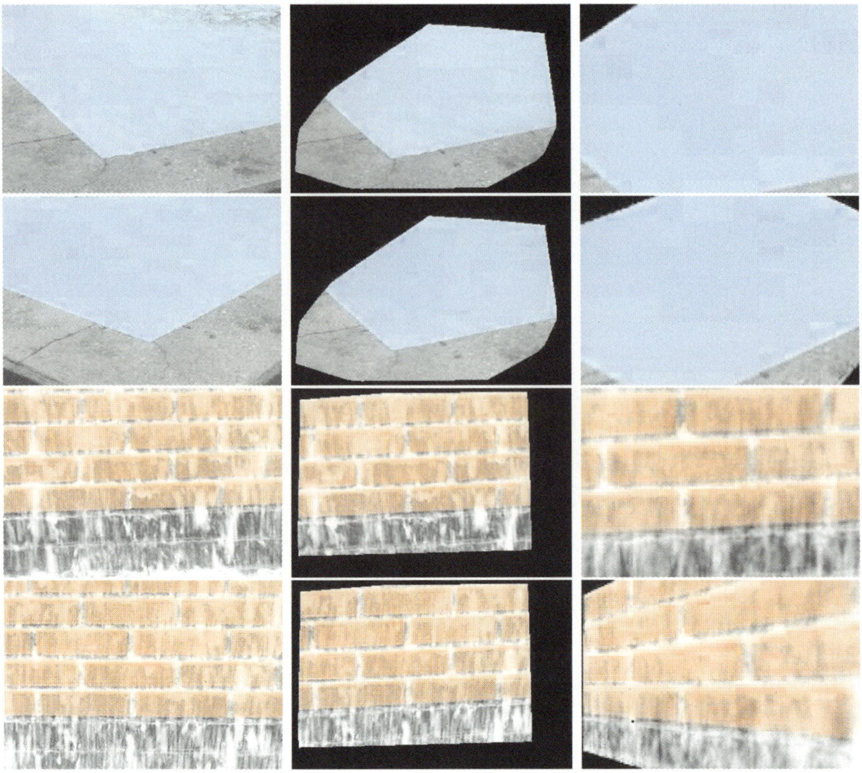

Fig. 9.7. **Pool, Waterfall.** For each sequence: Two samples of the original sequence (left column) and the same samples after the homography registration (middle column), and two samples of a synthesized sequence with synthetic camera motion (right column) (from Doretto and Soatto,[12] © 2006 IEEE).

shows two samples of the pool and waterfall sequences along with the same samples after the rectification with respect to the estimated homographies. For each sequence, Figure 9.7 also shows two extrapolated frames obtained by simulating the models and by imposing a synthetic motion.[k] The extrapolated movies are 200 frames long, and the frame dimension is 175×120 pixels. Notice that only the pixels in the domain Ω are displayed. For the pool sequence, the synthetic camera motion is such that the camera first zooms in, then translates to the left, turns to the left, right, and finally zooms out. For the waterfall sequence, the synthetic camera motion is such

[k]The interested reader is invited to visit the website `http://vision.ucla.edu/~doretto/` for demos on dynamic texture synthesis.

Table 9.1. Model complexity and fidelity. For every sequence: l_{LDT} is the state space dimension of the LDT model, l_{DSA} and k_{DSA} are the appearance and shape state dimensions of the DSA model, $\mathrm{RMSE}_{\mathrm{LDT}}$ and $\mathrm{RMSE}_{\mathrm{DSA}}$ are the normalized root mean square reconstruction errors per pixel using the LDT and DSA models respectively.

Sequence	l_{LDT}	l_{DSA}	k_{DSA}	$\mathrm{RMSE}_{\mathrm{LDT}}$	$\mathrm{RMSE}_{\mathrm{DSA}}$	$\mathrm{RMSE}_{\mathrm{LDT2}}$
flowers	22	19	6	1.57%	1.61%	1.73%
candle	11	7	7	0.83%	0.84%	1.14%
duck	16	11	6	0.66%	0.63%	0.73%
flag	18	10	8	1.17%	1.27%	1.42%

that the camera first zooms in, then translates to the left, down, right, up, and finally rotates to the left.

Although model (9.6) does not capture the physics of the scene, it is sufficient to "explain" the measured data and to extrapolate the appearance of the images in space and time. This model can be used for instance, for the purpose of video editing, as it allows controlling the motion of the vantage point of a virtual camera looking at the scene, but also for video stabilization of scenes with complex dynamics.

9.9. Validation of the Dynamic Shape and Appearance Model

Table 9.1 summarizes some differences between the linear dynamic texture (LDT) model and the dynamic shape and appearance (DSA) model extracted from four different real sequences that we call flowers, duck, flag, and candle. For each of the sequences, the LDT and the DSA models were learnt with the following choice of normalized cutoff thresholds: $\gamma_\rho = 0.01$ for the appearance space, and $\gamma_w = 0.03$ for the shape space.[1] In Table 9.1, l_{LDT} indicates the dimension of the state of the LDT model, whereas l_{DSA} and k_{DSA} indicate the appearance and shape state dimensions of the DSA model. Since the majority of the model parameters is used to encode either the principal components of the LDT model, or the principal templates of the DSA model, comparing l_{LDT} and l_{DSA} is informative of the reduction of the complexity of the DSA model. As expected, at this reduction corresponds an increase of the shape state dimension, going from zero to k_{DSA}. In particular, Table 9.1 suggests the following empirical relationship: $l_{\mathrm{LDT}} \approx l_{\mathrm{DSA}} + k_{\mathrm{DSA}}$.

[1]Note that for learning the LDT model the threshold is not used because the shape space is assumed to have dimension $k = 0$.

Table 9.1 also reports data about the fidelity in the reconstruction of the training sequences from the inferred models. In particular, the last three columns report the normalized root mean square reconstruction errors (RMSE) per pixel. $\mathrm{RMSE}_{\mathrm{LDT}}$ and $\mathrm{RMSE}_{\mathrm{LDT2}}$ are the errors for the LDT model with state dimension l_{LDT} and l_{DSA} respectively, whereas $\mathrm{RMSE}_{\mathrm{DSA}}$ is the error for the DSA model. One may notice that $\mathrm{RMSE}_{\mathrm{DSA}}$ and $\mathrm{RMSE}_{\mathrm{LDT}}$ are fairly similar. This is not surprising since the models are inferred while retaining principal components and templates that are above the same cutoff threshold. On the other hand, the comparison between $\mathrm{RMSE}_{\mathrm{LDT}}$ and $\mathrm{RMSE}_{\mathrm{LDT2}}$ highlights the degradation of the reconstruction error when the LDT model is forced to have the same state dimensionality of the appearance state.

Like in Section 9.7, Figure 9.8 and Figure 9.9 show results on the ability of the DSA model to capture the spatio-temporal properties of a video sequence by using the model to extrapolate new video clips.[m] For the four test sequences the figures show frames of the original sequence (top left), the same frames with the triangulated mesh representing the estimated shape w_t (top right), frames synthesized with the LDT model (bottom left), and frames synthesized with the DSA model (bottom right). Even if the reconstruction errors of the two models are comparable, the simulation reveals that the DSA model outperforms the simpler LDT model. This is true especially when a video sequence contains moving objects with defined structure and sharp edges, suggesting that the DSA model can capture the higher-order temporal statistical properties of a video sequence.

The fact that the DSA model has superior generative power and less complexity of the LDT model does not come for free. In fact, the two models have a different algorithmic complexity with respect to learning. While the LDT model can be inferred very efficiently with a closed-form procedure that takes a few seconds to run,[4] the procedure highlighted in Section 9.5 typically requires a few dozens of iterations to converge, which translates into a couple of hours of processing on a high-end PC. The situation is different with respect to reconstruction or extrapolation. The DSA model, as well as the LDT model, is a parametric model with a per-frame simulation cost dominated by the generation of the appearance of an image ρ_t, which involves $O(pl)$ multiplications and additions. The LDT model has the same simulation cost, which can be higher if the statedimension l_{LDT}

[m]The interested reader is invited to visit the website `http://vision.ucla.edu/~doretto/` for demos on dynamic texture synthesis.

Fig. 9.8. **Flowers, Duck, Flag.** For each sequence: Original frames (top left), original frames with estimated shape w_t (top right), frames synthesized with the LDT model (bottom left), frames synthesized with the DSA model (bottom right) (from Doretto,[11] © 2005 IEEE).

Fig. 9.9. **Candle:** Original frames (top left), original frames with the estimated shape w_t (top right), frames synthesized with the LDT model (bottom left), frames synthesized with the DSA model (bottom right) (from Doretto,[11] © 2005 IEEE).

is significantly higher than l_{DSA}. This complexity, as mentioned before, enables real time simulation.

9.10. Discussion

This chapter, which draws on a series of works published recently,[4,8,11,12,39,40] illustrates a model for portions of image sequences where shape, motion and appearance can be represented by conditionally linear models, and illustrates how this model can specialize into linear dynamic texture models, or models that account for view-point variation. We have seen how the linear dynamic texture model have proven successful at capturing the phenomenology of some very complex physical processes, such as water, smoke, fire etc., indicating that such models may be sufficient to support detection and recognition tasks and, to a certain extent, even synthesis and animation.[13] We have also seen that the general dynamic shape and appearance model can be used to model large enough regions of the image (in fact, the entire image), including significant changes in shape (e.g. a waving flag), motion (e.g. a floating duck), and appearance (e.g. a flame). This model can be thought of as extending the work on Active Appearance Models[6,28] to the temporal domain, or extending Dynamic Texture Models[4] to the spatial domain.

Eventually, this framework will be used to model segments of videos, which can be found by a segmentation procedure, which we have not addressed here. The interested reader can consult Refs. 3, 31, 32 and 41 for seed work in that direction, but significant work remains to be done in order to integrate the local models we describe into a more general modeling framework.

Appendix A. Image Formation Model and Assumptions

The goal of this appendix is to describe the conditions under which model (9.1) is valid. We start from a model that is standard in Computer Graphics: A collection of "objects" (closed, continuous but not necessarily smooth surfaces embedded in $\mathbb{R}^3$) S_i, $i = 1, \cdots, N_o$, the number of objects. Each surface is described relative to a Euclidean reference frame $g_i \in SE(3)$, a rigid motion in space,[34] which together with S_i, describes the *geometry* of the scene. In particular we call g_i the *pose* of the i-th object, and S_i its *shape*. Objects interact with light in ways that depend upon their material properties. We make the assumption that the light leaving a point $p \in S_i$ towards any direction depends solely on the incoming light directed towards p: Then each point p on S_i has associated with it a function $\beta_i : \mathbb{H}^2 \times \mathbb{H}^2 \to \mathbb{R}_+$; $(v, l) \mapsto \beta_i(v, l)$ that determines the portion of light coming from a direction l that is reflected in the direction v, each of them represented as a point on the hemisphere $\mathbb{H}^2$ centered at the point p. This *bidirectional reflectance distribution function* (BRDF), describes the reflective properties of the materials, neglecting diffraction, absorbtion, subsurface scattering and other aberrations. The *light source* is the collection of objects that can radiate energy, i.e. the scene itself, $L = \bigcup_{i=1}^{N_o} S_i$. The light element $\mathrm{d}E(q, l)$ accounts for light radiated by $q \in L$ in a direction $l \in \mathbb{H}^2$. $\mathrm{d}E$ can be described by a distribution on $L \times \mathbb{H}^2$ with values in $\mathbb{R}_+$. It depends on the properties of the light source that are described by its *radiance*. The collection $\beta_i : \mathbb{H}^2 \times \mathbb{H}^2 \to \mathbb{R}_+$, $i = 1, \cdots, N_o$, and $\mathrm{d}E : L \times \mathbb{H}^2 \to \mathbb{R}_+$ describes the *photometry* of the scene (reflectance and illumination).

In principle, we would want to allow S_i, g_i, β_i, and $\mathrm{d}E$ to be functions of time. In practice, instead of allowing the surface S_i to deform arbitrarily in time according to $S_i(t)$, and moving rigidly in space via $g_i(t) \in SE(3)$, we lump the pose $g_i(t)$ into S_i and, without loss of generality, describe the surface in the fixed reference frame via $S_i(t)$. Therefore, we use $S_i = S_i(t)$,

$\beta(v, l) = \beta(v, l, t)$, and $\mathrm{d}E(q, l) = \mathrm{d}E(q, l, t)$, $t = 1, \cdots, \tau$, to describe the *dynamics* of the scene. Now that we have defined geometry, photometry, and dynamics of the scene, we want to establish how they are related to the measured images.

As it is customary in computer vision, we make the assumption that the set of objects that act as light sources and those that act as light sinks are disjoint, i.e. we ignore inter-reflections. This means that we can divide the objects in two groups, the light source $L = \bigcup_{i=1}^{N_L} S_i$, and the shape $S = \bigcup_{i=N_L+1}^{N_o} S_i$ with its corresponding BRDF $\beta = \bigcup_{i=N_L+1}^{N_o} \beta_i$, where $S \cap L = \emptyset$. Note that S needs not be simply connected. We can also choose, as fixed reference frame, the one corresponding to the position and orientation of the viewer at the initial time instant t_0, and describe the position and orientation of the camera at time t, relative to the camera at time t_0, using a moving Euclidean reference frame $g(t) \in SE(3)$.

The image $I(\mathbf{x}, t)$ is obtained by summing the energy coming from the scene:

$$\begin{cases} I(\mathbf{x}, t) = \int_{L(t)} \beta(g_p x, g_p q, t) \langle \nu_p, l_{pq} \rangle \, \mathrm{d}E(q, g_q p, t) \\ \mathbf{x} = \pi(g(t)p) \ , \ p \in S(t) \end{cases} \tag{A.1}$$

where $q \in L(t)$, and x is a point in the three-dimensional Euclidean space that corresponds to the position of the pixel $\mathbf{x}$ (see Figure A.1). The quantities $g_p x$, $g_p q$, $g_q p \in \mathbb{H}^2$, represent unit vectors that indicate the directions from p to x, from p to q, and from q to p respectively. The unit vectors $\nu_p, l_{pq} \in \mathbb{H}^2$, represent the outward normal vector of $S(t)$ at point p, and the direction from p to q; $\pi : \mathbb{R}^3 \to \mathbb{R}^2$ denotes the *standard (or "canonical") perspective projection*, which consists in scaling the coordinates of p in the reference frame $g(t)$ by its depth, which naturally depends on $S(t)$.

Note that Equation (A.1) does not take into account the visibility of the viewer, and the light source. In fact, one should add to the equation two characteristic function terms: $\chi_v(x, t)$ outside the integral, which models the visibility of the scene from the pixel $\mathbf{x}$, and $\chi_s(p, q)$ inside the integral to model the visibility of the light source from a scene point (cast shadow). We are omitting these terms here for simplicity, and assume that there are no self-occlusions.

The image formation model (A.1), although derived with some approximations, is still an overkill because the variability in the image can be attributed to different factors. In particular, there is an ambiguity between reflectance and illumination if we allow either one to change arbitrarily, since only their convolution, or *radiance* affects the images. In this case,

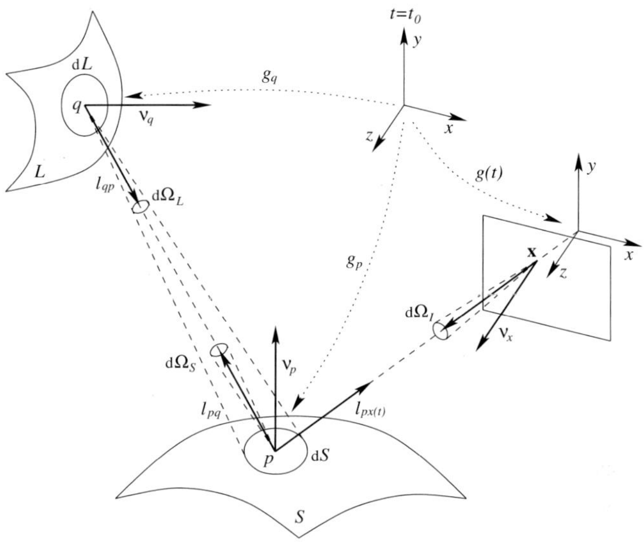

Fig. A.1. Geometric relation between light source, shape of the scene, and camera view point (from Doretto and Soatto,[12] © 2006 IEEE).

one can assume without loss of generality that the scene is Lambertian, or even self-luminous, and model deviations from the model as temporal changes in albedo, or radiance. Therefore, we can forego modeling illumination altogether and concentrate on modeling radiance directly. More precisely we have $\beta(v, l) \doteq \frac{\rho_a(p)}{\pi}, \quad p \in S$, where $\rho_a(p) : \mathbb{R}^3 \to \mathbb{R}_+$ is a scalar function called *surface albedo*, which is the percentage of incident irradiance reflected in any direction. Therefore, the first equation in (A.1) becomes $I(\mathbf{x}, t) = \frac{\rho_a(p,t)}{\pi} \int_{L(t)} \langle \nu_p, l_{pq} \rangle \, \mathrm{d}E(q, g_q p, t)$. With constant illumination we have $L(t) = L$ and $\mathrm{d}E(q, g_q p, t) = \mathrm{d}E(q, g_q p)$. A good approximation of the concept of *ambient light* can be produced through large sources that have diffusers whose purpose is to scatter light in all directions, which, in turn, gets reflected by the surfaces of the scene (inter-reflection). Instead of modeling such a complicated situation, we can look at the desired effect of the sources: to achieve a uniform light level in the scene. Therefore, as a further simplification, we postulate an ambient light intensity which is the same at each point in the environment. This hypothesis corresponds to saying that every surface point $p \in S(t)$ receives the same irradiance from every possible direction. In formulas, this means that the integral in the Lambertian model becomes a constant E_0, i.e. $\int_L \langle \nu_p, l_{pq} \rangle \, \mathrm{d}E(q, g_q p) \doteq E_0$.

By setting $\rho_I(p) \doteq E_0\rho_a(p)/\pi$, we obtain the following reduced image formation model

$$\begin{cases} I(\mathbf{x},t) = \rho_I(p,t) \\ \mathbf{x} = \pi(g(t)p) \ , \ p \in S(t) \ . \end{cases} \tag{A.2}$$

In addition to the reflectance/illumination ambiguity, which is resolved by modeling their product, i.e. radiance, there is an ambiguity between shape and motion. First, we parameterize S: a point $p \in S$ can be expressed, using a slight abuse of notation, by a parametric function $S(t) : B \subset \mathbb{R}^2 \to \mathbb{R}^3$; $u \mapsto S(u,t)$. This parametrization could be learned during the inference process according to a certain optimality property, like we do in Section 9.5. For now, we can choose a parametrization induced by the image plane $\Omega \subset \mathbb{R}^2$ at a certain instant of time t_0, where a point $p \in S(t)$ is related to a pixel position $\mathbf{x}_0 \in \Omega$ according to $\mathbf{x}_0 \doteq \pi(p)$, and the parametric function representing the shape is given by $S(t) : \Omega \to \mathbb{R}^3$; $\mathbf{x}_0 \mapsto S(\mathbf{x}_0,t)$. With this assumption the second equation in model (A.2) becomes $\mathbf{x} = \pi(g(t)S(\mathbf{x}_0,t))$. This equation highlights an ambiguity between shape $S(t)$ and motion $g(t)$. More precisely, *the motion of the point* $\mathbf{x}$ *in the image plane at time* t *could be attributed to the motion of the camera, or to the shape deformation.* Unfortunately we have access only to their composition. For this reason we lump these two quantities into one that we call $w(t) : \Omega \to \Omega$; $\mathbf{x}_0 \mapsto w(\mathbf{x}_0,t) \doteq \pi(g(t)S(\mathbf{x}_0,t))$.

The parametrization of the shape induces a parametrization of the irradiating albedo, which can be expressed as $\rho_I(S(\mathbf{x}_0,t),t) = I(\mathbf{x},t)$. This equation highlights another ambiguity between irradiating albedo $\rho_I(t)$ and shape $S(t)$. In particular, *the variability of the value of the pixel at position* $\mathbf{x}$ *could be attributed to the variability of the irradiating albedo, or to the shape deformation.* Again, since we measure only their composition, we lump these two quantities into one, and define $\rho(t) : \Omega \to \mathbb{R}_+$; $\mathbf{x}_0 \mapsto \rho(\mathbf{x}_0,t) \doteq \rho_I(S(\mathbf{x}_0,t),t)$. Note that the domain of $\rho(t)$ is $\Omega \subset \mathbb{R}^2$, while the domain of $\rho_I(t)$ is $S(t) \subset \mathbb{R}^3$. Finally, we rewrite model (A.2) in the form that we use throughout the chapter[n]:

$$\begin{cases} I(\mathbf{x}(t),t) = \rho(\mathbf{x}_0,t) \ , \ \mathbf{x}_0 \in \Omega \subset \mathbb{R}^2 \\ \mathbf{x}(t) = w(\mathbf{x}_0,t) \ , \qquad t = 1,\ldots,\tau \end{cases} \tag{A.3}$$

If we think of an image $I(t)$ as a function defined on a domain Ω and with a range $\mathbb{R}_+$, the model states that shape and motion are warped together

[n]In order to lighten the notation, in the body of the chapter the time variable will appear as a subscript, and pixel positions will not be in boldface.

to model the domain deformation $w(t)$, while shape and irradiating albedo are merged together to model the range deformation $\rho(t)$. We will refer to these two quantities as the *shape*° and *appearance* of the image $I(t)$, respectively.

We conclude by making explicit one last assumption, that becomes obvious once we try to put together shape (or warping) $w(t)$, and appearance $\rho(t)$ to generate an image $I(t)$. In fact, to perform this operation we need the warping to be invertible. More precisely, it has to be a homeomorphism. This ensures that the spaces Ω and $w(\Omega, t)$ are topologically equivalent, so the scene does not get crinkled, or folded by the warping. This condition is verified if the shape $S(t)$ is smooth with no self-occlusions. Therefore, in (A.3) the temporal variation due to occlusions is not modeled by variations of the shape (warping), but by variations of the appearance.

Acknowledgements

This work is supported by NSF grant EECS-0622245.

References

1. H. Jin, S. Soatto, and A. J. Yezzi, Multi-view stereo reconstruction of dense shape and complex appearance, *International Journal of Computer Vision.* **63**(3), 175–189, (2005).
2. J. Rissanen, Modeling by shortest data description, *Automatica.* **14**, 465–471, (1978).
3. G. Doretto, E. Jones, and S. Soatto. Spatially homogeneous dynamic textures. In *Proceedings of European Conference on Computer Vision*, vol. 2, pp. 591–602, (2004).
4. G. Doretto, A. Chiuso, Y. N. Wu, and S. Soatto, Dynamic textures, *International Journal of Computer Vision.* **51**(2), 91–109, (2003).
5. M. Turk and A. Pentland, Eigenfaces for recognition, *Journal of Cognitive Neuroscience.* **3**(1), 71–86, (1991).
6. T. F. Cootes, G. J. Edwards, and C. J. Taylor, Active appearance models, *IEEE Transactions on Pattern Analysis and Machine Intelligence.* **23**(6), 681–685, (2001).
7. T. K. Carne, The geometry of shape spaces, *Proceedings of the London Mathematical Society.* **3**(61), 407–432, (1990).
8. S. Soatto, G. Doretto, and Y. N. Wu. Dynamic textures. In *Proceedings of IEEE International Conference on Computer Vision*, vol. 2, pp. 439–446, (2001).

°Note that this concept of shape does not have to be confused with the concept of three-dimensional shape $S(t)$ that we have introduced at the beginning of the appendix.

9. T. Vetter and T. Poggio, Linear object classes and image synthesis from a single example image, *IEEE Transactions on Pattern Analysis and Machine Intelligence.* **19**(7), 733–742, (1997).
10. B. Schölkopf and A. Smola, *Learning with kernels: SVM, regularization, optimization, and beyond.* (The MIT press, 2002).
11. G. Doretto. Modeling dynamic scenes with active appearance. In *Proceedings of International Conference on Computer Vision and Pattern Recognition*, vol. 1, pp. 66–73, (2005).
12. G. Doretto and S. Soatto, Dynamic shape and appearance models, *IEEE Transactions on Pattern Analysis and Machine Intelligence.* **28**(12), 2006–2019, (2006).
13. G. Doretto and S. Soatto. Editable dynamic textures. In *Proceedings of International Conference on Computer Vision and Pattern Recognition*, vol. 2, pp. 137–142, (2003).
14. P. Saisan, G. Doretto, Y. N. Wu, and S. Soatto. Dynamic texture recognition. In *Proceedings of International Conference on Computer Vision and Pattern Recognition*, vol. 2, pp. 58–63, (2001).
15. B. Julesz, Visual pattern discrimination, *IEEE Transactions on Information Theory.* **8**(2), 84–92, (1962).
16. J. Portilla and E. Simoncelli, A parametric texture model based on joint statistics of complex wavelet coefficients, *International Journal of Computer Vision.* **40**(1), 49–71, (2000).
17. R. C. Nelson and R. Polana, Qualitative recognition of motion using temporal texture, *Computer Vision, Graphics, and Image Processing: Image Understanding.* **56**(1), 78–89, (1992).
18. M. Szummer and R. W. Picard. Temporal texture modeling. In *Proceedings of IEEE International Conference on Image Processing*, vol. 3, pp. 823–826, (1996).
19. Z. Bar-Joseph, R. El-Yaniv, D. Lischinski, and M. Werman, Texture mixing and texture movie synthesis using statistical learning, *IEEE Transactions on Visualization and Computer Graphics.* **7**(2), 120–135, (2001).
20. A. Fitzgibbon. Stochastic rigidity: image registration for nowhere-static scenes. In *Proceedings of IEEE International Conference on Computer Vision*, vol. 1, pp. 662–669, (2001).
21. Y. Z. Wang and S. C. Zhu. A generative method for textured motion: analysis and synthesis. In *Proceedings of European Conference on Computer Vision*, pp. 583–598, (2002).
22. Y. Z. Wang and S. C. Zhu. Modeling complex motion by tracking and editing hidden Markov graphs. In *Proceedings of International Conference on Computer Vision and Pattern Recognition*, vol. 1, pp. 856–863, (2004).
23. L. Yuan, F. Wen, C. Liu, and H. Y. Shum. Synthesizing dynamic texture with closed-loop linear dynamic systems. In *Proceedings of European Conference on Computer Vision*, vol. 2, pp. 603–616, (2004).
24. A. Schödl, R. Szeliski, D. H. Salesin, and I. Essa. Video textures. In *Proceedings of SIGGRAPH*, pp. 489–498, (2000).

25. L. Y. Wei and M. Levoy. Fast texture synthesis using tree-structured vector quantization. In *Proceedings of SIGGRAPH*, pp. 479–488, (2000).
26. V. Kwatra, A. Schödl, I. Essa, G. Turk, and B. A. F. Graphcut textures: image and video synthesis using graph cuts. In *Proceedings of SIGGRAPH*, pp. 277–286, (2003).
27. K. S. Bhat, S. M. Seitz, J. K. Hodgins, and P. K. Khosla. Flow-based video synthesis and editing. In *Proceedings of SIGGRAPH*, pp. 360–363, (2004).
28. S. Baker, I. Matthews, and J. Schneider, Automatic construction of active appearance models as an image coding problem, *IEEE Transactions on Pattern Analysis and Machine Intelligence.* **26**(10), 1380–1384, (2004).
29. T. Cootes, S. Marsland, C. Twining, K. Smith, and C. Taylor. Groupwise diffeomorphic non-rigid registration for automatic model building. In *Proceedings of European Conference on Computer Vision*, pp. 316–327, (2004).
30. N. Campbell, C. Dalton, D. Gibson, and B. Thomas. Practical generation of video textures using the autoregressive process. In *Proceedings of the British Machine Vision Conference*, pp. 434–443, (2002).
31. J. Y. A. Wang and E. H. Adelson, Representing moving images with layers, *IEEE Transactions on Image Processing.* **3**(5), 625–638, (1994).
32. J. D. Jackson, A. J. Yezzi, and S. Soatto. Dynamic shape and appearance modeling via moving and deforming layers. In *Proceedings of the Workshop on Energy Minimization in Computer Vision and Pattern Recognition (EMMCVPR)*, pp. 427–448, (2005).
33. P. Van Overschee and B. De Moor, Subspace algorithms for the stochastic identification problem, *Automatica.* **29**(3), 649–660, (1993).
34. Y. Ma, S. Soatto, J. Kosecká, and S. S. Sastry, *An invitation to 3D vision: from images to geometric models.* (Springer-Verlang New York, Inc., 2004).
35. T. J. R. Hughes, *The Finite Element Method - linear static and dynamic finite element analysis.* (Dover Publications, Inc., 2000).
36. L. Ljung, *System identification: theory for the user.* (Prentice-Hall, Inc., 1999), 2nd edition.
37. T. Kailath, *Linear systems.* (Prentice Hall, Inc., 1980).
38. G. H. Golub and C. F. Van Loan, *Matrix computations.* (The Johns Hopkins University Press, 1996), 3rd edition.
39. G. Doretto. *DYNAMIC TEXTURES: modeling, learning, synthesis, animation, segmentation, and recognition.* PhD thesis, University of California, Los Angeles, CA (March, 2005).
40. G. Doretto and S. Soatto. Towards plenoptic dynamic textures. In *Proceedings of the 3rd International Workshop on Texture Analysis and Synthesis*, pp. 25–30, (2003).
41. G. Doretto, D. Cremers, P. Favaro, and S. Soatto. Dynamic texture segmentation. In *Proceedings of IEEE International Conference on Computer Vision*, vol. 2, pp. 1236–1242, (2003).

CHAPTER 10

DIVIDE-AND-TEXTURE: HIERARCHICAL TEXTURE DESCRIPTION

Geert Caenen[1], Alexey Zalesny[2], and Luc Van Gool[1,2]

[1]*ESAT/PSI Visics, Univ. of Leuven, Belgium*
[2]*D-ITET/BIWI, ETH Zurich, Switzerland*
E-mails: geert.caenen@esat.kuleuven.ac.be
zalesny@vision.ee.ethz.ch
vangool@vision.ee.ethz.ch, luc.vangool@vision.ee.ethz.ch

Many textures require complex models to describe their intricate structures, or are even still beyond the reach of current texture synthesis. Their modeling can be simplified if they are considered composites of simpler subtextures. After an initial, unsupervised segmentation of the composite texture into subtextures, it can be described at two levels. One is a label map texture, which captures the layout of the different subtextures. The other consists of the different subtextures. Models can then be built for the "texture" representing the label map and for each of the subtextures separately. Texture synthesis starts by creating a virtual label map, which is subsequently filled out by the corresponding, synthetic subtextures. In order to be effective, this scheme has to be refined to also include mutual influences between textures, mainly found near their boundaries. The proposed composite texture model also includes these. Obviously, one could consider such a strategy with sub-subtextures. Several experiments are shown, for example synthetic textures that represent entire landscapes.

10.1. Introduction

Many textures are so complex that for their analysis and synthesis they can better be considered a composition of simpler subtextures. A good case in point is landscape textures. Open pastures can be mixed with patches of forest and rock. The direct synthesis of the overall texture would defy existing methods, which is in compliance with observations in [8] stating that the textures are as a rule intermediate objects between homogeneous fields and complicated scenes, and the analysis/synthesis of the totally averaged behavior can fail in reproducing important texture features. The whole only appears to be one texture at a very coarse scale. In terms of intensity, colors, and simple filter outputs such scene can not be considered "homogeneous". The homogeneity rather exists in terms of the regularity (in a structural or stochastic sense) in the layout of simpler subtextures as well as in the properties of the subtextures themselves. We propose such hierarchical approach to texture synthesis. We show that this approach can be used to synthesize intricate textures and even complete scenes.

Figure 10.1 shows an example texture image. A model for this texture was extracted using a method in [17]. This method will be referred to as the "basic method", and such model as a "basic model".

(a) original (b) synthesis from basic model

Fig. 10.1. The image on the left shows a complex landscape texture; the image on the right shows the result of attempting to synthesize similar texture from its basic model that considers the original as one, single texture.

Figure 10.1 also shows a texture that has been synthesized on the basis of this model. As can be seen, the result is not entirely convincing. The problem is that the pattern in the example image is too complicated to be dealt with as a single texture. In cases like this a more sophisticated texture model is needed. As mentioned, the idea explored in this chapter is that a prior decomposition of such textures into their subtextures (e.g. grass, sand, bush, rock, *etc.* in the example image) is useful. As mentioned in [12], distinguishing between subtextures, i.e. decomposing or segmenting, is in general easier than texture synthesis. This allows to separate both procedures and use much more complex iterative modeling/generating algorithms only for analysis/synthesis. Despite the fact, that simple pairwise pixel statistics are used for modeling, their optimal combination yields a powerful generative model of textures, whereas for segmentation it is enough to use a preselected filter bank.

The layout of these subtextures can be described as a “label map”, where pixels are given integer labels corresponding to the subtexture they belong to. This label map can be considered as a texture in its own right, which can be modeled using an approach for simple textures such as our basic modeling scheme and of which more can then be synthesized. Also the subtextures can be modeled using their basic model and these subtextures can be filled in at the places prescribed by the synthesized label map.

The creation of a composite texture model starts with one or more example images of that texture as the only input. A first step is the decomposition of the texture into its subtextures. This is the subject of Section 10.3. We propose an unsupervised segmentation scheme, which calculates pixel similarity scores on the basis of color and local image structure and which uses these to group pixels through efficient clique partitioning. Once this decomposition has been achieved, the hierarchical texture model can be extracted. This process is described in Section 10.2.

Based on such model, texture synthesis amounts to first synthesizing a label map, and then synthesizing the subtextures at the corresponding places. Results are shown in Section 10.4. Section 10.5 concludes the chapter.

An idea similar to our composite texture approach has been propounded independently in [10], but their “texture by numbers” scheme (based on smart copying from the example [4, 16]) did not include the automated extraction or synthesis of the label maps (they were hand drawn).

10.2. Composite Texture Modeling

This section focuses on the construction of the composite texture model, on the basis of an example image and its segmentation. We start with a short description of the "basic model", used for the description of simple textures. Then, interdependencies between subtextures are noted to be an issue. After these introductory sections the actual composite texture modeling process is described. Finally, it is explained how the model is used for the synthesis of composite textures.

10.2.1. *The basic texture model*

Before explaining the composite texture algorithm, we concisely describe our basic texture model for single textures, in order to make this chapter more self-contained and to introduce some of the concepts that will also play an important role with the composite texture scheme. The point of departure of the basic model is the co-occurrence principle. Simple statistics about the colors at pixel pairs are extracted, where the pixels take on carefully selected, relative positions. The approach differs in this selectivity from more broad-brush co-occurrence methods [6, 7], where all possible pairs are considered. Every different type of pair – i.e. every different relative position – is referred at as a clique type. The notion "clique" is meant in a graph-theoretical sense where pixels are nodes, and arcs connect those pixels into pairs whose statistics are used in the texture model. This way one obtains the so-called neighborhood graph where pairs are second-order cliques. Figure 10.2 exemplifies clique types assuming the translation invariance scheme.

Fig. 10.2. Clique type assignment for the translation invariant scheme.

The statistics gathered for these cliques are the histograms of the intensity differences between the head and tail pixels of the pairs, and this for all three color bands R, G, and B. Clique types are selected mutually dependent, one-by-one, each time adding the type with statistics computed from the current synthesis deviating most from those of the target texture. The initial set of clique types is restricted only by the maximal clique length, which is proportional to the size of the image under consideration. After the clique selection process is over, all clique types have statistics similar to those of the target texture, but only a small fraction of the types needed to be included in the model, which therefore is very compact. Hence, the basic model consists of a selection of cliques (the so-called "neighborhood system") and their color statistics (the so-called "statistical parameter set"). A more detailed explanation about these basic models and how they are used for texture synthesis is given in [17].

10.2.2. *Subtexture interactions*

A straightforward implementation for composite texture synthesis would use the basic method first to synthesize a novel label map, after which it would be applied to each of the subtextures separately, in order to fill them in at the appropriate places. In reality, subtextures are not stationary within their patch boundaries. Typically there are natural processes at work (geological, biological, *etc.*) that cause interactions between the subtextures. There are transition zones around some of the subtexture boundaries. Figure 10.3 illustrates such transition effect. The image on the left is an original image of zebra fur. The image in the middle is the result of taking the left image label map (consisting of the black and white stripes) and filling in the black and white subtextures. The boundaries between the two look unnatural. The image on the right has been synthesized taking the subtexture interactions into account, using the algorithm proposed in this chapter. The texture looks much better now.

In [18] we have proposed a scheme that orders the subtextures by complexity, and then embarks on a sequential synthesis, starting with the simplest. Only interactions with subtextures that have been synthesized already are taken into account. In this chapter we propose an alternative, parallel approach, where all subtextures and their interactions are taken care of simultaneously, both during modeling and synthesis. The sequential aspect that remains, is that first the label texture is synthesized and only then the subtextures.

(a) original

(b) subtexture synthesis without interactions

(c) subtexture synthesis with interactions

Fig. 10.3. Composite texture synthesis of zebra fur with and without subtexture interactions demonstrates the importance of the latter.

10.2.3. *A parallel composite texture scheme*

The parallel composite texture scheme is a generalization of the basic scheme in [17]. It is also based on the careful selection of cliques and the statistics of their head-tail intensity differences. Yet, for composite texture a distinction will be made between “intra-label” and “inter-label” cliques. Intra-label cliques have both their head and tail pixels within the same subtexture. Inter-label cliques have their head and tail pixels within different subtextures.

The parallel composite texture modeling scheme takes the following steps:

1. Segment the example image of the composite texture (see Section 10.3). The image and the resulting label map are the input for the modeling procedure. Let K be the number of subtextures and B the number of image color bands.

2. Calculate the intensity difference histograms for all inter-label and intra-label clique types that occur in the example image, up to a maximal, user-specified head-tail distance (the clique length); calculate the intensity histograms for all color bands. They all will be referred to as reference histograms. After this step the example image is no longer needed.

3. Construct an initial composite texture model containing the $K \times B$ intensity histograms for each subtexture and each color band, $K \times (B^2\text{-}B)/2$ intensity difference histograms for each subtexture and each band-band connection (so-called vertical cliques), as well as $2K \times B$ clique types and their statistics: for each subtexture/band the shortest horizontal and shortest vertical cliques are added to the model, i.e., the head and tail pixels are direct neighbors.

   Loop:

4. Synthesize a texture using the input label map and the current composite texture model, as discussed further on.

5. Calculate the intensity difference histograms for all inter-label and intra-label clique types from the image synthesized in step 4, up to a maximal, user-specified clique length. They will be referred to as current histograms.

6. Measure the histogram distances – a weighted (see below) Euclidean distance between the reference and current histograms.

7. If the maximal histogram distance is less than a threshold go to the step 9.

8. Add the following $2K$ histograms to the composite model: (a) K intra-label ones, for each subtexture the one with the largest histogram distance; (b) K inter-label ones, those with the largest histogram distance for pairs of subtextures (k,n) for all n and one fixed k at a time.

   Loop end.

9. Model the label map as a normal non-composite texture (i.e. using the basic model), except that instead of intensity difference histograms co-occurrence matrices are used.

Stop.

The number of image bands could vary in general, including for example multispectral images or even additional heterogeneous image properties like filter responses *etc.* In the latter case the intensity differences can be substituted by other statistics including the complete or quantized co-occurrence.

The statistical data kept for the cliques normally consist of intensity histograms, but for the label map texture model a complete label co-occurrence matrix is stored. Indeed, the label map generation is driven by label co-occurrences and not differences because the latter are meaningless in that case. Also, there are only a few labels in a typical segmentation and, hence, taking the full co-occurrence matrix rather than only difference histograms into account comes at an affordable cost. We now concisely describe how texture synthesis is carried out, and how the histogram distances are calculated.

10.2.4. *Composite texture synthesis*

Texture synthesis is organized as an iterative procedure that generates an image sequence, where histogram distances for the clique types in the model decrease with respect to the corresponding reference histograms. This evolution is based on non-stationary, stochastic relaxation, underpinned by Markov Random Field theory. Non-stationary means that the control parameters of the synthesizer (in our case these are so-called Gibbs parameters of the random field) are changed based on the comparison of the reference and current histograms. A more detailed account is given in [17].

A separate note on the synthesis of subtexture interactions is in order here. Even if the modeling procedure selects quite a few inter-label clique types, they still represent a very sparse sample from all possible such clique types, as there are of the order of K^2 subtexture pairs, as opposed to K subtextures, for which just as many clique types were selected. Thus, many subtexture pairs do not interact according to the composite texture model, i.e. there are no cliques in the model corresponding to the label pair under consideration. For such pairs, subtexture knitting – a predefined type of interaction – is used. During knitting neighboring pixels outside the subtexture's area are nevertheless treated as if they lay within, and this for all clique types of that subtexture. The intensity difference is calculated and its entry in the histogram for the given subtexture is used. Knitting produces smooth transitions between subtextures. In case clique types describing the interaction between a subtexture pair have been included in the model, their statistical data are used instead and knitting is turned off for that pair. During normal synthesis, the composite texture model is available from the start and all subtexture pairs without modeled interactions are known beforehand. Hence, knitting is always applied to the same subtexture pairs, i.e., it is static. During the texture modeling stage the set of selected clique types will be constantly updated and the knitting is adaptive. Knitting will be automatically switched off for subtexture pairs with a selected inter-label clique type. This will also happen for subtexture pairs that do not interact, e.g. a texture that simply occludes another one. This is because during the composite texture modeling process knitting is turned on for all pairs which are left without an inter-label clique type. Knitting will not give good results for independent pairs though, as it blends the textures near their border. Hence, a clique type will be selected for such pairs, as the statistics near the border are being driven away from reality under the influence of knitting. The selection of this clique type turns off further knitting, and will itself prescribe statistics that are in line with the subtextures' independence. This process may not be very elegant in the case of independent subtextures, but it works.

10.2.5. *Histogram distances*

The texture modeling algorithm heavily relies on histogram distances. For intra-label cliques, these are weighted Euclidean distances, where the weight is calculated as follows:

$$\mathrm{weight}(k,k,type) = \frac{N\,(k,k,type)}{N_{\max}}, \tag{10.1}$$

where the clique count $N(\cdot)$ is the number of cliques of this type having both the head and the tail inside the label class k, and $N_{\max}$ is the maximum clique count reached over all clique types. The rationale behind this weighing is that types with low clique counts must not dominate the model, as the corresponding statistical relevance will be wanting. This weight also reduces the influence of long clique types, which tend to have lower clique counts. For the inter-label cliques, this effect is achieved by making the weights dependent on clique length explicitly:

$$\text{weight}(k, n, type) = \left(1 - \frac{l^2(type)}{(l_{\max} + 1)^2}\right) \frac{N_{\max}(k, n)}{N_{\max}}, \quad (10.2)$$

where $N_{\max}(k, n)$ is the maximal clique count among the types for the given subtexture pair, $l(type)$ is the clique length, and $l_{\max}$ is the maximal clique length taken over all types present in the example texture. Such weighing again increases the statistical stability and gives preference to shorter cliques, which seems natural as the mutual influence of the subtextures can be expected to be stronger near their boundary.

10.2.6. *Parallel vs. sequential approach*

As mentioned before, prior to this work we have proposed a sequential composite texture scheme [17]. The main advantage of the parallel approach discussed here is that all bidirectional, pairwise subtexture interactions can be taken into account. This, in general, results in better quality and a more compact model. Additionally, there is a disturbing asymmetry between the model extraction and subsequent texture synthesis procedures with the sequential approach. During modeling the surrounding subtextures are ideal, i.e. taken from the reference image. This is not the case during the synthesis stage, where the sequential method has to build further on the basis of previously synthesized subtextures. There is a risk that the sequentially generated subtextures will be of lower and lower quality, due to error accumulation. The parallel approach, in contrast, is free from these drawbacks, as both the modeling and synthesis stages operate under similar conditions. The advantage of the sequential modeling step (but not the synthesis one!) is that every subtexture can be modeled simultaneously, distributed over different computers. But as speed is more crucial during synthesis, this advantage is limited in practice. During model extraction, the foremost problem is the clique type selection. This problem is more complicated in the parallel case, as there are many more clique types to choose from. At every iteration of the modeling algorithm a choice can be made between all inter- and intra-label cliques.

10.3. Texture Decomposition

In order for the texture modeling and synthesis approach to work, the decomposition of the texture into its subtextures needs to be available. We propose an unsupervised segmentation scheme, which calculates pixel similarity scores on the basis of color and local image structure and which uses these to group pixels through efficient clique partitioning. Once this decomposition has been achieved, the hierarchical texture model can be extracted. The approach is unsupervised in the sense that neither the number nor the sizes of subtextures are given to the system.

Important to mention is that, in contrast with traditional segmentation schemes, we envisage a clustering that is not necessarily semantically correct. Our goal is to reduce the complexity of the texture in terms of structure and color properties.

10.3.1. *Pixel similarity scores*

For the description of the subtextures, both color and structural information is taken into account. Local statistics of the (L, a, b) color coordinates and response energies of a set of Gabor filters $(f_1, \ldots, f_n)$ are chosen, but another wavelet family or filter bank could be used to optimize the system.

The initial (L, a, b)-color and $(f_1, \ldots, f_n)$-structural feature vector of an image pixel i are both referred to as $\mathbf{x}_i$, for the sake of simplicity. The local statistics of the vectors $\mathbf{x}_j$ near the pixel i are captured by a local histogram p_i.

To avoid problems with sparse high-dimensional histograms, we first cluster both feature spaces separately. For the structural features this processing is done in the same vein as the texton analysis in [11]. The cluster centers are obtained using the k-means algorithm and will serve as bin centers for the local histograms.

Instead of assigning a pixel to a single bin, each pixel is assigned a vector of weights that express its affinity to the different bins. The weights are based on the Euclidean distances to the bin centers: if $d_{ik} = \|\mathbf{x}_i - \mathbf{b}_k\|$ is the distance between a feature value $\mathbf{x}_i$ and the k-th bin center, we compute the corresponding weight as

$$w_{ik} = e^{-d_{ik}^2/2\sigma^2} . \tag{10.3}$$

The resulting local *weighted histogram* p_i of pixel i is obtained by averaging the weights over a region R_i :

$$p_i(k) = \frac{1}{|R_i|} \sum_{j \in R_i} w_{jk} . \tag{10.4}$$

In our experiments, R_i was chosen a fixed shape: a disc with a radius of 8 pixels. The values $p_i(k)$ can therefore be computed for all pixels at once (denoted $P(k)$), using the convolution:

$$P(k) = W_k * \chi_D \text{ with } W_k(i) = w_{ik} \text{ and } \chi_D(i) = \begin{cases} 1 \text{ if } i \in D, \\ 0 \text{ if } i \notin D, \end{cases} \tag{10.5}$$

where $D = \{i \mid \|i\| < 8\}$.

The resulting weighted histogram can be considered a smooth version of the traditional histogram. The weighting causes small changes in the feature vectors (e.g. due to non-uniform illumination) to result in small changes in the histogram. In traditional histograms this is often not the case as pixels may suddenly jump to another bin. Figure 10.4 illustrates this by computing histograms of two rectangular patches from a single Brodatz texture. These patches have similar texture, only the illumination is different. Clearly the weighted histograms (right) are less sensitive to this difference. This is reflected in a higher Bhattacharyya score (10.6).

Color and structural histograms are computed separately. In a final stage, the color and structure histograms are simply concatenated into a single, longer histogram and the $p_i(k)$ are scaled to ensure the sum to 1.

In order to compare the feature histograms, we have used the Bhattacharyya coefficient ρ. Its definition for two frequency histograms $p = (p_1, \dots, p_n)$ and $q = (q_1, \dots q_n)$ is:

$$\rho(p,q) = \sum_i \sqrt{p_i q_i} . \tag{10.6}$$

This coefficient is proven to be more robust [1] in the case of zero count bins and non-uniform variance than the more popular chi-squared statistic (denoted χ^2). In fact, after a few manipulations one can show the following relation in case the histograms are sufficiently similar:

$$\rho(p,q) \approx 1 - \frac{1}{8}\sum_i \frac{(q_i - p_i)^2}{p_i} = 1 - \frac{1}{8}\chi^2(p,q). \tag{10.7}$$

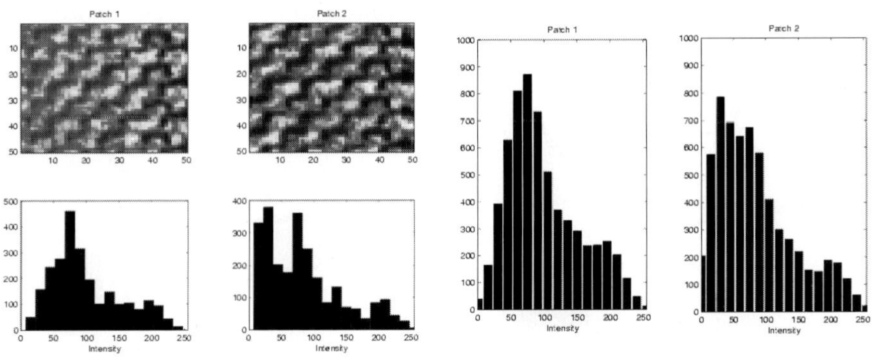

Fig. 10.4. Top left: patches with identical texture and different illumination; bottom left: traditional intensity histograms of the patches; right: weighted histograms of the patches.

Another advantage of the Bhattacharyya coefficient over the χ^2-measure is that it is symmetric, which is more natural when similarity has to be expressed.

In order to evaluate the similarity between two pixels, their feature histograms are not simply compared. Rather, the comparison of the histogram for the first pixel is made with those of all pixels in a neighborhood of the second. The best possible score is taken as the similarity $S'(i,j)$ between the two pixels. This allows the system to assess similarity without having to collect histograms from large regions R_i. Additional advantages of such approach are that boundaries between subtextures are slightly better located and narrow subtextures can still be distinguished. Figure 10.5 illustrates the behavior near texture boundaries and an example of an improved segmentation as well as a comparison with Normalized Cuts is shown in Fig. 10.6.

Using the shifting strategy has three major effects on the similarity scores, depending on the location of the pixels:

1. Pixels that lie *in the interior of a subtexture* only have strong similarities with this texture.

2. Pixels *near a texture border* (Fig. 10.5) attain an increased similarity score when compared to the particular subtexture they belong to. Comparisons made with the neighboring texture will also yield higher scores, yet less extreme ones.

3. Pixels *on a texture border* are very similar to both adjacent textures.

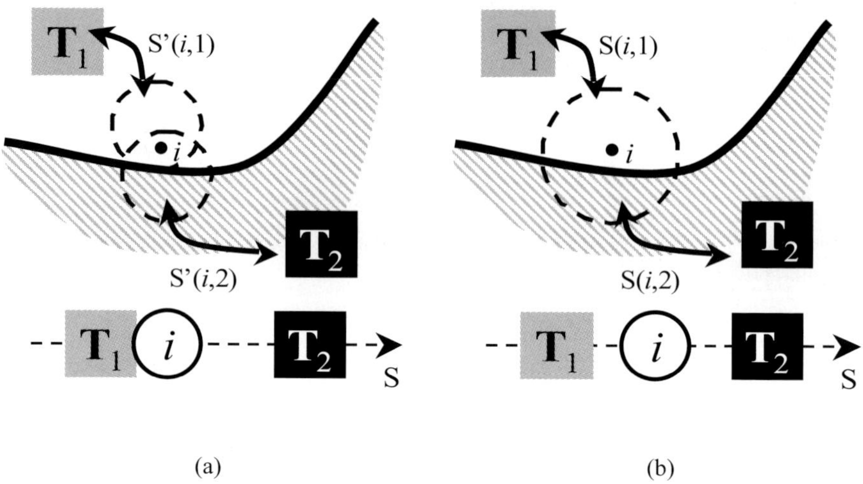

Fig. 10.5. (a) Comparison between two pixels using shifted matching; the dashed lines indicate the supports of the histograms that yield optimal similarities between i and subtextures $\mathbf{T}_1$ and $\mathbf{T}_2$; (b) comparison without shifts. The similarity scores $S'(i,1)$ and $S'(i,2)$ for (a), although *both* significantly higher than $S(i,1)$ and $S(i,2)$ in (b), are proportionally closer to the desired similarities, as is indicated schematically.

To fully exploit this shifted matching result we transform our similarity scores using $S'(i,j) \rightarrow S'(i,j)^n$, with $n = 10$ in our experiments. This causes the similarities established between pixels of type 2 and their neighbor texture to decrease significantly.

The search for the location with the best matching histogram close to the second pixel is based on the mean shift gradient to maximize the Bhattacharyya measure [3]. This avoids having to perform an exhaustive search.

A final refinement is by defining a symmetric similarity measure S: $S(i,j) = S(j,i) = \max\{S'(i,j), S'(j,i)\}$.

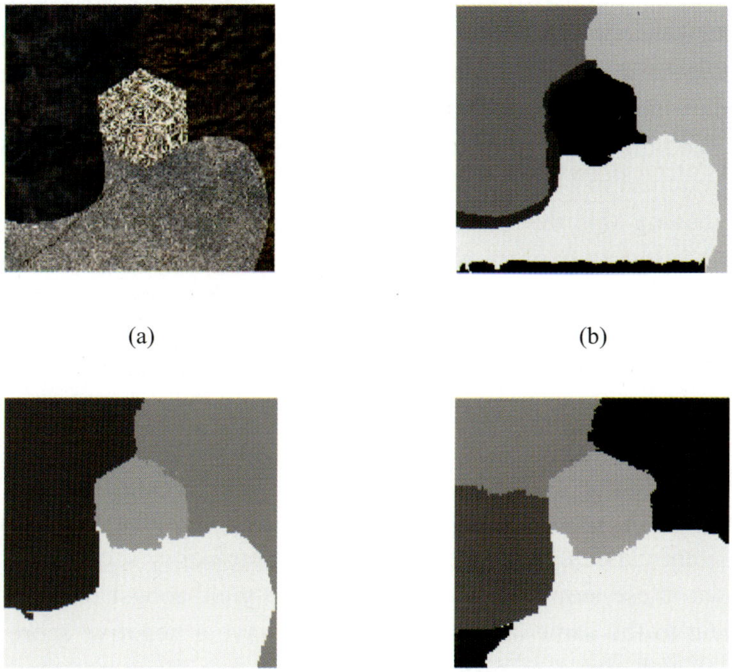

(a) (b) (c) (d)

Fig. 10.6. (a) Original image (texture collage) and segmentations obtained: (b) with CP, larger regions, and no shifted matching; (c) using CP and shifted matching (smaller regions, mean shift optimization); and (d) using a version of Normalized Cuts along with its standard parameter set available at http://www.cs.berkeley.edu.

As shifted matches cause neighboring pixels to have an exact match, the similarity scores are only computed for a subsample (a regular grid) of the image pixels, which also yields a computational advantage. Yet, after segmentation of this sample, a high-resolution segmentation map is obtained as follows. The histogram of each pixel is first compared to each entry in the list of neighboring sample histograms. The pixel is then assigned to the best matching class in the list.

Our particular segmentation algorithm requires a similarity matrix S with entries ≥ 0 indicating that pixels are likely to belong together and entries < 0 indicating the opposite. The absolute value of the entry is a measure of confidence. So far, all the similarities S have positive values. We subtract a constant value, which was determined experimentally and kept the same in all our experiments. With this fixed value images with different numbers of subtextures could be segmented successfully. Hence, the number of subtextures was not given to the system, as would e.g. be required in k-means clustering. As it will be illustrated in Section 10.4.2, having this threshold in the system can be an advantage, as it allows the user to express what he or she considers being perceptually similar: the threshold determines the simplicity or homogeneity of each subtexture or in other words, the level of hierarchy.

10.3.2. *Pixel grouping*

In order to achieve the intended, unsupervised segmentation of the composite textures into simpler subtextures, pixels need to be grouped into disjoint classes, based on their pairwise similarity scores. Taken on their own, these similarities are too noisy to yield robust results. Pixels belonging to the same subtexture may e.g. have a negative score (false negative) and pixels of different subtextures may have positive scores (false positives). Nevertheless, taken altogether, the similarity scores carry quite reliable information about the correct grouping. The transitivity of subtexture membership is crucial: if pixels i and j are in the same class and j and k too, then i, j and k must belong to the same class. Even if one of the pairs gets a falsely negative score, the two others can override a decision to split. Next, we formulate the texture segmentation problem so as to exploit transitivity to detect and avoid false scores. We present a time-optimized adaptation of the grouping algorithm we first introduced in [5]. We construct a complete graph G where each vertex represents a pixel and where edges are weighted with the pairwise similarity scores. We partition G into completely connected disjoint subsets of vertices (usually also cliques but please note the different meaning in this context) through edge removal so as to maximize the total score on the remaining edges (Clique Partitioning, or CP). As to avoid confusion with a clique concept defined earlier, we will use the word "component" instead of clique here. The transitivity property is ensured by the component constraint: every two vertices in a component are connected, and no two vertices from different components are connected. The CP formulation of texture segmentation is made possible by the presence of positive *and* negative weights: they naturally lead to the definition of a *best solution* without the need of knowing the number of components (subtextures) or the introduction of artificial stopping criteria as in other graph-based approaches based on strictly positive weights [15, 2]. On the other hand, our approach needs the parameter t_0 that determines the splitting point between positive and negative scores. But, as our experiments have shown, the same parameter value yields good results for a wide range of images. Moreover, the same value yields good results for examples with a variable number of subtextures. This is much better than having to specify this number, as would e.g. be necessary in a *k*-means clustering approach.

CP can be solved by Linear Programming [9] (LP). Let w_{ij} be the weight of the edge connecting (i, j), and $x_{ij} \in \{1, 0\}$ indicate whether the edge exists in the solution ($0 = no,\ 1 = yes$). The following LP can be established:

$$\text{maximize} \sum_{1 \le i < j \le n} w_{ij} x_{ij} \text{ subject to } \begin{cases} x_{ij} + x_{jk} - x_{ik} \le 1, \forall 1 \le i < j < k \le n, \\ x_{ij} - x_{jk} - x_{ik} \le 1, \forall 1 \le i < j < k \le n, \\ -x_{ij} + x_{jk} + x_{ik} \le 1, \forall 1 \le i < j < k \le n, \\ x_{ij} \in \{0, 1\}, \forall 1 \le i < j \le n. \end{cases} \tag{10.8}$$

The inequalities express the transitivity constraints, while the objective function to be maximized corresponds to the sum of the intra-component edges.

Unfortunately CP is an NP-hard problem [9]: LP (10.8) has worst case exponential complexity in the number n of vertices (pixels), making it impractical for large n. The challenge is to find a practical way out of this complexity trap. The correct partitioning of the example in Fig. 10.7 is $\{\{1,3\},\{2,4,5\}\}$. A simple greedy strategy merging two vertices (i, j) if $w_{ij} > 0$ fails because it merges $(1, 2)$ as its first move. Such an approach suffers from two problems: the generated solution depends on the *order* by which vertices are processed and it looks only at *local* information.

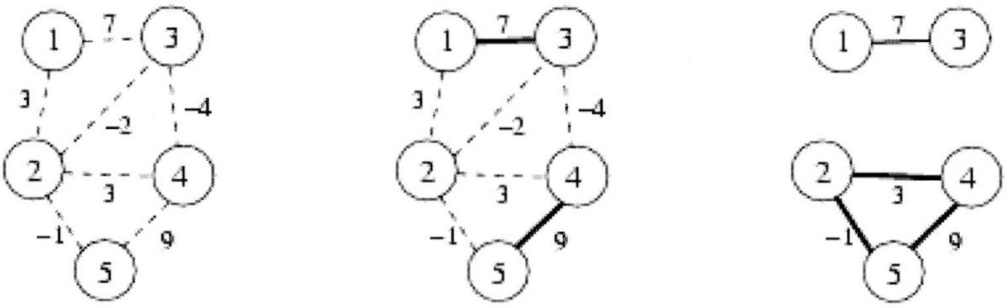

Fig. 10.7. An example graph and two iterations of our heuristic. Edges that are not displayed have zero weight.

We propose the following iterative heuristic. The algorithm starts with the partition

$$\Phi = \{\{i\}\}_{1\leq i\leq n} \tag{10.9}$$

composed of n singleton components each containing a different vertex. The function

$$m(c_1, c_2) = \sum_{i\in c_1, j\in c_2} w_{ij} \tag{10.10}$$

defines the cost of merging components c_1, c_2. We consider the functions

$$\begin{aligned} b(c) &= \max\nolimits_{t\in\Phi} m(c,t), \\ d(c) &= \arg\max\nolimits_{t\in\Phi} m(c,t), \end{aligned} \tag{10.11}$$

representing, respectively, the score of the best merging choice for component c and the associated component to merge with. We merge components c_i, c_j if and only if the three following conditions are met simultaneously

$$d(c_i) = c_j,\ d(c_j) = c_i,\ b(c_i) = b(c_j) > 0. \tag{10.12}$$

In other words, two components are merged only if each one represents the best merging option for the other and if merging them increases the total score. At each iteration the functions $b(c)$, $d(c)$ are computed, and all pairs of components fulfilling the criteria are merged. The algorithm iterates until no two components can be merged. The function m can be progressively computed from its values in the previous iteration. The basic observation is that for any pair of merged components $c_k = c_i \cup c_j$, the function changes to $m(c_l, c_k) = m(c_l, c_i) + m(c_l, c_j)$ for all $c_l \notin \{c_i, c_j\}$. This strongly reduces the number of operations needed to compute m and makes the algorithm much faster than in [5].

Figure 10.7 shows an interesting case. In the first iteration $\{1\}$ is merged with $\{3\}$ and $\{4\}$ with $\{5\}$. Notice how $\{2\}$ is, correctly, not merged with $\{1\}$ even though $m(\{1\},\{2\}) = 3 > 0$. In the second iteration $\{2\}$ is correctly merged with $\{4,5\}$, resisting the (false) attraction of $\{1,3\}$ ($b(\{1,3\},\{2\}) = 1$, $d(\{1,3\}) = \{2\}$). The algorithm terminates after the third iteration because $m(\{1,3\},\{2,4,5\}) = -3 < 0$. The second iteration shows the power of CP. Vertex 2 is connected to unreliable edges (w_{12} is false positive, w_{25} is false negative. Given vertices $\{1,2,3\}$ only, it is not possible to derive the correct partitioning $\{\{1,3\},\{2\}\}$; but, as we add vertices $\{4,5\}$, the *global information* increases and CP arrives at the correct partitioning.

The proposed heuristic is *order independent*, takes a more global view than a direct greedy strategy, and resolves several ambiguous situations while maintaining polynomial complexity. Analysis reveals that the exact amount of operations depends on the structure of the data, but it is at most $4n^2$ in the average case. Moreover, the operations are simple: only comparisons and sums of real values (no multiplication or division is involved).

In the first iterations, being biased toward highly positive weights, the algorithm risks to take wrong merging decisions. Nevertheless our merging criterion ensures this risk to quickly diminish with the size of the components in the correct solution (number of pixels forming each subtexture) and at each iteration, as the components grow and increase their resistance against spurious weights.

10.4. Results

In this section we first present the results of experiments that test the effectiveness of the CP algorithm as a substitute for the much slower LP algorithm, as proposed in Section 10.3. Once the viability of this approach for the creation of label maps has been established, a second section describes results of our parallel composite texture synthesis.

10.4.1. *Performance of the CP approximation*

The practical shortcut for the implementation of CP may raise some questions as to its performance. In particular, how much noise on the edge weights (i.e. uncertainty on the similarity scores) can it withstand? And, how well does the heuristic approximation approach the true solution of CP?

We tested both LP and the heuristic on random instances of the CP problem. Graphs with *a priori* known, correct partitioning were generated. Their sizes differed in that both the number of components and the total number of vertices (all components had the same size) were varied. Intra-component weights were uniformly distributed in $[-a, 9]$ with a real number, while inter-component weights were uniformly distributed in $[-9, a]$, yielding an ill-signed edge percentage of $a/(a+9)$. This *noise level* could be controlled by varying the parameter a. Let the *difference between two partitionings* be the minimum amount of vertices that should change their component membership in one partitioning to get the other. The quality of the produced partitionings is evaluated in terms of *average percentage of misclassified vertices*: the difference between the produced partitioning and the correct one, averaged over 100 instances and divided by the total number of vertices in a single instance.

Table 10.1 reports the performance of our approximation for larger problem sizes. Given 25% noise level, the average error already becomes negligible with component sizes between 10 and 20 (less than 0.5%). In problems of this size, or larger, the algorithm can withstand even higher noise levels, still producing high quality solutions. In the case of 1000 vertices and 10 components, even with 40% noise level ($a = 6$), the algorithm produces solutions, which are closer than 1% to the correct one. This case is of particular interest as its size is similar to the typical texture segmentation problems.

Table 10.2 shows a comparison between our approximation to CP and the optimal solution computed by LP on various problem sizes, with constant noise level set to 25% ($a = 3$). In all cases the partitionings produced by the two algorithms are virtually identical: the average

Table 10.1. Performance of the CP approximation algorithm on various problem sizes.

Vertices	Components	Noise Level	Err% Approx
40	4	25	0.33
60	4	25	0.1
60	4	33	2.1
120	5	36	1.6
1000	10	40	0.7

Table 10.2. Comparison of LP and our approximation. The noise level is 25%. Diff % is the average percentual difference between the partitionings produced by the two algorithms. The two Err columns report the average percentage misclassified vertices for each algorithm.

Vert.	Components	Diff%	Err% LP	Err% Approx
15	3	0.53	6.8	6.93
12	2	0.5	2.92	3.08
21	3	0.05	2.19	2.14
24	3	0.2	1.13	1.33

percentual difference is very small as shown in the third column of the table. Due to the very high computational demands posed by LP, the largest problem reported here has only 24 vertices. Beyond that point, computation times run into the hours, which we consider as too impractical. Note that the average percentage of misclassifications quickly drops with the size of the components.

The proposed heuristic is fast: it completed these problems in less than 0.1 seconds, except for the 1000 vertices one, which took about 4 seconds on the average. The ability to deal with thousands of vertices is particularly important in our application, as every pixel to be clustered will correspond to a vertex. Figure 10.8 shows the average error for a problem with 100 vertices and 5 components as a function of the noise level (a varies from 3 to 5.5). Although the error grows faster than linearly, and the problem has a relatively small size, the algorithm produces high quality solutions in situations with as much as 36% of noise.

These encouraging results show CP's robustness to noise and support our heuristic as a good approximation. Components in these experiments were only given the same size to simplify the discussion. The algorithm itself deals with differently sized components.

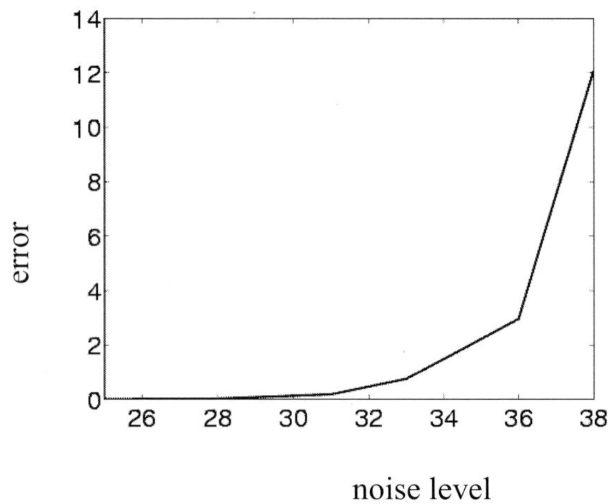

Fig. 10.8. Relationship between noise level and error, for a 100 vertices, 5 component problem. The average percentage of misclassified vertices (X-axis) is still low with as much as 36% noise level.

10.4.2. *Composite texture synthesis results*

This section presents some of the results obtained with the parallel composite texture synthesis as described in the chapter. The various stages of our method will be systematically explained through an example. Afterwards we will focus on the different aspects that were touched upon in the chapter using adequate examples.

The Complete Scheme – The landscape shown in Fig. 10.9 (top left) is clearly too complex to be synthesized when regarded as a single texture. Therefore, in keeping with the propounded composite texture

Fig. 10.9. Real landscape (top left) and label map (top right); synthetic landscape when keeping this label map (bottom).

approach, it is decomposed by analyzing the local color and structural properties. The CP-algorithm yields a label map based on the homogeneity of these properties, as shown in Fig. 10.9 (top right). Based on this label map and the example image, a model for the subtextures and their interactions is learned. In order to show the effectiveness of the texture synthesis, we also show the same landscape layout, but with the label regions filled with textures generated on the basis of this model

(Fig. 10.9 bottom). Of course, it is the very goal of the approach to go one step further and to create wholly new patterns. To that end, a *new* label map is generated, as shown in Fig. 10.10 (top), and this is filled with the corresponding subtextures (Fig. 10.10 bottom). The overall impression is quite realistic. The label map is capable to capture the main, systematic aspects of the layout. The sky is, e.g. created at the top, and also the different land cover types keep their natural, overall configuration.

Fig. 10.10. Synthetic label map (top) and completely synthetic landscape (bottom).

Fig. 10.11. Landscape texture synthesis. Left: original images with three different subtextures for the top landscape and two subtextures for the bottom landscape; middle: results with the older, sequential approach, right: parallel composite texture synthesis with better, more natural texture transitions.

Parallel vs. Sequential Approach – Figure 10.11 shows three images of two landscapes. The ones on the left are the original images, used as the sole examples. The images in the middle show the result of our previous, sequential texture synthesis method [18] applied to a synthesized label map. The images on the right show the same experiment, but now with textures synthesized by the parallel approach described in this chapter. The overall results of the parallel method look better. In particular, unnaturally sharp transitions between the subtextures have been eliminated. This can e.g. be seen at the boundaries between the bush and grass textures of the top row. Also, the shadowing effects, learned as an interaction between bush and stone, added more reality to that result. In the sequential approach, only interactions with previously synthesized textures can be taken into account, not with those to come later in the process.

Dealing with Semantics – Figure 10.12 shows a synthetic example of zebra fur. The label map for this example was synthesized only including information from the original image (Fig. 10.3). Apparently this did not suffice to capture sufficient statistics for the stripe layout (corresponding to the two subtextures in the label map). Without any further semantic knowledge, the system has generated one stripe, which is too wide, giving an unnatural impression. A larger texture sample should be provided as an example to resolve this. Figure 10.13 shows another example where the model fails to pick up the underlying semantics. Despite the globally satisfying impression of the landscape, the model failed to "understand" the road separating the vineyard from the slope. Nevertheless the road was partially reconstructed as a transition effect when incorporating the subtexture interactions.

Fig. 10.12. Synthetic zebra fur based on a synthetic layout label map, demonstrates the importance of presenting a sufficiently large example image (cf. Fig. 10.3). One stripe is unnaturally wide.

Fig. 10.13. Left: original aerial image of a landscape, right: image synthesized based on the original label map. The overall impression is satisfactory, but a semantic concept like road continuity was – of course – not picked up.

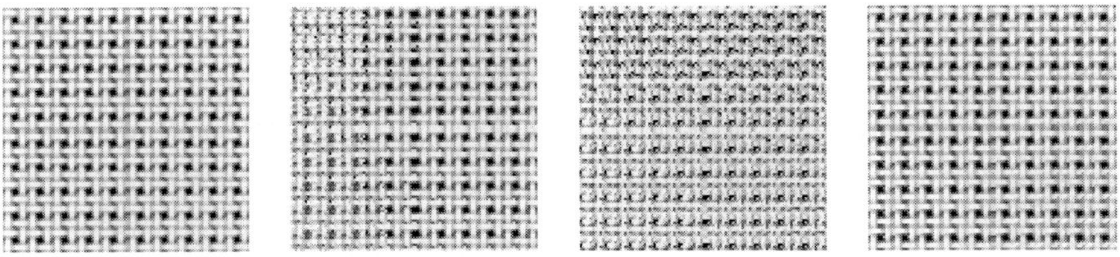

(a) original | (b) synthesis as a single texture, 3000 iterations | (c) synthesis as a single texture, 500 iterations | (d) synthesis as a composite texture

Fig. 10.14. Patterns that are traditionally considered as a single texture can benefit from the composite texture approach just the same. (a) original image; (b) synthesis using basic model with 3000 iterations; (c) synthesis using basic model with 500 iterations; (d) composite texture based synthesis (two subtextures).

Processing Simple Textures as Composite Textures – Figure 10.14 illustrates that the composite texture approach even holds good promise for "simple" textures. Given the example on the left, a basic model was extracted and used to synthesize the two middle textures. For the texture (b) 59 cliques were selected and the synthesis was allowed to run over 3000 iterations. The image (c) shows the result if the number of iterations with the basic model is restricted to 500. Quality has clearly suffered. The image on the right is the result of a composite texture synthesis. Bright and dark regions were distinguished as two subtextures. Not only is this latter result better, it also took only 100 iterations, while the total number of cliques (for the two subtextures and their interactions) was still limited to 59. The computational complexity of the parallel approach is lower, because every pixel is involved in about only half as many cliques.

Multiple Level Decomposition – We will now briefly illustrate the potential of increasing the number of layers in the composite texture description. So far, we have considered only two: the label map and directly beneath the subtextures. On the other hand, Fig. 10.14 has demonstrated that it may be useful to also subdivide the subtextures themselves. This is in agreement with the strategy as originally described, i.e., to decompose until a level of sufficient homogeneity in terms of simple properties is achieved. The sponge texture in the center

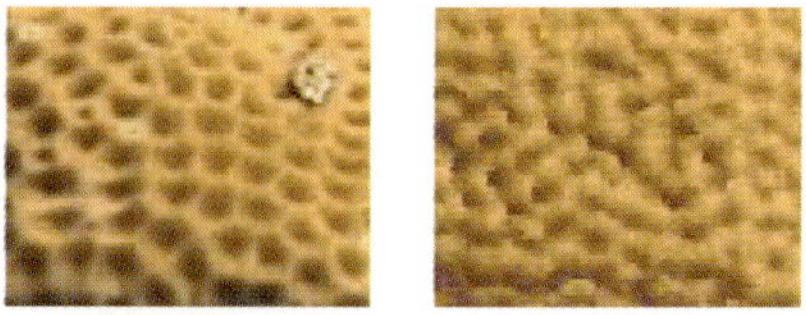

Fig. 10.15. The sea sponge texture with cavities cannot be synthesized as a single subtexture with the basic model.

(a) (b)

(c)

Fig. 10.16. (a) original image; (b) label map of the sponge texture after the extra decomposition into two subtextures; (c) synthesis based on the original label map using this extra level of decomposition. The cavities of the sponge are recovered.

of Fig. 10.16(a) is quite intricate. The cavities show patterns that have to be captured quite precisely and simultaneously their structure varies over the texture, due to perspective effects and changing orientations. Figure 10.15 shows a cutout of the sponge texture and a synthetic result, based on the basic model for this texture. The result more or less averages out the cavity variations in the example. The sponge is segmented out as a separate subtexture by an initial segmentation. Now, by lowering the threshold introduced at the end of Section 10.3.1 for this part, a further decomposition is achieved (Fig. 10.16(b)). In Fig. 10.16(c) the result of the synthesis based on this additional decomposition is shown. Clearly, the cavities have been recovered. This result is however preliminary as we don't have a systematic way of deciding where to stop the decomposition. This will be the subject of future research.

10.5. Conclusions

We have described a hierarchical texture synthesis approach, that considers textures as composites of simpler subtextures, that are studied in terms of their own statistics, that of their interactions, and that of their layout. The approach supports the fully automated synthesis of complex textures from example images, without verbatim copying.

The following observation made this hierarchical approach possible: it is easier to distinguish textures than to synthesize them. It is in a full agreement with the complexity comparison between the segmenting and synthesizing stages. Segmentation uses fixed filters, which are texture- and mutually-independent, while the synthesis uses an optimal texture- and mutually-dependent pixel pair type selection obtained during the analysis-by-synthesis procedure. Despite a seeming simplicity of the pairwise statistics they, if taken together, represent much more intricate pixel interdependency compared to the segmenting filters.

In the current approach only one level of the hierarchy is thoroughly explored and a promising extension towards multiple levels is suggested. Future research will crack down on this problem of how to optimize the trade-off between the complexity of the label maps and the homogeneity of the subtextures they contain.

Acknowledgments

The authors gratefully acknowledge support by the Swiss National Foundation Project ASTRA (200021-103850).

References

1. Aherne, F., Thacker, N., and Rockett, P. 1998. The Bhattacharyya Metric as an Absolute Similarity Measure for Frequency Coded Data. Kybernetika 34, No. 4, pp.363-368.
2. Aslam, J., Leblanc, A., and Stein, C. A New Approach to Clustering. Workshop on Algorithm Engineering, 2000.
3. Comaniciu, D. and Meer, P. Real-Time Tracking of Non-Rigid Objects using Mean Shift. In Proc. ICPR, Vol. 3, pp. 629-632 (2000).
4. Efros, A. and Leung, T. Texture Synthesis by Non-Parametric Sampling. In Proc. ICCV, Vol. 2, pp. 1033-1038 (1999).
5. Ferrari, V., Tuytelaars, T., and Van Gool, L. Real-time affine region tracking and coplanar grouping. In Proc. CVPR, Vol. II, pp. 226-233 (2001).
6. Gagalowicz, A. and Ma, S.D. Sequential Synthesis of Natural Textures. Computer Vision, Graphics, and Image Processing, Vol. 30, pp. 289-315 (1985).
7. Gimel'farb, G. *Image Textures and Gibbs Random Fields*. Kluwer Academic Publishers: Dordrecht, 250 p. (1999).
8. Gousseau, Y. Texture synthesis through level sets. In Proc. Texture 2002 workshop, pp. 53-57 (2002).
9. Graham, R., Groetschel, M., and Lovasz, L. (eds.) *Handbook of Combinatorics*. Elsevier, Vol. 2, pp. 1890-1894 (1995).
10. Hertzmann, A., Jacobs, C., Oliver, N., Curless, B., and Salesin D. Image Analogies. In Proc. SIGGRAPH, pp. 327-340 (2001).
11. Malik, J., Belongie, S., Leung, T., and Shi, J. *Contour and Texture Analysis for Image Segmentation. Perceptual Organization for Artificial Vision Systems*. Boyer and Sarkar, eds. Kluwer (2000).
12. Paget, R. *Nonparametric Markov Random Field Models for Natural Texture Images*. PhD Thesis, University of Queensland, February 1999.
13. Puzicha, J., Hofmann, T., and Buhmann, J. Histogram Clustering for Unsupervised Segmentation and Image Retrieval. Pattern Recognition Letters, 20(9), pp. 899-909 (1999).
14. Puzicha, J. and Belongie, S. Model-based Halftoning for Color Image Segmentation (2000).
15. Shi, J. and Malik, J. Normalized Cuts and Image Segmentation. In Proc. CVPR, pp. 731-737 (1997).

16. Wei, L.-Y. and Levoy, M. Fast Texture Synthesis Using Tree-Structured Vector Quantization. In Proc. SIGGRAPH, pp. 479-488 (2000).
17. Zalesny, A. and Van Gool, L. A Compact Model for Viewpoint Dependent Texture Synthesis. SMILE 2000, Workshop on 3D Structure from Images, Lecture Notes in Computer Science 2018, M. Pollefeys et al. (Eds.), pp. 124-143 (2001).
18. Zalesny, A., Ferrari, V., Caenen, G., Auf der Maur, D., and Van Gool, L. Composite Texture Descriptions. In Proc. ECCV, pp. 180-194 (2002).

Chapter 11

A Tutorial on the Practical Implementation of the Trace Transform

Maria Petrou and Fang Wang

Communications and Signal Processing Group,
Electrical and Electronic Engineering Department,
Imperial College,
London SW7 2AZ, UK

The trace transform is a generalisation of the Radon transform. It consists of tracing an image with straight lines along which certain functionals of the image function are calculated. When a second functional is applied over all values computed along parallel lines, a function of the orientation of the parallel lines is produced. When a third functional over the values of this function is applied, a so called "triple feature" is produced. Different combinations of the three successive functionals used may be chosen so that the triple feature is invariant to rotation, translation, scaling or affine transform of the imaged object. The theory of triple feature construction, however, is accurate in the continuous domain. The application of the process in the digital domain may lead to severe loss of the desired properties of the computed features. This chapter first reviews the trace transform from the theoretical and applications point of view, and then shows how to implement it in practice, so the desirable properties of the triple features are retained. Finally, it presents an application of the theory to the problem of texture feature extraction.

11.1. Introduction

It has been known for some time that a 2D function may be fully reconstructed from the knowledge of its integrals along straight lines defined in its domain. This is the well known Radon transform[5] which has found significant applications recently in computer tomography.[19] Consider a 3D object, eg somebody's head. Imagine an X-ray beam entering it at a point and exiting it from the other end (see figure 11.1). The difference between the intensity of the beam when it exits the object from its intensity when it

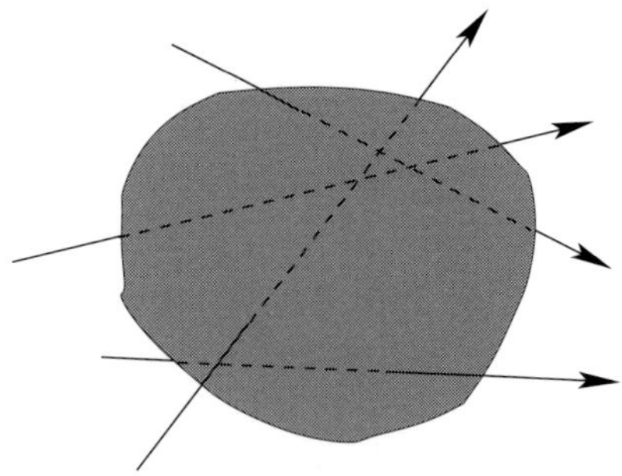

Fig. 11.1. In computer tomography a 3D object is crossed by lines along many different orientations and the integral of some function defined inside the volume of the object is measured along each path.

entered it is equal to the total intensity of the X-ray absorbed by the object along the ray's path. For different beam directions we shall have different absorbencies integrated along the path of each ray across the object. If we record the difference in intensity for every possible ray that crosses the head and store it as a function of the parameters of the path of the ray, we produce the so called "sinogram" of the particular object. So, sinogram is the jargon term for the Radon transform of a function defined inside the volume of the imaged object. The function in this particular example is the absorption of X-rays by the material of the object at each location inside the object. If all X-rays used lie on the same plane, each path is characterised by two parameters and the sinogram is 2D. If the X-rays used are not coplanar, each path is characterised by four parameters and the sinogram is 4D. The Radon transform (ie the sinogram) is invertible, so from the knowledge of the integrated absorbency values along the X-ray paths, the absorbency value at each point inside the object may be computed and a tomographic image of the object may be produced, with the grey value indicating the X-ray absorbency of the material at each voxel.

A derivative of the Radon transform is the Hough transform which is a variation appropriate for sparse images like edge maps.[4] The trace transform proposed in Ref. 6 is only similar to the Radon transform in the sense that it also calculates functionals[a] of the image function along lines criss-crossing its domain. We call the functional computed along a tracing line

[a]A functional requires the values of a function at all points in order to be computed, while a function returns the value at a single point only. So, $f(x) = x^2$ is a function, but $\max(f(x))$ is a functional because one has to know all the values of $f(x)$ to choose its maximum.

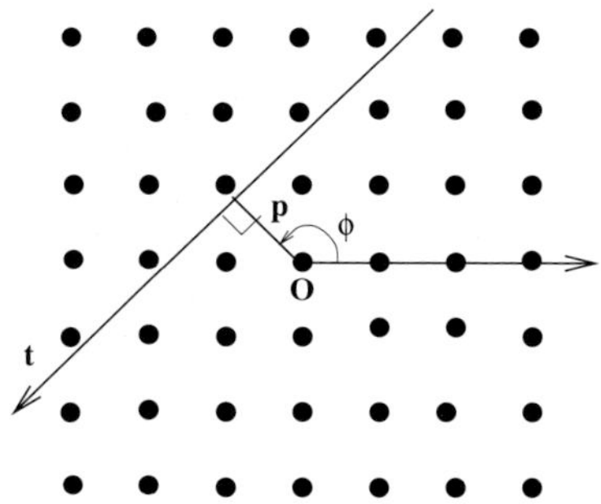

Fig. 11.2. Definition of the parameters of an image tracing line. The black dots represent the image pixels.

"trace" functional. The Radon transform uses a specific trace functional, namely the integral of the function. The Radon transform, therefore, is a special case of the trace transform. The trace transform, however, has so far only been developed in 2D, and no 3D version exists yet (see, however, Ref. 3). Further, there is no general theory about the invertibility of the trace transform. As one obtains a different trace transform for each trace functional used, if one is interested in the inverse transform, one has to investigate it for each functional separately. In the next section we shall also see that the trace transform has another important difference from the Radon transform in terms of its size. The trace transform may use trace functionals that are sensitive to the direction in which a tracing line is traversed and so it traces all lines in two directions. The integral is a functional that retains the same absolute value whichever way the tracing line is traversed and so each line has only to be considered once. So, the trace transform has double the size of the Radon transform.

With the trace transform, the image is transformed into another "image" which is a 2D function depending on parameters (ϕ, p) that characterise each line. Figure 11.2 defines these parameters. Parameter t is defined along the line with its origin at the foot of the normal. As an example, figure 11.3 shows a texture image and one of its trace transforms,[b] which is a function of (ϕ, p). We may further apply a second functional, called "diametric" functional, to each column of the trace transform, (ie along the p direction) to yield a string of numbers that is a function of ϕ. Note that fixing ϕ is equivalent to considering all tracing lines that are par-

[b]Note that a different trace transform is produced for each different trace functional computed along the tracing lines.

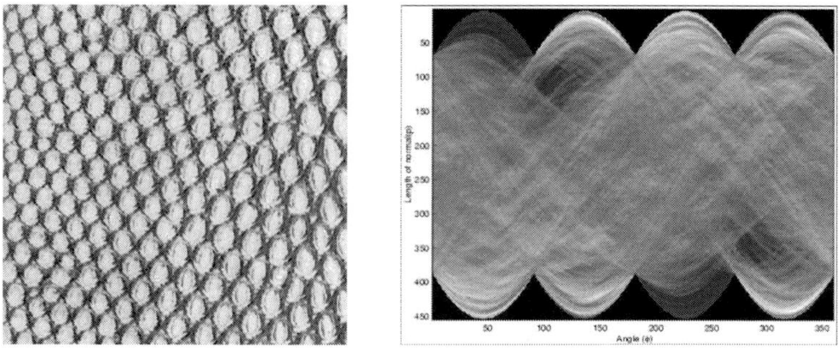

Fig. 11.3. A texture image and a trace transform of it.

allel to each other with common orientation ϕ. So, the diametric functional yields a single value for each batch of parallel lines. These values make up a function of ϕ, called the "circus function". Finally, we may compute from the circus function a third functional, called "circus" functional, to yield a single number, the so called "triple feature". Figure 11.4 shows this process schematically. With the appropriate choice of the functionals we use, the triple feature may have the properties we desire. For example, in Ref. 6 it was shown how to choose the three functionals in order to produce triple features that are invariant to rotation, translation and scaling of the imaged object. In Ref. 14 it was shown how to choose the three functionals in order to produce triple features that are invariant to affine transforms and robust to gradual changes of illumination and minor to moderate occlusions of the imaged object.

If one knows how to produce invariant features, one may also work out how to produce features sensitive to a particular transformation. In Ref. 17 it was shown how to produce rotationally sensitive features in order to distinguish Alzheimer patients from normal controls from the sinograms of their 3D brain scans, because previous studies had indicated that the brains of Alzheimer patients appear more isotropic than the brains of normal subjects.[9] In Ref. 8 it was shown how to select functionals that allow one to infer the affine parameters between two images for the purpose of image registration.

In Ref. 6 it was also shown that the trace transform can be used to produce thousands of features by simply combining any functionals we think of, and then performing feature selection to identify those features that correlate with a certain phenomenon we wish to monitor. For example, when wishing to produce indicators that correlate with the level of use of

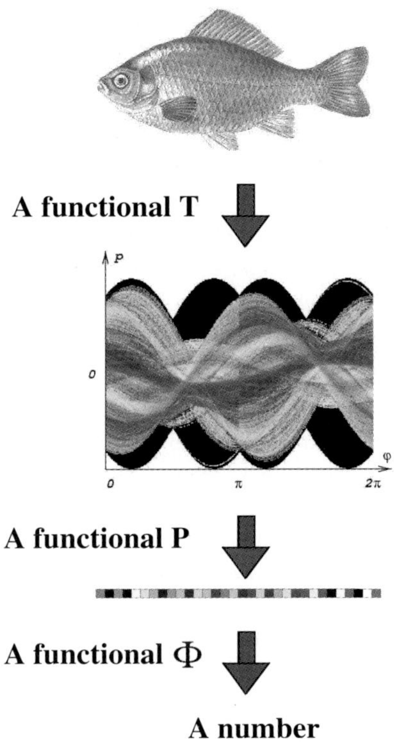

Fig. 11.4. How to produce triple features.

a car park from aerial images of it, we proceed by using, say, A number of trace functionals, B number of diametric functionals and C number of circus functionals in all possible combinations, to produce ABC number of triple features. These features are all diverse in nature and all somehow characterise the image from which they are computed. We may then select from these features the ones that produce values which correlate with the sequence of images we have, say in decreasing or increasing level of usage of the car park. These features may subsequently be used as indicators to monitor new images which have not been previously seen by the system. In Ref. 16 this method was used to select features that rank textures in order of similarity in the same way humans do. The features were selected by using the first 56 textures of the Brodatz album and tested on the remaining 56, ie on textures that had never been seen by the system. This was a form of reverse engineering the human vision system, since it allowed the authors to identify functionals and their combinations that produced rankings that the humans produce. Finally, in Ref. 18 the trace transform was used to produce features that helped identify faces with accuracy two orders of magnitude better than other competing methods (see also Ref. 11 for blind test assessment). In this case, however, the features were not triple features, but directly the raw values of the trace transform, selected for their stability over time and over different images of the same face.

These successes of the trace transform rely on the multiplicity of the representations it offers for the same data. Each representation presents the information through a different "pair of eyes", salienating different aspects of it, while suppressing others. For example, in Ref. 18, 22 different trace transforms were used to represent the same face, adding robustness to the system. Note that multiresolution approaches also rely on multiple representations, the difference being that all features in that case are of the same nature, eg amplitude in some frequency band. The multi-representation analysis performed by the use of several trace transforms allows the use of many different features of very diverse nature.

Table 11.1 lists some functionals one may use to construct the trace transform. Some of the functionals included in this table involve the calculation of a weighted median. The median of values $y_1, y_2, \ldots, y_n$ with non-negative weights $w_1, w_2, \ldots, w_n$, denoted by $median(\{y_k\}_k, \{w_k\}_k)$, is defined as the median of the sequence created when y_k is repeated w_k times. Assuming that the values have been sorted in ascending order, and that any values with 0 weight have been removed, the weighted median is defined by identifying the maximal index m for which

$$\sum_{k<m} w_k \leq \frac{1}{2} \sum_{k\leq n} w_k \,. \tag{11.1}$$

If the inequality above is strict, the median is y_m. If the inequality above is actually an equality, the median is $(y_m + y_{m-1})/2$.

A very important characteristic of the trace transform is that it is defined in the continuous domain. It effectively assumes that one has at one's disposal an instrument that computes the necessary functionals along tracing lines directly from the scene.[c] In reality, of course, one does not have such an instrument. All we have is the samples of the digitised scene. An important issue then is to overcome this drawback. How, can we un-do

[c]In computer tomography we do have such an instrument that allows us to measure directly the integral of the absorption function along each X-ray path.

Table 11.1. Some functionals that can be used to produce triple features. In this table $\xi(t)$ represents the values of the image function along the tracing line. The first functional produces the Radon transform of the image. $\xi(t)'$ is the first derivative of the image function along the tracing line. Parameter q may take values like 4, 2, 1 etc. Parameter c is the median of the values of t, t_k along the tracing line, defined as: $c \equiv \text{median}(\{t_k\}_k, \{|\xi(t_k)|\}_k)$, where $\xi(t_k)$ is the value of the image at sample point t_k, along the tracing line; c_1 is another median of these samples, $c_1 \equiv \text{median}(\{t_k\}_k, \{|\xi(t_k)|^{1/2}\}_k)$. In all definitions $r \equiv t - c$ and $r_1 \equiv t - c_1$. In all cases R_+ means that the integration is over the positive values of the variable of integration.

F_1	$\int \xi(t)dt$
F_2	$\frac{\int t\xi(t)dt}{\int \xi(t)dt}$
F_3	$(\int \lvert\xi(t)\rvert^q dt)^{1/q}$
F_4	$\int \lvert\xi(t)'\rvert dt$ or $\sum_k \lvert\xi(t_{k+1}) - \xi(t_k)\rvert$
F_5	$\int \left(t - \frac{\int t\xi(t)dt}{\int \xi(t)dt}\right)^2 \xi(t)dt$
F_6	$\sqrt{\frac{\int \left(t - \frac{\int t\xi(t)dt}{\int \xi(t)dt}\right)^2 \xi(t)dt}{\int \xi(t)dt}}$
F_7	$\max(\xi(t))$
F_8	$\max(\xi(t)) - \min(\xi(t))$
F_9	Amplitude of 1st harmonic of $\xi(t)$
F_{10}	Amplitude of 2nd harmonic of $\xi(t)$
F_{11}	Amplitude of 3rd harmonic of $\xi(t)$
F_{12}	Amplitude of 4th harmonic of $\xi(t)$
F_{13}	x^* so that $\int_{-\infty}^{x^*} \xi(t)dt = \int_{x^*}^{+\infty} \xi(t)dt$
F_{14}	x^* so that $\int_{-\infty}^{x^*} \lvert\xi(t)'\rvert dt = \int_{x^*}^{+\infty} \lvert\xi(t)'\rvert dt$
F_{15}	Phase of 1st harmonic of $\xi(t)$
F_{16}	Phase of 2nd harmonic of $\xi(t)$
F_{17}	Phase of 3rd harmonic of $\xi(t)$
F_{18}	Phase of 4th harmonic of $\xi(t)$
F_{19}	$\int_{R_+} t\xi(t)dt$
F_{20}	$\int_{R_+} t^2\xi(t)dt$
F_{21}	$\text{median}\big(\{\lvert\xi(t_k - c)\rvert\}_{t_k>0}, \{\lvert\xi(t_k - c)\rvert^{1/2}\}_{t_k>0}\big)$
F_{22}	$\text{median}\big(\{\lvert(t_k - c_1)\xi(t_k - c_1)\rvert\}_{t_k>0}, \{\lvert\xi(t_k - c_1)\rvert^{1/2}\}_{t_k>0}\big)$
F_{23}	$\lvert\int_{R_+} e^{i4\ln r_1} r_1{}^{0.5}\xi(r_1)dr_1\rvert$
F_{24}	$\lvert\int_{R_+} e^{i3\ln r_1}\xi(r_1)dr_1\rvert$
F_{25}	$\lvert\int_{R_+} e^{i5\ln r_1} r_1\xi(r_1)dr_1\rvert$
F_{26}	$\text{median}(\{\xi(t_k)\}_k, \{\lvert\xi(t_k)\rvert\}_k)$
F_{27}	$\int \lvert FourierTransf(\xi(t))(\omega)\rvert^4 d\omega$
F_{28}	Standard deviation of $\{\xi(t_k)\}_k$
F_{29}	$\text{median}(\{\xi(t_k)\}_k, \{\lvert\xi'(t_k)\rvert\}_k)$

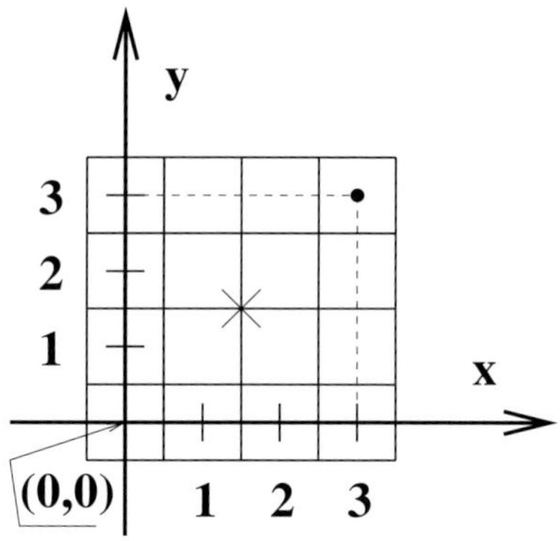

Fig. 11.5. The pixels of a 4×4 image ($M = N = 4$) are considered as tiles of size 1×1. The values of the pixels are assumed to be sample values of the continuous scene at the centre of each tile. A continuous coordinate system (x, y) is placed at the centre of the bottom left pixel. The coordinates of the centre of the top right pixel, marked here with a black dot, then are $(M-1, N-1) = (3, 3)$. The centre of the image, marked with a cross, has coordinates $(C_x, C_y) = (1.5, 1.5)$. Half of the image size along each axis is $M_H = C_x + 0.5 = 2$ and $N_H = C_y + 0.5 = 2$.

the damage done by sampling and digitising the scene? This issue is dealt with in the next section. In section 11.3 then we present some examples of taking the trace transforms of texture images and list functionals that have been proven to be useful in texture analysis. We conclude in section 11.4.

11.2. From the Continuous Theory to the Digital Application

Let us assume that we have an image of size $M \times N$. Each pixel may be thought of as a tile of size 1×1. The sampled value of the pixel corresponds to the value at the centre of the tile. We may easily see that if we set the origin of the axes at the centre of the bottom left pixel, the coordinates of the top right pixel will be $(M-1, N-1)$ (see figure 11.5). The centre of the image will be at coordinates $(C_x, C_y) \equiv \left(\frac{M-1}{2}, \frac{N-1}{2}\right)$. Half of the image size then will be $M_H \equiv C_x + 0.5$ and $N_H \equiv C_y + 0.5$.

When performing calculations in the digital domain, a pixel is treated like a point. This is far too gross for the calculations involved in the production of the triple features: if one performs calculations along digital lines, one will never reproduce results compatible with the theoretical predictions. Much higher accuracy is needed. All calculations have to be performed along continuous lines. However, all calculations performed by computers are of finite accuracy, and one has to choose *a priori* the accuracy with which one will perform these calculations. This is equivalent to saying that one has to choose the size of the tile that will represent an ideal point of zero size in one's calculations. This again is equivalent to saying that one has to impose a fine grid over which the calculations will be performed, in order to retain the desired accuracy. What we shall do here is to consider carefully the various issues concerning the accuracy of the performed calculations and decide upon this fine grid we shall be using.

Computers tend to be slow when they execute floating point arithmetic. Speed is very important when computing the trace transform, so we must try to perform all calculations in integer arithmetic. This, however, should not be done at the expense of accuracy. So, in order to use integer arithmetic and at the same time to retain as many significant points as possible in our calculations, we introduce a fine grid over the image grid, by replacing each pixel tile with $B_N \times B_N$ finer tiles. The size of the fine grid then is $(MB_N) \times (NB_N)$.

One has to be careful on the choice of B_N. As we are going to use tracing lines that cross the image in all possible directions, and as we shall be measuring locations along these lines, we must consider the largest possible value we may measure along any line. Given that we start measuring parameter t from the foot of the normal along the line and parameter p from the centre of the image, the maximum possible value for either of these parameters is $\sqrt{M_H^2 + N_H^2}$. To be on the safe side and not to move outside the image border, we may decrease this number by a small quantity, say $\epsilon \sim 10^{-3}$, and say that the maximum allowable value of t or p is

$$P_{max} \equiv \sqrt{M_H^2 + N_H^2} - 0.001 \tag{11.2}$$

So, when we increase the linear dimensions of our image by B_N, this number becomes $P_{max}B_N$. If we perform our operations using two-byte (ie 16-bit) signed integers, the range of allowed values is $[-2^{15}, 2^{15} - 1]$. If one of our numbers falls outside this range, significant errors will occur. For example, if a number arises that is $-2^{15} - 1$, this number will be misread, it might even be wrapped round to $2^{15} - 1$ and this will cause problems. An example will make this clearer. Consider that we have a computer that can only do integer arithmetic using 3 bits. The allowed numbers then can only be $[-2^2, 2^2 - 1]$, ie $[-4, 3]$, since 3 bits allows us to write only unsigned integers $0, 1, 2, \ldots, 7$ and signed $-4, -3, \ldots, 3$. Any number outside this range will be misread, creating significant errors.

So, to avoid such errors, for two-byte arithmetic, we must have

$$P_{max} B_N < 2^{15} \tag{11.3}$$

If we are going to use four-byte (ie 32-bit) signed integers, then this number should not exceed 2^{31}, as the allowed range of signed integers is $[-2^{31}, 2^{31} - 1]$. So, for four-byte arithmetic, we must have

$$P_{max} B_N < 2^{31} \tag{11.4}$$

Each of the fine tiles we introduced has size $\frac{1}{B_N} \times \frac{1}{B_N}$. In all our calculations such a tile will represent a point. In other words, we have introduced a very fine grid to represent the continuous domain, but still a grid, given that it is not possible with computers to have infinite accuracy. A mathematical point in the continuous domain has zero size, but in the domain we shall operate is a small tile of size $\frac{1}{B_N} \times \frac{1}{B_N}$. If the centre of this fine tile corresponds to the ideal mathematical point of the continuous calculation, the sides of the tile being at most $\pm \frac{1}{2B_N}$ away from its centre, represent the limits of error within which the true value lies. So, $\frac{1}{2B_N}$ represents the error per point with which we shall perform all our calculations. As we shall be using several points along a line, the total error will be in the worst case equal to the number of points times the error per point. Let us say that we shall sample the tracing line with steps in the t parameter equal to Δt. Then in a length of $2P_{max}$ we shall be using $\frac{2P_{max}}{\Delta t} + 1$ points. The factor of 2 appears here because P_{max} refers to only half of the image diagonal and in practice we shall be covering the whole length of the diagonal. The total error we expect to commit, therefore, is:

$$E \equiv \frac{1}{2B_N} \times \left(\frac{2P_{max}}{\Delta t} + 1 \right) \tag{11.5}$$

Let us say that we shall sample each tracing line in steps of 1, ie $\Delta t = 1$. Let us also say that we wish the total error never to exceed 0.5. Then we may write:

$$E = \frac{P_{max}}{B_N} + \frac{1}{2B_N} < 0.5 \tag{11.6}$$

As $1/(2B_N)$ is much smaller than $\frac{P_{max}}{B_N}$, the second term may be omitted on the left-hand side of the above inequality. So, we may write:

$$\frac{P_{max}}{B_N} < 0.5 \Rightarrow P_{max} < \frac{B_N}{2} \tag{11.7}$$

In order to make sure that we satisfy the constraints of the hardware we use, expressed either by (11.3) or by (11.4), and at the same time make sure that our maximum accumulated error is less than 0.5, we must make sure that the upper limit of P_{max}, given by (11.7), does not violate either (11.3) or (11.4) ie that either $B_N^2 < 2^{16}$ or that $B_N^2 < 2^{32}$. These statements are equivalent to $\log_2 B_N < 8$ or $\log_2 B_N < 16$.

The analysis above means that if we choose $B_N = 2^{12}$, we may perform the calculations with signed integers of four-bytes and be sure that the total error will always be less than 0.5. As this total error refers to the extreme values of the various parameters, and in order to guard ourselves from reaching it, we trim the image all around by E as given by (11.5). For a typical image of 256×256, ie $M = N = 256$, $C_x = C_y = 127.5$, $M_H = N_H = 128$ and $P_{max} = \sqrt{128^2 + 128^2} - 0.001 = 181.018335984$. For $B_N = 2^{12}$ then $E = 0.044316$. The product $P_{max} B_N \simeq 741,451 < 2^{31} = 2,147,483,648$. For a 1024×1024 image, $P_{max} = 724.076343935$, which when multiplied with $B_N = 2^{12}$ gives $P_{max} B_N \simeq 2,965,816 < 2^{31} = 2,147,483,648$. The error E in this case is $E = 0.176898521$. These error values indicate the accuracy with which invariant features are expected to be constructed.

11.2.1. *Ranges of parameter values*

Parameter p is the distance of the centre of the image from the tracing line, and so it is expected to take only positive values. However, negative values are also allowed. This is because the tracing lines are characterised by their direction as well, which for some functionals matters and for some it does not matter. For example, if along the line the integral of the image values is computed, direction does not matter, but if the functional is equal to the index of the point with the maximal grey value, then direction matters. So, each tracing line should be scanned along two directions, one of the directions corresponding to negative p values. This distinction becomes clear with the example shown in figure 11.6.

We shall work out next the coordinates of the points we shall be using in terms of the original image coordinates and the ranges of values p and t. For a start, we said earlier that t is sampled at intervals $\Delta t = 1$. We use the same sampling rate for p, ie $\Delta p = 1$. However, we shall keep our analysis general, for arbitrary Δt and Δp. We also said that we restrict the space over which we perform our calculations in the range $\pm(M_H - E) \equiv \pm M_{HE}$

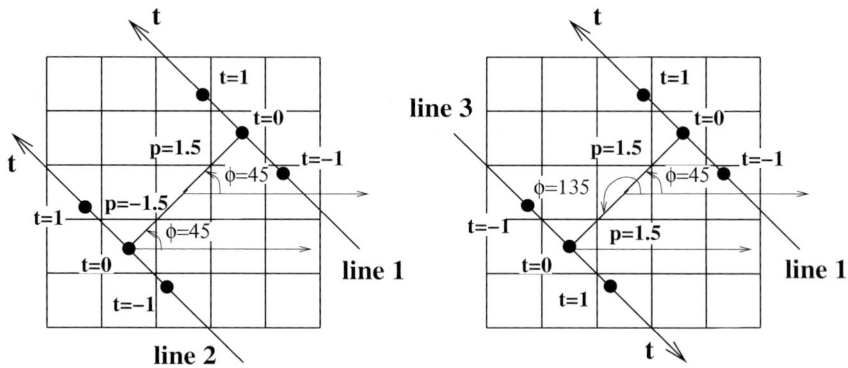

Fig. 11.6. On the left, two tracing lines with the same orientation ϕ but positive and negative values of p with the same absolute value. On the right, two lines with the same positive value of p but different orientations ϕ. When the direction along which we retrieve the image values along the line matters in the calculation of the functional, lines 2 and 3 represent different lines. Both are necessary for the complete representation of the image. Examples of functionals for which direction matters are functionals F_{19} and F_{20} in Table 11.1.

for the x coordinate and $\pm(N_H - E) \equiv \pm N_{HE}$ for the y coordinate, leaving out a strip of width E around the image border.

We wish to work out the relationship between the "continuous" variables that will be used in computing the various functionals and the coordinates of the original pixels in the input image. Note that the word "continuous" is inside quotes because it refers simply to the fine grid we are using rather than to continuous numbers in the strict mathematical sense. Let us call B the point of the line from which the calculation of the functional will start.

Let us consider first lines with $\phi = 0°$, with the help of figure 11.7. The maximum value of p then, p_{max} will be equal to M_{HE}. The maximum number of intervals Δp we can fit in this length is $N_p \equiv \left\lfloor \frac{p_{max}}{\Delta p} \right\rfloor$. This corresponds to $2N_p + 1$ lines, N_p of them with p value $-N_p\Delta p \leq p < 0$, N_p of them with p value $0 < p \leq N_p\Delta p$ and one with $p = 0$.

The fine grid (or "continuous") coordinates of point B in relation to point O (see figure 11.7) are (x_B, y_B). As $p = 0$ at the centre of the image, we may easily work out that

$$x_B = \lfloor (C_x + p)B_N + 0.5 \rfloor + \frac{B_N}{2} \tag{11.8}$$

Note that the floor operator in the first term produces the integer part of number $(C_x + p)B_N + 0.5$. This is equivalent to rounding number $(C_x + p)B_N$

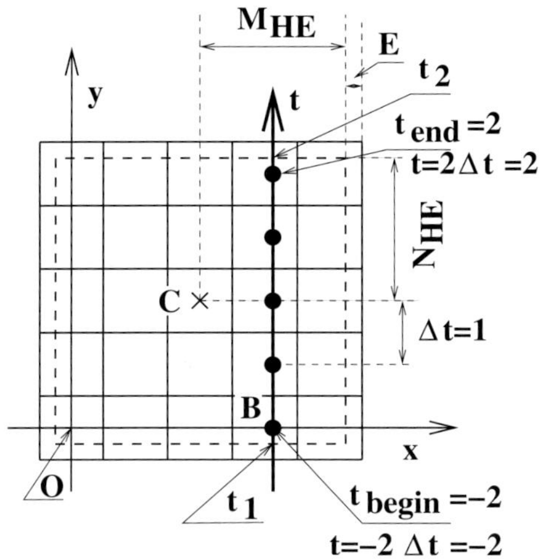

Fig. 11.7. A line at $\phi = 0^o$. The dashed rectangle indicates the region over which all calculations will take place. Note the strip of width E that has been omitted all around. t_1 and t_2 are the values of t when the tracing line intersects that border. The black dots are the sampling points used along the tracing line. The bottom-most of these points is at the most negative value of t allowed and it corresponds to t_{begin}. The top-most of the dots is the maximum positive value allowed for t and it is marked as t_{end}. Note that the centre C is marked by a cross and it is at coordinate position (C_x, C_y), with respect to the origin O. The point with $t = t_{begin}\Delta t$ is point B, ie the starting point of the line. Its y coordinate is at position $C_y - |t_{begin}| \times \Delta t$ with respect to the continuous coordinate system indicated here. As t_{begin} is negative, the coordinate position of point B in the continuous domain is $C_y + t_{begin}\Delta t$. In the finely discretised space, it will be this number multiplied with B_N rounded to the nearest integer and adding $B_N/2$ to account for the fine pixels below the Ox axis. Note also that point B, in general, is not expected to be on the x axis, as it happens to be here. It simply is the extreme starting point of the tracing line that is used in the calculations, given that Δt has to fit an integer number of times in the line, starting from the foot of the normal.

to the nearest integer.[d] The second term adds the number of fine bins that are on the left of the Oy axis, ie in the half of the bottom left pixel at the negative x coordinate values. The following example will make this point clear. Consider the image of figure 11.5. Let us say that we choose $B_N = 2^2 = 4$. Figure 11.8 shows the relationship between the original image pixels, the fine pixels and the continuous coordinates.

[d]Consider for example number 7.3. When rounded it should produce 7. The integer part of $7.3 + 0.5 = 7.8$ is indeed 7. So, in this case, the floor operator produces the right answer either we add 0.5 to the number or not. However number 7.6 is rounded to 8. Taking simply its floor we shall get 7, which is the wrong answer. To make sure we get its nearest integer, as opposed to taking its integer part, we have to add 0.5 and then take the floor, ie we have to take the integer part of: $\lfloor 7.6 + 0.5 \rfloor = 8$.

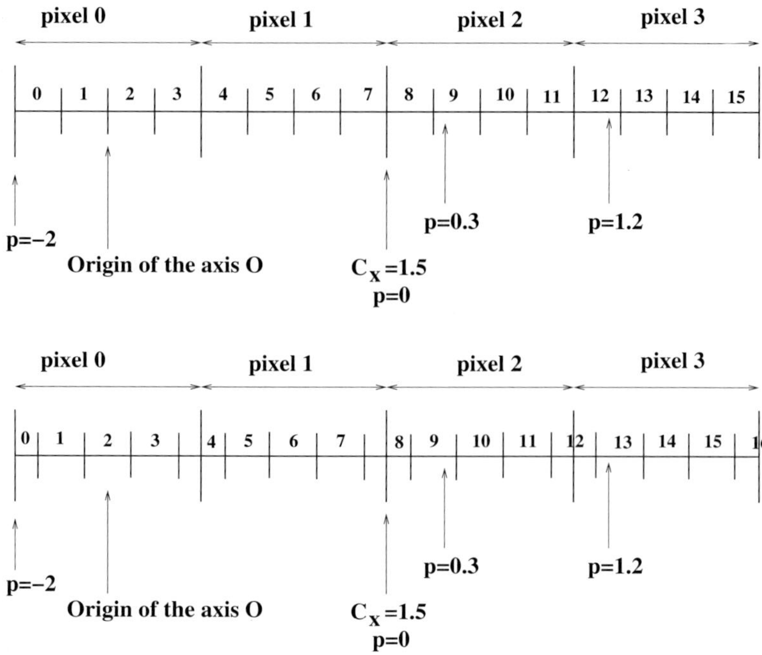

Fig. 11.8. In a 4×4 image, the centre of the image along the x axis is at $C_x = 1.5$ because the origin of the continuous coordinates is in the middle of the first pixel, point O. If $B_N = 4$, each pixel is divided along the x axis into 4 fine pixels (top graph). The total number of fine pixels is $4 \times 4 = 16$ and these are numbered sequentially here from left to right. Note, however, that as B_N is an even number, the centre of each pixel will always fall at the boundary between two fine pixels: the actual points at which we have values from the sampled scene, instead of being represented by the finite points we use for our calculations, are represented at shifted positions. So, to correct for this error, we have to shift the fine grid by half a fine pixel, so the points for which we know the values exactly are placed in the middle of the finite "points" we use to perform the continuous calculations. The shifted grid is shown at the bottom graph. When the continuous variable p takes various values with its 0 being at the centre C, our task is to find the right fine pixel in which this value falls. Let us say that $p = -2$. Formula (11.8) will give $\lfloor (1.5 - 2)4 + 0.5 \rfloor + 2 = \lfloor -1.5 \rfloor + 2 = -2 + 2 = 0$, ie this point will be in the 0th fine bin, which is correct. When $p = 0.3$, formula (11.8) gives $\lfloor (1.5 + 0.3)4 + 0.5 \rfloor + 2 = \lfloor 7.7 \rfloor + 2 = 7 + 2 = 9$, ie this point falls in the 9th fine pixel, which is correct. One can easily check that $p = 1.2$ corresponds to the 13th fine pixel. Note that we have 2 fine pixels on the left of the origin O which the formula accounts for by the inclusion of term $B_N/2$.

All points of such a line will have the same x coordinate. This coordinate corresponds to integer pixel coordinate i given by

$$i = \left\lfloor \frac{x_B}{B_N} \right\rfloor \tag{11.9}$$

In the example of figure 11.8 the point with $p = -2$ has $x_B = 0$ and so it corresponds to the $\lfloor 0/4 \rfloor = 0^{th}$ pixel of the original image, the point with $p = 0.3$ has $x_B = 9$ and so it corresponds to the $\lfloor 9/4 \rfloor = 2^{nd}$ pixel of the original image and the point with $p = 1.2$ has $x_B = 13$ and so it corresponds to the $\lfloor 13/4 \rfloor = 3^{rd}$ pixel of the original image.

In general, parameter t along a tracing line is allowed to take values in the range $[t_1, t_2]$. For lines with $\phi = 0^o$, $t_1 = -N_{HE}$ and $t_2 = N_{HE}$ (see figure 11.7). If we sample continuous t in steps of Δt, the extreme values of t are at $t_{begin} = -\left\lfloor \frac{|t_1|}{\Delta t} \right\rfloor = -\left\lfloor \frac{N_{HE}}{\Delta t} \right\rfloor$ and $t_{end} = \left\lfloor \frac{t_2}{\Delta t} \right\rfloor = \left\lfloor \frac{N_{HE}}{\Delta t} \right\rfloor$ steps away from the foot of the normal on either side of it. Between two successive values of t there are $\Delta t B_N$ fine pixels. So, point B is below the centre of the image $t_{begin} \times \Delta t B_N$ fine pixels. This means that point B has fine grid coordinates given by

$$y_B = \lfloor (C_y + t_{begin}\Delta t)B_N + 0.5 \rfloor + \frac{B_N}{2} \tag{11.10}$$

All other points I in this line needed for the calculation of the functionals have coordinates $x_I = x_B$ and

$$y_I = y_B + \lfloor I \Delta t B_N \rfloor \tag{11.11}$$

where I takes values in the range $[0, t_{end} - t_{begin}]$. The corresponding index of the original image pixels will be:

$$j = \left\lfloor \frac{y_I}{B_N} \right\rfloor \tag{11.12}$$

All these become clearer with the example of figure 11.9.

We shall consider next how we deal with a line at a random orientation $0^o < \phi < 90^o$. First of all, we must decide what the maximum value of p is for such a line. From figure 11.10 we can see that

$$p_{max} = M_{HE} \cos\phi + N_{HE} \sin\phi \qquad \text{for } 0^o < \phi < 90^o \tag{11.13}$$

It can easily be checked with the help of figures similar to figure 11.10, that in order for such a relationship to be valid for ϕ in all quadrants, it should be written as

$$p_{max} = M_{HE}|\cos\phi| + N_{HE}|\sin\phi| \qquad \text{for } 0^o \leq \phi < 360^o \tag{11.14}$$

Next, we must find the range of values t takes along such a line. Remember that the extreme values of t are determined by the points where the tracing line intersects the usable part of the image, ie the dashed frame in figure 11.11. From figure 11.11 we can see that for each extreme value

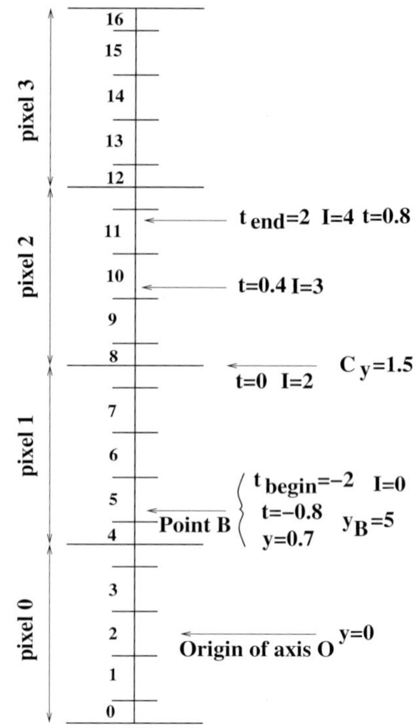

Fig. 11.9. Consider the 4×4 image of figure 11.5. Assume that $B_N = 4$. The vertically written numbers from bottom to top enumerate the 16 fine pixels one can fit in the original 4 pixels. (Note the shifting by 0.5 used to make sure that the centres of the original pixels coincide with centres of the fine pixels. Note also that fine pixels labelled 0 and 16 are half fine pixels.) It can be worked out that $N_H = 2$, $P_{max} = 2.83$, $E = 0.83$, $N_{HE} = 1.17$ and $t_1 = -1.17$. Assume that $\Delta t = 0.4$. Then $t_{begin} = -2$. This means that the most negative value of t considered will be $-2\Delta t = -0.8$ and it will correspond to index $I = 0$. The continuous y value of the B point will be $1.5 - 0.8 = 0.7$ and the coordinate of the same point in the fine grid will be $y_B = 5$, while in the grid of the original pixels it will be at the pixel with $j = 1$.

there are two cases: the negative part of the line crosses either the right border or the bottom border, and the positive part of the line crosses either the top border or the left border. Both options should be considered and the values with the minimum absolute value should be adopted as the limiting values of t.

In order to compute the t value of intersection between the image border and a tracing line with random orientation $0^\circ < \phi < 90^\circ$, we work in conjunction with figure 11.12. Note that t_{1x} is the negative t value for which the tracing line intersects the bottom edge of the usable image, t_{1y} is

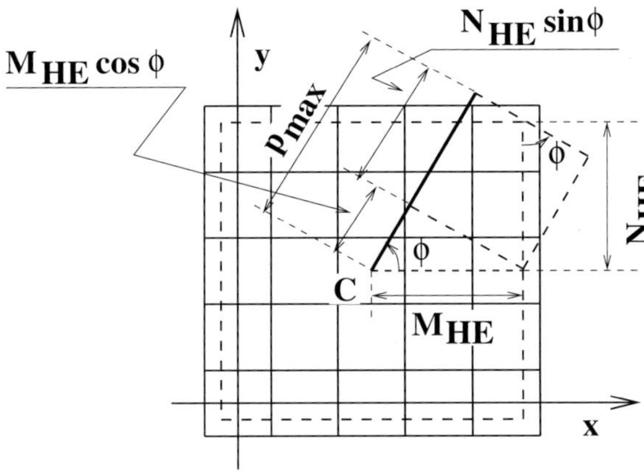

Fig. 11.10. For an angle $0^o < \phi < 90^o$ the maximum value of p is given by (11.13).

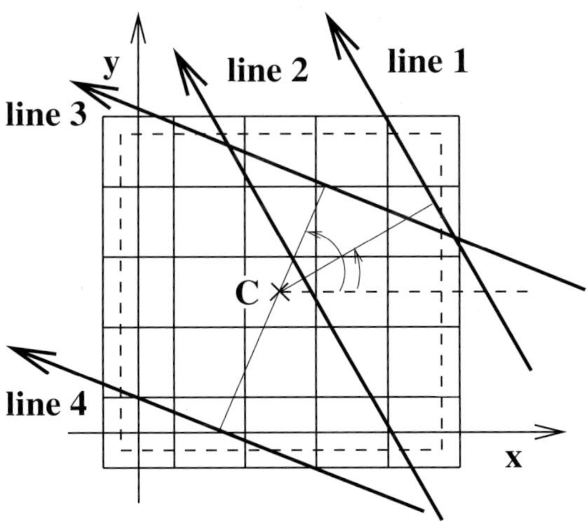

Fig. 11.11. For $0^o < \phi < 90^o$ it is possible for the negative part of the line to intersect either the right or the bottom border of the image (lines 1 and 2) and the positive part of the line to intersect either the left or the top border of the image (lines 3 and 4).

the negative t value for which the tracing line intersects the right edge of the usable image, t_{2x} is the positive value for which the tracing line intersects the top edge of the usable image and t_{2y} is the positive value for which the tracing line intersects the left edge of the usable image.

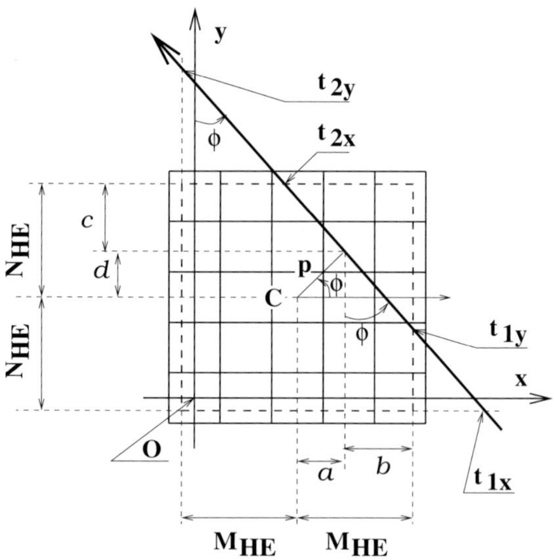

Fig. 11.12. Lengths a, b, c and d help us identify the t value of the points where the tracing line intersects the usable image border marked by the dashed rectangle.

We can see that

$$\begin{aligned} a = p\cos\phi \Rightarrow b = M_{HE} - p\cos\phi \\ d = p\sin\phi \Rightarrow c = N_{HE} - p\sin\phi \end{aligned} \tag{11.15}$$

Then

$$\begin{aligned} t_{1y} = -\frac{b}{\sin\phi} &\Rightarrow t_{1y} = -\frac{M_{HE} - p\cos\phi}{\sin\phi} \\ t_{1x} = -\frac{N_{HE} + d}{\cos\phi} &\Rightarrow t_{1x} = -\frac{N_{HE} + p\sin\phi}{\cos\phi} \\ t_{2x} = \frac{c}{\cos\phi} &\Rightarrow t_{2x} = \frac{N_{HE} - p\sin\phi}{\cos\phi} \\ t_{2y} = \frac{M_{HE} + a}{\sin\phi} &\Rightarrow t_{2y} = \frac{M_{HE} + p\cos\phi}{\sin\phi} \end{aligned} \tag{11.16}$$

The final t_1 value for a tracing line is chosen to be $t_1 = \max\{t_{1x}, t_{1y}\}$ and the t_2 value is $t_2 = \min\{t_{2x}, t_{2y}\}$. The above formulae are valid also when $\phi \to 0°$, in which case t_{1y} becomes positive, and when $\phi \to 90°$, in which case t_{2x} is negative. For the other three quadrants the formulae are as follows.

For $90^\circ < \phi < 180^\circ$:

$$\begin{aligned} t_{1y} &= -\frac{M_{HE} - p\cos\phi}{\sin\phi} \\ t_{1x} &= \frac{N_{HE} - p\sin\phi}{\cos\phi} \\ t_{2x} &= -\frac{N_{HE} + p\sin\phi}{\cos\phi} \\ t_{2y} &= \frac{M_{HE} + p\cos\phi}{\sin\phi} \end{aligned} \tag{11.17}$$

For $180^\circ < \phi < 270^\circ$:

$$\begin{aligned} t_{1y} &= \frac{M_{HE} + p\cos\phi}{\sin\phi} \\ t_{1x} &= \frac{N_{HE} - p\sin\phi}{\cos\phi} \\ t_{2x} &= -\frac{N_{HE} + p\sin\phi}{\cos\phi} \\ t_{2y} &= -\frac{M_{HE} - p\cos\phi}{\sin\phi} \end{aligned} \tag{11.18}$$

For $270^\circ < \phi < 360^\circ$:

$$\begin{aligned} t_{1y} &= \frac{M_{HE} + p\cos\phi}{\sin\phi} \\ t_{1x} &= -\frac{N_{HE} + p\sin\phi}{\cos\phi} \\ t_{2x} &= \frac{N_{HE} - p\sin\phi}{\cos\phi} \\ t_{2y} &= -\frac{M_{HE} - p\cos\phi}{\sin\phi} \end{aligned} \tag{11.19}$$

From the knowledge of t_1 and t_2 one can work out the extreme indices of t along each line, called t_{begin} and t_{end}, respectively. Note that because there is the possibility of both t_1 and t_2 being positive, or both being negative, we identify these extreme indices using

$$t_{begin} = \left\lceil \frac{t_1}{\Delta t} \right\rceil \qquad t_{end} = \left\lfloor \frac{t_2}{\Delta t} \right\rfloor \tag{11.20}$$

For example, if t_1 is negative and Δt fits in it 3.5 times, taking the ceiling of $t_1/\Delta t = -3.5$ yields -3, which is the correct number of Δts we should consider on the negative part of the tracing line. If t_1 is positive and Δt fits in it 3.5 times, taking the ceiling of $t_1/\Delta t = 3.5$ yields 4, which again is the correct number of Δts we have to move away from the foot of the normal to start the calculations. When t_2 is positive and Δt fits in it 2.5 times, taking the floor of $t_2/\Delta t = 2.5$ yields 2, which is the correct number of Δts we should consider after the foot of the normal. Finally, if t_2 is negative and Δt fits in it 2.5 times, taking the floor of $t_2/\Delta t = -2.5$ yields -3, which again is correct and indicates the number of Δts away from the foot of the normal at which the calculation should stop. Figure 11.13 shows two cases where t_1 and t_2 are either both positive or both negative.

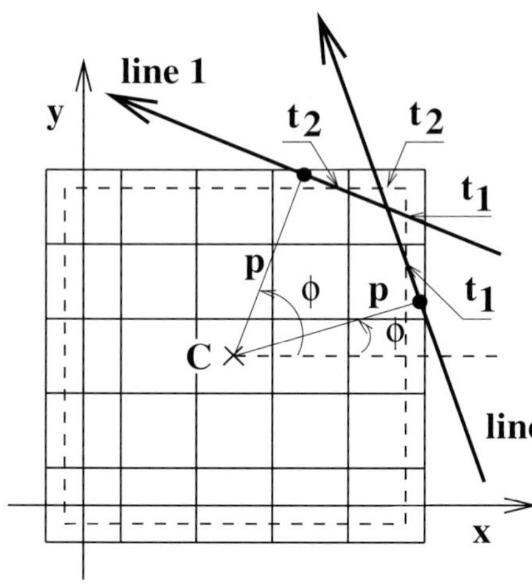

Fig. 11.13. Line 1 has both t_1 and t_2 negative, while line 2 has both t_1 and t_2 positive. For both lines the black dot indicates the foot of the normal where $t = 0$.

To move from point with $t = t_{begin}\Delta t$ to point with $t = t_{end}\Delta t$ along the line, we must consider increments of the coordinates of the first point B, (x_B, y_B) given by:

$$x_{inc} = -\Delta t \sin\phi B_N \qquad y_{inc} = \Delta t \cos\phi B_N \tag{11.21}$$

The coordinates of the starting point B for the calculations along the line are:

$$\begin{aligned} x_B &= \lfloor (C_x + p\cos\phi) B_N + x_{inc} t_{begin} + 0.5 \rfloor + \frac{B_N}{2} \\ y_B &= \lfloor (C_y + p\sin\phi) B_N + y_{inc} t_{begin} + 0.5 \rfloor + \frac{B_N}{2} \end{aligned} \tag{11.22}$$

The successive points we consider then along the line will have coordinates

$$x_I = x_B + \lfloor I x_{inc} \rfloor$$
$$y_I = y_B + \lfloor I y_{inc} \rfloor \tag{11.23}$$

where I is an index identifying the point along the line and taking values in the range $[0, t_{end} - t_{begin}]$. For $I = 0$ we get the B point.

The indices (i, j) of the corresponding original pixel are given by

$$i = \left\lfloor \frac{x_I}{B_N} \right\rfloor \qquad j = \left\lfloor \frac{y_I}{B_N} \right\rfloor \tag{11.24}$$

Equations (11.21)–(11.24) are valid for all quadrants.

Finally, let us consider the case of a line at orientation $\phi = 90^\circ$ (see figure 11.14). For such a line all points have the same y coordinate, ie $y_{inc} = 0$. The x coordinate, on the other hand, of the points considered along the line is incremented by

$$x_{inc} = -\Delta t B_N \tag{11.25}$$

The maximal value of p is $p_{max} = N_{HE}$ and the range of allowed continuous values of t is from $t_1 = -M_{HE}$ to $t_2 = M_{HE}$. The extreme samples along the line will be

$$t_{begin} = \left\lceil \frac{t_1}{\Delta t} \right\rceil \tag{11.26}$$

and

$$t_{end} = \left\lfloor \frac{t_2}{\Delta t} \right\rfloor \tag{11.27}$$

number of Δts away from the foot of the normal and on either side of it. The starting point B, ie the point with $t = t_{begin}\Delta t$, will have coordinates:

$$x_B = \lfloor C_x B_N + x_{inc} t_{begin} + 0.5 \rfloor + \frac{B_N}{2}$$
$$y_B = \lfloor (C_y + p) B_N + 0.5 \rfloor + \frac{B_N}{2} \tag{11.28}$$

The other points considered along the line will have coordinates

$$x_I = x_B + \lfloor I x_{inc} \rfloor$$
$$y_I = y_B \tag{11.29}$$

where index I identifies the points along the line and takes values in the range $[0, t_{end} - t_{begin}]$.

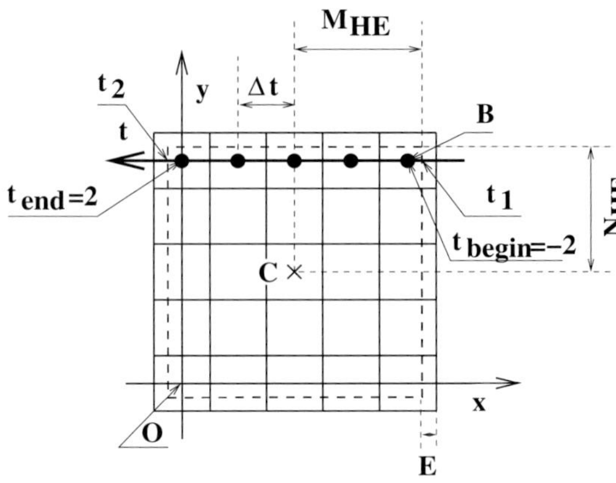

Fig. 11.14. A tracing line at $\phi = 90^{o}$.

For all other orientations ϕ we use the same procedure as for the first quadrant. Significant gains in computation time may be achieved if symmetries are considered so the parameters of the lines in the remaining quadrants are worked out from the parameters of the lines in the first quadrant. However, note that for fixed size images, the line parameters may be computed off line once and stored for use for all images of the same size.

In general, the maximum number of lines for a given orientation can be found by dividing p_{max} with Δp and taking the integer part of it. We usually use $\Delta p = 1$, so for a given ϕ we use $\lfloor p_{max} \rfloor$ lines with positive p and equal number of lines with negative p and of course one line with $p = 0$. The two sets of lines coincide in direction, but they are distinct in the way they are traversed by variable t (the t_1 value of one corresponds to the t_2 value of its counterpart).

Parameter ϕ may be sampled every $\Delta\phi$ degrees. We may choose $\Delta\phi = 1.5^{o}$. This will give 240 orientations.

It is possible to use a functional as a trace functional, or as a circus functional, or as a diametric one. When applied as a trace functional, the independent variable is obviously t and its discrete counterpart takes values that are integer multiples of Δt, with the integer multiplier taking values in the range $[t_{begin}, t_{end}]$. When applied as a circus functional, the independent variable is ϕ and its discrete counterpart takes values that are integer multiples of $\Delta\phi$, with the integer multiplier taking values from 0 to $\lfloor 360/\Delta\phi \rfloor$. Finally, when the functional is applied as a diametric functional, the independent variable is p and its discrete counterpart takes values that are integer multiples of Δp, with the integer multiplier varying from $-\lfloor p_{max}/\Delta p \rfloor$ to $\lfloor p_{max}/\Delta p \rfloor$.

11.2.2. *Summary of the algorithm*

(1) Input parameters: M, N, B_N, Δp, Δt.
(2) Precompute the following parameters:

$$\begin{aligned}
C_x &= \tfrac{M-1}{2} \\
C_y &= \tfrac{N-1}{2} \\
M_H &= C_x + 0.5 \\
N_H &= C_y + 0.5 \\
P_{max} &= \sqrt{M_H^2 + N_H^2} - 0.001 \\
E &= \frac{1}{2B_N}\left(\frac{2P_{max}}{\Delta t} + 1\right) \\
M_{HE} &= M_H - E \\
N_{HE} &= N_H - E \\
M_{B_N} &= MB_N \\
N_{B_N} &= NB_N
\end{aligned} \tag{11.30}$$

(3) Precompute the parameters you need for all tracing lines with $\phi = 0^o$:

$$\begin{aligned}
N_p &= \left\lfloor \frac{M_{HE}}{\Delta p} \right\rfloor \\
N_P &= 2N_p + 1 \\
t_{end} &= \left\lfloor \frac{N_{HE}}{\Delta t} \right\rfloor \\
t_{begin} &= -t_{end} \\
x_{inc} &= 0 \\
y_{inc} &= \Delta t B_N \\
y_B &= \lfloor (C_y + t_{begin}\Delta t)B_N + 0.5 \rfloor + \frac{B_N}{2}
\end{aligned} \tag{11.31}$$

(4) For p varying from $-N_p\Delta p$ to $N_p\Delta p$, compute the x_B value of the corresponding line:

$$
\begin{aligned}
p_J &= -N_p\Delta p + (J-1)\Delta p \qquad \text{for } J = 1, \ldots, N_P \\
x_B &= \lfloor (C_x + p_J)B_N + 0.5 \rfloor + \frac{B_N}{2}
\end{aligned}
\tag{11.32}
$$

Each such line is characterised by the value of p (index J). For each such line store:
the value of angle ϕ, N_P, x_{inc}, y_{inc};
for every value of index J, store:
t_{begin}, t_{end}, x_B and y_B.

(5) Precompute the parameters you need for all tracing lines with $0^\circ < \phi < 90^\circ$. For every different value of ϕ you have to compute:

$$
\begin{aligned}
p_{max} &= M_{HE}|\cos\phi| + N_{HE}|\sin\phi| \\
N_p &= \left\lfloor \frac{p_{max}}{\Delta p} \right\rfloor \\
N_P &= 2N_p + 1 \\
t_{1y} &= -\frac{M_{HE} - p\cos\phi}{\sin\phi} \\
t_{1x} &= -\frac{N_{HE} + p\sin\phi}{\cos\phi} \\
t_{2y} &= \frac{M_{HE} + p\cos\phi}{\sin\phi} \\
t_{2x} &= \frac{N_{HE} - p\sin\phi}{\cos\phi} \\
t_{begin} &= \left\lceil \frac{\max(t_{1y}, t_{1x})}{\Delta t} \right\rceil \\
t_{end} &= \left\lfloor \frac{\min(t_{2y}, t_{2x})}{\Delta t} \right\rfloor \\
x_{inc} &= -\Delta t \sin\phi B_N \\
y_{inc} &= \Delta t \cos\phi B_N
\end{aligned}
\tag{11.33}
$$

(6) For every different value of ϕ you will have to consider all values of p given by

$$
p_J = -N_p\Delta p + (J-1)\Delta p \qquad \text{for } J = 1, 2, \ldots, N_P \tag{11.34}
$$

and compute the corresponding x_B and y_B values of each line:

$$\begin{aligned} x_B &= \lfloor (C_x + p_J \cos\phi) B_N + 0.5 + x_{inc} t_{begin} \rfloor + \frac{B_N}{2} \\ y_B &= \lfloor (C_y + p_J \sin\phi) B_N + 0.5 + y_{inc} t_{begin} \rfloor + \frac{B_N}{2} \end{aligned} \tag{11.35}$$

Each such line is characterised by the value of p (index J). For each such line store:
the value of angle ϕ, N_P, x_{inc}, y_{inc};
for every value of index J, store:
t_{begin}, t_{end}, x_B and y_B.

(7) Precompute the parameters you need for all tracing lines with $\phi = 90^\circ$:

$$\begin{aligned} N_p &= \left\lfloor \frac{N_{HE}}{\Delta p} \right\rfloor \\ N_P &= 2N_p + 1 \\ t_{end} &= \left\lfloor \frac{M_{HE}}{\Delta t} \right\rfloor \\ t_{begin} &= -t_{end} \\ t_{endbeg} &= t_{end} - t_{begin} \\ x_{inc} &= -\Delta t B_N \\ y_{inc} &= 0 \\ x_B &= \lfloor C_x B_N + x_{inc} t_{begin} + 0.5 \rfloor + x_{inc} B_N + \frac{B_N}{2} \end{aligned} \tag{11.36}$$

(8) For p varying from $-N_p\Delta p$ to $N_p\Delta p$, compute:

$$\begin{aligned} p_J &= -N_p \Delta p + (J-1)\Delta p \qquad \text{for } J = 1, \ldots, N_P \\ y_B &= \lfloor (C_y + p_J) B_N + 0.5 \rfloor + \frac{B_N}{2} \end{aligned} \tag{11.37}$$

Each such line is characterised by the value of p (index J). For each such line store:
the value of angle ϕ, N_P, x_{inc}, y_{inc};
for every value of index J, store:
t_{begin}, t_{end}, x_B and y_B.

(9) Lines with $90^\circ < \phi < 180^\circ$. Follow the calculations of steps 5 and 6, but replace the equations for t_{1x}, t_{1y}, t_{2x} and t_{2y} with equations (11.17).

(10) Lines with $\phi = 180^o$. These are like the $\phi = 0^o$ lines pointing downwards (see figure 11.7). If we use a superscript to identify the angle to which each value refers, we may easily verify that

$$\begin{aligned} t_{begin}^{180} &= -t_{end}^{0} \\ t_{end}^{180} &= -t_{begin}^{0} \\ N_p^{180} &= N_p^0 \\ N_P^{180} &= N_P^0 \end{aligned} \tag{11.38}$$

Further, we may easily work out that

$$\begin{aligned} x_{inc} &= 0 \\ y_{inc} &= -\Delta t B_N \\ y_B &= \left\lfloor (C_y - t_{begin}^{180}\Delta t)B_N + 0.5 \right\rfloor + \frac{B_N}{2} \end{aligned} \tag{11.39}$$

(11) For J varying from 1 to N_P^{180} then we work out

$$\begin{aligned} p_J &= -N_p^{180}\Delta p + (J-1)\Delta p \\ x_B &= \lfloor (C_x - p_J)B_N + 0.5 \rfloor + \frac{B_N}{2} \end{aligned} \tag{11.40}$$

Each such line is characterised by the value of p (index J). For each such line store:
the value of angle ϕ, N_P^{180}, x_{inc}, y_{inc};
for every value of index J, store:
t_{begin}^{180}, t_{end}^{180}, x_B and y_B.

(12) Lines with $180^o < \phi < 270^o$. Follow the calculations of steps 5 and 6, but replace the equations for t_{1x}, t_{1y}, t_{2x} and t_{2y} with equations (11.18).

(13) Lines with $\phi = 270^o$. These are like the $\phi = 90^o$ lines pointing to the right (see figure 11.14). If we use a superscript to identify the angle to which each value refers, we may easily verify that

$$\begin{aligned} t_{begin}^{270} &= -t_{end}^{90} \\ t_{end}^{270} &= -t_{begin}^{90} \\ N_p^{270} &= N_p^{90} \\ N_P^{270} &= N_P^{90} \end{aligned} \tag{11.41}$$

Further, we may easily work out that

$$\begin{aligned} x_{inc} &= \Delta t B_N \\ y_{inc} &= 0 \\ x_B &= \left\lfloor C_x B_N + x_{inc} t^{270}_{begin} + 0.5 \right\rfloor + \frac{B_N}{2} \end{aligned} \tag{11.42}$$

(14) For J varying from 1 to N_P^{270} then we work out

$$\begin{aligned} p_J &= -N_p^{270}\Delta p + (J-1)\Delta p \\ y_B &= \lfloor (C_y - p_J)B_N + 0.5 \rfloor + \frac{B_N}{2} \end{aligned} \tag{11.43}$$

Each such line is characterised by the value of p (index J). For each such line store:
the value of angle ϕ, N_P^{270}, x_{inc}, y_{inc};
for every value of index J, store:
t^{270}_{begin}, t^{270}_{end}, x_B and y_B.

(15) Lines with $270^\circ < \phi < 360^\circ$. Follow the calculations of steps 5 and 6, but replace the equations for t_{1x}, t_{1y}, t_{2x} and t_{2y} with equations (11.19).

All the above calculations may be done off line. The parameters produced may be used to compute the trace transform of any image of size $M \times N$.

The main program then that computes the trace transform reads the parameters stored for each line and from those it works out the values of the points along each line needed for the calculation of each functional as follows. For index I taking values from 0 to $t_{end} - t_{begin}$, the t_I values of the points along the line and their corresponding (i, j) pixel coordinates are given by:

$$\begin{aligned} t_I &= (t_{begin} + I)\Delta t \\ x_I &= x_B + \lfloor I x_{inc} \rfloor \\ y_I &= y_B + \lfloor I y_{inc} \rfloor \\ i_I &= \left\lfloor \frac{x_I}{B_N} \right\rfloor \\ j_I &= \left\lfloor \frac{y_I}{B_N} \right\rfloor \end{aligned} \tag{11.44}$$

The (i_I, j_I) pixel coordinates are used to obtain the grey value of the image at point with $t = t_I$. These values are used for the calculation of the functionals. If more than one trace functionals are to be used, they should all be computed simultaneously.

11.3. Application to Texture Analysis

First of all, we demonstrate in figure 11.15 the invariance to rotation, translation and scaling of some features constructed from the trace transform. These features are from Ref. 6 and they are constructed by taking ratios of triple features. They are identified in Ref. 6 as Π_1, Π_2, Π_3, Π_4 and Π_5. We do not include their definition formulae here because they cannot be presented without going into the properties of functionals. The interested reader can find the details in Ref. 6. All we wish to demonstrate here is that the trace transform may be used to construct invariant features that capture both shape and texture information.

So, the next question that arises is how much the value of such a feature is influenced by texture and how much by shape. Figure 11.16 shows some shapes filled with a texture from the Brodatz album and filled with random Gaussian noise.

Having shown how invariant features behave, we wish to stress now that for texture analysis we may use features that are not invariant. Note that the invariance of features constructed from the trace transform is based on the assumption that the imaged object is 2D, flat, "painted" on a flat surface. Texture is usually a much more complex surface property, depending on surface roughness and imaging geometry. As such, texture may appear very different in different scales and rotations. There is no point in taking a texture image and digitally rotating and scaling it to demonstrate feature invariance. A texture image rotated is different from a rotated texture imaged. So, the usefulness of invariant features (not only those constructed from the trace transform) in texture characterisation is meaningless. The relevance of the trace transform to texture characterisation lies in the production of many features of diverse nature from which features may be selected that can be used for specific tasks. For texture analysis the functionals that should be used should be chosen to be more sensitive to texture than the shape of the object. Such functionals are various types of differentiators. Functionals useful for texture analysis are listed in Tables 11.2–11.4. More may be devised. Combinations of functionals that led to good texture triple features are listed in Table 11.5. Note that these

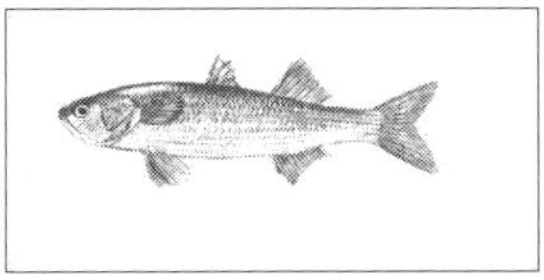

$\Pi_1 = 0.849452$
$\Pi_2 = 15.834468$
$\Pi_3 = 0.904226$
$\Pi_4 = 1.063229$
$\Pi_5 = 0.621326$

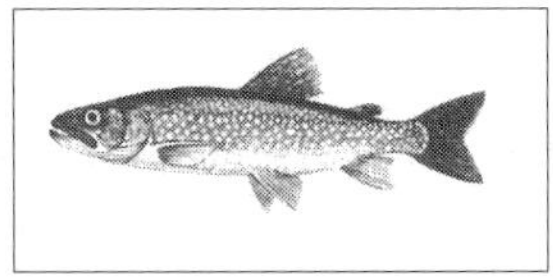

$\Pi_1 = 0.867079$
$\Pi_2 = 18.214664$
$\Pi_3 = 0.891661$
$\Pi_4 = 0.914598$
$\Pi_5 = 0.598998$

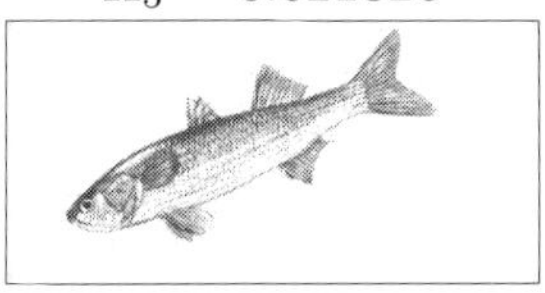

$\Pi_1 = 0.852330(0.3\%)$
$\Pi_2 = 15.618398(-1.4\%)$
$\Pi_3 = 0.903188(-0.1\%)$
$\Pi_4 = 1.064443(0.1\%)$
$\Pi_5 = 0.615897(-0.9\%)$

$\Pi_1 = 0.867799(0.1\%)$
$\Pi_2 = 17.815078(-2.2\%)$
$\Pi_3 = 0.891784(0.0\%)$
$\Pi_4 = 0.915794(0.1\%)$
$\Pi_5 = 0.598337(-0.1\%)$

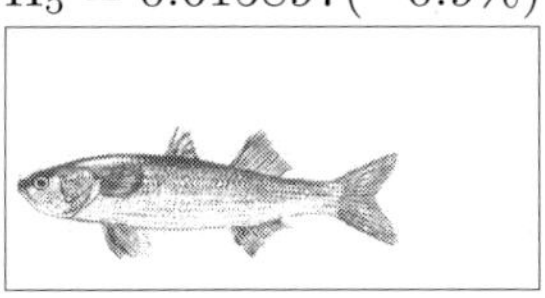

$\Pi_1 = 0.850505(0.1\%)$
$\Pi_2 = 15.816426(-0.1\%)$
$\Pi_3 = 0.904131(-0.0\%)$
$\Pi_4 = 1.063807(0.1\%)$
$\Pi_5 = 0.620088(-0.0\%)$

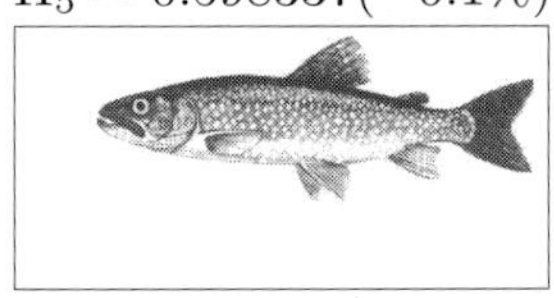

$\Pi_1 = 0.867060(-0.0\%)$
$\Pi_2 = 17.807729(-2.2\%)$
$\Pi_3 = 0.892320(0.1\%)$
$\Pi_4 = 0.915167(0.1\%)$
$\Pi_5 = 0.599341(0.1\%)$

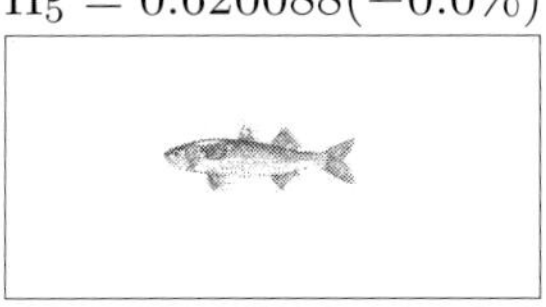

$\Pi_1 = 0.851853(0.3\%)$
$\Pi_2 = 15.901972(0.4\%)$
$\Pi_3 = 0.903605(-0.1\%)$
$\Pi_4 = 1.076698(1.3\%)$
$\Pi_5 = 0.626116(0.8\%)$

$\Pi_1 = 0.869238(0.2\%)$
$\Pi_2 = 17.880884(-1.8\%)$
$\Pi_3 = 0.894285(0.3\%)$
$\Pi_4 = 0.913650(-0.1\%)$
$\Pi_5 = 0.598815(-0.0\%)$

Fig. 11.15. Demonstrating the invariance of the features when the object is rotated, translated or scaled. The numbers in brackets are the percentage change with respect to the original values.

$\Pi_1 = 0.885608$	$\Pi_1 = 0.910648(2.8\%)$	$\Pi_1 = 0.733789(17\%)$
$\Pi_2 = 14.767812$	$\Pi_2 = 11.175148(24\%)$	$\Pi_2 = 35.879023(142\%)$
$\Pi_3 = 0.93099$	$\Pi_3 = 0.928244(0.3\%)$	$\Pi_3 = 0.920856(1\%)$
$\Pi_4 = 0.656298$	$\Pi_4 = 0.681161(3.8\%)$	$\Pi_4 = 1.042226(59\%)$
$\Pi_5 = 0.660066$	$\Pi_5 = 0.6564(0.6\%)$	$\Pi_5 = 0.470670(7\%)$

Fig. 11.16. Triple features capture both shape and texture content of an object. The numbers in brackets indicate the percentage change in relation to the first set of values.

combinations do **not** produce invariant features. They produce texture features that can be used to rank textures in terms of their similarity, in sequences similar to those created by human ranking.

11.4. Conclusions

The trace transform offers the option to construct features from an image that have predescribed desirable properties. Commonly required properties are invariance to various types of transformation. The trace transform is particularly suited to construct features that are invariant to rotation, translation, scaling and affine transforms. However, these are not the only properties one may wish the constructed features to have. It may be desirable to construct features that have other properties, not parametrically expressed: for example to correlate with certain image characteristics in a sequence of images ranked according to some property. Such features may be constructed by the thousands, having as diverse nature as the engineering instinct of the researcher allows. The creation of such features may then be followed by a feature selection scheme where the features that correlate with the image characteristic of interest are identified and kept for use with hitherto unseen images. It is this property of the trace transform-based features that we consider most relevant to texture analysis, rather than the platform it offers for the construction of invariant features. Unless textures are flat patterns painted on flat surfaces, rotation, scaling and translation of the imaged object does not result in rotation translation and scaling of the produced image. So, in order to describe in an invariant way real textures, ie rough surface textures, as opposed to flat image textures, one has to invoke other techniques, like for example photometric stereo techniques.[1,2,10,12,13]

Table 11.2. Some trace functionals T that may be used for texture analysis. In this table x_i refers to the grey value of the image at point i along the tracing line and N is the total number of points considered along the tracing line.

1	$\sum_{i=1}^{N} x_i$
2	$\sum_{i=1}^{N} i x_i$
3	$\frac{1}{N}\sqrt{\sum_{i=1}^{N}(x_i - \hat{x})^2}$
4	$\sqrt{\sum_{i=1}^{N} x_i^2}$
5	$Max_{i=1}^{N} x_i$
6	$\sum_{i=1}^{N-1} \|x_{i+1} - x_i\|$
7	$\sum_{i=1}^{N-1} \|x_{i+1} - x_i\|^2$
8	$\sum_{i=4}^{N-3} \|x_{i-3} + x_{i-2} + x_{i-1} - x_{i+1} - x_{i+2} - x_{i+3}\|$
9	$\sum_{i=3}^{N-2} \|x_{i-2} + x_{i-1} - x_{i+1} - x_{i+2}\|$
10	$\sum_{i=5}^{N-4} \|x_{i-4} + x_{i-3} + ... + x_{i-1} - x_{i+1} - ... - x_{i+3} - x_{i+4}\|$
11	$\sum_{i=6}^{N-5} \|x_{i-5} + x_{i-4} + ... + x_{i-1} - x_{i+1} - ... - x_{i+4} - x_{i+5}\|$
12	$\sum_{i=7}^{N-6} \|x_{i-6} + x_{i-5} + ... + x_{i-1} - x_{i+1} - ... - x_{i+5} - x_{i+6}\|$
13	$\sum_{i=8}^{N-7} \|x_{i-7} + x_{i-6} + ... + x_{i-1} - x_{i+1} - ... - x_{i+6} - x_{i+7}\|$
14	$\sum_{i=5}^{N-4} \sum_{k=1}^{4} \|x_{i-k} - x_{i+k}\|$
15	$\sum_{i=6}^{N-5} \sum_{k=1}^{5} \|x_{i-k} - x_{i+k}\|$
16	$\sum_{i=7}^{N-6} \sum_{k=1}^{6} \|x_{i-k} - x_{i+k}\|$
17	$\sum_{i=8}^{N-7} \sum_{k=1}^{7} \|x_{i-k} - x_{i+k}\|$
18	$\sum_{i=11}^{N-10} \sum_{k=1}^{10} \|x_{i-k} - x_{i+k}\|$
19	$\sum_{i=16}^{N-15} \sum_{k=1}^{15} \|x_{i-k} - x_{i+k}\|$
20	$\sum_{i=21}^{N-20} \sum_{k=1}^{20} \|x_{i-k} - x_{i+k}\|$
21	$\sum_{i=26}^{N-25} \sum_{k=1}^{25} \|x_{i-k} - x_{i+k}\|$
22	$\sum_{i=11}^{N-10}((1 + \sum_{k=1}^{10} \|x_{i-k} - x_{i+k}\|)/(1 + \sum_{k=-10}^{9} \|x_{i-k} - x_{i+k}\|))$
23	$\sum_{i=11}^{N-10} \sqrt{(\sum_{k=1}^{10} \|x_{i-k} - x_{i+k}\|)^2/(1 + \sum_{k=-10}^{9} \|x_{i-k} - x_{i+k}\|)}$
24	$\sum_{i=1}^{N-2} \|x_i - 2x_{i+1} + x_{i+2}\|$
25	$\sum_{i=1}^{N-3} \|x_i - 3x_{i+1} + 3x_{i+2} - x_{i+3}\|$
26	$\sum_{i=1}^{N-4} \|x_i - 4x_{i+1} + 6x_{i+2} - 4x_{i+3} + x_{i+4}\|$
27	$\sum_{i=1}^{N-5} \|x_i - 5x_{i+1} + 10x_{i+2} - 10x_{i+3} + 5x_{i+4} - x_{i+5}\|$
28	$\sum_{i=1}^{N-2} \|x_i - 2x_{i+1} + x_{i+2}\|x_{i+1}$
29	$\sum_{i=1}^{N-3} \|x_i - 3x_{i+1} + 3x_{i+2} - x_{i+3}\|x_{i+1}$
30	$\sum_{i=1}^{N-4} \|x_i - 4x_{i+1} + 6x_{i+2} - 4x_{i+3} + x_{i+4}\|x_{i+2}$
31	$\sum_{i=1}^{N-5} \|x_i - 5x_{i+1} + 10x_{i+2} - 10x_{i+3} + 5x_{i+4} - x_{i+5}\|x_{i+2}$

Table 11.3. Some diametric functionals P that may be used for texture analysis. In this table x_i refers to the value of the trace transform at row i along the column to which the functional is applied and N is the total number of rows of the trace transform. Here $\hat{x}$ is the mean of the x_i values.

1	$Max_{i=1}^{N} x_i$
2	$Min_{i=1}^{N} x_i$
3	$\sqrt{\sum_{i=1}^{N} x_i^2}$
4	$\frac{\sum_{i=1}^{N} i x_i}{\sum_{i=1}^{N} x_i}$
5	$\sum_{i=1}^{N} i x_i$
6	$\frac{1}{N} \sum_{i=1}^{N} (x_i - \hat{x})^2$
7	c so that: $\sum_{i=1}^{c} x_i = \sum_{i=c}^{N} x_i$
8	$\sum_{i=1}^{N-1} \lvert x_{i+1} - x_i \rvert$
9	c so that: $\sum_{i=1}^{c} \lvert x_{i+1} - x_i \rvert = \sum_{i=c}^{N-1} \lvert x_{i+1} - x_i \rvert$
10	$\sum_{i=1}^{N-4} \lvert x_i - 4x_{i+1} + 6x_{i+2} - 4x_{i+3} + x_{i+4} \rvert$

Table 11.4. Some circus functionals Φ that may be used for texture analysis. In this table x_i refers to the value of the circus function at angle i and N is the total number of columns of the trace transform.

1	$\sum_{i=1}^{N-1} \lvert x_{i+1} - x_i \rvert^2$
2	$\sum_{i=1}^{N-1} \lvert x_{i+1} - x_i \rvert$
3	$\sqrt{\sum_{i=1}^{N} x_i^2}$
4	$\sum_{i=1}^{N} x_i$
5	$Max_{i=1}^{N} x_i$
6	$Max_{i=1}^{N} x_i - Min_{i=1}^{N} x_i$
7	i so that $x_i = Min_{i=1}^{N} x_i$
8	i so that $x_i = Max_{i=1}^{N} x_i$
9	i so that $x_i = Min_{i=1}^{N} x_i$ without the first harmonic
10	i so that $x_i = Max_{i=1}^{N} x_i$ without the first harmonic
11	Amplitude of the first harmonic
12	Phase of the first harmonic
13	Amplitude of the second harmonic
14	Phase of the second harmonic
15	Amplitude of the third harmonic
16	Phase of the third harmonic
17	Amplitude of the fourth harmonic
18	Phase of the fourth harmonic

Table 11.5. This table shows the combinations of functionals that were shown in Refs. 15 and 16 to produce good triple features for texture discrimination. The numbers identify the corresponding functionals in Tables 11.2–11.4.

Trace Functionals	Diametric Functionals	Circus Functionals
6	1	1
6	2	1
6	2	17
6	5	1
14	10	13
23	6	13
24	2	1
25	5	1
31	2	13

Acknowledgements

This work was supported by an RCUK Basic Technology grant on "Reverse Engineering the human vision system".

References

1. S Barsky and M Petrou, 2003. "The 4-source photometric stereo technique for three-dimensional surfaces in the presence of highlights and shadows". IEEE Transactions on Pattern Analysis and Machine Intelligence, PAMI-25, pp 1239–1252.
2. M J Chantler, M Petrou, A Penirsche, M Schmidt and G McGunnigle, 2005. "Classifying Surface Texture While Simultaneously Estimating Illumination Direction". International Journal of Computer Vision, Vol 62, pp 83–96.
3. P Daras, D Zarpalas, D Tzovaras and M Strintzis, 2006. "Efficient 3D model search and retrieval using generalised 3D Radon transforms". IEEE Transactions on Multimedia, Vol 8, pp 101–114.
4. S R Deans, 1981. "Hough Transform from the Radon Transform". IEEE PAMI, Vol 3, pp 185–188.
5. S R Deans, 1983. "The Radon Transform and some of its applications". Krieger Publishing Company.
6. A Kadyrov and M Petrou, 2001. "The Trace transform and its applications". IEEE Transactions on Pattern Analysis and Machine Intelligence, PAMI, Vol 23, pp 811–828.
7. A Kadyrov, A Talebpour and M Petrou, 2002. "Texture classification with thousands of features", British Machine Vision Conference, P L Rosin and D Marshall (eds), 2–5 September, Cardiff, ISBN 1 901725 19 7, Vol 2, pp 656–665.

8. A Kadyrov and M Petrou, 2006. “Affine parameter Registration from the trace transform”. IEEE Transactions on Pattern Analysis and Machine Intelligence, Vol 28, pp 1631–1645.
9. V A Kovalev, M Petrou and Y S Bondar, 1999. “Texture anisotropy in 3D images”. IEEE Transactions on Image Processing, Vol 8, pp 346–360.
10. X Llado, M Petrou and J Marti, 2005. “Texture recognition by surface rendering”. Optical Engineering journal, Vol 44, No 3, pp 037001-1–037001-16.
11. K Messer, J Kittler, M Sadeghi, S Marcel, C Marcel, S Bengio, F Cardinaux, C Sanderson, J Czyz, L Vandendorpe, S Srisuk, M Petrou, W Kurutach, A Kadyrov, R Paredes, B Kepenekci, F B Tek, G B Akar, F Deravi, N Mavity, 2003. “Face Verification Competition on the XM2VTS Database”, Proceedings of the 4th International Conference on Audio and Video-based Biometric Person Authentication, University of Surrey, Guildford, UK June 9–11, pp 964–974.
12. A Penirschke, M J Chantler and M Petrou, 2002. “Illuminant rotation invariant classification of 3D surface textures using Lissajou’s ellipses”. Proceedings Texture 2002, The 2nd International workshop on texture analysis and synthesis, 1 June, Copenhagen, Denmark, pp 103–107.
13. M Petrou, S Barsky and M Faraklioti, 2001. “Texture analysis as 3D surface roughness”. Pattern Recognition and Image Analysis, Vol 11, No 3, pp 616–632.
14. M Petrou and A Kadyrov, 2004. “Affine invariant features from the Trace transform”. IEEE Transactions on Pattern Analysis and Machine Intelligence, PAMI-26, pp 30–44.
15. M Petrou, R Piroddi and A Talebpour, 2006. “Texture recognition from sparsely and irregularly sampled data”. Computer Vision and Image Understanding, Vol 102, pp 95–104.
16. M Petrou, A Talebpour and A Kadyrov, 2007. “Reverse Engineering the way humans rank textures”. Pattern Analysis and Applications, Vol 10, No 2, pp 101–114.
17. A Sayeed, M Petrou, N Spyrou, A Kadyrov and T Spinks, 2002. “Diagnostic features of Alzheimer’s disease extracted from PET sinograms”. Physics in Medicine and Biology, Vol 47, pp 137–148.
18. S Srisuk, M Petrou, W Kurutach and A Kadyrov, 2005. “A face authentication system using the trace transform”. Pattern Analysis and Applications, Vol 8, pp 50–61.
19. P Toft, 1996. “The Radon Transform: Theory and Implementation”. PhD thesis, Technical University of Denmark.

Chapter 12

Face Analysis Using Local Binary Patterns

A. Hadid*, G. Zhao, T. Ahonen, and M. Pietikäinen

Machine Vision Group
Infotech Oulu, P.O. Box 4500
FI-90014, University of Oulu, Finland
http://www.ee.oulu.fi/mvg

Local Binary Pattern (LBP) is a simple yet very efficient texture operator which labels the pixels of an image by thresholding the neighborhood of each pixel with the value of the center pixel and considers the result as a binary number. Due to its discriminative power and computational simplicity, LBP texture operator has become a popular approach in various applications. This chapter presents the LBP methodology and its application to face image analysis problems, demonstrating that LBP features are also efficient in nontraditional texture analysis tasks. We explain how to easily derive efficient LBP based face descriptions which combine into a single feature vector the global shape, the texture and eventually the dynamics of facial features. The obtained representations are then applied to face and eye detection, face recognition and facial expression analysis problems, yielding in excellent performance.

12.1. Introduction

Texture analysis community has developed a variety of approaches for different biometric applications. A notable example of recent success is iris recognition, in which approaches based on multi-channel Gabor filtering have been highly successful. Multi-channel filtering has also been widely used to extract features e.g. in fingerprint and palmprint analysis. However, face analysis problem has not been associated with progress in texture analysis field as it has not been investigated from such point of view.

*Corresponding author: hadid@ee.oulu.fi, Phone:+358 8 553 2809, Fax:+358 8 553 2612

Automatic face analysis has become a very active topic in computer vision research as it is useful in several applications, like biometric identification, visual surveillance, human-machine interaction, video conferencing and content-based image retrieval. Face analysis may include face detection and facial feature extraction, face tracking and pose estimation, face and facial expression recognition, and face modeling and animation.[1,2] All these tasks are challenging due to the fact that a face is a dynamic and non-rigid object which is difficult to handle. Its appearance varies due to changes in pose, expression, illumination and other factors such as age and make-up. Therefore, one should derive facial representations that are robust to these factors.

While features used for texture analysis have been successfully used in many biometric applications, only relatively few works have considered them in facial image analysis. For instance, the well-known Elastic Bunch Graph Matching (EBGM) method used Gabor filter responses at certain fiducial points to recognize faces.[3] Gabor wavelets have also been used in facial expression recognition yielding in good results.[4] A problem with the Gabor-wavelet representations is their computational complexity. Therefore, simpler features like Haar wavelets have been considered in face detection resulting in a fast and efficient face detector.[5]

Recently, the local binary pattern (LBP) texture method has provided excellent results in various applications. Perhaps the most important property of the LBP operator in real-world applications is its robustness to monotonic gray-scale changes caused, for example, by illumination variations. Another important property is its computational simplicity, which makes it possible to analyze images in challenging real-time settings.[6–8]

This chapter considers the application of local binary pattern approach to face analysis, demonstrating that texture based region descriptors can be very useful in recognizing faces and facial expressions, detecting faces and different facial components, and in other face related tasks.

The rest of this chapter is organized as follows: First, basic definitions and motivations behind local binary patterns in spatial and spatiotemporal domains are given in Section 12.2. Then, we explain how to use LBP for efficiently representing faces (Section 12.3). Experimental results and discussions on applying LBP to face and eye detection, and face and facial expression recognition are presented in Section 12.4. This section also includes a short overview on the use of LBP in other face analysis related tasks. Finally, Section 12.5 concludes the chapter.

12.2. Local Binary Patterns

12.2.1. *LBP in the spatial domain*

The LBP texture analysis operator, introduced by Ojala *et al.*,[7,8] is defined as a gray-scale invariant texture measure, derived from a general definition of texture in a local neighborhood. It is a powerful means of texture description and among its properties in real-world applications are its discriminative power, computational simplicity and tolerance against monotonic gray-scale changes.

The original LBP operator forms labels for the image pixels by thresholding the 3×3 neighborhood of each pixel with the center value and considering the result as a binary number. The histogram of these $2^8 = 256$ different labels can then be used as a texture descriptor. See Fig. 12.1 for an illustration of the basic LBP operator.

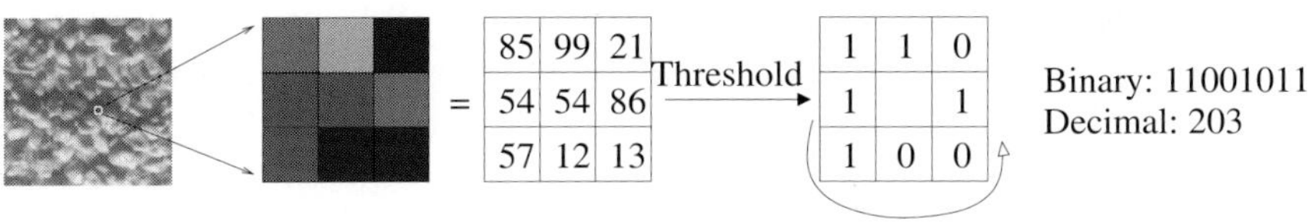

Fig. 12.1. The basic LBP operator.

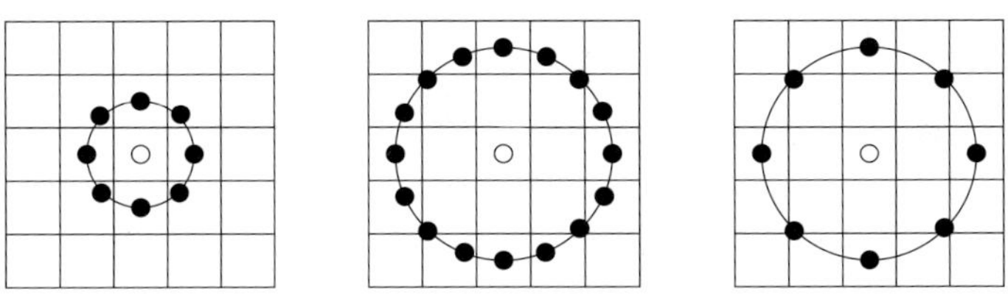

Fig. 12.2. Neighborhood set for different (P,R). The pixel values are bilinearly interpolated whenever the sampling point is not in the center of a pixel.

The operator has been extended to use neigborhoods of different sizes.[8] Using a circular neighborhood and bilinearly interpolating values at non-integer pixel coordinates allow any radius and number of pixels in the neighborhood. In the following, the notation (P, R) will be used for pixel neighborhoods which means P sampling points on a circle of radius of R. See Fig. 12.2 for an example of circular neighborhoods.

Another extension to the original operator is the definition of so called *uniform patterns*.[8] This extension was inspired by the fact that some binary patterns occur more commonly in texture images than others. A local binary pattern is called uniform if the binary pattern contains at most two bitwise transitions from 0 to 1 or vice versa when the bit pattern is traversed circularly. For example, the patterns 00000000 (0 transitions), 01110000 (2 transitions) and 11001111 (2 transitions) are uniform whereas the patterns 11001001 (4 transitions) and 01010011 (6 transitions) are not. In the computation of the LBP labels, uniform patterns are used so that there is a separate label for each uniform pattern and all the non-uniform patterns are labeled with a single label. For example, when using $(8, R)$ neighborhood, there are a total of 256 patterns, 58 of which are uniform, which yields in 59 different labels.

Ojala *et al.* noticed in their experiments with texture images that uniform patterns account for a little less than 90% of all patterns when using the (8,1) neighborhood and for around 70% in the (16,2) neighborhood. We have found that 90.6% of the patterns in the (8,1) neighborhood and 85.2% of the patterns in the (8,2) neighborhood are uniform in case of preprocessed FERET facial images.[9] Each bin (LBP code) can be regarded as a micro-texton. Local primitives which are codified by these bins include different types of curved edges, spots, flat areas etc. Fig. 12.3 shows some examples.

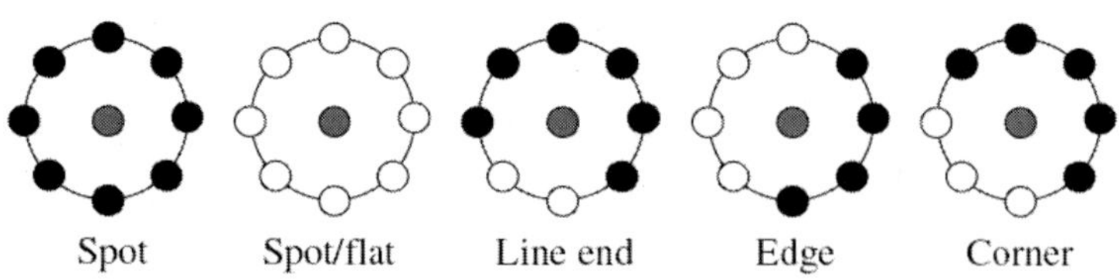

Fig. 12.3. Examples of texture primitives which can be detected by LBP (white circles represent ones and black cirlces zeros).

We use the following notation for the LBP operator: $\text{LBP}^{u2}_{P,R}$. The subscript represents using the operator in a (P, R) neighborhood. Superscript $u2$ stands for using only uniform patterns and labeling all remaining patterns with a single label.

After the LBP labeled image $f_l(x, y)$ has been obtained, the LBP histogram can be defined as

$$H_i = \sum_{x,y} I\{f_l(x, y) = i\}, i = 0, \ldots, n - 1, \tag{12.1}$$

in which n is the number of different labels produced by the LBP operator and

$$I\{A\} = \begin{cases} 1, & \text{A is true} \\ 0, & \text{A is false.} \end{cases}$$

When the image patches whose histograms are to be compared have different sizes, the histograms must be normalised to get a coherent description:

$$N_i = \frac{H_i}{\sum_{j=0}^{n-1} H_j}. \tag{12.2}$$

12.2.2. *Spatiotemporal LBP*

The original LBP operator was defined to only deal with the spatial information. Recently, it has been extended to a spatiotemporal representation for dynamic texture analysis (DT). This has yielded the so called Volume Local Binary Pattern operator (VLBP).[10] The idea behind VLBP consists of looking at dynamic texture as a set of volumes in the (X,Y,T) space where X and Y denote the spatial coordinates and T denotes the frame index (time). The neighborhood of each pixel is thus defined in three dimensional space. Then, similarly to LBP in spatial domain, volume textons can be defined and extracted into histograms. Therefore, VLBP combines motion and appearance together to describe dynamic texture.

Later, to make the VLBP computationally simple and easy to extend, the co-occurrences of the LBP on three orthogonal planes (LBP-TOP) was also introduced.[10] LBP-TOP consists then of considering three orthogonal planes: XY, XT and YT, and concatenating local binary pattern co-occurrence statistics in these three directions as shown in Fig. 12.4. The circular neighborhoods are generalized to elliptical sampling to fit to the space-time statistics.

Figure 12.5 shows example images from three planes. (a) shows the image in the XY plane, (b) in the XT plane which gave the visual impression of one row changing in time, while (c) describes the motion of one column in temporal space. The LBP codes are extracted from the XY, XT and YT planes, which are denoted as $XY - LBP$, $XT - LBP$ and $YT - LBP$, for all pixels, and statistics of three different planes are obtained, and then concatenated into a single histogram. The procedure is shown in Fig. 12.6. In such a representation, DT is encoded by the $XY - LBP$, $XT - LBP$ and $YT - LBP$, while the appearance and motion in three directions of DT are considered, incorporating spatial domain information ($XY - LBP$) and two spatial temporal co-occurrence statistics ($XT - LBP$ and $YT - LBP$).

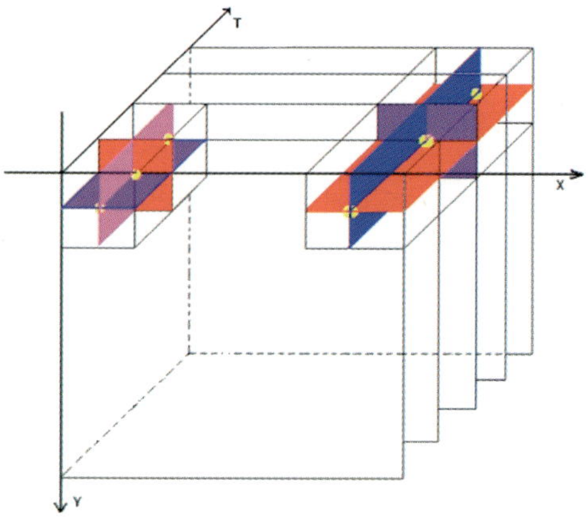

Fig. 12.4. Three planes in DT to extract neighboring points.

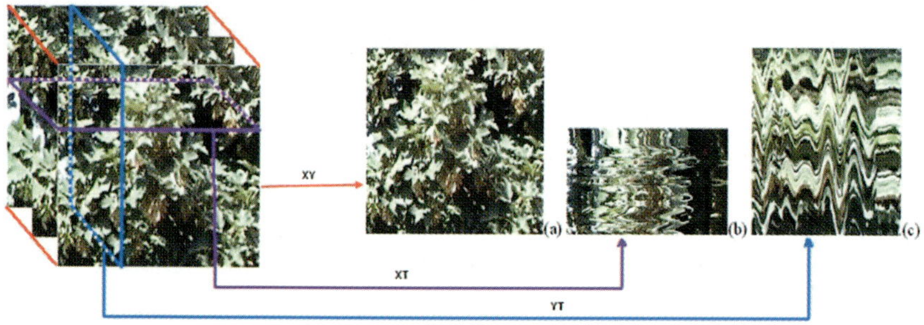

Fig. 12.5. (a) Image in XY plane (400 × 300) (b) Image in XT plane (400 × 250) in $y = 120$ (last row is pixels of $y = 120$ in first image) (c) Image in TY plane (250 × 300) in $x = 120$ (first column is the pixels of $x = 120$ in first frame).

Setting the radius in the time axis to be equal to the radius in the space axis is not reasonable for dynamic textures.[10] So we have different radius parameters in space and time to set. In the XT and YT planes, different radii can be assigned to sample neighboring points in space and time.

More generally, the radii in axes X, Y and T, and the number of neighboring points in the XY, XT and YT planes can also be different, which can be marked as R_X, R_Y and R_T, P_{XY}, P_{XT} and P_{YT}. The corresponding feature is denoted as $LBP-TOP_{P_{XY},P_{XT},P_{YT},R_X,R_Y,R_T}$.

Let us assume we are given an $X \times Y \times T$ dynamic texture ($x_c \in \{0, \cdots, X-1\}, y_c \in \{0, \cdots, Y-1\}, t_c \in \{0, \cdots, T-1\}$). A histogram of

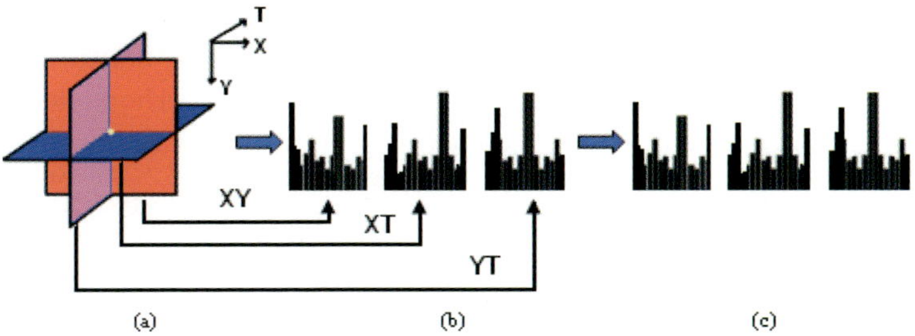

Fig. 12.6. (a) Three planes in dynamic texture (b) LBP histogram from each plane (c) Concatenated feature histogram.

the DT can be defined as

$$H_{i,j} = \sum_{x,y,t} I\{f_j(x,y,t) = i\}, \quad i = 0, \cdots, n_j - 1; j = 0, 1, 2 \tag{12.3}$$

in which n_j is the number of different labels produced by the LBP operator in the jth plane ($j = 0 : XY,\ 1 : XT\ and\ 2 : YT$), $f_i(x, y, t)$ expresses the LBP code of central pixel (x, y, t) in the jth plane.

When the DTs to be compared are of different spatial and temporal sizes, the histograms must be normalized to get a coherent description:

$$N_{i,j} = \frac{H_{i,j}}{\sum_{k=0}^{n_j-1} H_{k,j}}. \tag{12.4}$$

In this histogram, a description of DT is effectively obtained based on LBP from three different planes. The labels from the XY plane contain information about the appearance, and in the labels from the XT and YT planes co-occurrence statistics of motion in horizontal and vertical directions are included. These three histograms are concatenated to build a global description of DT with the spatial and temporal features.

12.3. Face Description Using LBP

In the LBP approach for texture classification,[6] the occurrences of the LBP codes in an image are collected into a histogram. The classification is then performed by computing simple histogram similarities. However, considering a similar approach for facial image representation results in a loss of spatial information and therefore one should codify the texture information while retaining also their locations. One way to achieve this goal is to use the LBP texture descriptors to build several local descriptions of the face and combine them into a global description. Such local descriptions have been gaining interest lately which is understandable given the limitations of the holistic representations. These local feature based methods seem to be more robust against variations in pose or illumination than holistic methods.

Another reason for selecting the local feature based approach is that trying to build a holistic description of a face using texture methods is not reasonable since texture descriptors tend to average over the image area. This is a desirable property for textures, because texture description should usually be invariant to translation or even rotation of the texture and, especially for small repetitive textures, the small-scale relationships determine the appearance of the texture and thus the large-scale relations do not contain useful information. For faces, however, the situation is different: retaining the information about spatial relations is important.

The basic methodology for LBP based face description is as follows: The facial image is divided into local regions and LBP texture descriptors are extracted from each region independently. The descriptors are then concatenated to form a global description of the face, as shown in Fig. 12.7.

The basic histogram that is used to gather information about LBP codes in an image can be extended into a *spatially enhanced histogram* which encodes both the appearance and the spatial relations of facial regions. As the facial regions $R_0, R_1, \ldots R_{m-1}$ have been determined, the spatially enhanced histogram is defined as

$$H_{i,j} = \sum_{x,y} I\{f_l(x,y) = i\} I\{(x,y) \in R_j\}, i = 0, \ldots, n-1, j = 0, \ldots, m-1.$$

This histogram effectively has a description of the face on three different levels of locality: the LBP labels for the histogram contain information about the patterns on a pixel-level, the labels are summed over a small region to produce information on a regional level and the regional histograms are concatenated to build a global description of the face.

It should be noted that when using the histogram based methods the regions $R_0, R_1, \ldots R_{m-1}$ do not need to be rectangular. Neither do they need to be of the same size or shape, and they do not necessarily have to cover the whole image. It is also possible to have partially overlapping regions.

This outlines the original LBP based facial representation[11,12] that has been later adopted to various facial image analysis tasks. Figure 12.7 shows an example of an LBP based facial representation.

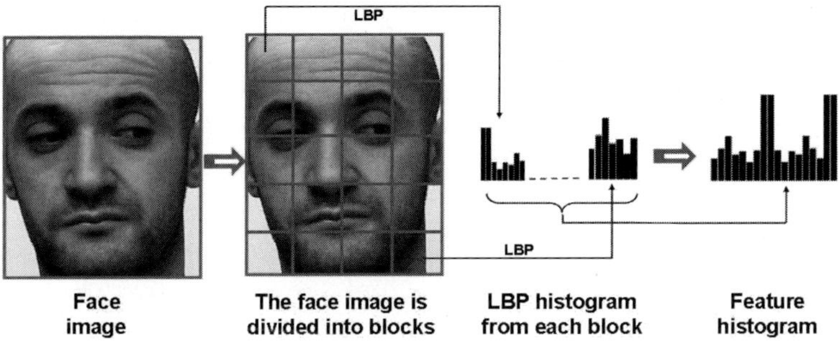

Fig. 12.7. Example of an LBP based facial representation.

12.4. Applications to Face Analysis

12.4.1. *Face recognition*

This section describes the application of LBP based face description to face recognition. Typically a nearest neighbor classifier is used in the face recognition task. This is due to the fact that the number of training (gallery) images per subject is low, often only one. However, the idea of a spatially enhanced histogram can be exploited further when defining the distance measure for the classifier. An indigenous property of the proposed face description method is that each element in the enhanced histogram corresponds to a certain small area of the face. Based on the psychophysical findings, which indicate that some facial features (such as eyes) play a more important role in human face recognition than other features,[2] it can be expected that in this method some of the facial regions contribute more than others in terms of extrapersonal variance. Utilizing this assumption the regions can be weighted based on the importance of the information they contain. For example, the weighted Chi square distance can be defined as

$$\chi_w^2(\mathbf{x}, \boldsymbol{\xi}) = \sum_{j,i} w_j \frac{(x_{i,j} - \xi_{i,j})^2}{x_{i,j} + \xi_{i,j}}, \tag{12.5}$$

in which $\mathbf{x}$ and $\boldsymbol{\xi}$ are the normalized enhanced histograms to be compared, indices i and j refer to i-th bin in histogram corresponding to the j-th local region and w_j is the weight for region j.

We tested the proposed face recognition approach using the FERET face images.[9] The details of these experiments can be found in Refs. 11–13. The recognition results (rank curves) are plotted in Fig. 12.8. The results clearly show that LBP approach yields higher recognition rates than the control

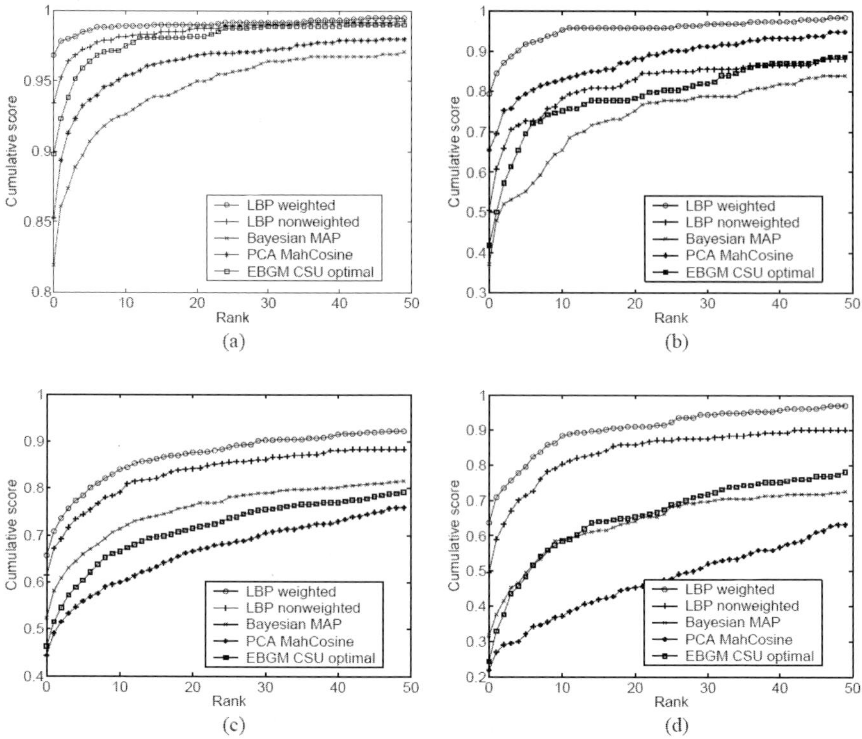

Fig. 12.8. The cumulative scores of the LBP and control algorithms on the (a) *fb*, (b) *fc*, (c) *dup I* and (d) *dup II* probe sets.

algorithms (PCA,[14] Bayesian Intra/Extrapersonal Classifier (BIC)[15] and Elastic Bunch Graph Matching EBGM[3]) in all the FERET test sets including changes in facial expression (*fb* set), lighting conditions (*fc* set) and aging (*dup I* & *dup II* sets). The results on the *fc* and *dup II* sets show that especially with weighting, the LBP based description is robust to challenges caused by lighting changes or aging of the subjects.

To gain better understanding on whether the obtained recognition results are due to general idea of computing texture features from local facial regions or due to the discriminatory power of the local binary pattern operator, we compared LBP to three other texture descriptors, namely the gray-level difference histogram, homogeneous texture descriptor[16] and an improved version of the texton histogram.[17] The details of these experiments can be found in Ref. 13. The results confirmed the validity of the

Table 12.1. The recognition rates obtained using different texture descriptors for local facial regions. The first four columns show the recognition rates for the FERET test sets and the last three columns contain the mean recognition rate of the permutation test with a 95 % confidence interval.

Method	fb	fc	dup I	dup II	lower	mean	upper
Difference histogram	0.87	0.12	0.39	0.25	0.58	0.63	0.68
Homogeneous texture	0.86	0.04	0.37	0.21	0.58	0.62	0.68
Texton Histogram	0.97	0.28	0.59	0.42	0.71	0.76	0.80
LBP (nonweighted)	0.93	0.51	0.61	0.50	0.71	0.76	0.81

LBP approach and showed that the performance of LBP in face description exceeds that of other texture operators LBP was compared to, as shown in Table 12.1. We believe that the main explanation for the better performance of the local binary pattern operator over other texture descriptors is its tolerance to monotonic gray-scale changes. Additional advantages are the computational efficiency of the LBP operator and that no gray-scale normalization is needed prior to applying the LBP operator to the face image.

Additionally, we experimented with the Face Recognition Grand Challenge Experiment 4 which is a difficult face verification task in which the gallery images have been taken under controlled conditions and the probe images are uncontrolled still images containing challenges such as poor illumination or blurring. We considered the FRGC Ver 1.0 images. The gallery set consists of 152 images representing separate subjects and the probe set has 608 images. Figure 12.9 shows an example of gallery and probe images from the FRGC database.

Fig. 12.9. Example of Gallery and probe images from the FRGC database, and their corresponding filtered images with Laplacian-of-Gaussian filter.

In our preliminary experiments to compensate for the illumination and blurring effects, the images were filtered with Laplacian-of-Gaussian filters of three different sizes ($\sigma = \{1, 2, 4\}$) and LBP histograms were computed from each of these images using a rectangular grid of 8×8 local regions and $LBP^{u2}_{8,2}$. This resulted in recognition rate of 54% which is a very significant increase over the rate of the basic setup of[11] which was only 15%. Though even better rates have been reported for the same test data, this result shows that a notable gain can be achieved in the performance of LBP based face analysis by using suitable preprocessing. Currently we are working on finding better classification schemes and also incorporating the preprocessing into the feature extraction step.

Since the publication of our preliminary results on the LBP based face description,[11] our methodology has already attained an established position in face analysis research. Some novel applications of the same methodology to problems such as face detection and facial expression analysis are discussed in other sections of this chapter.

In face recognition, Zhang *et al.*[18] considered the LBP methodology for face recognition and used AdaBoost learning algorithm for selecting an optimal set of local regions and their weights. This yielded in a smaller feature vector length representing the facial images than that used in the original LBP approach.[11,12] However, no significant performance enhancement has been obtained. More recently, Huang *et al.*[19] proposed a variant of AdaBoost called JSBoost for selecting the optimal set of LBP features for face recognition.

Zhang *et al.*[20] proposed the extraction of LBP features from images obtained by filtering a facial image with 40 Gabor filters of different scales and orientations. Excellent results have been obtained on all the FERET sets. A downside of the method lies in the high dimensionality of the feature vector (LBP histogram) which is calculated from 40 Gabor images derived from each single original image. To overcome this problem of long feature vector length, Shan *et al.*[21] presented a new extension using Fisher Discriminant Analysis (FDA) instead of the χ^2 (Chi-square) and histogram intersection which have been previously used in Ref. 20. The authors constructed an ensemble of piecewise FDA classifiers, each of which is built based one segment of the high-dimensional LBP histograms. Impressive results were reported on the FERET database.

In Ref. 22, Rodriguez and Marcel proposed an approach based on adapted, client-specific LBP histograms for the face verification task. The method considers local histograms as probability distributions and computes a log-likelihood ratio instead of χ^2 similarity. A generic face model is considered as a collection of LBP histograms. Then, a client-specific model is obtained by an adaptation technique from the generic model under a probabilistic framework. The reported experimental results show that the proposed method yields excellent performance on two benchmark databases (XM2VTS and BANCA).

12.4.2. *Face detection*

The LBP based facial description presented in Section 12.3 and used for recognition in Section 12.4.1 is more adequate for larger-sized images. For example, in the FERET tests the images have a resolution of 130×150 pixels and were typically divided into 49 blocks, leading to a relatively long feature vector typically containing thousands of elements. However, in many applications such as face detection, the faces can be on the order of 20×20 pixels. Therefore, such representation cannot be used for detecting (or even recognizing) low-resolution face images.

In Ref. 23, we derived another LBP based representation which is suitable for low-resolution images and has a short feature vector needed for fast processing. A specific aspect of this representation is the use of overlapping regions and a 4-neighborhood LBP operator ($LBP_{4,1}$) to avoid statistical unreliability due to long histograms computed over small regions. Additionally, we enhanced the holistic description of a face by including the global LBP histogram computed over the whole face image.

We considered 19×19 as the basic resolution and derived the LBP facial representation as follows (see Fig. 12.10): We divided a 19×19 face image into 9 overlapping regions of 10×10 pixels (overlapping size=4 pixels). From each region, we computed a 16-bin histogram using the $LBP_{4,1}$ operator and concatenated the results into a single 144-bin histogram. Additionally, we applied $LBP_{8,1}^{u2}$ to the whole 19×19 face image and derived a 59-bin histogram which was added to the 144 bins previously computed. Thus, we obtained a (59+144=203)-bin histogram as a face representation.

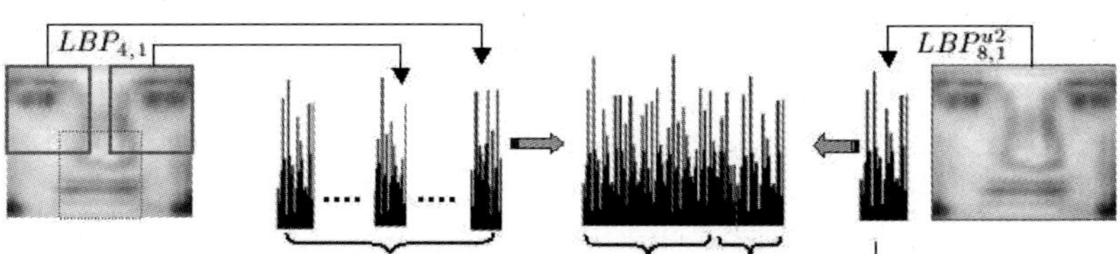

Fig. 12.10. Facial representation for low-resolution images: a face image is represented by a concatenation of a global and a set of local LBP histograms.

To assess the performance of the new representation, we built a face detection system using LBP features and an SVM (Support Vector Machine) classifier.[24] Given training samples (face and nonface images) represented by their extracted LBP features, an SVM classifier finds the separating hyperplane that has maximum distance to the closest points of the training set. These closest points are called *support vectors*. To perform a nonlinear separation, the input space is mapped onto a higher dimensional space using Kernel functions. In our approach, to detect faces in a given target image, a 19×19 subwindow scans the image at different scales and locations. We considered a downsampling rate of 1.2 and a moving scan of 2 pixels. At each iteration, the representation $LBP(w)$ is computed from the subwindow and fed to the SVM classifier to determine whether it is a face or not ($LBP(w)$ denotes the LBP feature vector representing the region scanned by the subwindow).

Additionally, given the results of the SVM classifier, we perform a set of heuristics to merge multiple detections and remove the false ones. For a given detected window, we count the number of detections within a neighborhood of 19×19 pixels (each detected window is represented by its center). The detections are removed if their number is less than 3. Otherwise, we merge them and keep only the one with the highest SVM output.

From the collected training sets, we extracted the proposed facial representations. Then, we used these features as inputs to the SVM classifier and trained the face detector. The system was run on several images from different sources to detect faces. Figures 12.11 and 12.12 show some detection examples. It can be seen that most of the upright frontal faces are detected. For instance, Fig. 12.12.g shows perfect detections. In Fig. 12.12.f, only one face is missed by the system. This miss is due to occlusion. A similar situation is shown in Fig. 12.11.a in which the missed face is due to a large in-plane rotation. Since the system is trained to detect only in-plane rotated faces up to $\pm 18^o$, it succeeded to find the slightly rotated faces in Fig. 12.11.c, Fig. 12.11.d and Fig. 12.12.h and failed to detect largely rotated ones (as those in 12.11.e and 12.11.c). A false positive is shown in Fig. 12.11.e while a false negative is shown in Fig. 12.11.d. Notice that this false negative is expected since the face is pose-angled (*i.e.* not in frontal position). These examples summarize the main aspects of our detector using images from different sources.

In order to further investigate the performance of our approach, we implemented another face detector using the same training and test sets. We considered a similar SVM based face detector but using different features as

Fig. 12.11. Detection examples in several images from different sources. The images c, d and e are from the World Wide Web. Note: excellent detections of upright faces in a; detections under slight in-plane rotation in a and c; missed faces in c, e and a because of large in-plane rotation; missed face in a because of a pose-angled face; and a false detection in e.

inputs and then compared the results to those obtained using the proposed LBP features. We chose the normalized pixel features as inputs since it has been shown that such features perform better than the gradient and wavelet based ones when using with an SVM classifier.[25] We trained the system using the same training samples. The experimental results clearly showed the validity of our approach which compared favorably against the state-of-the-art algorithms. Additionally, by comparing our results to those obtained using normalized pixel values as inputs to the SVM classifier, we confirmed the efficiency of an LBP based facial representation. Indeed, the results showed that: (i) The proposed LBP features are more discriminative than the normalized pixel values; (ii) The proposed representation is more compact as, for 19×19 face images, we derived a 203-element feature vector

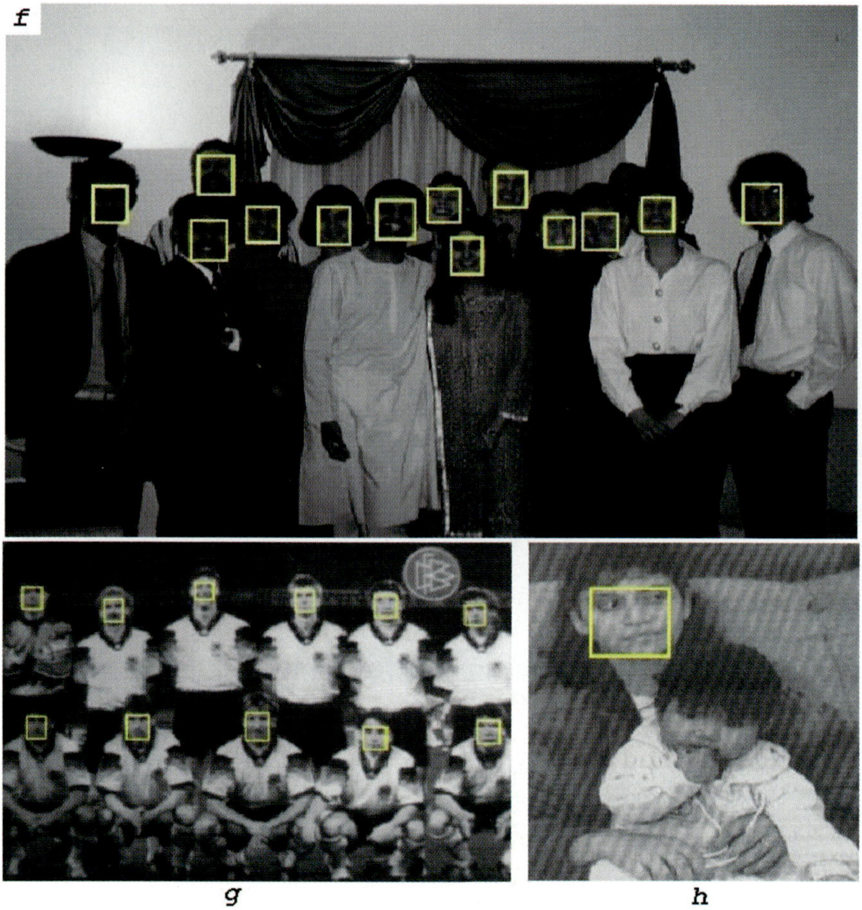

Fig. 12.12. Detection examples in several images from the subset of MIT-CMU tests. Note: excellent detections of upright faces in f and g; detection under slight in-plane rotation in h; missed face in f because of occlusion.

while the raw pixel features yield a vector of 361 elements; and (iii) Our approach did not require histogram equalization and used a smaller number of support vectors. More details on these experiments can be found in Ref. 23.

Recently, we extended the proposed approach with an aim to develop a real-time multi-view detector suitable for real world environments such as video surveillance, mobile devices and content based video retrieval. The new approach uses LBP features in a coarse-to-fine detection strategy (pyramid architecture) embedded in a fast classification scheme based on AdaBoost learning. A real-time operation was achieved with as a good detection accuracy as the original, which was a much slower approach. The system handles out-of-plane face rotations in the range of $[-60^o, +60^o]$ and in-plane rotations in the range of $[-45^o, +45^o]$. As done by S. Li and Zhang in Ref. 26, the in-plane rotation is achieved by rotating the original images by $\pm 30^o$. Some detection examples on CMU Rotated and Profile Test Sets are shown in Fig. 12.13. The results are comparable to the state-of-the-art, especially in terms of detection accuracy. In terms of speed, our approach might be slightly slower than the system proposed by S. Li and Zhang in Ref. 26. However, it is worth mentioning that comparing the results of face detection methods is not always fair because of the differences in the number of training samples, in the post processing procedures which are applied to merge or delete multiple detections and in the definition itself of what is the meaning of correct face detection.[27]

LBP based face description has been also considered in other works. For instance, in Ref. 28, a variant of LBP based facial representation, called Improved LBP, was adopted for face detection. In ILBP, the 3×3 neighbors of each pixel are not compared to the center pixel as in the original LBP, but to the mean value of the pixels. The authors argued that ILBP captures more information than LBP does. However, using ILBP, the length of the histogram increases rapidly. For instance, while $\text{LBP}_{8,1}$ uses a 256-bin histogram, $\text{ILBP}_{8,1}$ computes 511 bins. Using the ILBP features, the authors have considered a Bayesian framework for classifying the ILBP representations. The face and non-face classes were modeled using multivariable Gaussian distributions while the Bayesian decision rule was used to decide on the "faceness" of a given pattern. The reported results are very encouraging. More recently,[29] the authors proposed another approach to face detection based on boosting ILBP features.

12.4.3. *Eye detection*

Inspired by the works of Viola and Jones on the use of Haar-like features with integral images[5] and that of Heusch *et al.* on the use of LBP as a preprocessing step for handling illumination changes,[30] we developed a robust approach for eye detection using Haar-like features extracted from LBP images. Thus, in our system, the images are first filtered by LBP operator ($LBP_{8,1}$) and then Haar-like features are extracted and used with AdaBoost for building a cascade of classifiers.

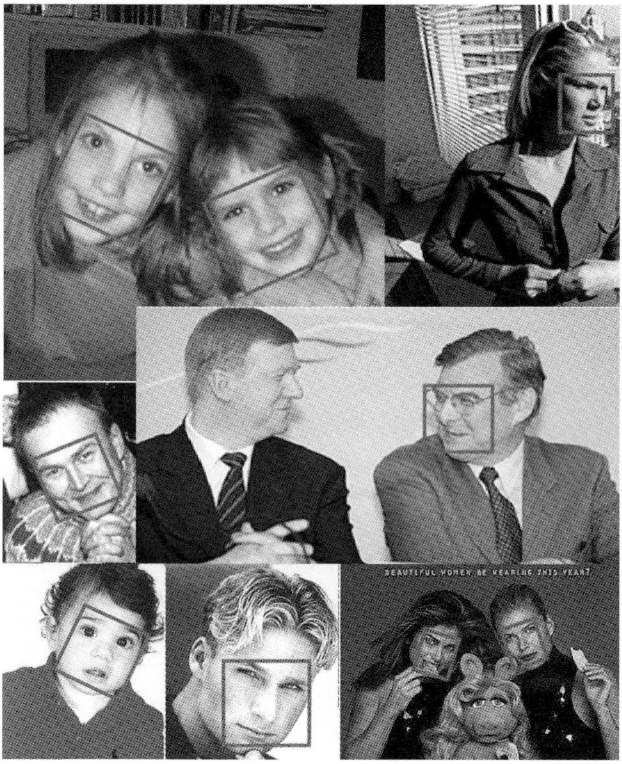

Fig. 12.13. Examples of face detections on the CMU Rotated and Profile Test Sets.

During training, the boostrap strategy is used to collect the negative examples. First, we randomly extracted non-eye samples from a set of natural images which do not contain eyes. Then, we trained the system, run the eye detector, and collected all those non-eye patterns that were wrongly classified as eyes and used them for training. Additionally, we considered negative training samples extracted also from the facial regions because it has been shown that this can enhance the performance of the system. In total, we trained the system using 3,116 eye patterns (positive samples) and 2,461 non-eye patterns (negative samples). Then, we tested our system on a database containing over 30,000 frontal face images and compared the results to those obtained by using Haar-like features and LBP features separately. Detection rates of 86.7%, 81.3% and 80.8% were obtained when considering LBP/Haar-like features, LBP only and Haar-like features only, respectively. Some detection examples, using the combined

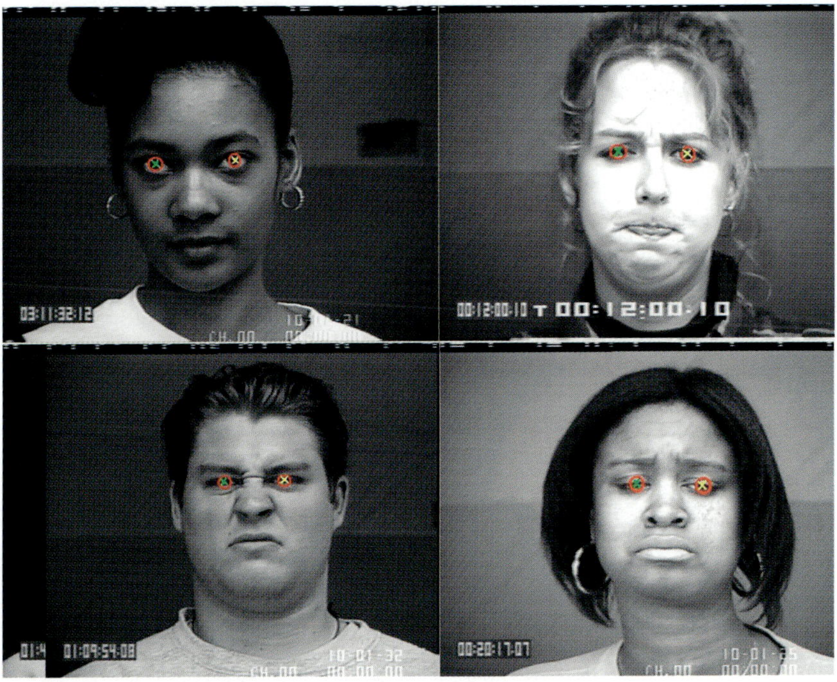

Fig. 12.14. Examples of eye detections.

approach, are shown in Fig. 12.14. The results assess the efficiency of combining LBP and Haar-like features (86.7%) while LBP and Haar-like features alone gave a lower performance. The ongoing experiments aim to handle more challenging cases such as detecting of partially occluded eyes.

12.4.4. *Facial expression recognition using spatiotemporal LBP*

This section considers the LBP based representation for dynamic texture analysis, described in Section 12.2.2, and applies it to the problem of facial expression recognition from videos.[10] The goal of facial expression recognition is to determine the emotional state of the face, for example, happiness, sadness, surprise, neutral, anger, fear, and disgust, regardless of the identity of the face. Psychological studies [31] have shown that facial motion is fundamental to the recognition of facial expressions and humans do better job in recognizing expressions from dynamic images as opposed to mug shots.

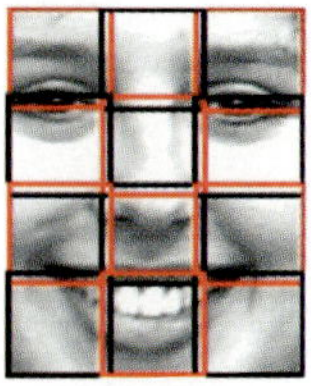

Fig. 12.15. Overlapping blocks (4 × 3, overlap size = 10).

Considering the motion of the facial region, we consider here region-concatenated descriptors on the basis of simplified VLBP. Like in Ref. 12, an LBP description computed over the whole facial expression sequence encodes only the occurrences of the micro-patterns without any indication about their locations. To overcome this effect, a representation in which the face image is divided into several overlapping blocks is used. Figure 12.15 depicts overlapping 4 × 3 blocks with an overlap of 10 pixels. The LBP-TOP histograms in each block are computed and concatenated into a single histogram, as Fig. 12.16 shows. All features extracted from each block volume are connected to represent the appearance and motion of the facial expression sequence, as shown in Fig. 12.17. The basic VLBP features are also extracted on the basis of region motion in same way as the LBP-TOP features.

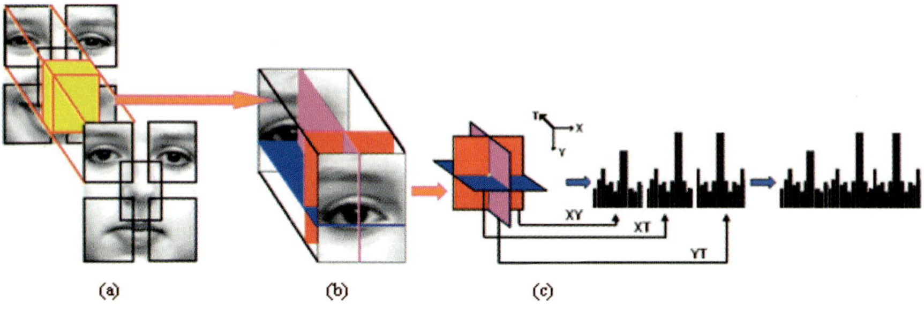

Fig. 12.16. Features in each block volume. (a) Block volumes; (b) LBP features from three orthogonal planes; (c) Concatenated features for one block volume with the appearance and motion.

We experimented with the Cohn-Kanade database[32] which consists of 100 university students with age ranging from 18 to 30 years. Sixty-five percent were female, 15 percent African-American, and three percent Asian or Latino. Subjects were instructed by an experimenter to perform a series

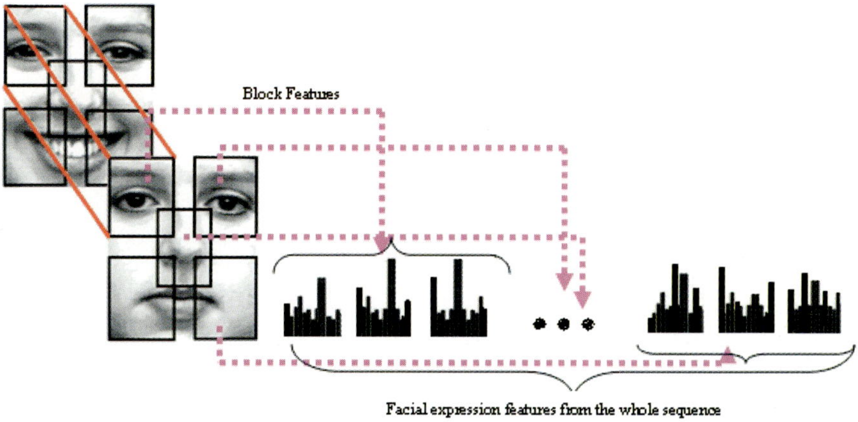

Fig. 12.17. Facial expression representation.

of 23 facial displays that included single action units and combinations of action units, six of which were based on descriptions of prototypic emotions, anger, disgust, fear, joy, sadness, and surprise. For our study, 374 sequences from the dataset were selected from the database for basic emotional expression recognition. The selection criterion was that a sequence to be labeled is one of the six basic emotions. The sequences came from 97 subjects, with one to six emotions per subject. Just the positions of the eyes from the first frame of each sequence were used to determine the facial area for the whole sequence. The whole sequence was used to extract the proposed LBP-TOP and VLBP features.

Figure 12.18 summarizes the confusion matrix obtained using a ten-fold cross-validation scheme on the Cohn-Kanade facial expression database. The model achieved a 96.26% overall recognition rate of facial expressions. The details of our experiments and comparison with other dynamic and static methods can be found in Ref. 10. These experimental results clearly showed that the LBP based approach outperforms the other dynamic and static methods.[33–37] Our approach is quite robust with respect to variations of illumination and skin color, as seen from the pictures in Fig. 12.19. It also performed well with some in-plane and out-of-plane rotated sequences. This demonstrates robustness to errors in alignment.

LBP has been also considered for facial expression recognition in other works. For instance, in Ref. 38, an approach to facial expression recognition from static images was developed using LBP histograms computed

	Surprise	Happiness	Sadness	Fear	Anger	Disgust
Surprise	98.65		1.35			
Happiness		96.04		2.97		0.99
Sadness	1.37		95.89		2.74	
Fear		3.57	1.79	94.64		
Anger			3.12		96.88	
Disgust			2.63		2.63	94.74

Fig. 12.18. Confusion matrix.

Fig. 12.19. Variation of illumination.

over non-overlapping blocks for face description. The Linear Programming (LP) technique was adopted to classify seven facial expressions: anger, disgust, fear, happiness, sadness, surprise and neutral. During the training, the seven expression classes were decomposed into 21 expression pairs such as anger-fear, happiness-sadness etc. Thus, twenty-one classifiers were produced by the LP technique, each corresponding to one of the 21 expression pairs. A simple binary tree tournament scheme with pairwise comparisons was used for classifying unknown expressions. Good results (93.8%) were obtained for the Japanese Female Facial Expression (JAFFE) database used in the experiments. The database contains 213 images in which ten persons are expressing three or four times the seven basic expressions. Another approach to facial expression recognition using LBP features was proposed in Ref. 39. Instead of the LP approach, template matching with weighted Chi square statistic and SVM are adopted to classify the facial expressions using LBP features. Extensive experiments on the Cohn-Kanade database confirmed that LBP features are discriminative and more efficient than

Gabor-based methods especially at low image resolutions. Boosting LBP features has also been considered for facial expression recognition in Ref. 40.

12.4.5. *LBP in other face related tasks*

The LBP approach has been also adopted to several other facial image analysis tasks such as near-infrared based face recognition,[41] gender recognition,[42] iris recognition,[43] head pose estimation[44] and 3D face recognition.[45] A bibliography of LBP-related research can be found at

http://www.ee.oulu.fi/research/imag/texture/lbp/bibliography/

For instance, in Ref. 46, LBP is used with Active Shape Model (ASM) for localizing and representing facial key points since an accurate localization of such points of the face is crucial to many face analysis and synthesis problems such as face alignment. The local appearance of the key points in the facial images are modeled with an Extended version of Local Binary Patterns (ELBP). ELBP was proposed in order to encode not only the first derivation information of facial images but also the velocity of local variations. The experimental analysis showed that the combination ASM-ELBP enhances the face alignment accuracy compared to the original method used in ASM. Later, Marcel *et al.*[47] further extended the approach to locate facial features in images of frontal faces taken under different lighting conditions. Experiments on the standard and darkened image sets of the XM2VTS database assessed that the LBP-ASM approach gives superior performance compared to the basic ASM.

In our recent work, we experimented with a Volume LBP based spatiotemporal representation for face recognition from videos. The experimental analysis showed that, in some cases, the methods which use only the facial structure (such as PCA, LDA and the original LBP) can outperform the spatiotemporal approaches. This can be explained by the fact that some facial dynamics is not useful for recognition. In other terms, this means that some part of the temporal information is useful for recognition while another part may also hinder the recognition. Obviously, the useful part defines the extra-personal characteristics while the non-useful one concerns the intra-class information such as facial expressions and emotions. For recognition, one should then select only the extra-personal characteristics. To tackle the problem of selecting only the spatiotemporal information which is useful for recognition, we used AdaBoost learning technique. The goal is to classify the facial information into intra and extra classes, and then use only the extra-class LBP features for recognition. We considered one-against-all classification scheme with AdaBoost and obtained a significant increase in the recognition rates on MoBo video face database.[48] The significant increases in the recognition rates can be explained by the following: (*i*) the LBP based spatiotemporal representation, in contrast to the HMM based approach, is very efficient as it codifies the local facial dynamics and structure, (*ii*) the temporal information extracted by the volume LBP features consists of both intra and extra personal dynamics (facial expression and identity). Therefore, there was need for performing feature selection. This yielded in our proposed approach with excellent results outperforming the state-of-the-art on the considered test data.

12.5. Conclusion

Face images can be seen as a composition of micro-patterns which can be well described by LBP texture operator. We exploited this observation and proposed efficient face representations which have been successfully applied to various face analysis tasks, including face and eye detection, face recognition, and facial expression analysis problems. The extensive experiments have clearly shown the validity of LBP based face descriptions and demonstrated that texture based region descriptors can be very useful in nontraditional texture analysis tasks.

Among the properties of the LBP operator are its tolerance against monotonic gray-scale changes, discriminative power, and computational simplicity which makes it possible to analyze images in challenging real-time settings. Since the publication of our preliminary results on the LBP based face description, the methodology has already attained an established position in face analysis research. This is attested by the increasing number of works which adopted a similar approach. Additionally, it is worth mentioning that the LBP methodology is not limited to facial image analysis as it can be easily generalized to other types of object detection and recognition tasks.

References

1. S. Z. Li and A. K. Jain, Eds., *Handbook of Face Recognition*. (Springer, New York, 2005).
2. W. Zhao, R. Chellappa, P. J. Phillips, and A. Rosenfeld, Face recognition: A literature survey, *ACM Computing Surveys*. **34(4)**, 399–458, (2003).

3. L. Wiskott, J.-M. Fellous, N. Kuiger, and C. von der Malsburg, Face recognition by elastic bunch graph matching, *IEEE Transactions on Pattern Analysis and Machine Intelligence.* **19**, 775–779, (1997).
4. Y.-L. Tian, T. Kanade, and J. F. Cohn. Facial expression analysis. In eds. S. Z. Li and A. K. Jain, *Handbook of Face Recognition*, pp. 247–275. Springer, (2005).
5. P. Viola and M. Jones. Rapid object detection using a boosted cascade of simple features. In *Computer Vision and Pattern Recognition*, pp. 511–518, (2001).
6. T. Mäenpää and M. Pietikäinen. Texture analysis with local binary patterns. In eds. C. Chen and P. Wang, *Handbook of Pattern Recognition and Computer Vision, 3rd ed*, pp. 197–216. World Scientific, Singapore, (2005).
7. T. Ojala, M. Pietikäinen, and D. Harwood, A comparative study of texture measures with classification based on feature distributions, *Pattern Recognition.* **29**, 51–59, (1996).
8. T. Ojala, M. Pietikäinen, and T. Mäenpää, Multiresolution gray-scale and rotation invariant texture classification with local binary patterns, *IEEE Transactions on Pattern Analysis and Machine Intelligence.* **24**, 971–987, (2002).
9. P. Phillips, H. Moon, S. A. Rizvi, and P. J. Rauss, The FERET evaluation methodology for face-recognition algorithms, *IEEE Transactions on Pattern Analysis and Machine Intelligence.* **22**, 1090–1104, (2000).
10. G. Zhao and M. Pietikäinen, Dynamic texture recognition using local binary patterns with an application to facial expressions, *IEEE Transactions on Pattern Analysis and Machine Intelligence.* **29**(6), 915–928, (2007).
11. T. Ahonen, A. Hadid, and M. Pietikäinen. Face recognition with local binary patterns. In *8th European Conference on Computer Vision*, pp. 469–481 (May, 2004).
12. T. Ahonen, A. Hadid, and M. Pietikäinen, Face description with local binary patterns: Application to face recognition, *IEEE Transactions on Pattern Analysis and Machine Intelligence.* **28(12)**, 2037–2041, (2006).
13. T. Ahonen, M. Pietikäinen, A. Hadid, and T. Mäenpää. Face recognition based on the appearance of local regions. In *17th International Conference on Pattern Recognition*, vol. 3, pp. 153–156, (2004).
14. M. Turk and A. Pentland, Eigenfaces for recognition, *Journal of Cognitive Neuroscience.* **3**, 71–86, (1991).
15. B. Moghaddam, C. Nastar, and A. Pentland. A bayesian similarity measure for direct image matching. In *3th International Conference on Pattern Recognition*, vol. II, pp. 350–358, (1996).
16. B. S. Manjunath, J. R. Ohm, V. V. Vinod, and A. Yamada, Color and texture descriptors, *IEEE Trans. Circuits and Systems for Video Technology, Special Issue on MPEG-7.* **11**(6), 703–715 (Jun, 2001).
17. M. Varma and A. Zisserman. Texture classification: Are filter banks necessary? In *Proceedings of the IEEE Conference on Computer Vision and Pattern Recognition*, vol. 2, pp. 691–698 (Jun, 2003).
18. G. Zhang, X. Huang, S. Z. Li, Y. Wang, and X. Wu. Boosting local binary pattern LBP-based face recognition. In *Advances in Biometric Person Au-*

thentication: 5th Chinese Conference on Biometric Recognition, pp. 179–186, (2004).

19. X. Huang, S. Li, and Y. Wang. Jensen-Shannon boosting learning for object recognition. In *Proc. IEEE International Conference on Computer Vision and Pattern Recognition(CVPR 2005)*, pp. II: 144–149, (2005).
20. W. Zhang, S. Shan, W. Gao, X. Chen, and H. Zhang. Local gabor binary pattern histogram sequence (LGBPHS): A novel non-statistical model for face representation and recognition. In *Proceedings of the Tenth IEEE International Conference on Computer Vision (ICCV05)*, pp. 1:786–791, (2005).
21. S. Shan, W. Zhang, Y. Su, X. Chen, and W. Gao. Ensemble of piecewise FDA based on spatial histograms of local (gabor) binary patterns for face recognition. In *Proc. 18th International Conference on Pattern Recognition (ICPR 2006)*, pp. IV: 606–609, (2006).
22. Y. Rodriguez and S. Marcel. Face authentication using adapted local binary pattern histograms. In *Proc. 9th European Conference on Computer Vision (ECCV 2006), 2006*, pp. 321–332, (2006).
23. A. Hadid, M. Pietikäinen, and T. Ahonen. A discriminative feature space for detecting and recognizing faces. In *IEEE Conference on Computer Vision and Pattern Recognition*, vol. II, pp. 797–804, (2004).
24. V. Vapnik, Ed., *Statistical Learning Theory.* (Wiley, New York, 1998).
25. B. Heisele, T. Poggio, and M. Pontil. Face detection in still gray images. Technical Report 1687, Center for Biological and Computational Learning, MIT, (2000).
26. S. Z. Li and Z. Zhang, FloatBoost learning and statistical face detection, *IEEE Transactions on Pattern Analysis and Machine Intelligence.* **26**(9), 1112–1123, (2004).
27. V. Popovici, J.-P. Thiran, Y. Rodriguez, and S. Marcel. On performance evaluation of face detection and localization algorithms. In *Proc. 17th International Conference on Pattern Recognition (ICPR 2004)*, pp. 313–317, (2004).
28. H. Jin, Q. Liu, H. Lu, and X. Tong. Face detection using improved LBP under Bayesian framework. In *Third International Conference on Image and Graphics (ICIG 04)*, pp. 306–309, (2004).
29. H. Jin, Q. Liu, X. Tang, and H. Lu. Learning local descriptors for face detection. In *Proc. IEEE International Conference on Multimedia and Expo*, pp. 928– 931, (2005).
30. G. Heusch, Y. Rodriguez, and S. Marcel. Local binary patterns as an image preprocessing for face authentication. In *7th International Conference on Automatic Face and Gesture Recognition (FG2006)*, pp. 9–14, (2006).
31. J. Bassili, Emotion recognition: The role of facial movement and the relative importance of upper and lower areas of the face, *Journal of Personality and Social Psychology.* **37**, 2049–2059, (1979).
32. T. Kanade, J. F. Cohn, and Y. Tian. Comprehensive database for facial expression analysis. In *IEEE Int. Conf. on Automatic Face and Gesture Recognition*, pp. 46–53, (2000).
33. S. Aleksic and K. Katsaggelos. Automatic facial expression recognition us-

ing facial animation parameters and multi-stream HMMs. In *IEEE Trans. Information Forensics and Security.* **1**(1), 3–11, (2006).
34. M. Yeasin, B. Bullot, and R. Sharma. From facial expression to level of interest: A spatio-temporal approach. In *Proc. Conf. Computer Vision and Pattern Recognition*, pp. 922–927, (2004).
35. Y. Tian. Evaluation of face resolution for expression analysis. In *Proc. IEEE Workshop on Face Processing in Video*, (2004).
36. G. Littlewort, M. Bartlett, I. Fasel, J. Susskind, and J. Movellan. Dynamics of facial expression extracted automatically from video. In *Proc. IEEE Workshop Face Processing in Video*, (2004).
37. M. Bartlett, G. Littlewort, I. Fasel, and R. Movellan. Real time face detection and facial expression recognition: Development and application to human computer interaction. In *Proc. CVPR Workshop on Computer Vision and Pattern Recognition for Human-Computer Interaction*, (2003).
38. X. Feng, M. Pietikäinen, and A. Hadid, Facial expression recognition with local binary patterns and linear programming, *Pattern Recognition and Image Analysis.* **15**(2), 546–548, (2005).
39. C. Shan, S. Gong, and P. W. McOwan. Robust facial expression recognition using local binary patterns. In *Proc. IEEE International Conference on Image Processing (ICIP 2005)*, Vol. 2, pp. 370–373, (2005).
40. C. Shan, S. Gong, and P. McOwan. Conditional mutual infomation based boosting for facial expression recognition. In *Proc. of British Machine Vision Conference*, (2005).
41. S. Z. Li, R. Chu, S. Liao, and L. Zhang, Illumination invariant face recognition using near-infrared images, *IEEE Trans. Pattern Analysis and Machine Intelligence.* **29**(4), 627–639, (2007).
42. N. Sun, W. Zheng, C. Sun, C. Zou, and L. Zhao. Gender classification based on boosting local binary pattern. In *Proc. 3rd International Symposium on Neural Networks (ISNN 2006)*, pp. 194–201, (2006).
43. Z. Sun, T. Tan, and X. Qiu. Graph matching iris image blocks with local binary pattern. In *Proc. International Conference on Biometrics(ICB 2006)*, pp. 366–373, (2006).
44. B. Ma, W. Zhang, S. Shan, X. Chen, and W. Gao. Robust head pose estimation using LGBP. In *Proc. 18th International Conference on Pattern Recognition (ICPR 2006)*, pp. II: 512–515, (2006).
45. S. Li, C. Zhao, X. Zhu, and Z. Lei. Learning to fuse 3D + 2D based face recognition at both feature and decision levels. In *Proc. of IEEE International Workshop on Analysis and Modeling of Faces and Gestures (AMFG 2005)*, pp. 44–54, (2005).
46. X. Huang, S. Z. Li, and Y. Wang. Shape localization based on statistical method using extended local binary pattern. In *Proc. Third International Conference on Image and Graphics (ICIG 04)*, pp. 184–187, (2004).
47. S. Marcel, J. Keomany, and Y. Rodriguez. Robust-to-illumination face localisation using active shape models and local binary patterns. Technical Report IDIAP-RR 47, IDIAP Research Institute (July, 2006).
48. R. Gross and J. Shi. The CMU Motion of Body (MoBo) database. Technical Report CMU-RI-TR-01-18, Robotics Institute, CMU (June, 2001).

Chapter 13

A Galaxy of Texture Features

Xianghua Xie and Majid Mirmehdi
Department of Computer Science, University of Bristol
Bristol BS8 1UB, England
E-mail: {xie,majid}@cs.bris.ac.uk

The aim of this chapter is to give experienced and new practitioners in image analysis and computer vision an overview and a quick reference to the "galaxy" of features that exist in the field of texture analysis. Clearly, given the limited space, only a corner of this vast galaxy is covered here! Firstly, a brief taxonomy of texture analysis approaches is outlined. Then, a list of widely used texture features is presented in alphabetical order. Finally, a brief comparison of texture features and feature extraction methods based on several literature surveys is given.

13.1. Introduction

The aim of this chapter is to give the reader a comprehensive overview of texture features. This area is so diversive that it is impossible to cover it fully in this limited space. Thus only a list of widely used texture features is presented here. However, before that, we will first look at how these features can be used in texture analysis. With reference to several survey papers,[1–6] we categorise these texture features into four families: statistical features, structural features, signal processing based features, and model based features. It is worth noting that this categorisation is not a crisp classification. There are techniques that generate new features from two or more of these categories for texture analysis, e.g. Ref. 7 applies statistical co-occurrence measurements on wavelet transformed detail images. At the end of this chapter, a very brief comparison of texture features and feature extraction methods will be given based on several literature surveys.

13.1.1. *Statistical features* ♠

Statistical texture features measure the spatial distribution of pixel values. They are well rooted in the computer vision literature and have been extensively applied to various tasks. Texture features are computed based on the statistical distribution of image intensities at specified relative pixel positions. A large number of these features have been proposed, ranging from first order statistics to higher order statistics depending on the number of pixels for each observation.

The image histogram is a first order statistical feature that is not only computationaly simple, but also rotation and translation invariant; it is thus commonly used in various vision applications, e.g. image indexing and retrieval. Second order statistics examine the relationship between a pair of pixels across the image domain, for example through autocorrelation. One of the most well-known second order statistical features for texture analysis is the co-occurrence matrix.[8] Several statistics, such as energy and entropy, can be derived from the co-occurrence matrix to characterise textures. Higher order statistical features explore pixel relationships beyond pixel pairs and they are generally less sensitive to image noise.[9,10] The Gray level run length[11] and local binary patterns (LBP)[12] can also be considered higher order statistical features.

13.1.2. *Structural features* ♡

From the structural point of view, texture is characterised by *texture primitives* or texture elements, and the spatial arrangement of these primitives.[4] Thus, the primary goals of structural approaches are firstly to extract texture primitives, and secondly to model or generalise the spatial placement rules. The texture primitive can be as simple as individual pixels, a region with uniform graylevels, or line segments. The placement rules can be obtained through modelling geometric relationships between primitives or learning their statistical properties.

A few example works are as follows. Zucker[13] proposed that natural textures can be treated as ideal patterns that have undergone certain transformations. The placement rule is defined by a graph that is isomorphic to a regular or semi-regular tessellation which is transformable to generate variant natural textures. Fu[14] considered a texture as a string of a language defined by a tree grammar which defines the spatial placement rules, and its terminal symbols are the texture primitives that can be individual pixels, connected or isolated. Marr[15] proposed a symbolic description, the primal sketch, to represent spatial texture features, such as edges, blobs, and bars. In Ref. 16, Julesz introduced the concept of textons as fundamental image structures, such as elongated blobs, bars, crosses, and terminators (more details later in this chapter). The textons were considered as atoms of pre-attentive human visual perception. The idea of describing texture using local image patches and placement rules has also been practiced in texture synthesis, e.g. Ref. 17.

13.1.3. *Signal processing based features* ◇

Most signal processing based features are commonly extracted by applying filter banks to the image and computing the energy of the filter responses. These features can be derived from the spatial domain, the frequency domain, and the joint spatial/spatial-frequency domain.

In the spatial domain, the images are usually filtered by gradient filters to extract edges, lines, isolated dots, etc. Sobel, Robert, Laplacian, Laws filters have been routinely used as a precursor to measuring edge density. In Ref. 18, Malik and Perona used a bank of differences of offset Gaussian function filters to model pre-attentive texture perception in human vision. Ade [19] proposed eigenfilters, a set of masks obtained from the Karhunen-Lóeve (KL) transform [20] of local image patches, for texture representation.

Many other features are derived by applying filtering in the frequency domain, particularly when the associated kernel in the spatial domain is difficult to obtain. The image is transformed into the Fourier domain, multiplied with the filter function and then re-transformed into the spatial domain saving on the spatial convolution operation. Ring and wedge filters are some of the most commonly used frequency domain filters, e.g. Ref. 21. D'Astous and Jernigan [22] used peak features, such as strength and area, and power distribution features, such as power spectrum eigenvalues and circularity, to discriminate textures.

The Fourier transform has relatively poor spatial resolution, as Fourier coefficients depend on the entire image. The classical way of introducing spatial dependency into Fourier analysis is through the windowed Fourier transform. If the window function is Gaussian, the windowed Fourier transform becomes the well-known Gabor transform. Psychophysiological findings of multi-channel, frequency and orientation analysis in the human vision system have strongly motivated the use of Gabor analysis, along with other multiscale techniques. Turner [23] and Clark and Bovik [24] first proposed the use of Gabor filters in texture analysis.

Carrying similar properties to the Gabor transform, wavelet transform representations have also been widely used for texture analysis, e.g. Refs. 25, 7, 26 and 27. Wavelet analysis uses approximating functions that are localised in both spatial and spatial-frequency domain. The input signal is considered as the weighted sum of overlapping wavelet functions, scaled and shifted. These functions are generated from a basic wavelet (or mother wavelet) by dilation and translation.

Dyadic transformation is one of the most commonly used, however, its frequency and orientation selection are rather coarse. Wavelet packet decomposition,[28] as a generalisation of the discrete wavelet transform, is one of the extensions to improve the selectivity where at each stage of the transform, the signal is split into low-pass and high-pass orthogonal components. The low-pass is an approximation of the input signal, while the high-pass contains the missing signals from the approximation. Finer frequency selectivity can be further obtained by dropping the constraints of orthogonal decomposition.

13.1.4. *Model based features* ♣

Model based methods include, among many others, fractal models,[29] autoregressive models,[30,31] random field models,[32] and the epitome model.[33] They generally use stochastic and generative models to represent images, with the estimated model parameters as texture features for texture analysis.

The fractal model is based on the observation of self-similarity and has been found useful in modelling natural textures. Fractal dimension and lacunarity are the two most popular fractal features. However, this model is generally considered not suitable for representing local image structures. Random field models, including autoregressive models, assume that local information is sufficient to achieve a good global image representation. One of the major challenges is to efficiently estimate the model parameters. The establishment of the equivalence between Markov random fields and Gibbs distributions provided tractable statistical analysis using random field theories. Recently, Jojic *et al.*[33] proposed a generative model called *epitome* which is a miniature of the original image and extracts its essential textural and shape characteristics. This model also relies on the local neighbourhood.

13.2. Texture Features and Feature Extraction Methods

In this section, a number of of commonly used texture features are presented in alphabetical order. Additionally, we also outline several feature extraction methods. Each feature or feature extraction method has one or more symbols noted after it signifying which typical feature categories it can be associated with. The symbol ♠ denotes a statistical approach, ♡ denotes a structural approach, ◇ represents a signal processing approach, and ♣ represents a model based approach. In what follows $\mathbf{I}$ denotes a $w \times h$ image in which individual pixels are addressed by $\mathbf{I}(x, y)$, however, when convenient, other appropriate terminology may also be used.

(1) **Autocorrelation** (♠ − −−)
The autocorrelation feature is derived based on the observation that some textures are repetitive in nature, such as textiles. It measures the correlation between the image itself and the image translated with a displacement vector, $\mathbf{d} = (dx, dy)$ as:

$$\rho(\mathbf{d}) = \frac{\sum_{x=0}^{w} \sum_{y=0}^{h} \mathbf{I}(x, y)\mathbf{I}(x + dx, y + dy)}{\sum_{x=0}^{w} \sum_{y=0}^{h} \mathbf{I}^2(x, y)}. \tag{13.1}$$

Textures with strong regularity will exhibit peaks and valleys in the autocorrelation measure. This second order statistic is clearly sensitive to noise interference. Higher order statistics, e.g. Refs. 34 and 10, have been investigated, for example, Huang and Chan[10] used fourth-order cumulants to extract harmonic peaks and demonstrated the method's ability to localise defects in textile images.

(2) **Autoregressive** model (− − −♣)
The autoregressive model is usually considered as an instance of the Markov Random Field model. Similar to autocorrelation, autoregressive models also exploit the linear dependency among image pixels. The basic autoregressive model for texture analysis can be formulated as:[30]

$$g(\mathbf{s}) = \mu + \sum_{\mathbf{d}\in\Omega} \theta(\mathbf{d})g(\mathbf{s} + \mathbf{d}) + \varepsilon(\mathbf{s}), \tag{13.2}$$

where $g(\mathbf{s})$ is the gray level value of a pixel at site $\mathbf{s}$ in image $\mathbf{I}$, $\mathbf{d}$ is the displacement vector, θ is a set of model parameters, μ is the bias that depends on the mean intensity of the image, $\varepsilon(\mathbf{s})$ is the model error term, and Ω is the set of neighbouring pixels at site $\mathbf{s}$. A commonly used second order neighbourhood is a pixel's 8-neighbourhood. These model parameters can be considered as a characterisation of a texture, thus, can be used as texture features.
Autoregressive models have been applied to texture synthesis,[35] texture segmentation,[1] and texture classification.[30] Selection of the neighbourhood size is one of the main design issues in autoregressive models. Multiresolution methods have been used to alleviate the associated difficulties, such as in Ref. 30.

(3) **Co-occurrence matrices** (♠ − −−)
Spatial graylevel co-occurrence matrices (GLCM)[8] are one of the most well-known and widely used texture features. These second order statistics are accumulated into a set of 2D matrices, $\mathbf{P}(r, s|\mathbf{d})$, each of which measures the spatial dependency of two graylevels, r and s, given a displacement vector

$\mathbf{d} = (d, \theta) = (dx, dy)$. The number of occurrences (frequencies) of r and s, separated by distance $\mathbf{d}$, contributes the (r, s)th entry in the co-occurrence matrix $\mathbf{P}(r, s|\mathbf{d})$. A co-occurrence matrix is given as:

$$\mathbf{P}(r, s|\mathbf{d}) = \|\{((x_1, y_1), (x_2, y_2)) : \mathbf{I}(x_1, y_1) = r, \mathbf{I}(x_2, y_2) = s\}\| \qquad (13.3)$$

where $(x_1, y_1), (x_2, y_2) \in w \times h$, $(x_2, y_2) = (x_1 \pm dx, y_1 \pm dy)$ and $\|.\|$ is the cardinality of a set. Texture features, such as energy, entropy, contrast, homogeneity, and correlation, are then derived from the co-occurrence matrix. Example successful applications on texture analysis using co-occurrence features can be found in Refs. 8, 36 and 37.

Co-occurrence matrix features can suffer from a number of shortcomings. It appears there is no generally accepted solution for optimising $\mathbf{d}$.[6,38] The number of graylevels is usually reduced in order to keep the size of the co-occurrence matrix manageable. It is also important to ensure the number of entries of each matrix is adequate to be statistically reliable. For a given displacement vector, a large number of features can be computed, which implies dedicated feature selection procedures.

(4) **Difference of Gaussians filter** $(- - \diamond -)$

This is the one of the most common filtering techniques to extract texture features. Smoothing an image using different Gaussian kernels followed by computing their difference is used to highlight image features, such as edges at different scales. As Gaussian smoothing is low pass filtering, difference of Gaussians is thus effectively band pass filtering. Its kernel (see Fig. 13.1) can be simply defined as:

$$DoG = G_{\sigma_1} - G_{\sigma_2}, \qquad (13.4)$$

where G_{σ_1} and G_{σ_2} are two different Gaussian kernels. Difference of Gaussians is often used as an approximation of Laplacian of Gaussian. By varying σ_1 and σ_2, we can extract textural features at particular spatial frequencies. Note this filter is not orientation selective. Example applications can be found in the scale-space primal sketch[39] and SIFT feature selection.[40]

(5) **Difference of offset Gaussians filters** $(- - \diamond -)$

This is another simple filtering technique which provides useful texture features, such as edge orientation and strength. Similar to difference of Gaussians filters, the filter kernel is obtained by subtracting two Gaussian functions. However, the centre of these two Gaussian functions are displaced by a vector $\mathbf{d} = (dx, dy)$:

$$DooG_\sigma(x, y) = G_\sigma(x, y) - G_\sigma(x + dx, y + dy). \qquad (13.5)$$

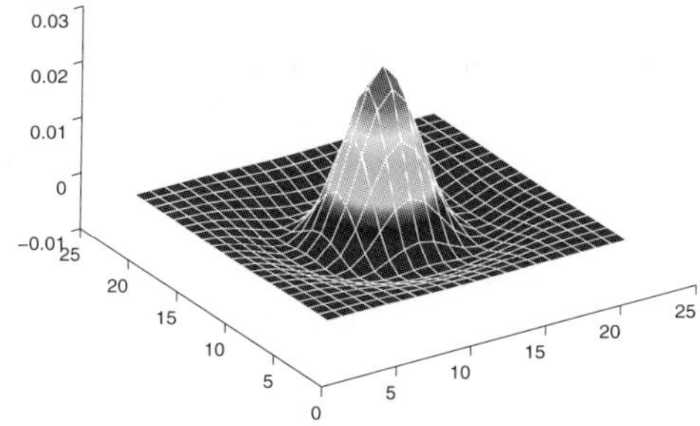

Fig. 13.1. 3D visualisation of a difference of Gaussians filter kernel.

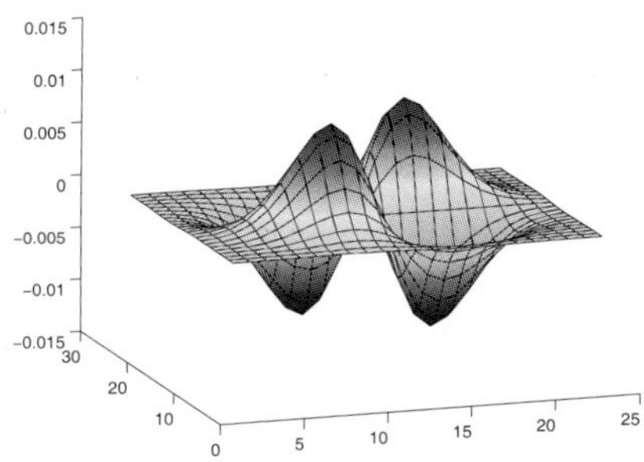

Fig. 13.2. 3D visualisation of a difference of offset Gaussian filters kernel.

Figure 13.2 shows an example difference of offset Gaussians filter kernel in 3D. For an example application of these filters to texture analysis see Ref. 18.

(6) **Derivative of Gaussian filters** (– – ◇–)

Edge orientation or texture directionality is one of the most important cues to understand textures. Derivative filters, particularly derivative of Gaussian filters, are commonly applied to highlight texture features at different orientations. By varying their kernel bandwidth, these filters can also selectively highlight texture features at different scales. Given a Gaussian function $G_\sigma(x, y)$, its first derivatives in x and y directions are:

$$D_x(x, y) = -\frac{x}{\sigma^2} G_\sigma(x, y), \quad D_y(x, y) = -\frac{y}{\sigma^2} G_\sigma(x, y). \tag{13.6}$$

Convolving an image with Gaussian derivative kernels is equivalent to smoothing the image using a Gaussian kernel and then computing its derivatives. These oriented filters have been widely used in texture analysis, for example in Refs. 41 and 42. Also see "Steerable filter".

(7) **Eigenfilter** (– – ♢–)
Most filters used for texture analysis are non-adaptive, i.e. the filters are pre-defined and often not directly associated with the textures. However, the eigenfilter, first introduced to texture analysis by Ade,[19] is an exception. Eigenfilters are considered adaptive as they are data dependent and they can highlight the dominant features of the textures. The filters are usually generated through the KL transform. In Ref. 19, the eigenfilters are extracted from autocorrelation functions. Let $\mathbf{I}^{(x,y)}$ be the original image without any displacement, and $\mathbf{I}^{(x+n,y)}$ be the shifted image along the x direction by n pixel(s). For example, if n takes a maximum value of 2, the eigenvectors and eigenvalues are computed from this 9×9 autocorrelation matrix:

$$\begin{bmatrix} E[\mathbf{I}^{(x,y)}\mathbf{I}^{(x,y)}] & \dots & E[\mathbf{I}^{(x,y+2)}\mathbf{I}^{(x,y)}] & \dots & E[\mathbf{I}^{(x+2,y+2)}\mathbf{I}^{(x,y)}] \\ \vdots & & \vdots & & \vdots \\ E[\mathbf{I}^{(x,y+2)}\mathbf{I}^{(x,y)}] & \dots & E[\mathbf{I}^{(x,y+2)}\mathbf{I}^{(x,y+2)}] & \dots & E[\mathbf{I}^{(x,y+2)}\mathbf{I}^{(x+2,y+2)}] \\ \vdots & & \vdots & & \vdots \\ E[\mathbf{I}^{(x+2,y+2)}\mathbf{I}^{(x,y)}] & \dots & E[\mathbf{I}^{(x+2,y+2)}\mathbf{I}^{(x,y+2)}] & \dots & E[\mathbf{I}^{(x+2,y+2)}\mathbf{I}^{(x+2,y+2)}] \end{bmatrix}, \tag{13.7}$$

where $E[.]$ denotes expectation. The 9×1 eigenvectors are rearranged in the spatial domain resulting in 3×3 eigenfilters. The number of eigenfilters selected can be determined by thresholding the sum of eigenvalues. The filtered images, usually referred to as basis images, can be used to reconstruct the original image. Due to their orthogonality, they are considered as an optimised representation of the image. Example applications can be found in Refs. 19 and 43.

(8) **Eigenregion** (♠♡ – –)
Eigenregions are geometrical features that encompass area, location, and shape properties of an image.[44] They are generated based on image prior-segmentation and principal component analysis. The images are firstly segmented and the regions within are downsampled to much smaller patches, such as 5×5. Then principal components are obtained from these simplified image regions and used for image classification. A similar approach has been presented in Ref. 45 for image segmentation.

(9) **Epitome model** (– – –♣)
The epitome, described in Ref. 33, is a small, condensed representation of a given image containing its primitive shapes and textural elements. The mapping from the epitome to its original pixels is hidden, and several images may share the same epitome by varying the hidden mapping. In this model, raw pixel values are used to characterise textural and colour prop-

Fig. 13.3. Epitome - from left: Original colour image, its 32 × 32 epitome, and its 16 × 16 epitome (generated with the software provided by the authors in Ref. 33).

erties, (e.g. instead of filtering responses). The epitome is derived using a generative model. It is assumed that image patches from the original image are produced from the epitome by copying pixel values from it with added Gaussian noise. Thus, as a learning process various sizes of patches from the image are taken and are forced into the epitome, a much smaller image, by examining the best possible match. The epitome is then updated accordingly when new image patches are sampled. This process iteratively continues until the epitome is stabilised. Figure 13.3 shows an example image and two epitomes at different sizes. We can see that the epitomes are relatively compact representations of the image.

The authors of the epitome model have demonstrated its ability in texture segmentation, image denoising, and image inpainting.[33] Stauffer[46] also used epitomes to measure the similarity between pixels and patches to perform image segmentation. Cheung *et al.*[47] further extended the epitome model for video analysis.

(10) **Fractal model** (− − −♣)

Fractals, initially proposed by Mandelbrot,[29] are geometric primitives that are self-similar and irregular in nature. Fragments of a fractal object are exact or statistical copies of the whole object and they can match the whole by stretching and shifting. Fractal dimension is one of the most important features in the fractal model as a measure of complexity or irregularity. Pentland[48] used the Fourier power spectral density to estimate the fractal dimension for image segmentation. The image intensity is modelled as 3D fractal Brownian motion surfaces. Gangepain and Roques-Carmes[49] proposed the

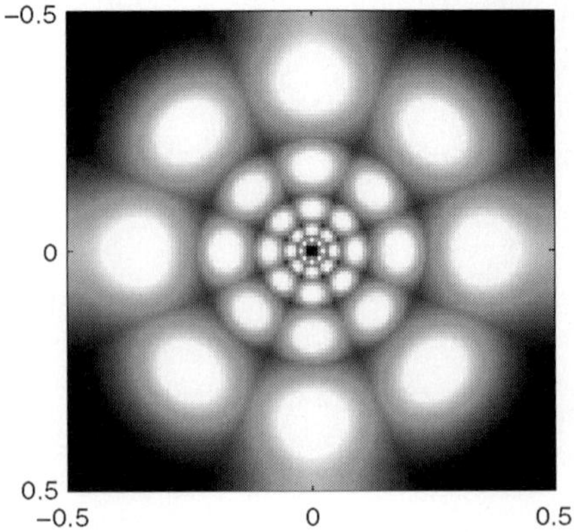

Fig. 13.4. The frequency response of the dyadic bank of Gabor filters. The maximum amplitude response over all filters is plotted. Each filter is represented by one centre-symmetric pair of lobes. The axes are in normalised spatial frequencies (reproduced with permission from Ref. 56).

box-counting method which was later improved by Voss [50] and Keller *et al.*[51] Super and Bovik[52] proposed the use of Gabor filters to estimate the fractal dimension in textured images. Lacunarity is another important measurement in fractal models. It measures the structural variation or inhomogeneity and can be calculated using the gliding-box algorithm.[53]

(11) **Gabor filters** ($- - \diamond -$)

Gabor filters are used to model the spatial summation properties of simple cells in the visual cortex and have been adapted and popularly used in texture analysis, for example see Refs. 23, 24, 54 and 55. They have been long considered as one of the most effective filtering techniques to extract useful texture features at different orientations and scales. Gabor filters can be categorised into two components: a real part as the symmetric component and an imaginary part as the asymmetric component. The 2D Gabor function can be mathematically formulated as:

$$G(x, y) = \frac{1}{2\pi\sigma_x\sigma_y} \exp\left[-\frac{1}{2}\left(\frac{x^2}{\sigma_x^2} + \frac{y^2}{\sigma_y^2}\right)\right] \exp(2\pi j u_0 x), \qquad (13.8)$$

where σ_x and σ_y define the Gaussian envelope along the x and y directions respectively, u_0 denotes the radial frequency of the Gabor function, and $j = \sqrt{-1}$. Figure 13.4 shows the frequency response of the dyadic Gabor filter bank with the centre frequencies $\{2^{-\frac{11}{2}}, 2^{-\frac{9}{2}}, 2^{-\frac{7}{2}}, 2^{-\frac{5}{2}}, 2^{-\frac{3}{2}}\}$, and orientations $\{0°, 45°, 90°, 135°\}$.[56]

(12) **Gaussian Markov random field (GMRF)** – see "Random field models".

(13) **Gaussian pyramid features** $(- - \diamond -)$

Extracting features in multiscale is an efficient way of analysing image texture. The Gaussian pyramid is one of the simplest multiscale transforms. Let us denote $\mathbf{I}^{(n)}$ as the nth level image of the pyramid, l as the total number of levels, and $S^{\downarrow}$ as the down-sampling operator. We then have

$$\mathbf{I}^{(n+1)} = S^{\downarrow} G_{\sigma}(\mathbf{I}^{(n)}), \qquad \forall n, n = 1, 2, ..., l-1, \tag{13.9}$$

where G_{σ} denotes the Gaussian convolution. The finest scale layer is the original image, $\mathbf{I}^{(1)} = \mathbf{I}$. As each level is a low pass filter version of the previous level, the low frequency information is repeatedly represented in the Gaussian pyramid.

(14) **Gray level difference matrix** $(\spadesuit - --)$

Gray level difference statistics are considered a subset of the co-occurrence matrix.[57] They are based on the distribution of pixel pairs separated by $\mathbf{d} = (dx, dy)$ and having gray level difference k, and represented as:

$$\mathbf{P}(k|\mathbf{d}) = \|\{((x_1, y_1), (x_2, y_2)) : |\mathbf{I}(x_1, y_1) - \mathbf{I}(x_2, y_2)| = k\}\|, \tag{13.10}$$

where $(x_2, y_2) = (x_1 \pm dx, y_1 \pm dy)$. Various properties then can be extracted from this matrix, such as angular second moment, contrast, entropy, and mean, for texture analysis purposes.

(15) **Gibbs random field** – see "'Random field models'

(16) **Histogram features** $(\spadesuit - --)$

Commonly used histogram features include range, mean, geometric mean, harmonic mean, standard deviation, variance, and median. Despite their simplicity, histogram techniques have proved their worth as a low cost, low level approach in various applications, such as Ref. 58. They are invariant to translation and rotation, and insensitive to the exact spatial distribution of the colour pixels. Table 13.1 lists some similarity measurements of two distributions, where r_i and s_i are the number of events in bin i for the first and second datasets, respectively, $\overline{r}$ and $\overline{s}$ are the mean values, n is the total number of bins, and $r_{(i)}$ and $s_{(i)}$ denote the sorted (ascending order) indices. Note EMD is the Earth Mover's Distance.

(17) **Laplacian of Gaussian** $(- - \diamond -)$

Laplacian of Gaussian is another simple but useful multiscale image transformation. The transformed data contains basic but also useful texture features. The 2D Laplacian of Gaussian with zero mean and Gaussian standard

Table 13.1. Some histogram similarity measurements.

Measurement	Formula
L_1 norm	$L_1 = \sum_{i=1}^{n} \lvert r_i - s_i \rvert$
L_2 norm	$L_2 = \sqrt{\sum_{i=1}^{n} (r_i - s_i)^2}$
Mallows or EMD distance	$M_p = \left(\frac{1}{n} \sum_{i=1}^{n} \lvert r_{(i)} - s_{(i)} \rvert^p\right)^{1/p}$
Bhattacharyya distance	$B = -\ln \sum_{i=1}^{n} \sqrt{r_i s_i}$
Matusita distance	$M = \sqrt{\sum_{i=1}^{n} (\sqrt{r_i} - \sqrt{s_i})^2}$
Divergence	$D = \sum_{i=1}^{n} \left((r_i - s_i) \ln \frac{r_i}{s_i}\right)$
Histogram intersection	$H = \frac{\sum_{i=1}^{n} \min(r_i, s_i)}{\sum_{i=1}^{n} r_i}$
Chi-square	$\chi^2 = \sum_{i=1}^{n} \frac{(r_i - s_i)^2}{r_i + s_i}$
Normalised correlation coefficient	$r = \frac{\sum_{i=1}^{n} (r_i - \bar{r})(s_i - \bar{s})}{\sqrt{\sum_{i=1}^{n} (r_i - \bar{r})^2} \sqrt{\sum_{i=1}^{n} (s_i - \bar{s})^2}}$

deviation σ is defined as:

$$LoG_{\sigma}(x, y) = -\frac{1}{\pi\sigma^4}\left[1 - \frac{x^2 + y^2}{2\sigma^2}\right] e^{-\frac{x^2+y^2}{2\sigma^2}}. \qquad (13.11)$$

Figure 13.5 plots a 3D visualisation of such a function. Laplacian of Gaussian calculates the second spatial derivative of an image, and is closely related to the difference of Gaussians function. It is often used in low level feature extraction, e.g. Ref. 59.

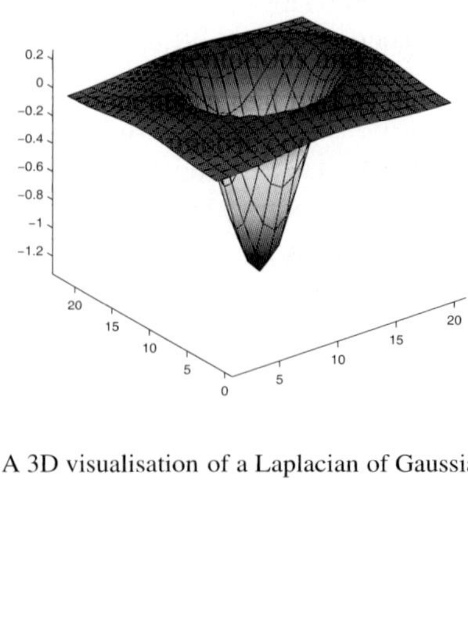

Fig. 13.5. A 3D visualisation of a Laplacian of Gaussian filter kernel.

(18) **Laplacian pyramid** ($- - \diamond -$)

Decomposing an image so that redundant information is minimised and characteristic features are thus preserved and highlighted is a common way of analysing textures. The Laplacian pyramid was applied by Burt and Adelson[60] to image compression to remove redundancy. Compared to the Gaussian pyramid, the Laplacian pyramid is a more compact representation. Each level of a Laplacian pyramid contains the difference between a low pass filtered version and an upsampled "predication" from coarser level, e.g.:

$$\mathbf{I}_L^{(n)} = \mathbf{I}_G^{(n)} - S \uparrow \mathbf{I}_G^{(n+1)}, \tag{13.12}$$

where $\mathbf{I}_L^{(n)}$ denotes the nth level in a Laplacian pyramid, $\mathbf{I}_G^{(n)}$ denotes the nth level in a Gaussian pyramid of the same image, and $S \uparrow$ represents upsampling using nearest neighbours.

(19) **Laws operators** ($\spadesuit - \diamond -$)

These texture energy measures were developed by Laws[61] and are considered as one of the first filtering approaches to texture analysis. The Laws texture energy measures are computed first by applying a bank of separable filters, followed by a nonlinear local window based transform. The most commonly used five element kernels are as follows:

$$\begin{array}{lclrrrrrl} L5 & = & [& 1 & 4 & 6 & 4 & 1 &] \\ E5 & = & [& -1 & -2 & 0 & 2 & 1 &] \\ S5 & = & [& -1 & 0 & 2 & 0 & -1 &] \\ W5 & = & [& -1 & 2 & 0 & -2 & 1 &] \\ R5 & = & [& 1 & -4 & 6 & -4 & 1 &], \end{array} \tag{13.13}$$

where the initial letters denote Level, Edge, Spot, Wave, and Ripple, respectively. From these five 1D operators, a total of 25 2D Laws operators can be generated by convolving a vertical 1D kernel with a horizontal 1D kernel, for example convolving the vertical L5 with a horizontal W5.

(20) **Local binary patterns (LBP)** ($\spadesuit\heartsuit - -$)

The LBP operator was first introduced by Ojala *et al.*[12] as a shift invariant complementary measure for local image contrast. It uses the graylevel of the centre pixel of a sliding window as a threshold for surrounding neighbourhood pixels. Its value is given as a weighted sum of thresholded neighbouring pixels.

$$\mathcal{L}_{P,R} = \sum_{p=0}^{P-1} sign(g_p - g_c) 2^p, \tag{13.14}$$

where g_c and g_p are the graylevels of centre pixel and neighbourhood pixels respectively, P is the total number of neighbourhood pixels, R denotes the radius, and $sign(.)$ is a sign function such that

$$sign(x) = \begin{cases} 1 \text{ if } x \geq 0 \\ 0 \text{ otherwise.} \end{cases} \tag{13.15}$$

Figure 13.6 shows an eight-neighbours LBP calculation. A simple local contrast measurement, $C_{P,R}$, is derived from the difference between the average gray levels of pixels brighter than centre pixel and those darker then centre pixel, i.e. $C_{P,R} = \sum_{p=0}^{P-1}(sign(g_p - g_c)g_p/M - sign(g_c - g_p)g_p/(P - M))$ where M denote the number of pixels that brighter than the centre pixel. It is calculated as a complement to the LBP value in order to characterise local spatial relationships, together called LBP/C.[12] Two-dimensional distributions of the LBP and local contrast measures are used as texture features.

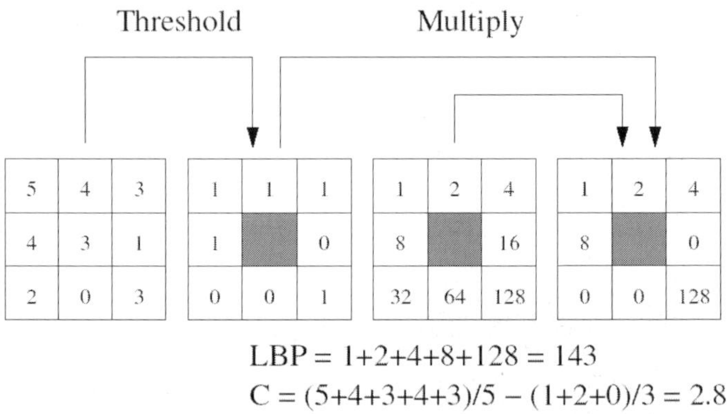

Fig. 13.6. Calculating LBP code and a contrast measure (*reproduced with permission from Ref. 62*).

The LBP operator, with a radial symmetric neighbourhood, is invariant with respect to changes in illumination and image rotation (for example, compared to co-occurrence matrices), and computationally simple.[62] Ojala *et al.* demonstrated good performance for LBP in texture classification.

(21) **Markov random field (MRF)** – see "Random field models".

(22) **Oriented pyramid** (– – ◇–)

An oriented pyramid decomposes an image into several scales and different orientations. Unlike the Laplacian pyramid where there is no orientation information in each scale, in an oriented pyramid each scale represents textural energy at a particular direction. One way of generating an orientated pyramid is by applying derivative filters to a Gaussian pyramid or directional filters to a Laplacian pyramid, i.e. further decompose each scale. For an example of an oriented pyramid see Ref. 63. Also see "Steerable pyramids".

(23) **Power spectrum** $(- - \diamond -)$

The power spectrum depicts the energy distribution in the frequency domain. It is commonly generated using the discrete form of the Fourier transform: [64]

$$F(u, v) = \sum_{x=0}^{w-1} \sum_{y=0}^{h-1} \mathbf{I}(x, y) e^{-2\pi i (\frac{ux}{w} + \frac{vy}{h})}. \tag{13.16}$$

Then the power spectrum is obtained by computing the complex modulus (magnitude) of the Fourier transform, i.e. $P(u, v) = |F(u, v)|^2$. The radial distribution of energy in the power spectrum reflects the coarseness of the texture, and the angular distribution relates to the directionality. For example in Figure 13.7 the horizontal orientation of the texture features is reflected in the vertical energy distribution in the spectrum image. Thus, one can use these energy distributions to characterise textures. Commonly used techniques include applying ring filters, wedge filters, and peak extraction algorithms.

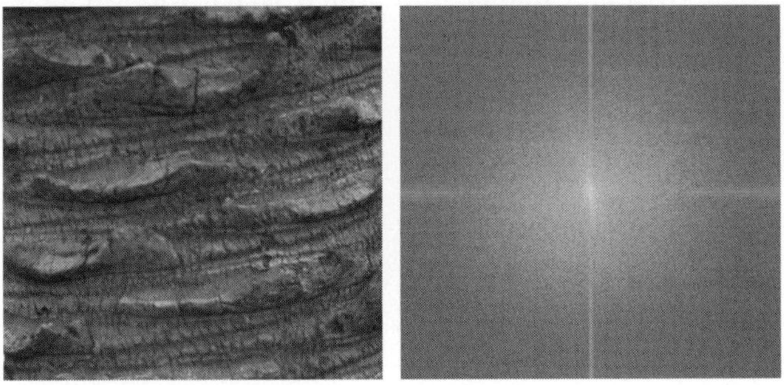

Fig. 13.7. Power spectrum image of a texture image - from left: the original image, and its Fourier spectrum image from which texture features can be computed.

(24) **Primal sketch** $(-\heartsuit - \clubsuit)$

Primal sketch attempts to extract distinctive image primitives as well as describe their spatial reletionship. Its concept was first introduced by Marr [65] as a symbolic representation of an image. It is considered as a representation of image primitives or textons, such as bars, edges, blobs, and terminators. An image primitive extraction process is usually necessary, followed by a process of pursuing the sketch. Then, statistics, such as amount of different types of primitives, element orientation, distribution of size parameters, distribution of contrast of primitives, and spatial density of elements, can be

Fig. 13.8. An example of "primal sketch" - from left: The original image and its primal sketch with each element represented by a bar or a circle (images reproduced with permission from Ref. 67).

extracted from the primal sketch for texture analysis.[66] Recently in Ref. 67, Guo *et al.* integrated sparse coding theory and the MRF concept as a primal sketch. The image was divided into sketchable regions, modelled using sparse coding, and non-sketchable regions, where the MRF based model was adopted. Textons were collected from the sketchable parts of the image. Figure 13.8 gives an example of a primal sketch with each element represented by bar or circles.

(25) **Radon transform** ($\spadesuit - - -$)

The Radon transform is an integral of a function over a set of all lines. A 2D Radon transform of an image $\mathbf{I}(x, y)$ can be defined as:

$$R[\mathbf{I}(x,y)](\rho,\theta) = \sum_{x}\sum_{y} \mathbf{I}(x,y)\delta(\rho - x\cos\theta - y\sin\theta), \qquad (13.17)$$

where θ is the angle between a line and the y-axis and ρ is the perpendicular distance of that line from the origin, which is the centre of the image. It can be used to detect linear trends in an image.[68] Thus, directional textures will exhibit "hot spots" in their Radon transform space. In Ref. 68, the Radon transform was used to find the dominant texture orientation which was later compensated to achieve rotational invariancy in texture classification. An example of the Radon transform of a texture is given in Fig. 13.9. The Radon transform is closely related to the Fourier, Hough, and Trace transforms.

(26) **Random field models** ($- - - \clubsuit$)

Markov Random Field (MRF) is a conditional probability model which provides a convenient way to model local spatial interactions among entities such as pixels. The establishment of the equivalence between MRFs and Gibbs distribution provided tractable means for statistical analysis as Gibbs distribution takes a much simpler form. Since then, MRFs have been applied

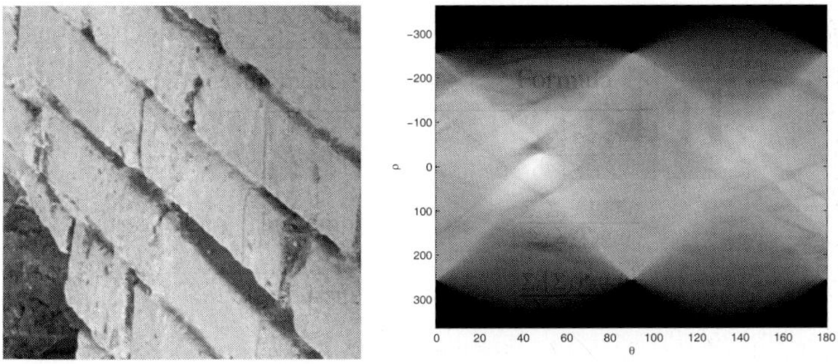

Fig. 13.9. An example of the Radon transform - from left: Original image and a visualisation of its Random transform.

to various applications, including texture synthesis[69] and texture classification.[35]

In MRF models, an image is represented by a finite rectangular lattice within which each pixel is considered as a site. Neighbouring sites then form cliques and their relationships are modelled in the neighbourhood system. Let the image **I** be represented by a finite rectangular $M \times N$ lattice $\mathcal{S} = \{s = (i, j) | 1 \leq i \leq M, 1 \leq j \leq N\}$, where s is a site in $\mathcal{S}$. A Gibbs distribution takes the following form

$$P(\mathbf{x}) = \frac{1}{Z} e^{-\frac{1}{T} U(\mathbf{x})}, \tag{13.18}$$

where T is a constant analogous to temperature, $U(\mathbf{x})$ is an energy function and Z is a normalising constant or *partition function* of the system. The energy is defined as a sum of *clique potentials* $V_c(\mathbf{x})$ over all possible cliques C:

$$U(\mathbf{x}) = \sum_{c \in C} V_c(\mathbf{x}). \tag{13.19}$$

If $V_c(\mathbf{x})$ is independent of the relative position of the clique c, the Gibbs random field (GRF) is said to be homogeneous. A GRF is characterised by its global property (the Gibbs distribution) whereas an MRF is characterised by its local property (the Markovianity).[32] Different distributions can be obtained by specifying the potential functions, such as Gaussian MRF (GMRF)[70] and the FRAME model.[71]

(27) **Random walk** (♠ – ––)

In Ref. 72, Kidode and Wechsler proposed a random walk procedure for texture analysis. The random walkers are moving in unit steps in one of the four given directions. The moving probabilities for a random walker

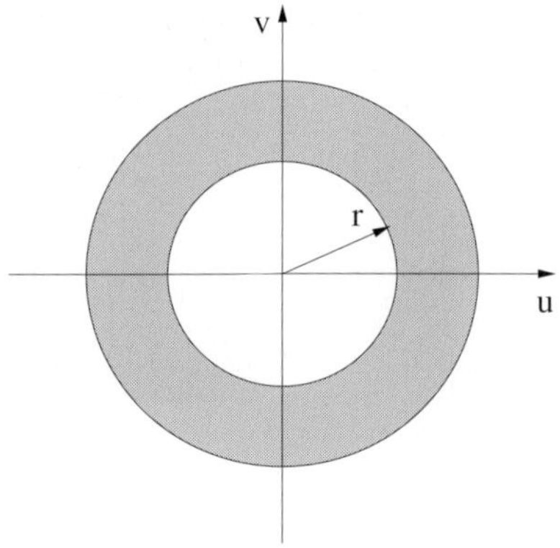

Fig. 13.10. A ring filter for power spectrum analysis.

at a given pixel to its four-connected neighbours are defined as a function of the underlying pixels. A very recent work on random walk based image segmentation can be found in Ref. 73, in which an image is treated as a graph with a fixed number of vertices and edges. Each edge is assigned a weight which corresponds to the likelihood a random walker will cross it. The user is required to select a certain number of seeds according to the number of regions to be segmented. Each unseeded pixel is assigned a random walker. The probilities for the random walker to reach those seed points are used to perform pixel clustering and image segmentation.

(28) **Relative extrema** (♠ − −−)
Relative extrema measures extract minimum and maximum values in a local neighbourhood. In Ref. 74, Mitchell *et al.* used relative frequency of the local gray level extremes to perform texture analysis. The number of extrema extracted from each scan line and their related threshold were used to characterise textures. This simple approach is a particularly useful trade-off in real-time applications.

(29) **Ring filter** (− − ◇−)
The Ring filter can be used to analyse texture energy distribution in the power spectrum as given in Eq. (13.16). In polar coordinates, it is defined as:

$$P(r) = 2\sum_{\theta=0}^{\pi} P(r,\theta), \tag{13.20}$$

where r denotes radius and θ is the angle. Figure 13.10 shows an example of a ring filter. The distribution of $P(r)$ indicates the coarseness of a texture. Also see the "Wedge filter".

Table 13.2. Some run length matrix features.

Measurement	Formula
Short runs emphasis	$\frac{\sum_i \sum_j \mathbf{P}_\theta(i,j)/j^2}{\sum_i, \sum_j \mathbf{P}_\theta(i,j)}$
Long runs emphasis	$\frac{\sum_i \sum_j j^2 \mathbf{P}_\theta(i,j)}{\sum_i \sum_j \mathbf{P}_\theta(i,j)}$
Gray level nonuniformity	$\frac{\sum_i \{\sum_j \mathbf{P}_\theta(i,j)\}^2}{\sum_i \sum_j \mathbf{P}_\theta(i,j)}$
Run length nonuniformity	$\frac{\sum_j \{\sum_i \mathbf{P}_\theta(i,j)\}^2}{\sum_i \sum_j \mathbf{P}_\theta(i,j)}$
Run percentage	$\frac{\sum_i \sum_j \mathbf{P}_\theta(i,j)}{wh}$

(30) **Run lengths** (♠ − −−)
The gray level run length was introduced by Galloway in Ref. 11. A run is defined as consecutive pixels with the same gray level, collinear in the same direction. The number of pixels in a run is referred to as run length, and the frequency at which such a run occurs is known as run length value. Let $\mathbf{P}_\theta(i, j)$ be the run length matrix, each element of which records the frequency that j pixels with the same gray level i continue in the direction θ. Some of the statistics commonly extracted from run length matrices for texture analysis are listed in Table 13.2.

(31) **Scale-space primal sketch** (−♡ − ♣)
In this scale-space analysis, an image is usually successively smoothed using Gaussian kernels so that the original image is represented in multiscale. The hierarchical relationship among image primitives at different scales are then examined. In Refs. 75 and 39, the authors demonstrated that the scale-space primal sketch enables explicit extraction of significant image structures, such as blob-like features, which can be later used to characterise their spatial displacement rules. Also see the "Primal sketch".

(32) **Spectral histogram** (− − ◇−)
The spectral histogram is translation invariant which is often a desirable property in texture analysis and with a sufficient number of filters it can uniquely represent any image up to a translation, as shown in Ref. 76. Essentially, a spectral histogram is a vector consisting of the marginal distribution of filter responses. It implicitly combines the local structure of an image through examining spatial pixel relationships using filter banks and global statistics by computing marginal distribution. Let $\{F^{(\alpha)}, \alpha = 1, 2, ..., K\}$ de-

note a bank of filters. The image is convolved with these filters, and each filtering response generates a histogram:

$$\mathbf{H}_{\mathbf{I}}^{(\alpha)}(z) = \frac{1}{|\mathbf{I}|} \sum_{(x,y)} \delta\left(z - \mathbf{I}^{(\alpha)}(x,y)\right), \tag{13.21}$$

where z denotes a bin of the histogram, $\mathbf{I}^{(\alpha)}$ is the filtered image, and $\delta(.)$ is the Dirac delta function. Thus, the spectral histogram for the chosen filter bank is defined as:

$$\mathbf{H}_{\mathbf{I}} = \left(\mathbf{H}_{\mathbf{I}}^{(1)}, \mathbf{H}_{\mathbf{I}}^{(2)}, ..., \mathbf{H}_{\mathbf{I}}^{(K)}\right). \tag{13.22}$$

An example of using spectral histograms for texture analysis can be found in Ref. 76.

(33) **Steerable filters** (− − ◇−)

The concept of steerable filters was first developed by Freeman and Adelson.[41] The steerable filters are a bank of filters with arbitrary orientations, each of which is generated using a linear combination of a set of basis functions. For example, we can use Gaussian derivative filters to generate steerable filters. For more general cases, please see Ref. 41. Let G_x and G_y denote the first x derivative and the first y derivative of a Gaussian function, respectively. Notably, G_y is merely a rotation of G_x. Then, a first derivative filter for any direction θ can be easily synthesised via a linear combination of G_x and G_y:

$$D_\theta = G_x \cos\theta + G_y \sin\theta, \tag{13.23}$$

where $\cos\theta$ and $\sin\theta$ are known as the interpolation functions of the basis functions G_x and G_y. Figure 13.11 illustrates our Gaussian derivative based steerable filters. The first two images in the top row show the basis functions, G_x and G_y. The next three are "steered" filters at $\theta = 30$, 80, and 140 respectively. The bottom row shows the original image and the corresponding responses of the three filters. As expected, the oriented filters exhibit selective responses at edges which is very useful for texture analysis. See Ref. 77 for a recent application of steerable filters to texture classification.

(34) **Steerable pyramid** (− − ◇−)

A steerable pyramid is another way of analysing texture in multiple scales and different orientations. This pyramid representation is a combination of multiscale decomposition and differential measurements.[78] Its differential measurement is usually based on directional steerable basis filters. The basis filters are rotational copies of each other, and any directional copy can

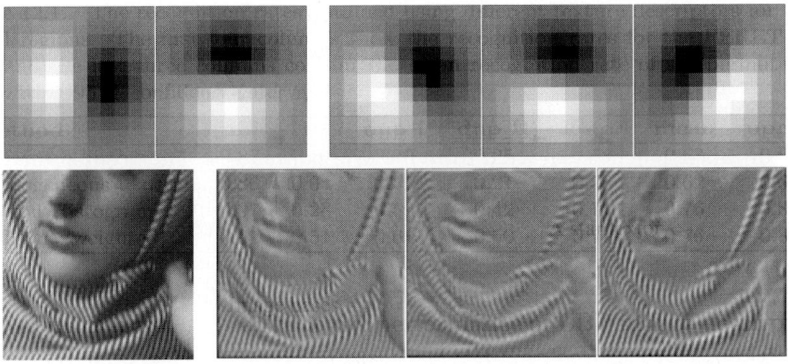

Fig. 13.11. A simple example of steerable filters - from left: The first row shows two basis functions, G_x and G_y, and three derived filters using basis functions at $\theta = 30$, 80, and 140; The next row shows the original image and the three filter responses.

Fig. 13.12. A steerable pyramid representation of the image shown in Fig. 13.11. The original image is decomposed into 4 scales with the last scale as an excessively low pass filtered version. At each scale, the image is further decomposed to 5 orientations (the images are generated using the software provided by the authors in Ref. 78).

be generated using a linear combination of these basis functions. The pyramid can have any number of orientation bands. As a result it does not suffer from aliasing, however, the pyramid is substantially over-complete which degrades its computational efficiency. Figure 13.12 gives an example steerable pyramid representation of the image shown in Fig. 13.11. Also see the "Steerable filter".

(35) **Texems** ($-\heartsuit - \clubsuit$)

In Ref. 79, Xie and Mirmehdi present a two layer generative model, called texems (short for texture exemplars), to represent texture images. Each texem, characterised by a mean and a covariance matrix, represents a class of image patches extracted from the original images. The original image is then described by a family of these texems, each of which is an implicit representation of a texture primitive. An example is given in Fig. 13.13 where four 7×7 texems are learnt from the given image. The notable difference between the texem and the texton is that the texem model relies directly on raw pixel values instead of composition of base functions and it does not explicitly describe texture primitives as in the texton model, i.e. multiple or only partial primitives may be encapsulated in each texem. In Ref. 79, two different mixture models were investigated to derive texems for both gray level and colour images. An application to novelty detection in random colour textures was also presented.

Fig. 13.13. Extracting texems from a colour image - from left: The original colour image and its four 7×7 texems, represented by mean and covariance matrices.

(36) **Textons** ($-\heartsuit - -$)

Textons were first presented by Julesz[16] as fundamental image structures and were considered as atoms of pre-attentive human visual perception. Leung and Malik[42] adopted a *discriminative* model to describe textons. Each texture image was analysed using a filter bank composed of 48 Gaussian filters with different orientations, scales and phases. Thus, a high dimensional feature vector was extracted at each pixel position. K-means was used to cluster those filter response vectors into a few mean vectors which were referred to as textons.

More recently, Zhu *et al.*[80] argued that textons could be defined in the context of a *generative* model of images. In their three-level generative model, an image I was considered as a superposition of a number of base functions that were selected from an over-complete dictionary $\mathbf{\Psi}$. These image bases, such as Gabor and Laplacian of Gaussian functions at various scales,

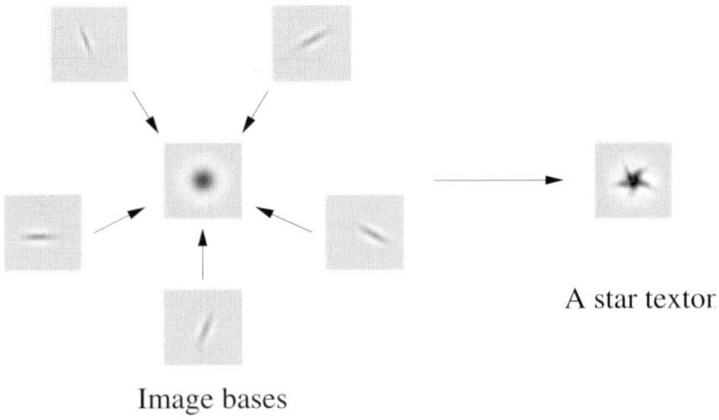

Fig. 13.14. A star texton configuration (*image adapted from*[80]).

orientations, and locations, were generated by a smaller number of texton elements which were in turn selected from a texton dictionary $\mathbf{\Pi}$. An image I is generated by a base map $\mathbf{B}$ which is in turn generated from a texton map $\mathbf{T}$, i.e:

$$\mathbf{T} \xrightarrow{\mathbf{\Pi}} \mathbf{B} \xrightarrow{\mathbf{\Psi}} \mathbf{I}, \tag{13.24}$$

where $\mathbf{\Pi} = \{\pi_i, i = 1, 2, ...\}$ and $\mathbf{\Psi} = \{\psi_i, i = 1, 2, ...\}$. Each texton, an instance in the texton map $\mathbf{T}$, is considered a combination of a certain number of base functions with deformable geometric configurations, e.g. star, bird, snowflake. This configuration is illustrated in Fig. 13.14 using a texton of a star shape. By fitting this generative model to observed images, the texton dictionary then is learnt as parameters of the generative model. Example applications of the texton model can be found in Refs. 42,81,82 and 83.

(37) **Texture spectrum** (♠♡ − −)
Similar to the texton approach, the texture spectrum method[84] considers a texture image a composition of texture units and uses the global distribution of these units to characterise textures. Each texture unit comprises a small local neighbourhood, e.g. 3×3, and the pixels within are thresholded according to the central pixel intensity in a very similar approach to LBP's approach. Pixels brighter or darker than the central pixel are set to 0 or 2 respectively, and the rest of the pixels are set to 1. These values are then vectorised to form a feature vector for the central pixel, the frequency of which is computed across the image to form the texture unit spectrum. Various characteristics from this spectrum are extracted to perform texture analysis, such as symmetricity and orientation.

(38) **Trace transform** (♠ − −−)
The trace transform[85] is a 2D representation of an image in polar coordinates

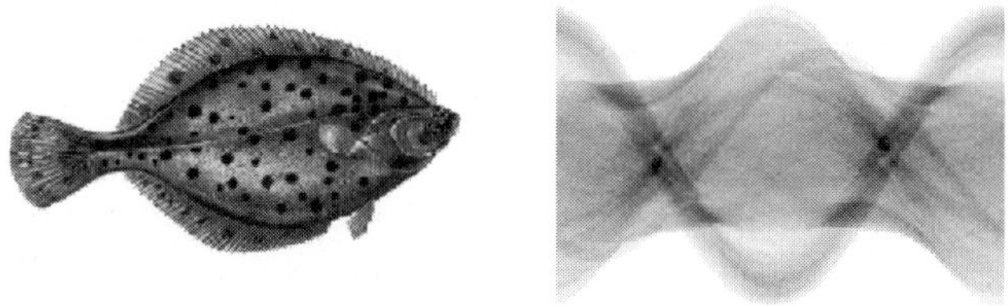

Fig. 13.15. An example of the trace transform (reproduced with permission from Ref. 85).

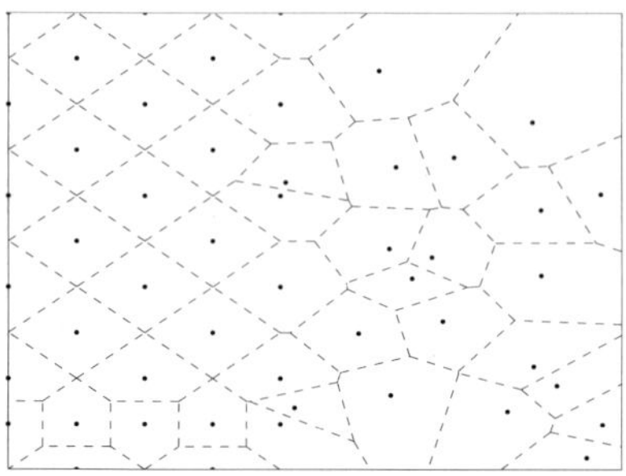

Fig. 13.16. An example of Voronoi tessellation - The dots are feature points, and the tessellation is shown in dashed lines. The points on the left hand are regularly distributed and those on the right randomly placed. These are reflected in the shape and distribution of the polygonal regions.

with the origin in the centre of the image. Similar to the Radon transform, it traces lines from all possible directions originating from the centre but instead of computing the integral as in the Radon transform, it evaluates several other functionals along each trace line. Thus, it is considered as a generalisation of the Radon transform. In practice, different functionals are used to produce different trace transforms from the same image. Features can then be extracted from transformed images using diametrical and circus functionals. Figure 13.15 gives an example of the trace transform.

(39) **Voronoi tessellation** (−♡ − −)
Voronoi tessellation, introduced by Ahuja,[86] divides a domain into a number of polygonal regions based on a set of given points in this domain. Each polygon contains one given point only and any points that are closer to this given point than any others. The shape of the polygonal regions, or Voronoi pologons, reflect the local spatial point distributions. Figure 13.16 shows an example of Voronoi tessellation. In Ref. 59, Tuceryan and Jain first extracted texture tokens, such as local extrema, line segmentations, and terminations,

and then used Voronoi tessellation to divide the image plane. Features from this tessellation, such as area of the pologal regions, its shape and orientation, and relative position to the tokens, were used for texture segmentation.

(40) **Wavelets** $(- - \diamond -)$

Wavelet based texture analysis uses a class of functions that are localised in both spatial and spatial-frequency domain to decompose texture images. Wavelet functions belonging to the same family can be constructed from a basis function, known as "mother wavelet" or "basic wavelet", by means of dilation and translation. The input image is considered as the weighted sum of overlapping wavelet functions, scaled and shifted. Let $g(x)$ be a wavelet (in $1D$ for simplicity). The wavelet transform of a $1D$ signal $f(x)$ is defined as

$$W_f(\alpha, \tau) = \int_{-\infty}^{\infty} f(x) g^*(\alpha(x - \tau)) dx, \tag{13.25}$$

where $g(\alpha(x - \tau))$ is computed from the mother wavelet $g(x)$, and τ and α denote the translation and scale respectively. The discrete equivalent can be obtained by sampling the parameters α and τ. Typically, the sampling constraints require the transform to be a non-redundant complete orthogonal decomposition. Every transformed signal contains information of a specific scale and orientation. Popular wavelet transform techniques that have been applied to texture analysis include dyadic transform, pyramidal wavelet transform, and wavelet packet decomposition, e.g. Ref. 56.

(41) **Wedge filter** $(- - \diamond -)$

Along with the ring filter, the wedge filter is used to analyse energy distribution in the frequency domain. The image is transformed into the power spectrum, usually using the fast Fourier transform, and wedge filters are applied to examine the directionality of its texture. A wedge filter in polar coordinates can be defined as:

$$P(\theta) = \sum_{r=0}^{\infty} P(r, \theta), \tag{13.26}$$

where r denotes the radius and θ the angle. Figure 13.17 illustrates a wedge filter in a polar coordinates. Also see the "Ring filter".

(42) **Wigner distribution** $(- - \diamond -)$

The Wigner distribution also gives a joint representation in the spatial and spatial-frequency domain. It is sometimes described as a local spatial frequency representation. Considering a 1D case, let $f(x)$ denote a continuous,

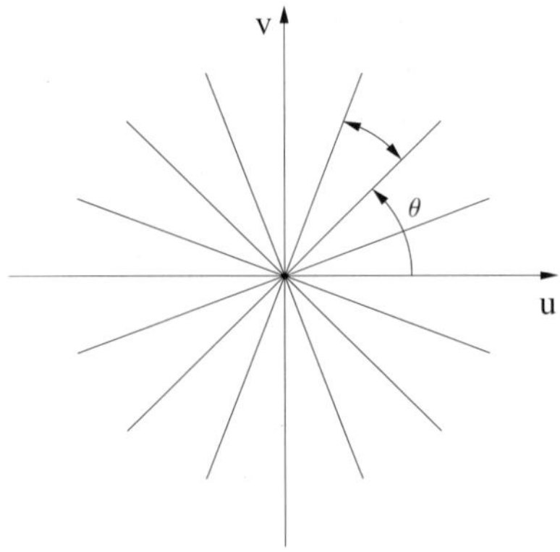

Fig. 13.17. A wedge filter for power spectrum analysis.

integrable and complex function. The Wigner distribution can be defined as:

$$WD(x, \omega) = \int_{-\infty}^{\infty} f(x + \frac{x'}{2}) f^*(x - \frac{x'}{2}) e^{-i\omega x'} dx', \tag{13.27}$$

where ω is the spatial frequency and $f^*(.)$ is the complex conjugate of $f(.)$. The Wigner distribution directly encodes the phase information and unlike the short time Fourier transform it is a real valued function. Example applications of Wigner distribution to feature extraction and image analysis can be found in Ref. 87. In Ref. 88, the authors demonstrated detecting cracks in random textures based on Wigner distrbution. Also see "Wavelets".

13.3. Texture Feature Comparison

There have been many studies comparing various subsets of texture features. As a pointer, here we briefly mention only some of these studies. In general, the results in most of these works much depend on the data set used, the set of parameters used for the methods examined, and the application domain.

In Ref. 89, Ohanian and Dubes compared the fractal model, co-occurrence matrices, the MRF model, and Gabor filtering for texture classification. The co-occurrence features generally outperformed other features in terms of classification rate. However, as pointed out in Ref. 6, they used raw Gabor filtered images instead of using empirical nonlinear transformations to obtain texture features.

Reed and Wechsler[90] performed a comparative study on various spatial and spatial-frequency representations and concluded that the Wigner distribution had the best joint resolution. In another related work, Pichler *et al.*[91] reported superior results using Gabor filtering over other wavelet transforms.

In Ref. 92, Chang *et al.* evaluated co-occurrence matrices, Laws texture energy measures, and Gabor filters for segmentation in natural and synthetic images. Gabor filtering again achieved best performance. Later, Randen and Husøy [56] performed an extensive evaluation of various filtering approaches for texture segmentation. The methods included Laws filters, ring and wedge filters, various Gabor filters, and wavelet transforms. No single approach was found to be consistently superior to the others on their twelve texture collages.

Singh and Singh[93] compared seven spatial texture analysis techniques, including autocorrelation, co-occurrence matrices, Laws filters, run lengths, and statistical geometrical (SG) features,[94] with the latter performing best in classifying VisTex and MeasTex[95] textures. In the SG based method, the image was segmented into a binary stack depending on the number of graylevels in the image. Then geometrical measurements of the connected regions in each stack were taken as texture features.

Recently, Varma and Zisserman[96] compared two statistical approaches to classify material images from the Columbia-Utrecht (CUReT)[81] texture database. Both approaches applied a filter bank consisting isotropic Gaussian, Laplacian of Gaussian, and orientated edge filters at various scales and orientations. However, the first method, following the work of Konishi and Yuille,[97] directly estimated the distribution of filtering responses and classified the texture images based on the class conditional probability using the Bayesian theorem. The second approach, adopted in Refs. 42, 98 and 99, clustered the filtering responses to generate texton representations and used texton frequency to classify textures based on the χ^2 distance measure. The results showed close performance of these two approaches. However, the Bayesian approach degraded quicker when less information in estimating the underlying distribution was available.

In Ref. 100, Drimbarean and Whelan presented a comparative study on colour texture classification. The local linear filter based on discrete Cosine transform (DCT), Gabor filters, and co-occurrence matrices were studied along with different colour spaces, such as RGB and $L^*a^*b^*$. The results showed that colour information was important in characterising textures. The DCT features were found the best of the three when classifying selected colour images from the VisTex dataset.[101]

References

1. R. Haralick, Statistical and structural approaches to texture, *Proceedings of the IEEE.* **67**(5), 786–804, (1979).
2. H. Wechsler, Texture analysis - a survey, *Signal Processing*. **2**, 271–282, (1980).

3. L. Van Gool, P. Dewaele, and A. Oosterlinck, Texture analysis, *Computer Vision, Graphics and Image Processing*. **29**, 336–357, (1985).
4. F. Vilnrotter, R. Nevatia, and K. Price, Structural analysis of natural textures, *IEEE Transactions on Pattern Analysis and Machine Intelligence*. **8**, 76–89, (1986).
5. T. Reed and J. Buf, A review of recent texture segmentation and feature extraction techniques, *Computer Vision, Image Processing and Graphics*. **57**(3), 359–372, (1993).
6. M. Tuceryan and A. Jain. Texture analysis. In *Handbook of Pattern Recognition and Computer Vision*, chapter 2, pp. 235–276. World Scientific, (1998).
7. L. Latif-Amet, A. Ertuzun, and A. Ercil, An efficient method for texture defect detection: Subband domain co-occurrence matrices, *Image and Vision Computing*. **18** (6-7), 543–553, (2000).
8. R. Haralick, K. Shanmugan, and I. Dinstein, Textural features for image classification, *IEEE Transactions on Systems, Man, and Cybernetics*. **3**(6), 610–621, (1973).
9. M. Tsatsanis and G. Giannakis, Object and texture classification using higher order statistics, *IEEE Transactions on Pattern Analysis and Machine Intelligence*. **14**(7), 733–750, (1992).
10. Y. Huang and K. Chan, Texture decomposition by harmonics extraction from higher order statistics, *IEEE Transactions on Image Processing*. **13**(1), 1–14, (2004).
11. R. Galloway, Texture analysis using gray level Run lengths, *Computer Graphics and Image Processing*. **4**, 172–179, (1974).
12. T. Ojala, M. Pietikäinen, and D. Harwood, A comparative study of texture measures with classification based on feature distribution, *Pattern Recognition*. **29**(1), 51–59, (1996).
13. S. Zucker, Toward a model of texture, *Computer Graphics and Image Processing*. **5**, 190–202, (1976).
14. K. Fu, *Syntactic Pattern Recognition and Applications*. (Prentice-Hall, 1982).
15. D. Marr, Early processing of visual information, *Philosophical Transactions of the Royal Society of London*. **B-275**, 483–524, (1976).
16. B. Julesz, Textons, the element of texture perception and their interactions, *Nature*. **290**, 91–97, (1981).
17. A. Efros and T. Leung. Texture synthesis by non-parametric sampling. In *IEEE International Conference on Computer Vision*, pp. 1033–1038, (1999).
18. J. Malik and P. Perona, Preattentive texture discrimination with early vision mechanisms, *Journal of the Optical Society of America, Series A*. **7**, 923–932, (1990).
19. F. Ade, Characterization of texture by 'eigenfilter', *Signal Processing*. **5**(5), 451–457, (1983).
20. I. Jolliffe, *Principal Component Analysis*. (Springer-Verlag, 1986).
21. J. Coggins and A. Jain, A spatial filtering approach to texture analysis, *Pattern Recognition Letters*. **3**, 195–203, (1985).
22. F. D'Astous and M. Jernigan. Texture discrimination based on detailed measures of the power spectrum. In *International Conference on Pattern Recognition*, pp. 83–86, (1984).
23. M. Turner, Texture discrimination by Gabor functions, *Biological Cybernetics*. **55**, 71–82, (1986).

24. M. Clark and A. Bovik, Texture segmentation using Gabor modulation/ demodulation, *Pattern Recognition Letters*. **6**(4), 261–267, (1987).
25. H. Sari-Sarraf and J. Goddard, Vision systems for on-loom fabric inspection, *IEEE Transactions on Industry Applications*. **35**, 1252–1259, (1999).
26. J. Scharcanski, Stochastic texture analysis for monitoring stochastic processes in industry, *Pattern Recognition Letters*. **26**, 1701–1709, (2005).
27. X. Yang, G. Pang, and N. Yung, Robust fabric defect detection and classification using multiple adaptive wavelets, *IEE Proceedings Vision, Image Processing*. **152** (6), 715–723, (2005).
28. R. Coifman, Y. Meyer, and V. Wickerhauser. Size properties of wavelet packets. In eds. M. Ruskai, G. Beylkin, R. Coifman, I. Daubechies, S. Mallat, Y. Meyer, and L. Raphael, *Wavelets and Their Applications*, pp. 453–470. Jones and Bartlett, (1992).
29. B. Mandelbrot, *The Fractal Geometry of Nature*. (W.H. Freeman, 1983).
30. J. Mao and A. Jain, Texture classification and segmentation using multiresolution simultaneous autoregressive models, *Pattern Recognition*. **25**(2), 173–188, (1992).
31. M. Comer and E. Delp, Segmentation of textured images using a multiresolution Gaussian autoregressive model, *IEEE Transactions on Image Processing*. **8**(3), 408–420, (1999).
32. S. Li, *Markov Random Filed Modeling in Image Analysis*. (Springer, 2001).
33. N. Jojic, B. Frey, and A. Kannan. Epitomic analysis of appearance and shape. In *IEEE International Conference on Computer Vision*, pp. 34–42, (2003).
34. C. Coroyer, D. Declercq, and P. Duvaut. Texture classification using third order correlation tools. In *IEEE Signal Processing Workshop on High-Order Statistics*, pp. 171–175, (1997).
35. A. Khotanzad and R. Kashyap, Feature selection for texture recognition based on image synthesis, *IEEE Transactions on Systems, Man, and Cybernetics*. **17**(6), 1087–1095, (1987).
36. L. Siew, R. Hodgson, and E. Wood, Texture measures for carpet wear assessment, *IEEE Transactions on Pattern Analysis and Machine Intelligence*. **10**, 92–105, (1988).
37. D. Clausi, An analysis of co-occurrence texture statistics as a function of grey level quantization, *Canadian Journal of Remote Sensing*. **28**(1), 45–62, (2002).
38. A. Monadjemi. *Towards Efficient Texture Classification and Abnormality Detection*. PhD thesis, University of Bristol, UK, (2004).
39. T. Lindeberg, Detecting salient blob-like image structures and scales with a scale-space primal sketch: A method for focus-of-attention, *International Journal of Computer Vision*. **11**(3), 283–318, (1993).
40. D. Lowe, Distinctive image features from scale-invariant keypoints, *International Journal of Computer Vision*. **60**(2), 91–110, (2004).
41. W. Freeman and E. Adelson, The design and use of steerable filters, *IEEE Transactions on Pattern Analysis and Machine Intelligence*. **13**(9), 891–906, (1991).
42. T. Leung and J. Malik, Representing and recognizing the visual appearance of materials using three-dimensional textons, *International Journal of Computer Vision*. **43** (1), 29–44, (2001).
43. A. Monadjemi, M. Mirmehdi, and B. Thomas. Restructured eigenfilter matching for

novelty detection in random textures. In *British Machine Vision Conference*, pp. 637–646, (2004).
44. C. Fredembach, M. Schröder, and S. Süsstrunk, Eigenregions for image classification, *IEEE Transactions on Pattern Analysis and Machine Intelligence*. **26**(12), 1645–1649, (2004).
45. L. Chang and C. Cheng. Multispectral image compression using eigenregion based segmentation. In *IEEE International Geoscience and Remote Sensing Symposium*, vol. 4, pp. 1844–1846, (2001).
46. C. Stauffer. Learning a probabilistic similarity function for segmentation. In *IEEE Workshop on Perceptual Organization in Computer Vision*, pp. 50–58, (2004).
47. V. Cheung, B. Frey, and N. Jojic. Video epitome. In *IEEE Conference on Computer Vision and Pattern Recognition*, vol. 1, pp. 42–49, (2005).
48. A. Pentland, Fractal-based description of nature scenes, *IEEE Transactions on Pattern Analysis and Machine Intelligence*. **9**, 661–674, (1984).
49. J. Gangepain and C. Roques-Carmes, Fractal approach to two dimensional and three dimensional surface roughness, *Wear*. **109**, 119–126, (1986).
50. R. Voss. Random fractals: Characterization and measurement. In eds. R. Pynn and A. Skjeltorp, *Scaling Phenomena in Disordered Systems*. Plenum, (1986).
51. J. Keller, S. Chen, and R. Crownover, Texture description and segmentation through fractal geometry, *Computer Vision, Graphics, and Image Processing*. **45**, 150–166, (1989).
52. B. Super and A. Bovik, Localizing measurement of image fractal dimension using Gabor filters, *Journal of Visual Communication and Image Representation*. **2**, 114–128, (1991).
53. C. Allain and M. Cloitre, Characterizing the lacunarity of random and deterministic fractal sets, *Physical Review*. **A-44**(6), 3552–3558, (1991).
54. A. Jain and F. Farrokhnia, Unsupervised texture segmentation using Gabor filters, *Pattern Recognition*. **24**, 1167–1186, (1991).
55. A. Kumar and G. Pang, Defect detection in textured materials using Gabor filters, *IEEE Transactions on Industry Applications*. **38**(2), 425–440, (2002).
56. T. Randen and J. Husøy, Filtering for texture classification: a comparative study, *IEEE Transactions on Pattern Analysis and Machine Intelligence*. **21**(4), 291–310, (1999).
57. R. Conners and C. Harlow, A theoretical comparison of texture algorithms, *IEEE Transactions on Pattern Analysis and Machine Intelligence*. **2**(3), 204–222, (1980).
58. M. Swain and D. Ballard, Indexing via color histograms, *International Journal of Computer Vision*. **7**(1), 11–32, (1990).
59. M. Tuceryan and A. Jain, Texture segmentation using voronoi polygons, *IEEE Transactions on Pattern Analysis and Machine Intelligence*. **12**, 211–216, (1990).
60. P. Burt and A. Adelson, The laplacian pyramid as a compact image code, *IEEE Transactions on Communications*. **31**, 532–540, (1983).
61. K. Laws. *Textured Image Segmentation*. PhD thesis, University of Southern California, USA, (1980).
62. T. Mäenpää and M. Pietikäinen. Texture analysis with local binary patterns. In eds. C. Chen and P. Wang, *Handbook of Pattern Recognition and Computer Vision*, pp. 197–216. World Scientific, 3 edition, (2005).

63. E. Simoncelli, W. Freeman, E. Adelson, and D. Heeger, Shiftable multi-scale transforms, *IEEE Transactions on Information Theory*. **38**(2), 587–607, (1992).
64. R. Gonzalez and R. Woods, *Digital Image Processing*. (Addison Wesley, 1992).
65. D. Marr, *Vision*. (W. H. Freeman and Company, 1982).
66. F. Tomita and S. Tsuji, *Computer Analysis of Visual Textures*. (Kluwer Academic Publisher, 1990).
67. C. Guo, S. Zhu, and Y. Wu. Towards a mathematical theory of primal sketch and sketchability. In *IEEE International Conference on Computer Vision*, vol. 2, pp. 1228–1235, (2003).
68. K. Jafari-Khouzani and H. Soltanian-Zadeh, Radon transform orientation estimation for rotation invariant texture analysis, *IEEE Transactions on Pattern Analysis and Machine Intelligence*. **27**(6), 1004–1008, (2005).
69. G. Cross and A. Jain, Markov random field texture models, *IEEE Transactions on Pattern Analysis and Machine Intelligence*. **5**, 25–39, (1983).
70. R. Chellappa. Two-dimensional discrete Gaussian Markov random field models for image processing. In eds. L. Kanak and A. Rosenfeld, *Progress in Pattern Recognition 2*. Elsevier, (1985).
71. S. Zhu, Y. Wu, and D. Mumford, FRAME: Filters, random field and maximum entropy - towards a unified theory for texture modeling, *International Journal of Computer Vision*. **27**(2), 1–20, (1997).
72. H. Wechsler and M. Kidode, A random walk procedure for texture discrimination, *IEEE Transactions on Pattern Analysis and Machine Intelligence*. **1**(3), 272–280, (1979).
73. L. Grady, Random walks for image segmentation, *IEEE Transactions on Pattern Analysis and Machine Intelligence*. **9**(11), 1768–1783, (2006).
74. O. Mitchell, C. Myers, and W. Boyne, A min-max measure for image texture analysis, *IEEE Transactions on Computers*. **C-26**, 408–414, (1977).
75. T. Lindeberg and J. Eklundh, Scale-space primal sketch: Construction and experiments, *Image and Vision Computing*. **10**(1), 3–18, (1992).
76. X. Liu and D. Wang, Texture classification using spectral histograms, *IEEE Transactions on Image Processing*. **12**(6), 661–670, (2003).
77. Y. Wu, K. Chan, and Y. Huang. Image texture classification based on finite gaussian mixture models. In *International Workshop on Texture Analysis and Synthesis*, pp. 107–112, (2003).
78. E. Simoncelli and W. Freeman. The steerable pyramid: A flexible architecture for multi-scale derivative computation. In *IEEE International Conference on Image Processing*, pp. 444–447, (1995).
79. X. Xie and M. Mirmehdi, TEXEM: Texture exemplars for defect detection on random textured surfaces, *IEEE Transactions on Pattern Analysis and Machine Intelligence*. (2007). to appear.
80. S. Zhu, C. Guo, Y. Wang, and Z. Xu, What are textons?, *International Journal of Computer Vision*. **62**(1-2), 121–143, (2005).
81. K. Dana, B. Ginneken, S. Nayar, and J. Koenderink, Reflectance and texture of real-world surfaces, *ACM Transactions on Graphics*. **18**(1), 1–34, (1999).
82. C. Schmid. Constructing models for content-based image retrieval. In *IEEE Conference on Computer Vision and Pattern Recognition*, vol. 2, pp. 39–45, (2001).

83. M. Varma and A. Zisserman, A statistical approach to texture classification from single images, *International Journal of Computer Vision*. **61**(1/2), 61–81, (2005).
84. D. He and L. Wang, Texture features based on texture spectrum, *Pattern Recognition*. **24**(5), 391–399, (1991).
85. A. Kadyrov and M. Petrou, The trace transform and its applications, *IEEE Transactions on Pattern Analysis and Machine Intelligence*. **23**(8), 811–828, (2001).
86. N. Ahuja, Dot pattern processing using voronoi neighbourhoods, *IEEE Transactions on Pattern Analysis and Machine Intelligence*. **4**, 336–343, (1982).
87. G. Cristobal, C. Gonzalo, and J. Bescos. Image filtering and analysis through the wigner distribution. In ed. P. Hawkes, *Advances in Electronics and Electron Physics Series*, vol. 80, pp. 309–397. Academic Press, (1991).
88. C. Boukouvalas, J. Kittler, R. Marik, M. Mirmehdi, and M. Petrou. Ceramic tile inspection for colour and structural defects. In *Advances in Materials and Processing Technologies*, pp. 390–399, (1995).
89. P. Ohanian and R. Dubes, Performance evaluation for four classes of textural features, *Pattern Recognition*. **25**(8), 819–833, (1992).
90. T. Reed and H. Wechsler, Segmentation of textured images and gestalt organization using spatial/spatial-frequency representations, *IEEE Transactions on Pattern Analysis and Machine Intelligence*. **12**, 1–12, (1990).
91. O. Pichler, A. Teuner, and B. Hosticka, A comparison of texture feature extraction using adaptive Gabor filter, pyramidal and tree structured wavelet transforms, *Pattern Recognition*. **29**(5), 733–742, (1996).
92. K. Chang, K. Bowyer, and M. Sivagurunath. Evaluation of texture segmentation algorithms. In *IEEE Conference on Computer Vision and Pattern Recognition*, vol. 1, pp. 294–299, (1999).
93. M. Singh and S. Singh. Spatial texture analysis: A comparative study. In *International Conference on Pattern Recognition*, vol. 1, pp. 676–679, (2002).
94. Y. Chen, M. Nixon, and D. Thomas, Statistical geometrical features for texture classification, *Pattern Recognition*. **28**(4), 537–552, (1995).
95. G. Smith and I. Burns, Measuring texture classification algorithm, *Pattern Recognition Letters*. **18**, 1495–1501, (1997).
96. M. Varma and A. Zisserman, Unifying statistical texture classification frameworks, *Image and Vision Computing*. **14**(1), 1175–1183, (2004).
97. S. Konishi and A. Yuille. Statistical cues for domain specific image segmentation with performance analysis. In *IEEE Conference on Computer Vision and Pattern Recognition*, pp. 125–132, (2000).
98. O. Cula and K. Dana. Compact representation of bidirectional texture functions. In *IEEE Conference on Computer Vision and Pattern Recognition*, pp. 1041–1047, (2001).
99. M. Varma and A. Zisserman. Classifying images of materials from images: Achieving viewpoint and illumination independence. In *European Conference on Computer Vision*, pp. 255–271, (2002).
100. A. Drimbarean and P. Whelan, Experiments in colour texture analysis, *Pattern Recognition Letters*. **22**, 1161–1167, (2001).
101. MIT Media Lab. VisTex texture database, (1995). URL `http://vismod.media.mit.edu/vismod/imagery/VisionTexture/vistex.html`.

Index